King Kong on 4th Street

Institutional Structures of Feeling

George Marcus, Sharon Traweek, Richard Handler,
and Vera Zolberg, *Series Editors*

*King Kong on 4th Street: Families and
the Violence of Poverty on the Lower East Side,*
Jagna Wojcicka Sharff

Transcultural Space and Transcultural Beings, David Tomas

*Exposing Prejudice: Puerto Rican Experiences of
Language, Race, and Class,* Bonnie Urciuoli

Tango and the Political Economy of Passion, Marta E. Savigliano

*Culture and the Ad: Exposing Otherness in
the World of Advertising,* William M. O'Barr

Surrogate Motherhood: Conception in the Heart, Helena Ragoné

Vinyl Leaves: Walt Disney World and America, Stephen M. Fjellman

KING KONG ON
4TH STREET

Families and the
Violence of Poverty on
the Lower East Side

Jagna Wojcicka Sharff

WestviewPress

A Division of HarperCollinsPublishers

"Blue Bayou" written by Roy Orbison and Joe Melson. © Copyright 1961, renewed 1989 Acuff-Rose
Music, Inc. International Rights Secured. All Rights Reserved. Used by Permission.

Copyright © 1998 by Westview Press, A Division of HarperCollins Publishers, Inc.

Published in 1998 in the United States of America by Westview Press, 5500 Central Avenue, Boulder,
Colorado 80301-2877, and in the United Kingdom by Westview Press, 12 Hid's Copse Road, Cumnor
Hill, Oxford OX2 9JJ

Library of Congress Cataloging-in-Publication Data
Wojcicka Sharff, Jagna.
  King Kong on 4th Street : families and the violence of poverty on
the Lower East Side / Jagna Wojcicka Sharff.
      p.   cm. — (Institutional structures of feeling)
  Includes bibliographical references (p.   ) and index.
    ISBN 0-8133-2936-1 (hardcover). — ISBN 0-8133-2937-X (pbk.)
    1. Family—New York (State)—Lower East Side (New York)
2. Hispanic American families—New York (State)—Lower East Side
(New York)   3. Urban poor—New York (State)—Lower East Side (New
York)   4. Sex role—New York (State)—Lower East Side (New York)
5. Kinship—New York (State)—Lower East Side (New York)   6. Lower
East Side (New York, N.Y.)—Social conditions.   7. Lower East Side
(New York, N.Y.)—Economic conditions.   I. Series.
HQ557.N5W65   1998
306.85'09747'1—dc21   97-30479
                                                                                                        CIP

10   9   8   7   6   5   4   3   2   1

Contents

Acknowledgments ix

Introduction 1

1 You Can Hear the Birds Singing 8

2 Dancing 21

3 Homing Pigeons 35

4 A Gentle Young Man 44

5 Chulito Flying 57

6 Victoria's Baptism 69

 Reflection 1: Small Creatures 79

7 Blue Bayou 86

 Reflection 2: Slipknots and Lariats 100

8 A Dream-Come-True Apartment with a 1949 Stove 110

9 Summertime 120

10 Sometimes the War Close to Home Is the Most Difficult to See 135

11 The Day of the Big Gun 147

12 A Death Foretold 158

13 Settling a Blood Feud 165

14   King Kong on 4th Street   174

15   I, Miguel Valiente   189

16   Jail, Jail, All Your Life Jail   202

     Epilogue: Walking My Baby   218

Appendix A: Methodology   231
Appendix B: Changes in the Patterns of Incarceration in New York State   233
Notes   235
References   239
About the Book and Author   245
Index   247

Acknowledgments

Like all human tasks, this book owes its conception and completion to people who came before me, those who worked with me, and those who will continue on. My mother, who showed me what a woman alone can do by bringing my brother and me through the great war, and my father, who rescued us from the postwar chaos, stand first in line. Next, I thank Dr. Marvin Harris, an inspiring mentor and later the coprincipal investigator of the research project on which this book is based.

A number of people worked with me collecting the data, some intensively and extensively—especially the core research team members, Nilda Cortez, Paul Van Linden Tol, and Nilsa Velazguez Buon. Others who contributed their work and insight to the gathering of information include Bela Feldman Bianco and Margalit Berlin during the first phase of the research, and Bonnie Urciuoli and Ronna Berezin, both of whom participated in the second phase. Weaving in and out of the research site as guests and occasional participants were my children, Adrian and Jennifer Benepe and Matthew Sharff. Jennifer produced some fine photographs of the neighborhood and its people, and Matthew tutored some of the younger children in reading. Many women and some children and men residing in the research neighborhood of the Lower East Side of Manhattan contributed work and insights as well. They must remain anonymous, but to all the named and the unnamed I am deeply grateful.

Dr. Joan Vincent read the final project report and made a number of suggestions for expanding it into a book, as did Roger Sanjek. Some of their suggestions, in addition to comments from the anonymous reviewers of the subsequent manuscript, are incorporated into this book.

During the years of solitary fieldwork, analysis, and writing, I was sustained by my family, friends, and colleagues; by Paul, my coworker, and my two grandsons, Alex and Erik, who bring sunshine into my life; and by Muriel Smolen, an encouraging, loyal friend. The women of the Wednesday Meeting helped with the final push toward publication. Kisses and hugs to all of you.

Andree Pages worked on the manuscript intensely, editing out of it the weird phrasings and misspellings that I put there. Johanna Lessinger, who incisively told me what my book was *really* about after she read it, helped me to discard the old introduction and write a new one. The manuscript was guided to publication by

Karl Yambert, my new editor at Westview Press, with the able assistance of Jennifer Chen. Research support for the years 1974 to 1976 was provided by Narcotic and Drug Research, Inc.; from 1977 to 1980 the National Institute of Drug Abuse, Grant # 1-ROI 1DAO 1866, funded the research. I thank both institutions. The research I pursued by myself between 1980 and 1990 was done on the cheap: I worked part-time on it while conducting other research, or supported myself on adjunct wages while giving more time to the research and writing. The book cover was designed by Matthew Sharff.

This book is dedicated to the children of the Lower East Side and their children, to help you recall how your parents survived, so that you will make a difference.

Jagna Wojcicka Sharff

Introduction

This book documents the societal violence against poor people, especially children, living in one community in the United States during a particularly critical juncture in time: the mid-1970s. The last major phase of deindustrialization was occurring in New York City, and the modest economic prospects of the working poor were deteriorating as a result of the loss of the manufacturing jobs on which their income depended (Gordon 1996). My focus on the lives of residents in a predominantly Latino neighborhood of the Lower East Side of Manhattan parallels stories from other urban areas in the United States where changes in corporate investment policy and priorities produced massive economic and social misery among Black, white, and Latino working people. By contextualizing certain behaviors of the poor that have been labeled as "deviant," my aim is to reveal them as survival strategies in a situation of great economic distress.[1]

The theoretical framework and empirical data of my research are enfolded in the closely interconnected stories that move chronologically through time, given life by the people who lived them. I chose to carry the argument through a narrative flow to make it accessible to a wide range of readers, because it is more affecting and powerful than data that is presented either as faceless statistics or technical jargon. Arguments that advance economic equity using complicated or obtuse language are often rejected in favor of simpler and more convenient views that portray poor people as responsible for their own poverty. This book aims to add a perspective that lays the blame for poverty where it belongs: on the structural changes in the economy and their social consequences.

In spite of a flood of theoretical works challenging the labeling, poor people continue to be demonized by politicians as "the underclass." This divisive practice conceptually and in practice removes them from our shared social system, consigning them instead to the category of an "intractable" urban social problem (see also Gans 1995). It conjures up a gray, faceless mass, obscuring the variations among people classified as poor. Another aim of this book, then, is to bring individual women, men, and children into view to show through stories that span a time from three to fifteen years that poor people's lives contain myriad sets of goals, paths, and outcomes, even within the dreary constraints of material poverty. In the stories of the families we will also see some of the things and events that poor people find good, beautiful, admirable, and fun. The neighborhood residents get a lot of joy and amusement out of the ongoing, real-life drama around them.

Through a description of events and interactions, the stories told in this book reconstruct the making of a web of relationships that connect individuals and groups in the neighborhood: kinship, fictive kinship, friendship, and other bonds of sentiment or obligation. Behavior within these webs, whether mainstream or "deviant"—for example, door-to-door selling of clothing as compared to street-corner drug dealing, or childbirth to married couples in contrast to that among unmarried teenagers—is contextualized as age-, gender-, and circumstance-appropriate behavior, part of the strategic options utilized for subsistence and network building by people of the neighborhood. The narrative style tries to reproduce the immediacy of the daily life as caught in field notes, with a minimum of authorial interpretation, but at the same time includes a weaving of voices and interpretations by others. The new trend toward reflexivity in anthropology encouraged me to gather and include the residents' and other researchers' reactions to the ongoing situations and events I encountered. Faye Harrison describes this inclusiveness as "bifocality or reciprocity of perspectives . . . seeing others against a background of ourselves and ourselves against a background of others" (1995:235), which tries to capture these social relations in the process of their entwining.

I and several other researchers of diverse backgrounds carried out the research for this book under my direction, with Marvin Harris as coprincipal investigator. Compiling the empirical basis for this book, we collected ethnographic, linguistic, nutritional, and economic data that included information on drug use and commerce as well as household budgets from thirty-six families. During the subsequent decade, from 1980 to 1990, I continued to collect information on my own through contacts with families and individuals whom I had grown to know well.

In the mid-1970s, the Lower East Side was a low-income area. The principal shelter for hundreds of thousands of impoverished immigrants during the last decades of the nineteenth century, by 1910 its tenements housed over three hundred thousand people in densities rivaled today only in parts of Asia. But in the succeeding decades, restrictive immigration policies reduced the numbers of people finding their first footing in this New World neighborhood. The last migrants to the area were the Puerto Ricans who arrived by the thousands between the 1950s and 1960s from their colonized, impoverished island in search of manufacturing jobs in the city (Melendez and Melendez 1993). By 1961 they constituted one-fourth of the one hundred thousand people living in the area, sharing its dilapidated old buildings with older Jews, Poles, Ukrainians, and Italians who had been left behind by their upward-scrambling progeny.

The city built its first low-income housing, First Houses, for the elderly in the area in 1936. In the late 1950s, wider swaths of the eastern and southern edges were bulldozed and replaced with towering "projects" to house the poor from all over the city. People displaced by that "urban renewal," the old and the new immigrants, crammed into the tenement heart of the district, renaming it Loisaida.

Family and neighborhood life reemerged, as in the past, amidst turf-disputing gangs, competing community organizations, and the everyday exigencies of living in slums.

The big difference now was competition for diminishing jobs. The severe economic transformations of the late 1960s and 1970s would make a profound impact on the lives of the people of this neighborhood. The traditional immigrant entrance jobs dwindled as the city metamorphosed from a center of manufacturing into a "post-industrial" center for finance, communications, and insurance (Sassen 1991). Older workers were getting laid off, and younger ones had no opportunity for apprenticeship (Sullivan 1989) except in prison. Once-plentiful jobs were following better-educated suburbanites who had left the city on the wings of white flight, as many companies relocated to suburbia and then to the South. At the same time that unemployment and underemployment rates soared in the city, the value of public support programs shrank for those unable to work or to find jobs.[2] Inflation was eating away a good portion of the subsistence income, and there was little hope of help from the state legislature, dominated by upstate congressmen who lived far from the City (Dehavenon 1984). The subsequent overseas flight of industry, which undercut the wages and working conditions of the middle class as well, had its most severe impact on poor whites and minorities, those already underpaid and underrepresented in the labor market (Mullings 1987). In the neighborhood, the economic dislocation reached its low point during the city's "fiscal crisis" of the mid-1970s (Taub 1982). By 1980, the median household income of Lower East Side residents was $8,782, or only 63 percent of the median income of all New Yorkers; 32.8 percent of the population lived in poverty (DeGiovanni 1987:8).

The decolonization and political freedom movements of the 1960s and early 1970s ushered in a period of reflection among anthropologists and influenced a reevaluation of our relationships with informants, encouraging partnerships with the people studied (Berreman 1972). I was already convinced that this was the only way to conduct research with people *and* obtain reliable information, so from the outset I followed a policy of "giving back" to the community and encouraged it among my coworkers. The residents gave our research team information and insight into their social system, and in exchange the team provided tutoring, advocacy, and access to people "in power" and to institutions that might be forbidding and inaccessible to poor people. We accompanied residents to schools, hospitals, potential employers, welfare and housing offices, police stations, courts, jails, and prisons. We partook of their daily petty humiliations, practiced standing up for them (and ourselves), and together learned the skills that impart courage, passing them on to others.

A terrible event, the brutal murder of a teenage boy in the building where our office was located, contributed to our early focus on children and violence. The murder forced us to see how much the children were suffering, not only in the aftermath of violent events but because of the conditions of their daily lives.

Already in the mid-1970s, many children on the Lower East Side were malnourished and inadequately clothed for cold weather, and they lived in a risky, body- and soul-maiming environment. This situation did not improve with time, nor was it limited to this neighborhood. Today, some twenty years later, we are informed that the number of poor children in the United States grew from 3.5 million to 6.1 million between 1979 and 1994, that one in four children under the age of six in our country now lives in poverty (Herbert 1996), and that our children are the worst off in terms of the gap between the rich and the poor among the top eighteen industrialized nations (Bradsher 1995a, 1995b). That the violence of poverty in children's lives would be a major focus of our research was thus already clearly evident shortly after we began.

In retrospect, I also see that focusing on children as a first priority connected our efforts to the residents' primary concern and gave us an entry to firsthand information on household composition, kinship networks, and webs of obligation and reciprocity (or animosity) connecting and dividing the neighborhood. The murder also presented me with a hideous puzzle. How was it that a mellow young man as pleasant and gentle as Juan could be cut down with such ferocity and disdain? Always in the forefront with some horrible new trend, the Lower East Side in the late 1970s was soon to become famous for the high homicide rate of young Latino men. So violence became central to our inquiry, violence in its enormous range: the violence of the state, which couldn't care less if poor children hungered or went cold, which built prisons to contain their future; violence from the cops and of the enforcers working for the drug-trade elite, which went down the scale to the fraternal murder between violently competing corner groups; the violence of the stressed family, all the way down to the dog getting cuffed by the child who has just been smacked by his mother.

Minor themes are threaded among the larger aims of the book. One is that of gender roles, which among the Lower East Side Latinos are highly marked through gender-appropriate norms yet often breached in practice because of the dearth of adult males; they are either dead, in prison, or elsewhere searching for work or seeking shelter. The work of fathering falls on uncles, grandfathers, older cousins or brothers, stepfathers, or on the mothers themselves. An unusual but culturally permissible result of the scarcity of adult men is the strong mother-son bond, which is occasionally—and sometimes explosively—displaced by an older woman-younger man partnership.

Another theme developed here is that of roles in the family. This point relates to the previous one as it connects the fragility of the marriage bond to the insecure economic position of the men (Liebow 1967; Stack 1974; Wilson 1987) and their physical vulnerability. As a result, I show how, within the limits of this degraded environment, mothers discern, develop, and direct the talents of their children, almost like investment bankers, to create a panoply of options for the survival of the household. Without claiming that each household contains the personnel or the need to follow the "ideal" model I develop, I show how in a number of households children fall into the roles of either the "macho defender/avenger" of the family, the "scholar/advocate," the "child reproducer," or the "wage earner" (Sharff 1980, 1981).

The women presented in this book have to carry much responsibility on their shoulders because their mates have "disappeared." Ironically, the women seem to expand their field of action in the face of male absence by devising novel ways of preserving the safety of the neighborhood. As we shall see, the much-touted theoretical distinction that locates the women's sphere of action inside the home and the men's in the public is radically modified, at least in practice, in poor neighborhoods. The stories show how women create and carry out the roles of street watchers, monitors, and advance warning systems (screaming out the window to stop a thief, for example) but also how some women act as mediators, prosecutors, and informal street judges who defuse potentially fatal confrontations, help settle scores with material settlements, and separate combatants, with the help of older men, to give them a chance to cool off. Listening to the soothing advice given on the side makes very apparent that this is consciously intended mediation in practice.

Other themes include the centrality of kinship, real and fictive, in sustaining life, a theme so eloquently and movingly developed over twenty years ago by Carol Stack in *All Our Kin* (1974). I build on her arguments about the value of children as social connectors, adding observations about the importance of continuing fertility for the more traditional Latina women as a means of attracting and holding a partner, a value jeopardized by the high rates of sterilization as birth control, often without the women's informed consent (see also Lopez 1987).[3] Adding to the theoretical discourse on what constitutes a "normal" family, I also underscore the importance of lasting, monogamous unions to the neighborhood's residents, showing, however, that where bureaucratic rules make legal marriage economically prohibitive—by depriving the woman and her children of a modest governmental support for food, housing, and especially health care—common-law marriages become the acceptable and recognized norm (Sharff 1987).

The stories trace the process of household mutations: Nuclear families turn into matrifocal ones and within a brief period of time may again change to nuclear or extended forms. They also show how this process affects specific individuals with anger, anxiety, and sadness as people go through these economics-driven changes. Also evident is the residents' subtle recognition of insult added to injury when they are told that their family forms are abnormal—or even worse, that their family forms generate poverty when in fact they are the residents' lifeboats (Scheper-Hughes 1992).

Last but not least is the theme that underlies so many stories, that of "scuffling," or work combining many little jobs, a process Lambros Comitas described for rural Jamaican men (1973). I use the term to cover all sorts of jobs—legal, off-the books, quasi-legal, and illegal—that members of a household combine against the dual adversity of unemployment and underemployment and the capricious and

stingy government supports. As the stories reveal, the lack of decent or even indecent jobs sends many young men into a highly competitive spiral for any kind of
work, including the drug trade, in which they compete on the lowest, street-seller
level. I show these men's work in the context of the needs and contributions to
their families of origin and of procreation. In these stories, even selling drugs is
presented as a possible option in a range of strategies that span the economic
spectrum from legal to underground jobs. In this sense my work differs from recent ethnographies that are mainly focused on observation of drug dealers and
their frequently glamorized self-reports of experiences in the trade (see Bourgois
1995 and Williams 1989).[4]

As I show, older men had clung to marginal jobs in the disappearing manufacturing sector or, together with the majority of the young men, circulated in what
has been termed the secondary labor market (Harrison 1977).[5] Meanwhile,
women raising young children attempted to subsist on a government program
that paid for inadequate diet and substandard housing. If a woman had no contributing partner or working older son, it was difficult to feed her children, and
even with combined welfare grants and food stamps, her family would suffer
from hunger at the end of each month. Similarly, landlords knew what the state
allotted for the housing of a family, and they charged to the hilt. By 1979, when
our team was collecting household budgets, a family of four was allotted $214 a
month, which paid for a tiny, dark tenement apartment cohabited by rats and
roaches. Of the twenty-four families receiving Aid to Families with Dependent
Children (AFDC) we interviewed, a third were paying more than their maximum
allotment for rent, which meant that the balance of the rent money had to come
from their already inadequate food budget (see also Susser and Kreniske 1987).
Only five families residing in public housing paid considerably less (Sharff
1980:25). I calculated that these families spent an average of 87 percent of their
combined allotment on food and rent alone, leaving only 13 percent for clothing,
transportation, personal hygiene items, leisure, recreation, and so on, with money
for emergencies not even considered. When I added emergency spending into
their budgets, I came up with annual budget deficits that ranged from a high of
almost $4,000 for a family who buried a teenage son that year, to a low of less than
$200 for a family who received additional Supplemental Security payments for a
disabled worker (Sharff 1980:30).

In the last section of the book, which reports on my findings between 1980 and
1990, I show how the earlier trends visible for the neighborhood accelerated
markedly in the following decade. For example, between 1970 and 1996, maximum welfare benefits in New York State were effectively reduced 48 percent
(Kilborn 1996:3). The further loss of jobs and benefits and of purchasing power
led to an enormous expansion of the illegal sector, and in turn of the state's response—which instead of increasing the number of decent jobs increased the
space in prisons and filled it. By following up on the life of Miguel, a sweet boy I
met when he was eleven years old, we see how even individuals who begin life full

of promise and mainstream aspirations can end up tortured and seriously hurt by the system. Miguel is one of the many faceless young men who are described in the newspapers as the "people in jails and prisons [whose numbers] doubled over the last decade and tripled over the last twenty years" (Butterfield 1997:A17). The girls, though luckier, in many instances had to travel difficult roads in order to achieve, like some of the boys, modest upward mobility.

The core fieldwork for this project was done by a team of four compatible people, all of whom appear frequently and volubly in the text. In addition to myself, a Polish national who arrived in the United States in 1947 as a child on a refugee visa, the team included three primary researchers: Research assistant Nilda Cortez was born in Puerto Rico of a notable family and raised in East Harlem. As a teen her ideas were influenced by the presence of a Quaker settlement house active in the area. Nilda and I had met ten years prior to the start of the project through mutual Quaker friends. Nilda in turn recommended to me one of the twelve local residents who worked for us as census takers; and Paul Van Linden Tol, a Dutch national and political activist in the bohemian subculture of the Lower East Side for seven years before we met him, joined the core team as a researcher. Our youngest team member, Nilsa Velazques Buon, was born and raised in East Harlem by Pentecostal parents, completed her education in New York City's public schools, and was just starting college when the project began. I had met her in East Harlem five years before while doing my dissertation research; then fifteen, she had impressed me with her intelligence and strength. During the last year of formal research Bonnie Urciuoli, a graduate student in linguistics, joined the team.

The period of the research, from 1974 to about 1990, coincides with three national initiatives that affected poor people: the end of the War on Poverty, the flowering of "the war on drugs," and the ushering in of "the war on crime." Our team research and my follow-up work with selected families documents how this national 180-degree turn away from the goal of creating greater economic equality and ending poverty toward that of a virtual war on the poor had disastrous consequences for individuals and communities alike. I made a conscious choice to minimize lengthy academic analysis in this book in order to make it readable to lay audiences and college undergraduates. It is my hope that presenting the information in this way will enable people of good will to come to their own conclusions, perhaps better than I could foresee, and begin to think in collective terms about what actions are possible to create a more equitable society.

1

You Can Hear the Birds Singing

When I think of the Lower East Side, I think of Luz. Luz means clarity, light. I see Luz, or Lucita as everyone called her, then a little doll of a nine-year-old, with her shiny black braid, dark rosy face, and almond eyes, coming around the corner onto East Fourth Street. In my mind she is always carrying a bag of groceries from which a loaf of Italian bread is sticking out; though a block away, she is already smiling at me, this responsive and responsible woman-child.

One of those memories takes me back to a cold February day in 1978, about six months after our ethnographic project had started. The temperature had dipped to ten degrees, and I was hanging out on the corner of Fourth and Avenue B, trying to keep warm with a bunch of kids aged ten to fourteen. They were waiting for Isabel, Lucita's older sister, to go with them to see two horror films over on Delancey Street, and I was locked out of my office. Since it was Saturday, my research team members Nilda and Paul wouldn't be moseying in to work until afternoon; they spent long evening hours in the neighborhood on weekends. Nilsa, our youngest colleague, whose official title was secretary but who was also a terrific field worker, would not be coming in at all; her weekends were reserved for her husband and four-year-old son. My only hope of rescue was Emilio, a fifteen-year-old, who from the beginning of the project had declared himself our official housekeeper, and who had my keys to the office. Emilio, alas, was nowhere to be seen.

While waiting for Isabel the kids tried to keep warm by talking about the movies they were about to see. The oldest, skinny fourteen-year-old Lisa Moreno with golden hair, and her rotund twelve-year-old brother Paco, had seen the movies already twice and thrice respectively. Now they were recounting the gory details to twelve-year-old Ginny Cortez. Lisa narrated the story almost to the climax. "Wait till you see it. You gonna scream!"

She looked up toward the clock hanging over Hanover Bank on Third Street. "Where the fuck is Isa at? She was supposed to be here at twelve-thirty and it's almost one." She then dispatched Marco, Ginny's gentle younger brother, whose glasses were patched at the bridge with a Band-Aid, and her own usually mercurial younger brother Jimmy, who was too cold at the moment to give her back any lip, to Lucita's and Isabel's house. "Tell her she doesn't get her ass down here *now*, we're leaving without her."

In a few minutes we saw Lucita, her little round face beaming from a block away as she rounded the corner from Fifth Street, a burned-out block with one intact building in which her family lived. She was on her way to the Dulceria Bakery to get fragrant coffee and a loaf of bread for her mother's breakfast. She said Isabel would be down in a minute. "The landlord didn't give no heat or hot water this morning," the third day in a row. Isa was waiting to bathe in a friend's apartment on the next block. The others nodded. No self-respecting child would sally forth into the outside world without a daily bath.

The children stomped their feet. They were all wearing sneakers, the only all-weather shoes their mothers could afford to buy, except for Lisa, who was wearing Fourteenth Street plastic cheapo high heels. She had on a black cowl synthetic sweater under a lilac nylon blouse, rayon trousers, and a thin raincoat. All dressed up and shivering. Daniel, an African American fourteen-year-old who lived below Delancey, now sauntered up to the group, cool in his belted beige raincoat, no doubt an Orchard Street special, and asked what was happening. The kids told him they were going to see *Telefon* and *Carrie*. Pretending to have just been invited, Daniel apologized for not being able to go with them. With a charming smile and a bow toward Lisa, he said: "You refused my invitation last week, now I am forced to refuse yours." As he went on his way, Lisa smiled at him, obviously charmed. The rascal knew Puerto Rican etiquette from hanging around with the local boys. He was already of an age considered dangerous for young señoritas, so he would have needed permission from Lisa's family to go with her to the movies, even surrounded as she was by a crew of obnoxious, underaged dueñas. And even then, the question of Daniel's race and ethnicity would have needed to be thrashed out before he was allowed to do any courting, to say nothing of an examination of his extended family, and so on and so forth, all very complex and already being fine-tuned in these pubescents' social repertoire.

As usual, Lisa was getting a lot of attention today. Now Loopy, a hyper fourteen-year-old with acne, joined the group and started teasing Lisa about her father, who had left the family five years ago and now lived in New Jersey with another woman and her children. Loopy said he had seen her father's car when he came to take the children to the beach last summer. He extended one accusatory hand toward an old station wagon parked on the block—"It's an old wreck, like this one!"—and pointed the other toward an ancient heap, belching exhaust at the stop light: "And smoking like that one!" Paco gazed down at his sneakers, Lisa's eyes flashed, and at this point I entered the conversation, asking Loopy what he was doing in the neighborhood, my tone suggesting that the rumor that he had moved away to the Bronx would not cause extreme sadness among those presently assembled. This was enough to defuse a potentially awkward situation: Lisa could not allow her father to be maligned, nor could she count on mellow Paco to play the macho and be his avenger. My seemingly innocent question was enough to put Loopy in his place.

Lucita passed by again, returning with the groceries, and Lisa once more warned her, in tones even more ominous, about leaving Isabel's ass behind. Lucita smiled good-naturedly, nodded, and went on. Then the rest of them left to see if they could persuade yet another girl to go with them. I stood frozen, gazing down the street, wondering idly where the fuck Emilio was at with my keys, and then catching myself; in less than a year's time I had begun to employ the children's linguistic constructs, at least in my head.

When I was finally installed in the office two hours later, Lucita stopped by for a chat, as she and other members of her family often did. She was on her way to the Key Food store on Avenue A in hopes that she could work that day. The massive Jamaican security guard at the store, nicknamed Jumbo by the children, was often capricious about allowing the girls to pack groceries for customers in exchange for tips. He didn't allow the boys to even set foot in the store, being well acquainted with their appetites and nimble fingers, but with the girls he played favorites. He was the final authority on who could work, and he picked and chose at will from the large group of eager workers in the neighborhood.

When she was allowed to pack, Lucita earned $10 to $15 a week for twenty to thirty hours' work. With these earnings she purchased her own clothing and school supplies and even saved for special occasions, such as Christmas dinner, which required expensive ingredients. Before departing, Lucita commented about how cold the office was. Like hers, our landlord was "not giving no heat or hot water," and it had been going on for a week. She also admonished me to stop smoking. "It's a matter of life and death," she said, furrowing her delicate brow for emphasis.

Later in the afternoon, the horror movie bunch returned for a visit. They vied with each other in recounting the bloody details blow by blow, watching my face with the satisfaction children get from making an effect on adult sensibilities. I wondered if seeing abstract horror relieved them, somehow, from the recurring crises in their own neighborhood.

Luz had been the first in her family to start frequenting our storefront anthropological field office. Curious, bouncing, affectionate, she shone among the eager group of children of all ages who turned up after school for tutoring and game playing. When she wasn't working at Key Food, she hung around the office as much as she could, trying to be helpful, often late into the night. On occasion, we had to carry her out bodily before closing shop, and we usually had to search before starting meetings to see if Luz was again hiding with some other little children under benches or inside cupboards. I was never sure whether it was our status as relatively exotic strangers or our rather mellow attitudes that encouraged these unending games of hide-and-seek.

The rest of her family approached us more gradually and cautiously, familiar to us by sight before we discovered they belonged to Luz. Early on in the research I had noticed an emaciated barefoot old man asleep in a doorway on the block. Over time he became a well-known figure, shuffling between the doorway and the corner. His head was shaved, his cheeks were sunken, and a lot of his teeth were missing. He smiled sweetly and mumbled to himself. The kids called him *loco* (crazy) behind his back, or teased him, begging him to sing some romantic Spanish song. On one occasion he actually obliged, and I was surprised by the scratchy yet melodious quality of his voice, rendering the echo of some long-forgotten ballad. Looking closer, I realized he wasn't much over forty.

It took a few months before I found out that he was Luz's mother's brother, her uncle Pedro, who had indeed been a singer of note in the neighborhood when he was a younger man. He had also had a factory job then, had been married and the father of a little girl. One day when the little girl was six, a sanitation driver had carelessly backed his truck up a little too fast and too far onto the sidewalk, as they tend to do on the Lower East Side. It crushed Pedro's daughter's head.

Pedro went berserk, attacking a sanitation crew (perhaps a different one) with a knife. He was arrested and was only allowed to attend his daughter's wake for a few minutes some days later, handcuffed and escorted by police officers. As I later learned, the prevailing opinion in the neighborhood dated the onset of Pedro's *locura* (craziness) to this incident and especially to the fact that he hadn't been able to express his grief properly, with respect, in company with the rest of his kin at the funeral. From that moment on, it was said, Pedro went downhill, drinking like crazy, losing his job, his wife, and his talent.

By the time I learned Pedro's story, I also knew he was not an abandoned derelict like so many others in the adjacent area of the Bowery. He was carefully monitored from a close distance by his sister Meri and her children. Late at night one of Lucita's brothers, seventeen-year-old Julio, fourteen-year-old Richie, or twelve-year-old Miguel, would guide Pedro to his one-room apartment on Fifth Street, secured for him and maintained by Meri with a small public assistance grant. During the day either Luz or her fifteen-year-old sister Isabel would get money from their mother to buy him a big hamburger (his lack of teeth made it hard for him to chew) from the tiny Dominican greasy spoon around the corner on Avenue B. He was also watched by other adults on the block, who conversed with him sociably whenever he was in shape to converse. He was not exactly confined, but someone always had an eye on him. Periodically, when he stopped eating altogether and drank too much, Meri would call the police to take him to Manhattan State Hospital for a few weeks' rest in the ward for the mentally ill. She said she did it to "make him fat." To the cops she said he was crazy.

After Luz became comfortable in my office, she brought in her brother Miguel, then Richie and Julio, then Isabel, and finally her mother. One summer day, Meri came in shyly, encouraged by Julio, who was learning from Paul how to use a video camera. She was a compact, shapely woman in her early forties, with a beautiful, mature round face. It was easy to tell where Luz got her looks. She didn't say anything, but just stood in the doorway smiling and gazing curiously around the office. Needing to go on an errand, Paul and I excused ourselves and asked Julio to watch the office. Upon returning, we found Julio behind the camera in the midst of persuading his mother to sing. Startled by our reappearance, she retreated, laughing. But from that day on she became a daily visitor, and I learned a great deal about her life.

Both her parents came from large families in rural Puerto Rico. Her father, who had been a cane cutter, came to New York in the 1940s and got his first job as a house painter, a profession he kept for the next thirty years, until he was in his mid-seventies. Her mother, a young woman at that time, had arrived to join her own mother, who was working in a lamp factory. She met and married Meri's father, and then stopped working, after the first of their seven children was born.

Dependent only on the father's wages, the family's existence was very precarious. Meri remembered being embarrassed about going to school in the clothes she owned. When one of the teachers offered her a hand-me-down dress in front of the other children, she was so ashamed that she dropped out of school. "Ay, Jagna," she told me, "I couldn't go back to the class." For a time she helped her mother with the care of her younger siblings; then, at the age of sixteen, she went to work in a garment factory to bring in extra money.

On the job she met the father of her first child, whom she did not marry. She had her first son when she was twenty. That year her mother died. And that same year, the whole neighborhood in which she had grown up was bulldozed to make way for public housing. She resettled in an old tenement close by and over the years had moved from one apartment to another within a close perimeter of her old home turf, vainly trying to improve her housing situation.

When I met Meri, she had had an application on file with the Housing Authority to obtain public housing for the past ten years. Every week she stopped at a furniture store on Allen Street to deposit a few dollars on credit for furniture to furnish her dream-to-come apartment. Over the years she had saved up $1,000 worth of credit in this store and another $1,000 in a furniture store in Brooklyn. As I discovered, this type of "saving" is typical in the neighborhood because public assistance regulations forbid any bank savings.

Aside from being responsible for her own children and her brother Pedro, Meri was also saddled with the care of her now incontinent and brain-damaged father, a consequence, she was sure, of his inhalation of paint fumes. She had to feed him, change his diapers, and constantly either watch him or have one of the children watch him, for he was fond of smoking and wasn't particularly careful about the matches or butts. Occasionally, and only after a great deal of nagging, one of her younger married sisters would relieve her for a couple of months by taking him in, but then Meri would discover that his small social security benefit had been misspent on things needed by the sister's children. She would not consider putting her father in an old folks' home: He had spent his life sacrificing for his children and now deserved good care in return.

Meri's life was full of *problemas*. After separating from the father of her first child, she met and married Ricardo Valiente, a man with whom she would have four more children. He worked in a garment factory, not making much money, and in the end started living with another woman. Then, in an argument, he pushed the woman into the East River. He was arrested, sentenced, and sent up-state. (Meri was vague about whether the woman had drowned.) With her husband incarcerated, Meri and her children were vulnerable physically and economically. They had no one to protect them "in the street," and instead of receiving material support from her husband, Meri was now obliged—despite his former dalliance—to help him in prison with occasional visits and small gifts.

Also doing time upstate was Felipe, her younger brother, who Meri said had been framed for murder by his brother-in-law, for whom he was taking the rap because the latter threatened to harm his wife if Felipe told the truth. Every few months Meri went to visit Felipe, usually taking Lucita with her. They got up very early in the morning to take the special 6:00 A.M. bus from Columbus Circle along with other women going to visit their relatives at various prisons now dotting the bucolic former vacation paradise of the Catskills. Depending on what prison Felipe was currently in—prisoners were moved frequently so they didn't develop any lasting ties—Meri and Lucita would spend two to three hours visiting and then ride back, late into the night, on the same cheap 1950s-vintage bus. Meri had tried to get the pastor of St. Theresa's over on Seventh Street involved in obtaining a release for her brother. He promised, but her brother remained in prison.

Meri ascribed her problems to the premature death of her mother. She felt she had been too suddenly thrust into the role of feminine head of the family. She also missed the experience and practical help that in most Puerto Rican families a mother provides for her daughter's children. In addition, Meri thought her mother would have provided a moral backup to curb Meri's husband's behavior. Meri's sisters lived in Brooklyn, too far away to exert any influence through women's opinion networks, even if they had wanted to get involved. And they didn't. They were involved in their Pentacostal church communities. So Meri's life was a lonely saga, as she told it. In times of crises she had no one to lean on.

For example, when her fourth child, Miguel, was born, she was home alone. She gave birth all by herself, squatting by the bed and holding on to it. It was a terribly painful experience, but not as humiliating as giving birth at the hospital. Meri hated and mistrusted hospitals, saying that the personnel showed no respect. Nevertheless, after suffering the pain and fear of giving birth to Miguel alone at home, she returned to the hospital to have Lucita. After Lucita's birth, when she was still groggy, some doctor asked her to sign something. She did, and the next thing she knew when she woke up was that she had been "operated" on—sterilized.

La operación, as it was known in the neighborhood, was a matter of serious consequence.[1] Some of the younger, upwardly mobile women elected to do it, even traveling to Puerto Rico if they couldn't find a doctor to perform it here. But these were women who usually had some advantages: combined family support, a mother's help with child care, some higher education, a good job, or a middle-class husband whose job situation was secure. For other women, there was a high premium on fertility as a means of attracting and holding a potential spouse.[2] For the people of the neighborhood it was simple: Every man wants to father a child.

That way at least he has accomplished something in this life. Something to make him live on, even if he dies at a young age—which many do. And a woman needs a man, because she cannot survive on public assistance or the kinds of wages she could earn by herself. So Meri was bereft by *la operación*. For a few years she had a steady, common-law partner, Sito, fifteen years younger than she, but he eventually drifted off to a nubile younger woman who had only two children and would probably be willing to have more.

Meri's analysis of her own situation, while quite correct in pointing out the helpful role of a mother in a woman's life and the role of fertility in attracting and holding a mate, did not go much further. She made some astute observations about things currently happening to her, but she did not yet comprehend that the constant humiliations she experienced were systemic, experienced by other women of the neighborhood as well.

For example, four evenings a week she attended an adult education class. She was given a small stipend of $30 a week to attend, a very helpful addition to her tight budget. She knew that there was something wrong with the class because she had been given the same texts, the same lectures, and the same exercises in the same class for the past five years. Only the teachers had changed. There was no progress, no advance from one level to another, and there was no talk of even the possibility of obtaining a G.E.D., or high school equivalency diploma. Her current teacher joked and abused the women verbally, calling them "a bunch of clowns," a phrase that questioned Meri's dignity as an adult. "Me, a *clown*, Jagna? I am the mother of five children!" She continued going to school because of the money, knowing that no one expected or wanted her to learn anything. She did not connect this continuing miseducation to the miseducation she had been treated to as a young woman nor to the miseducation her own children were then suffering. She had no baseline for knowing what education should be like, and even if she had, as some women who had gone to school in Puerto Rico did, she did not have the resources to effect a change. She did not know that the elementary school that she and all her children subsequently attended continued to hover at the bottom of the list of all the Manhattan schools for grade-level reading scores.

As she did not connect the function of public education in keeping the neighborhood's residents in place, she didn't understand the other parameters of structural poverty that affected her and her children's lives. She didn't really know that the lack of decent jobs (or even indecent ones, after the manufacturing jobs fled New York City) had a strong impact even on such intimate relations as conjugal stability. She interpreted the phenomenon of a floating male population in terms of machismo and sexual intrigues, as did most of the other women in the neighborhood. Nor did she consciously confront the question of why the drug business exercised such a strong lure for the young men in the area, a lure that would eventually snare her sons. She only said she knew her sons loved her very much and felt a great responsibility to help her—which indeed they did.

Meri's way of coping with all these problems was to "drink" Valiums all day. A kindly psychiatrist in the neighborhood to whom she had been referred by a friend prescribed high dosages as often as she needed them. From time to time, because he had to do things right for Medicaid reimbursement, he would have a short session with Meri. "Damn, Jagna," she'd tell me after one of those sessions, "that man knows all my business. He must be reading my mind." Whether he did or not, the Valiums kept rolling in, and Meri used them.

Only when she reached moments of total desperation would she go to consult an *espiritista*. She went for a consultation when her young partner, Sito, started seeing a younger woman. Meri was afraid she would do something insane in her grief. Walk into the traffic. Leave her children orphaned. After drinking half a bottle of rum and entertaining these thoughts, she went for a consultation. It must have helped because she never drank again. The espiritista, a local woman, knew Meri was using Valium and told her that it was impossible to pursue spiritual healing and growth while under its influence. But Meri couldn't give it up. After all, a doctor had prescribed it, so it couldn't be bad. She was addicted and didn't know it.

Perhaps because she was the mother of Luz, I did what I could to help Meri. Wherever we went with Lucita in tow, people gravitated to this beautiful child. Meri would say, "See, Jagna, how everybody loves Lucita? I don't know why."

"Because she's like you," I'd say, meaning she was loving, devoted, funny. To help Meri, I tried to find jobs for the older boys, but the jobs I scrounged up were all outside of the neighborhood, where the boys felt very uneasy. An invisible ghetto wall seemed to surround the Latino Lower East Side, ensuring the perpetuation of sufficiently different modes of social interaction on the inside to make the inhabitants feel like strangers on the outside. In addition, the boys felt needed in the neighborhood as protectors for their mother, sisters, younger brother, and friends. At any moment there might be a fire, a threatened fight, or an accident that might require their immediate assistance. Also, it was easier and more profitable to deal with outsiders on the boys' own turf: One could make a little bit of money by escorting middle-class people to the sources of drugs they came to buy in the neighborhood. And if the cops came, there were places to hide within running distance.

My attempt to get Meri out of the stinking hole of an apartment she lived in was eventually a little more successful, though it took some string pulling and a couple of bizarre trips with Meri through the city's housing offices. But despite my support in trying to make the system work for her, Meri's attempts on her own behalf flowed from her analysis of the cause of her problems, and therefore focused on the search for a union with a man as the basis for stability. At the time I was irritated by the constant competition for a mate that Meri and other women in her situation engaged in, regarding it as an anachronistic remnant of a tradition driven by machismo and currently reinforced by Latino *novelas* (soap operas). In retrospect I see that for Meri it was a rational strategy. Lacking consanguineous social support, no matter how financially modest, which her mother's generation and networks would have provided had her mother not died prematurely, Meri sought affined connections with and through a man, because men, even when only sporadically employed, can count on some support from their natal units. Until her own sons were old enough to secure the extra resources needed for survival on the Lower East Side, a loyal adult male would be an important asset for her own and her children's security.

When I first met Meri she had been living with Sito for the past two years. He was a handsome young man in his mid-twenties, with divorced parents who both lived in the neighborhood. Sito worked as a construction group member for Adopt-a-Building, gutting old tenements that the organization was able to pry away from the city's stockpile of abandoned buildings and rehabilitating them for local housing needs. The work was sporadic because of constant red-tape delays in permits, inspections, and cash flow problems, but when Sito got up early and joined his buddies on Count Augusto's crew, he was ecstatic and generous. He played the role of father to Meri's children, buying them needed clothing and treats, taking the whole family on evening excursions to the neighborhood swimming pool (which was officially closed at night, so the children and women needed strong arms for boosts in scaling the fence), protecting the family from intruders in their dilapidated building, and because he worked in the neighborhood, being always close enough to attend to emergencies. For example, when Miguel, then eleven, cracked his head diving in a West Village municipal pool and the whole family stood around wringing their hands, Lucita asking, "Is he dead?" Sito was already on his way to the Ninth Precinct police station and was the first one in the emergency room at Bellevue Hospital, attending to Miguel as his wound was being stitched up. In times like this, Sito provided an important role model for responsible manhood. He extended his care to other younger people and was the first one to intervene, unfortunately too late, in the murder of poor Juan. In retrospect, I can see that the example of Sito's courage still animates Miguel's behavior as an adult.

But during the lay-off periods Sito was depressed. He hung listlessly around the apartment, resenting the fact that Meri was supplying him with food, cigarettes, and an occasional pink Champale, his favorite drink, and he picked little quarrels with her. Her decision to move into the public housing that I had helped her secure provided the occasion for their formal breakup a year later. He moved in with his father, who lived in another project in the neighborhood, and as Meri soon found out, started courting a woman his own age. It pained and annoyed me to see Meri so distraught that she stooped to spying on him, asking her boys to follow him (which they refused to do), so obsessed that she finally confronted the new woman with Sito's photograph, asking, "Is this the man you love? Well, he is my husband." The woman just laughed at her, confident in her own allure and ability to hold Sito. What had been missing from the equation that might have provided a stronger tie to Sito and his kin was a child between the two. Love, sex, and companionship alone were not strong enough to maintain enduring ties in the harsh social and economic climate of the neighborhood. Serial monogamy and modest contributions of money and clothing for a man's children were the best a woman could expect.

Six months after her breakup with Sito, and after weeks of not having been around, Meri came into the office beaming and holding hands with a man who looked to my eyes very surly. He was in his thirties, handsome in a dangerous sort of way. His very dark eyes glistened from under his hat. She introduced him as Julio, her fiancé. I invited Julio to sit down, which he did, and then he pulled out a pint bottle of rum, asking me if I would like a drink. I declined but brought him a glass, and he proceeded to drink while Meri and I chatted in the back office.

It turned out that Julio had just been released from an upstate prison. She had met him there, courtesy of her brother. Since all of his brothers were doing well by Lower East Side standards, and married, they did not invite him to live with them. His mother was also reluctant to take him in. She lived over on Ninth Street in a small apartment taking round-the-clock care of her dying twenty-year-old daughter. The daughter had worked in a doll factory, and her family believed that the chemicals used there had paralyzed her central nervous system. I saw her once, before her death, a piteous skeleton, more child than woman, contorted on a wide mahogany bed, her hands elongated frozen claws. Since she had worked "off the books," there was no question of workmen's compensation, even if anybody had been sophisticated enough to know about pursuing it. Her hands full, Julio's mother was relieved to hear he would be staying with Meri.

As an ex-con, Julio would have a difficult time finding a job in the already tight job market. In the meantime, the Human Resources Administration was dragging its feet about providing him with a minimal amount of "home relief" that would pay for a room. So, Meri told me, she supported him. They were now living together, and they would soon be married.

Luz came in from her work at Key Food during the last part of the conversation. She leaned into her mother's lap and looked from her to me with shining, happy eyes. Meri stroked her hair with long searching gestures as mothers tend to do with daughters. As daughters do with mothers. As sisters do with sisters and girl cousins with one another on the Lower East Side. Then Meri took her leave. She had to go home to cook for her man. In the meantime, he had polished off the rum. They all left together, stopping off for Isabel at Key Food. She had also been lucky that day, because Jumbo was in a good mood. The boys remained on the corner of Avenue B and Fourth Street. When I locked up the office after midnight, I saw them still there, open to whatever luck might bring. They gave me a cheerful grin.

The engagement lasted six months. It was terminated by Julio's suicide. Or perhaps murder? I was awakened early one morning by a call from Miguel. "Jagna, my mother wants me to tell you that Julio is dead."

"What? Julio?" I thought he was talking about his older brother.

"No," Miguel corrected me, "I mean Julio, my father." In the neighborhood, a mother's common-law spouse becomes "Father" to her children as soon as his intentions to perform the role are declared.

I told him I'd be right down. Meri met me dressed in a black blouse and black jeans, probably just purchased for the occasion. She was distraught, but not weeping, and it was obvious that the Valiums were doing their thing. We went over the details of what had happened step by step. While Meri talked, Luz tried to touch her mother's hair, but Meri pushed her hand roughly away. Both their faces were swollen from crying.

Julio had gotten into big trouble. Two days before his death he was supposed to have appeared in two different places at exactly the same time: one appointment directed him to meet his parole officer, and the other was for him to appear at the welfare office. If he didn't go to the parole officer a warrant might be issued for his rearrest. If he didn't appear at the welfare office, his case might again be postponed. The fact that he was depending on Meri for his support was weighing very heavily on his mind. He tried to change the appointment at both places but got the wrong people or wrong numbers and ran out of money in the public telephone booth. So that day he went to his parole officer, and then rushed over to welfare, but it was too late. They told him to come back the next day.

On his way home Julio held up a man in an alley and took his wallet. The man ran after him, somebody called the cops, and Julio was arrested. He called Meri from the Ninth Precinct. When she got there she was told he had been transferred to a precinct uptown. She went there also but was told he had been transferred to a third precinct. At this point, it was late at night and she went to Julio's mother's house to consult with and comfort her.

At about three o'clock in the morning, the police came knocking on his mother's door and announced that Julio had hung himself in the uptown precinct. Meri didn't believe it. Neither, really, did I. Julio did not have a winning way with cops. Once, as we watched an arrest going on near the office, I had observed him glaring at the cops, murder in his eyes. He had not looked like a man who would turn his rage against himself.

The next day we went from one precinct to another trying to find out what had happened: no luck. Meri wanted to be sure that a proper inquest would be held, and she tried to interest Julio's family to press for it. As a mere girlfriend, in the authorities' eyes she had no legal rights. And his family did not want any further trouble. Paul went to the Medical Examiner's office with Meri's son Julio; they were given a confirmation of the police story. It was hard to believe, especially in light of the two precinct transfers. Meri still didn't believe it, and neither did I. But who gives a damn about an ex-con stickup artist?

A few days later I went with Meri and Luz to the *funeraria*, the Fernandez Funeral Parlor on First Avenue. Julio's brothers were footing the bill for this rite of passage. I'd visited the place several times before, but this time it was harder than ever. There was Meri, dressed in her black jeans and blouse, clutching her perpetual brown paper bag in which she holds her entire identity. In it are her and her father's and children's birth certificates, her welfare card with her picture on it, her food stamps, her Medicaid card, her father's social security papers, Pedro's papers, her rent and Con Ed receipts, and of course, her Valium.

The undertaker's wife, solid Señora Fernandez, wearing house slippers, welcomed us in. The slippers add a back-home touch to the funeral parlor rites, making people remember that in Puerto Rico, *velorios* (wakes) were traditionally held at home. She and Meri held a whispered conference. Later I learned that Meri had been trying to find out whether Señor Fernandez had found any signs of violence on Julio's body while preparing it for the wake. The señora was sympathetic and diplomatic. If the family was really interested, they should take it up with the Medical Examiner.

I entered the main room of the funeral parlor with Luz. Isabel was already there, kneeling on a plush stool beside the gladiola-adorned open casket. Lucita went forward and knelt beside her sister. I approached more gingerly. All the murderous glare and dangerous good looks were gone from Julio's face. He was just lying there like a powdered, papier-mâché doll, dressed in a black suit, his lifeless hands enfolded around a rosary. His thick hair was slicked back. Isabel reached out to his hair and started to caress it. She went through it lovingly and thoroughly, strand by strand. I retreated to a seat, feeling sick. The room looked sinister, dark, with old Italian plaster saints staring into space. They had seen other ethnic groups go the way of all flesh. No sympathy.

Then the girls crossed themselves and walked over into the antechamber. They huddled together in an old velvet upholstered chair, whispering to each other and stroking each other's hair. Now Meri knelt by the casket. She crossed herself and presumably prayed, filling the plush stool, her I.D. bag beside her. Then she got up, stroked Julio's hair, and proceeded to roll up one of his sleeves, looking intently at his arm. Suddenly she motioned me to come over. Oh my God, I thought, she's going to show me evidence of murder. But no. As I came close she pointed to a tattoo on Julio's arm. It was a heart with the names of Julio and Meri needled into it.

I walked into the afternoon sunlight with Lucita, who seemed overwhelmed and gladly accepted an invitation to my house. Meri was willing to let her go. Thwarted by the police, the Medical Examiner's office, and Julio's family, the Valium not doing its job, she herself was headed to the espiritista for a consultation.

One day three years later, I picked Lucita up by car for another visit. She was now blooming into adolescence, round and full and bursting at the seams with life like her mother.

In the car, catching up on all the news, she told me that on one of the trips upstate Meri had been introduced by her still-incarcerated brother to another fellow prisoner. The man had no relatives willing to make the tedious bus ride upstate. In the coolly controlled atmosphere of the state prison, Meri fell in love with her brother's friend, and a few months later they were married by a prison chaplain.

Meri seemed to have found what she'd been seeking—a stable union that would provide her with the social status of a married woman. As a married prisoner, Meri's new husband got weekend privileges. One weekend out of four, if he behaved, he could use a private mobile home on the prison grounds to entertain his family for two days. Meri brought food and cooked her heart out; *arroz con gandules* (rice with peas), *pernil* (roasted fresh ham), and more.

"Jagna, it's so beautiful there, so peaceful," Luz told me. "There's grass and trees all over. You can see cows eating grass. You could hear the birds singing."

2

Dancing

On that cold February day, as I waited for Emilio and my keys, I passed the time peering at the street that by then should have been as familiar as my own. In the midst of fieldwork, it is seldom that one gets a chance to see the familiar with new eyes. So, my feet gradually freezing, I stood gazing at our beloved tenement from outside the *bodega* (grocery) across the street. Since all of the street phones had been mangled, I had gone in there to call Emilio's family, and I could now feel the bodega owners giving me the evil eye—as they usually did, whether I was inside their store or out. I didn't know the reason for their animosity, unless of course they suspected that I suspected that their commercial interests extended beyond tropical *vegetales* and bleeding *carne*.

The store looked like a normal bodega should. The meat, as was customary, sat in its little pool of blood in a refrigerated case; the sturdy Caribbean fruits and roots nestled in their crates, only slightly worn by their sea voyage; and an impressive array of cleansers and poisons for the daily battle with germs and pests graced the shelves. The front glass counter, below the cash register, was piled with jars of cookies and candies for the young sweet-tooths of the neighborhood. Because of the heavy patronage the bodega was blessed with, it was anyone's guess whether more mature cravings that went beyond beer were also being slaked by the store owners, two well-muscled dark men. I thought yes, and as I stood with my back to them, I could feel their hostile eyes right between my shoulder blades.

I hopped from foot to foot, doing a little jig because I couldn't feel my feet anymore, and I wasn't even wearing sneakers, like the children, but my Vermont hiking specials. On the telephone, Emilio's brother Pablo had politely told me he didn't know where Emilio was "at." He had left the usual obscenity out of the phrase, since he was a young man of nineteen talking to an older señora. Obligations had already been established between his family and our team, and although they were minimal, they had elevated me into the category of "señora." The initial deal struck with Emilio, who was first on the scene just about the moment we moved into our storefront office, was that he would help to keep it clean and orderly, in exchange for the use of our phone for romantic purposes and occasional "loans" of a quarter for sweets. From the moment he took the broom out of my hands and proceeded to sweep the floor with extravagant manly strokes I knew it was fate. Every evening from then on—and in between, as the mood struck him— he would enter into a whirlwind of cleaning, first emptying all the trash, including cigarette butts, onto the floor, and then raising it all into a neat twister that eventually spun out the open front door onto the sidewalk, to expire there and then be tracked back in by little feet. He also became very adept at finding and dragging out from inside the office cupboards and cabinets the stowaways who had hid there. Once he flushed out two little guys who had hid between the real and the fake ceilings of our office. With time, the scope of his helpfulness expanded.

One afternoon, while running along the East River park, Emilio encountered a very large and pitiful dog. The creature, part Arctic wolf, part Dr. Seuss cartoon, was shivering and starving, his hindquarters sloping down as if deformed by blows, physical or otherwise. For Emilio it was love at first sight. However, Señora Medina, as I knew her then, Emilio's mother, was adamant: Seven people living in a tiny two-bedroom apartment was enough. But being an immensely practical woman, she suggested that Emilio ask us to house Max the Wolf in our office, in exchange for heavy-duty cleaning over the weekends. I agreed, even though also being an immensely practical woman, I knew that the heavy-duty cleaning would mostly be needed on account of Max. But we both also knew that this was the next step toward deepening the relations between our team and Emilio's family, a minor variant of *compadrazco* (godparenthood), with me becoming something akin to a dog-mother to their Max.

Max was a people dog. In addition to arthritis, he suffered from slight incontinence, which flowered when he was locked up in our cavernous cold storefront within hearing range of children's voices upstairs, in the corridors, and on the street. Even though Emilio, armed with our keys when we were away, took him for walks and fed him, he pissed out of loneliness.

Not only did he piss, but he sprawled all over the new blue covers Nilsa had sewn in her off hours for the foam rubber pillows lining the benches Paul had built, leaving big clots of greyish wolfhound hair. During more desperate moments of longing, he gnawed at the legs of the sturdy octagonal tables Paul also had built, and finally started in on the fake "wood" paneling that encased the walls and doors of our office. I didn't feel too bad about the paneling because it had been installed by the previous tenants, a drug-dealing "social club." But the Sterns, our landlord and his mother, did mind. I myself had to admit that the inside of the front door, chewed off to the height of Max's snout, the spotty covers, and the rough-hewn table legs lent the place a less than classy appearance. I had hoped to establish a haven for the children and their parents; pretty, clean, peaceful, a place in which to discuss important things, to feel unstressed.

Although different from what I had had in mind, the storefront did become a haven. Noisy, contentious, messy, but homey nonetheless. The pillow covers got frequent washings from Señora Medina's washing machine upstairs, and Emilio asked me for money to buy an industrial-size mop and wringer/bucket, which he used incessantly when he wasn't in school or working. One of the very few boys lucky enough to have a real job, Emilio went to school from 8 A.M. until 1 P.M. and then worked in a drugstore, in a special work-study program, until evening. After work, he hung out with us, often getting help with his homework, and then enthusiastically helped to clean up and clear out the office at night. His stamina was a source of inspiration.

As I gazed from across the street at our storefront, its door fastened with two sturdy padlocks that were probably frozen, my sense of urgency was stimulated by the lonesome howls emanating from its interior. To get my mind off what Max might be up to in the office, I turned my attention to the tenement on its right, at the time owned by Chino, an Indian ethnic from Guyana who represented himself to us as a "socialist." His tenants represented him to us as another "lan'lo" who gave no heat or hot water, maybe worse than other landlords in the neighborhood. Myrna, who lived in his building, told our team member Nilda that he hadn't paid for the electricity in the hallways for years, hooking it up to the tenants' meters instead. She also told her she had recently slapped him while waiting for the mailman, because the building was freezing. Chino in turn told another member, Nilsa, that he was taking Myrna to court for assault and battery, adding gleefully: "Guess what her husband gave her for Christmas? Two black eyes. That's what she deserves!" He repeated a favorite assertion of his, that Myrna was an addict, just like the rest of his tenants. Although we had seen Myrna and a couple of the other younger women entering Ismael's little herb store next door, they did not seem to be addicted. More likely, Chino's hostility was based on the fact that the tenants, led by Myrna and Basia Plotek, a Polish widow, had recently organized themselves into a tenants' association.

Chino himself was no angel. Besides identifying himself as a socialist, he represented himself as a bachelor. He had asked Nilda, and then Nilsa, in separate tête-à-têtes, to join him on an all-expense-paid trip to Guyana in order to marry, in two different versions, either himself or his brother.

Quite aside from the fact that at that time a marriage of convenience to acquire legal U.S. immigration status by a noncitizen to a Puerto Rican woman fetched a going rate of $2,000, plus an all-expense-paid trip—and that it also had to be broached with respect and propriety, preferably couched in a romantic idiom—we all knew via the tenants' grapevine that Chino had a wife and child sequestered in his back, first-floor apartment. Indeed, the very morning that his wife was entering a taxi on the way to Bellevue to deliver their second child, Chino had arrived at our office to continue his seduction of Nilsa. Already informed of the situation chez Chino at our earlier weekly staff meeting, Nilsa cut him dead with a courteous "I understand congratulations are in order?"

After that he stopped visiting. But we kept abreast of his doings as the building briefly passed from his socialist hands into the bureaucratic hands of the city, which didn't give heat or hot water either, and back into his possession when he paid off some of his real estate taxes. By then he had acquired a fellow landsman as a partner, who, being a greenhorn, thought he had landed in the Wild West. We were to make the acquaintance of his gun some months later.

As I stood waiting, I noticed that the traffic entering Ismael's storefront, next door to Chino's building, was beginning to pick up. Like so many successful small businessmen, Ismael was a sociable guy. Soon after our arrival, his wife and two young children had decamped to live with her mother over on Avenue D. It was said she was getting worried about the children, considering Ismael's source of income. Aside from dabbling in spiritist practices, for which, according to a knowledgeable espiritista, he had neither vocation nor any proper apprenticeship,[1] he also had the oldest marijuana dealership in the neighborhood. He had a reputation for honesty and good product, was open long hours, and allowed older teenagers to smoke on his premises. His business seemed more stable than the other small enterprises in the neighborhood. He made small, steady profits as an outlet for local middlemen, and he apparently had no interest in branching out to other drugs and bigger earnings. You might say he was risk-averse, sticking only to grass, *la hierba*.

To the left of our office sat another thriving business, a car repair shop owned and operated by two reserved, middle-age Cubans. All day and all evening, behind the partially shut gate of the garage, all kinds of vehicles were getting repaired, repainted, revved up, customized, and transmogrified. We had made several attempts at neighborliness with the men, mainly by asking for various adjustments on our assorted wrecks, all initially rejected. It was only Count Augusto's intercession that finally got me some new shoes for my brakes. But even that service was completed with stony politeness in spite of my attempt to fraternize. We had to learn about their trade through observation enlivened by gossip, speculating on the occasional brand-new cars that entered their doors only to emerge some time later in different hues. But we didn't look too intensely. It was rumored that the men were practicing spiritists, not of the garden-variety Puerto Rican *espiritismo*, but of an afro-indio-cathlo-voodoo practice, requiring black roosters, goats, and human remains, preferably from Haitian cemeteries. Although the study of *voudoun* was at the time close to the cutting edge of ethnographic studies, we had enough to worry about, and so we kept our distance.

Next to the voodoo garage was a small, nondescript shop that seemed to change hands and purposes about every two months. At one time it sold coffee and hot dogs; at another, it was filled with pinball machines, and we were swamped by kids' requests for "loans" of quarters to play them. Next it sold plaster saints, incense, and other paraphernalia for home altars; then it went back to hot dogs. But whatever its official purpose, it remained a final destination point for the *bolita* man who made the rounds every day collecting money for the numbers game. The man, probably in his late forties and wearing a navy knit hat, had the looks of a favorite uncle, with his basset-hound jowls, sympathetic eyes, and good-sized *nariz* (nose). He made his rounds in and out of the stores, up and down the tenement stairs, and sideways into greasy spoons, genially greeting the men and señoras. Even the Cubans, out on a break in front of their garage in beach chairs, returned his friendly greetings and apparently invested.

The next building was owned by a woman named Dolly Greenberg, who currently lived on Long Island, as Paul found out from records at City Hall. We frequently saw Dolly sitting in an up-to-date Buick, palavering with an older, heavy-set man whom the kids had nicknamed "Padrone."

Padrone's sons, Freddie and Sam, when not in prison, were supers in Dolly's and our buildings. It was rumored that Dolly, a pale champagne blonde in her late fifties, was renting her apartments to drug dealers and that several apartments in her building had become shooting galleries. If true—and our observation of the steady stream of people into her building seemed to confirm the rumor—it showed that Dolly had a prescient sense for business, a few years ahead of the other "lan'lo's" in the neighborhood. Though the allotments that welfare provided for tenement housing were being eaten away by inflation, a landlord could still make some profit off impoverished tenants by "milking" his (or her) building, simply taking their rent money and not repairing, painting, or providing heat and hot water. However, it was already in the wind that drug dealers would pay two or three times the amount of rent for an apartment, no questions asked, no complaints about no heat.

The two buildings hugging the corner of Avenue B were owned by a German, apparently a fairly recent emigré, with a crew cut and cold eyes. Lisa and her family, who were his tenants, reported that he was punctilious about the rent. Now I wondered how he managed to ignore the stuff that was being sold from the small, awning-shaded, hole-in-the-wall shoppette in the corner of his building. It was rented and operated by Rocky, a solid, dependable young man who sold sweets, cigarettes, and joints by the piece, occasionally to the young scholars on unofficial breaks from the Immaculate Heart parochial school located next door to Ismael's—to say nothing of the male pubescents of our more immediate acquaintance. Rocky's younger brother, Olie, who was also Señora Medina's son-in-law, was cooling his heels in Puerto Rico, but due to return any day now.

Just when I thought I felt frostbite setting in, I heard a whistle and looked up to the third-floor window to see Pablo's head sticking out. He yelled down that he was throwing me the key to the lobby's door, the local air-express custom used in many transactions. A curtain parted in the window next to the Medinas' apartment, and I recognized Doña Mercedes, performing her street-watching duties as well as her religious ones, since she was all dressed in white. She wore white dresses on behalf of other women who had made a promise to a saint or to the Virgin to wear white in exchange for help with a life-threatening problem or to avert calamity, always just around the corner in the neighborhood. Since *la promesa* is serious business, requiring a prolonged period of time to discharge, and wearing white to a factory job—which the women occasionally wangled off the books—was not acceptable, Doña Mercedes carried out the vows, often for several women concurrently. She was also in demand for leading *rosarios*, chanted recitations of the rosary performed on nine consecutive evenings following the death of a family member. Her calling inspired the honorific title of Doña.

A celibate widow in her late fifties, Doña Mercedes was the mother of five children, three elder sons married and living in the neighborhood and two daughters, eighteen and sixteen, still at home. The younger one had Down's syndrome. Doña Mercedes supplemented her own small welfare benefit with her daughter's social security allotment for the disabled and modest gratuities from her religious practice, which were sometimes paid in money, sometimes in goods or reciprocal services. She was a woman of strict morals. Sometimes she spoke to Nilda of this woman or that with deep disapproval. She'd say, "This Sonia, you know the one from upstairs, went to bed with the Con Edison man, so he would read her meter wrong," or "*Esa rubia* (that blond one) gave the plumber some *crica* (pussy)," and so on. Her constant preoccupation, however, was "working on my sons' minds" to make them exact justice on behalf of the family. Her brother, the only *baron* (boy) in a family with six daughters, had been murdered in Puerto Rico by a man who at this very moment was walking free on the streets of the neighborhood. She told Nilda, "*Un ojo por ojo, un diente por diente*" (An eye for eye, a tooth for tooth). At this moment she had her *ojo* on me, and that was way too many ojos for comfort.

Pablo appeared in the downstairs lobby. I guessed that the family consensus upstairs had been that it was too familiar a gesture to pitch the key out. Despite the ten-degree weather and lack of heat, he was wearing sandals over his bare feet, jeans, and a short-sleeved shirt. He escorted me up the dog-piss stairs, into the family quarters. A considerable amount of activity must have taken place from the time I phoned to the time I was fetched. The place was very clean and in the process of being perfected. Señora Medina's older daughter, Clara, who lived above with her husband and three-year-old, Andres Jr., was remopping the floor, cold water pouring out of the kitchen faucet, as usual when Puerto Rican women are cleaning house full blast. She was wearing a blue baby-doll nightie and panties. The kitchen was steaming due to the two vats of water boiling on the stove in addition to a red-hot brick glowing on another burner and the wide open heat-exhaling oven. The internal climate of the apartment was decidedly Caribbean, even if the heated brick (*ladrillo*) and gas oven were recent cultural innovations.

The kitchen was furnished with a table, no chairs, a washing machine and refrigerator. Eti, or Señora Medina, as I then knew her, was standing by the kitchen sink, talking on the telephone. Her appearance was an absolute revelation to me. On previous occasions I had seen her in well-worn jeans and a cheap pea jacket, her hair pulled severely back under a kerchief, giving her face a hard, frozen look, the look of a woman *sufriendo*. Suffering is what most women over forty hailing from Catholic backgrounds, whether Spanish, Italian, or Polish, are supposed to do. Now she was transformed. She was wearing a raspberry-colored, low-cut nightgown that revealed a lithe brown body. She had a string of pearls around her neck and a heavy silver bracelet on her wrist. Tiny, perfectly shaped feet were visible below the hem of the raspberry gown, and her hair, now loose, hung heavily, black and lustrous, halfway down her back. I was amazed by the relaxed, finely carved beauty of her face. She smiled, and motioned graciously to me to pass into the front room.

Andres Jr. was sitting on the daybed, watching an old black-and-white movie on a small television set that sported a wire hanger antenna. Pablo indicated a comfortable old easy chair and told me he'd be right back. Feeling a little strange at invading a domestic scene, I looked out the window and saw Pablo go into the bodega, then emerge with a grocery bag crowned by two loaves of French bread. As we discovered after months of acquaintance, Pablo was the family drone. After graduating from high school, he had landed a dull, non-union job in a factory, turning his earnings over to his mother. His income provided the necessary unreported addition to the welfare allotment for the younger children that permitted her to balance her household budget. On weekends he shopped and ironed his younger brothers' clothes. He told Nilsa he resented not being able to go out to lunch with his coworkers and the fact that young women considered him a *bobo* (sissy).

While waiting for adult company, I looked around the room and into another, apparently Señora Medina's bedroom, which contained a huge mahogany bed covered with a red chenille bedspread. All the walls of the apartment were painted white with red trim on the woodwork, and the front window was draped in matching red fabric. Soon Pablo rejoined us, but he sat quietly watching the television as I attempted some conversation with Andres Jr. It soon became clear that this three-year-old not only knew what was happening in the film, "mi caballito come la luz" (my little horse is eating the light, and indeed the stupid horse was nibbling a light bulb), but also spoke better Spanish than I. Clara stuck her head into the room and, laughing, told him, "Esa Americana no habla espanol" ("This American woman doesn't speak Spanish"). Presently, Señora Medina asked me, in Spanish, if I would like some coffee. I said yes, if they were also having some, and soon I was invited back into the kitchen, where Pablo was dragging in heavy chairs, upholstered in red, from the bedroom. Meanwhile, Clara was fetching "good" cups from a glass cabinet in the front room. Señora Medina served me *café con leche*, and she also served junior, after some lengthy negotiations about the amount of milk he was willing to have in it. Finally, she sat down with a sigh to drink with me and detail the reasons for her late start of the weekend cleaning.

Sitting with one foot up on the chair, caressing it, she told me that she had stayed up very late the night before. On Friday nights she would go with her girlfriends dancing in a fashionable Spanish nightclub on the West Side. The club was frequented by South American businessmen here for short or longer visits. The women danced, kept an eye on each other, made sure to be properly introduced, and occasionally met a man they might date, or even better, marry. I understood her to mean that the marriage deals were usually arranged to provide the man with permanent residence, although the possibility of a true love, inspired by the novelas, seemed to be an aspiration among this group of women. Over subsequent months, Nilsa got to know them better, all mothers whose partners had moved on to younger women, premature death, or prison. Several of the core of six, connected through kinship or fictive "sister" ties, were able to establish semi-durable love relationships with men they met at the nightclub, which included courtship, the purchase of gifts for the woman and her children, and companionship. The women chose their partners carefully, hoping for a lasting relationship. But none of the friends found a man to marry; doubtless the large class difference between them and the men lowered their chances.[2]

Settling herself more comfortably, Eti Medina began to tell me her life story. I would later discover that this was a very edited version—the full extent of this woman's courage and devotion to her children would only be revealed after many years of friendship. That day she told me the following story: Her husband was an alcoholic and living somewhere in Puerto Rico with his mistress. After Eti and he had had seven children together, she started using birth control pills, in secret from her husband. The presumption among the men there, she said, was that a woman with access to pills would be unfaithful to her husband. He personally observed her menstrual calendar, marking the days with big crosses, and when she didn't conceive again, he repeatedly created scenes, hitting her and accusing her of using pills because she had a lover. She saved money from her job as a school cook/nutritionist, and when she had enough, she took her four youngest children and joined her sister-in-law on the Lower East Side.

Two of her other children later joined her, but she had not heard from her husband in the five years since her departure. "I don't even know whether he's well or ill. If I ever marry again, it won't be to a Puerto Rican," she said dreamily. She went on to say that she had met a very nice Portuguese man at the club, they had gone out "as friends" for over a year, but that now he was back in Portugal for a visit and she didn't know if he'd return. She told me she was now looking for a rich old man to marry, a man who needed a woman's care. And she laughed.

I told her that another woman I knew from El Barrio (Spanish Harlem), a widowed grandmother, had done exactly that: Like in a novela, she met a Greek millionaire and married him. Because these fairy-tale romances do occur, they acquire the status of Horatio Alger stories for impoverished women. But I went on to say that I personally preferred to depend on myself, not on any man. Eti said that she would also like to be in my position, but the thought of going back to school was very frightening, and with the credentials she already had, she could not find a job that paid enough to live on. She had obtained her G.E.D. in 1969 and had taken several college courses in nutrition in Puerto Rico. Concurrently, she had obtained a job as a nutritionist in a Head Start program. To prove this to me, she went into her bedroom and returned with a large old leather bag stuffed with documents. She showed me her diploma and certificates, proud of her accomplishments; then downcast, she told me how she had applied to many New York schools for a job preparing children's meals, without any luck. She sounded very depressed. She said it was probably because her English was not very good—she lacked the *facilidad* in speaking it, although she understood and read it well. The few English phrases she used sounded fine to me, but it did seem that her self-confidence was undermined, making the language problem loom large. Anyway, I told her, what kind of advanced linguistics did she need to prepare lunches for mostly Spanish-speaking children in the neighborhoods she applied for?

We chatted some more, about schools, children. She thought that the education she had received in Puerto Rico was superior to what her children were getting in New York City schools. The casualness with which truancy and dropping out were tolerated by the schools seemed to make her especially angry. "They don't really care whether our children come out educated or not. Maybe they even prefer to have us ignorant." Her eldest son, now an army officer, had completed some college in Puerto Rico, and the next two, her daughters Clara and Maria, had finished high school there. (Maria still lived there). The next in age, Pablo, had managed to finish high school here, but she was worried about the youngest three boys—even Emilio, whom she had once encountered on the street when he was supposed to be in school. She chased him with a broom, she said, all the way into the principal's office, where she gave him a big whacking. At the time I wondered why she was carrying a broom in the street, but in due time I realized that the chase-with-a-broom-into-the-principal's-office story was apocryphal: Señora Medina herself retold it with variations on the particular sons involved, and so did other conscientious mothers, as well as children, proud of their mother's concern. Although there was not really any onslaught of enraged mothers wielding broomsticks in principals' offices all over the Lower East Side, there was the need to try to connect with indifferent, impersonal school officials, to demonstrate to them dramatically how much the education of the children really mattered, that the mothers were on their side as adults with authority. But it was all in vain. The mothers were treated by school officials with contempt at worst, and with indulgent paternalism at best.

When I asked her about the red and white paint job in the apartment, Señora Medina told me she had done it with the boys. There had been a fire in the apartment next door, and her own apartment had sustained a lot of water damage. The landlord had sent someone over to do some essential (ugly) plastering, but he refused to repaint. She pointed to gaping cracks in the baseboards; rats came through them at night, she said.

Our conversation eventually turned to our plan for Nilsa to accompany Eti to Small Claims Court. Señora Medina was taking action against a furniture company where she had been saving for several years, a couple of dollars a week, until she had $1,400 saved up. Now the company was trying to stick her with some huge couch that wouldn't even fit through the door. Nilsa was a highly skilled advocate, having been trained by her mother from a young age, and possessed a fiery tongue, fierce disposition, and an uncommon sense of justice. Señora Medina's own daughter Clara, who had arrived from Puerto Rico with her husband only five months before, was still docile, lacking the Nuyorican women's assertiveness.

As we talked, Eti offered me bread with margarine; the others casually helped themselves. With housecleaning temporarily halted, Clara joined Junior and Pablo in the front room to watch a Vincent Price horror movie. I joined them when Señora Medina got a call from another potential millionaire-husband. "Henry? I don't know who is Henry. Ah, yes, I remember you, but you never came to take me to the party. . . . "

When Emilio finally showed up with my keys, about two hours later, I didn't complain too hard. I felt ebullient about getting to know Señora Medina, and the trust she had showed in telling me about her life.

As she walked me to the door I thanked her, and then sniffing smoke, asked her if she smelled it too. She nodded but seemed neither bothered nor inclined to explain her lack of worry. I later asked Emilio what it was.

"Oh, they're trying to kill people in the building."

Really alarmed, I said, "Who?"

He answered, laughing, that the espiritistas were making witchcraft, and what I smelled was burning incense.

As time passed, I heard newer, more extensive versions of Señora Medina's battle to preserve and enhance her children's lives and her own. As in a restored painting, the uncovered, deeper layers presented more vibrant colors than scenes painted over to conform to conventional morality. Time and the trust built through the staff's help, which continued long after the project was over and continues to this day, brought forward the most dramatic uncovering of the past. This was a sobering lesson to me as an anthropologist. What versions of reality do we report after only one or two years of study? And what are indigenous academics, of a higher class, willing to impart about their own poor, when as a group they must defend themselves against grave racist stereotypes?

The deeper version of Eti Medina's story after her arrival in the United States, as she recounted it to me during subsequent months of conversation, was short and bitter. She and her children had spent the first few months with her sister-in-law and three young adult children in a small apartment. At one point eleven people were living there, sleeping on the floors and in the bathtub. She applied for welfare to get herself on her feet, but the agency kept her waiting with constantly changing requests for additional documentation, some of it from Puerto Rico, and meanwhile she had no way to contribute to the food and rent money. She soon discovered that her sister-in-law was "cutting" heroin as a cottage-industry job at home, and her niece and nephews were selling it and other drugs on the street. Señora Medina's anxiety deepened when the older cousins stole her son's gold neck chain as he slept, and she began to suspect that the cousins were addicted. The theft, never discussed, added to the unspoken resentments, recriminations, and hostility between the sisters-in-law and their children, resulting in displaced quarrels over petty differences that the crowded living situation engendered. One of the tenets of *respeto* (respect), with which each child is imbued from a very young age, is that people may not be directly confronted or criticized to their face except in very extreme situations. An injured or outraged party should ideally remove herself from the situation, and after a sufficient amount of cooling-off time has elapsed, perhaps let it be known through a relative what has prompted her action. But Eti had nowhere to turn.

A dramatic event provided the opportunity. One day, a downstairs lookout yelled that the cops were on their way. One of Eti's nephews had only enough time to leap out the second-floor window with the drugs into the alley (breaking his leg, but taking off anyway) before undercover narcotics agents burst into the apartment. They bashed the women against the wall and terrorized the children, tore the furniture and bedding to pieces, ripped pictures off the walls, and smashed apart the refrigerator.

In an early version of the story, Eti said she subsequently spent a few more weeks helping her sister-in-law patch up the damage and giving her a hand at night, while the children supposedly innocently slept on, mixing heroin with additives and measuring it out into small envelopes for distribution. But she knew, she said, that it was only a matter of time before, first, her children found out and became ashamed of their mother, and second, that they would begin a life in the trade and end up as junkies or dead. So, as soon as she had enough money to pay a month's security and a month's rent in Mr. Stern's fine tenement, she moved out. And fortuitously, the welfare office approved her status and would pay the rent plus a modest allowance for her and the three youngest children.

The version that Eti told years later agrees with this first version up to the point of the police raid, but thereafter goes wildly off. In this final version, she said that a few days after the raid, while she was haggling again with the welfare office, Emilio at her side as advocate/translator, the sister-in-law moved out, drugs, children, and gold chains, leaving behind sticks of broken furniture and several months of unpaid rent and Con Edison bills. There was no note of farewell or forwarding address. A few days later, when Eti returned from pleading for emergency aid at the welfare office, she found her children sitting in front of the building on the pathetic pile of their scattered belongings in an affecting tableau of eviction misery. At the heart-wrenching sight of her children out on the street, Eti, once again put on hold by the city's bureaucracy, and abandoned by kin, boiled over.

She sent Emilio scampering to fetch another relative, her husband's brother (and ex-husband to her recently departed sister-in-law—in this there was some poetic justice), who owned a car, to come and get them off the street: She was ready to accept his offer of a job. A few hours later, after Emilio found him, the family was installed in the brother's second family's crowded apartment. Angel, a car mechanic by day, gave Eti a few rudimentary lessons on how to carry herself as his assistant in this moonlighting job, and off they went. For the next few months she assisted him in robbing gas stations in New Jersey, wearing a ski mask and toting a toy gun. The ski mask was a new cultural artifact for her, and the job was scary, but she knew she had to do it to provide for her kids. Within that time she put together her nest egg for a month's rent and security in Stern's tenement, and the welfare office finally "opened" her case. Here the versions converged again: Eti breathed a sigh of relief at the termination of her brief career as a bandit. Her biggest worry had been that she might either get shot or be arrested, bringing shame and/or orphan status onto her children, the shame being the worse of the two, she implied.

Now she was leading a precarious but much more steady life. Her two older daughters had partners; the younger children were all in school; and Pablo's income, unreported to welfare, helped to maintain a very modest budget. But unexpected crises often tipped the balance: the recurrent breakdown of her old car, the need for warm winter clothing for the children, a fire in the building. She had no cushion to tide her over during illness, or when welfare periodically terminated her benefits, "churning" clients on and off its rolls. She sometimes borrowed a social security card from one of her "sisters" and worked in one of the sweatshops dotting lower Manhattan that offer seasonal, temporary low-wage work. When her drug-dealing niece and nephew were killed in a shoot-out with a competing drug group, Eti's wages paid for two funeral wreaths and a contribution to the burial expenses. Then she adopted homeless, twelve-year-old Cheetah, and there was all the trouble with his stealing and court appointments, and problems with Olie, her daughter Maria's partner.

But apart from these unending troubles, through her relation to the team and especially her growing friendship with Nilsa, Eti began to enjoy her life. Although her friendship with the other women continued and was enhanced by blood ties (Pablo became the putative father of her flighty friend Cuckie's last child), she began to expand her personal life. She became the power behind our summer program for children, which with her in charge, employed three other mothers; took a firm hold of the summer lunch-distribution program for which our office became a sponsor; and acquired a steady, younger partner. The latter came about after Nilsa's husband, a union worker, found a union job for Pablo and he moved out to his own apartment. He continued to contribute some money to the family, though not as much as before, and his position as gofer in the family was filled by Miguel, a twenty-seven-year-old factory worker. Eti was then forty-six.

At home parties, with Willi Colon's music blaring, the men sipping beer and the women orange soda, I could see the pure joy that Eti expressed in her dancing. She was a wonderful dancer, whether the partner was Miguel or one of her younger sons, with whom she also danced close and sensuous. I watched and thought about the often remarked upon close bond between mother and sons, reinforced in front of my eyes, weaving a tie that would lead to later ambivalence and a conflict of loyalty between a young man's spouse and his mother. It would have been too easy to assume that the dearth of mature men enhanced this process or gave it life. Rather, women did what they could, given their situation. Young men were erotically drawn to their mothers, and mothers could thus count on their continuing loyalty and support. Incestuous behavior was displaced when the sons began relationships with older women, "just like mother"; and older women consummated and displaced their attraction to their sons by taking young lovers.

It worked, but not smoothly. There were eruptions of torrential jealousy that were never explained in terms of what was really the problem. Instead, small irritations or conflicts were seized upon as rationales, or completely irrelevant or fabricated past events were dragged in by the tail to obscure what was, after all, a potentially very explosive area. For example, a son might accuse his mother of having cheated on his father ten years earlier even though she was a paragon of faithfulness. Or a mother might throw a temper tantrum when her son bought new furniture for his partner. But given the level of poverty, the level of need, the question would not be limited to love and loyalty, but, even more basically, to love and loyalty as expressed in the allocation of one's resources and energy.

In Miguel's case, as in most, he remained Eti's active consort for about five years. For him, as for other young men who entered into partnerships with older women, this was a time to complete his social growth as a man of the house, in locus parenti; to evolve to sexual and emotional maturity; and to "get on his feet" in terms of occupation, in the relative security of a mothering woman. In exchange, he supplied not only additional resources for the household budget but also support and "representation" in the neighborhood. Having a man in the house, whether an older son or a sexual consort, signified social power for a woman in terms of protection and, if need be, vengeance, for herself and her children. Even if the man was seldom called upon to display or use physical strength, even if it was in fact the woman who manipulated dangerous situations for her children's safety, the man still retained a residual, titular "authority" that evoked respectful distance from other men. Even if he was a bobo, which Miguel sort of was.

Eventually, when he started seriously courting a young, nubile woman, Eti kicked him out. But by then he had advanced in his job, could take a woman out in style, buy her presents, and play the role of a father well. The novelas played a large part in promoting this romanticized, supposedly traditional, vision of a Latino male, simultaneously projecting an image of a female who needed wooing and protection, preferably by a rich, powerful male—and promoting all along, needless to say, material goods that accrue to people if only they have the right aspirations. In reality, only a small portion of the idealized behavior, without most of the trappings portrayed, were accessible to people with such limited incomes. Hence "mahogany" beds, purchased on credit over ten years, ensconced in tiny tenement bedrooms where they barely fit; hence dancing in nightclubs with well-heeled businessmen while visions of marriage danced in the head; hence stylish, cheap clothes that evoked glamour.

For young men the condition of poverty was particularly painful. Because it was hard for them to find jobs, it was almost impossible for them to woo young women "in style." Even "liberated" working girls expected to be taken out on dates and would not consider sharing the cost of an evening out. One afternoon when Emilio Medina was in the office, Nilda discussed dating with a pretty community organizer named Marta. They were both bewailing the lack of manners of the local men, their lack of style. Then Nilda, who had lived and studied in Europe, went on to describe how nice the European "boys" were, what fun it was to go out on dates there. She said she hadn't minded going "Dutch" with them because "you know, all those boys there are poor. They're students." Emilio, pretending to be studying for his exams but in fact all ears, bellowed, "POOR? What about US?!" And in spite of Nilda's and Marta's protestations that this was different, he didn't allow them to wiggle out from the double standard. He said, "All you women care about is money clinking in a man's pocket. You won't even look at us, give us the time of day—you are driving us to crime!" He laughed at his own tirade, but he was on to something.

It was not until a year later, after spending a summer becoming politically aware through the Encampment for Citizenship sponsored by the Ethical Culture Society, on a scholarship that Nilda obtained for him, that Emilio was able to understand the infrastructural forces that led young men to careers in crime by denying them legitimate avenues for earning and self-respect. That understanding, coupled with his mother's heroic strength, would provide him with a basis for a decent adulthood. Unlike many of the other boys we knew, he would not end up on drugs, or dealing, or imprisoned, or dead.

As it turned out, Eti Medina made sure that all of her children stayed away from illicit jobs. A union job she eventually got with Nilsa's help provided a basis for a modest life for her and her children. She didn't need a millionaire after all.

3

Homing Pigeons

Meri's son Ricardo, known as Richie, was the bane of our "lan'lo's" life. Harold Stern and his mother (whom he addressed as "*Mother!*") had their rental office around the corner on Avenue B. Harold was a roundish man in his late forties, partial to an off-white turtleneck sweater pulled down over his ample belly, a Tyrolean hat with a feather, and a dead-end cigar perpetually stuck in the corner of his mouth. He was fatherly with prospective tenants and charming to me. Whenever I showed up in his office complaining of no heat, he would motion me, the cigar for a moment ceremoniously extended, inside the swinging gate that separated him from visiting tenants and into a dusty back office and a beat-up imitation leather chair. Then he would explain patiently, once again, how an oil truck had gotten stuck in Brooklyn, how another one was just on its way.

Harold and Mother Stern owned our building and an unspecified number of others in Brooklyn. As Harold told it, the capital that started this far-flung empire was obtained by the lucky fact that his father ("May he rest in peace") had owned a small building on Avenue B in which he had a shoe shop that in time became an object of overwhelming desire for the Board of Education. The compensation was ample; the land was cleared and an elementary school built. Now the school stood half empty, the baby boom having gone bust and the local fecund population beginning to ebb into peripheral public housing and the outer boroughs.

Mother Stern was a fragile, blue-coiffed lady in her early seventies, with a slightly protruding belly that always ached and ill-fitting dentures that gave her speech a peculiar clack. Unlike many other absentee or corporate landlords, the Sterns had an intimate, if not always cordial, relationship with the neighborhood. They spent most of their waking hours in the area that had been home, and they were therefore available for tenant complaints as well as the occasional stronger display of emotion. Harold delegated rent collection and inspections to Mother, just to be sure to be out of wrath's reckoning. He was well aware that Latinos were less likely to assault an old lady than a man at the height of his powers. He was a cheerful man, always ready to look at the worse side of life. When Mother complained or tried to argue from the back of the office, where she seemed to be perpetually preparing a cup of tea on an electric ring, he'd say "Be quiet, Mother!" and continue where he'd left off. Sometimes I'd stop by to sound him out about a local event, say a murder or a big robbery. He'd shush her protestations and always tell me a better story. "Oh, that's nothing," he'd say. "You should hear what happened to my friend. He's got a good business, over on the Upper East Side. Not a two-bit affair like this one here"—pointing across the street to the ancient little hardware store over which two shaky old brothers hovered—"but a really classy business. That's a good neighborhood up there, nice customers. So, guess what, darling? My friend gets held up, they tie him up, they rob him. And that's a classy neighborhood. You see?"

One morning early on in our research, while the days were still warm, I took a chair across the street from our office to catch up on my tan and observe the action. I was waiting for the Sterns' plumber because the toilet in the apartment above our office had overflowed and was dripping onto my desk. But my attention was focused on Richie, who seemed to be having a very busy morning. It was late summer, school was about to start, he was about to reenter the eighth grade after dropping out last spring, and he needed some decent duds. He had been roaming the neighborhood, ranging as far as Orchard Street, pilfering whatever was not nailed down.

He had begun his day's work on the corner of Fourth and Avenue A, where he pinched a gallon of milk from a truck unloading at Key Food. He offered the milk to Chino-the-socialist, who was hanging out in his doorway. Chino declined. Then he tried to interest a few of the passing señoras, who also refused, and finally sold it to Basia Plotek, a Polish widow who had diabetes and lived in Chino's building with her heroin-addicted son. She had been waiting with several other women in the lobby for the postman, who might today bring her social security check. All over the Lower East Side women were waiting for the postman because all the mailboxes were busted. She gave Richie fifty cents for the milk.

Immediately he disappeared around the corner of Avenue B, returning shortly with eleven battered golf clubs. These, as I had noticed in passing, had until most recently graced the display table of the Salvation Army thrift store. He stopped at our stoop and tried to sell one of them to Count Augusto, who was just about to enter our office, no doubt in search of Nilda. Count Augusto, then approaching thirty, a man of handsome countenance, elegant manners, and gracious speech in spite of several missing teeth, was, however, not to be conned. He was a master con artist himself. Having in his youth acquired a taste for heroin, and having found inventive ways of financing his taste, he had subsequently spent a number of years in prison. While there, he had kicked the habit and acquired a wealth of knowledge, practical and theoretical, with which to make his way in the world. His gracious speech and manners, rooted in the base of an upwardly mobile Puerto Rican family (his twin sister was a teacher), had been more fully developed through his association with black Southerners in prison. He was a courtly man, and at the moment he was courting Nilda. (She had provided him with the nickname, which he carried with pride.) Count Augusto seldom complained about the ill luck that life had dealt him. Only when he drank too much would he let slip that his mother had favored his twin sister and that he had had to hustle on the street from the age of sixteen. All the family's combined income had been invested in the sister's education, and now she seldom invited him into her middle-class suburban life. He consoled himself with Bacardi rum and made radical political speeches about the "bourgeoisie" when under the influence. When he became too fiery his friends would soothe him with, "Gusto, Gusto, this isn't you speaking, man, it's Bacardi."

Now he was conning Richie out of one golf club, free, in exchange for an offer to "hold" the rest of them (thus freeing Richie for further productive work). I saw Nilda meet them at the door, and after a short and sweet exchange, stemming probably from our team's agreement to never knowingly allow into our office anything that smelled even remotely of being pinched, the count, golf bag over his shoulder, now set off in the direction of his apartment on Seventh Street. The place, painted in Disney-color stripes by the count himself, contained a collection of numerous other objects of suspect provenance that the count traded. I wondered who the hell would want to buy golf clubs on the Lower East Side. But it turned out, the clubs had been correctly assessed by both Richie and the count as very handy self-defense and offense implements. Within the week, everybody who was anybody among the young machos (including the top lieutenants of the Gatos, an aging gang) was sporting a golf club. You'd think the neighborhood was a country club.

Having temporarily disposed of the golf clubs, Richie now met up with his cousin from Brooklyn. The day before, he had asked me if he could call his aunt in Brooklyn from our office. I had heard him tell the person on the other end, "Meet you at the 'Interview.'" Now I realized that he had been talking to his cousin, Hector, and that the "Interview" was not some romantic café but our office. We had started interviewing young men a few weeks before (as it later turned out, they had been providing us with fake names and bull information, which we didn't find out until months later, when we got to know their mothers), hence the name. Hector, known as Heckie, to whom I had not yet been properly introduced, gave me a sly appraisal from across the street. His nickname fit him well. He looked like one of those cartoon crows, wearing a man's long floppy jacket, pants rolled up to the ankles, white socks, and sneakers on his oversized feet. Heckie was a trendsetter. Years later a whole new generation of white teenagers frequenting the "East Village" (as real estate developers would rechristen the run-down area to give it some of the cachet of Greenwich Village, its neighbor to the west) and calling themselves "punks" would be seen sporting Heckie's garb. Now he and Richie were getting ready for what turned out to be a sock-acquisition foray to Orchard Street. School was starting next week. You gotta wear new socks to school.

Just as they were setting off, Mother Stern rounded the corner. Richie veered toward her, passed by her a little too closely with a bright-eyed smile, and veered off again, saying something presumably pleasant. Then he and Heckie took off. Mother Stern yelled something in their general direction and crossed the street to where I was sitting.

"He should drop dead!" she said, teeth clacking.

I asked her why he should drop dead.

"Darling," she said, pinning me down with a bony finger while massaging her belly with the other hand, "you don't know what he did to me!" She went on to explain that Richie had installed a pair of homing pigeons in one of her empty apartments. "Two pigeons and a baby pigeon and the feed—you should have seen the feathers and the mess. Every day it's something else with those kids. It's eating me alive," she said, rubbing away at the eaten spot.

"But you're looking pretty good," I said.

She stopped complaining, smiled, knocked on the wood of my chair and said, "God only knows how I do it."

I asked her how she knew the pigeons belonged to Richie. She gave me a roguish wink and said, "How did I know? I asked them all 'Whose pigeons are these?' and everyone said 'Not mine!' so I said 'Okay, I'll give them away,' and Richie says 'Give 'em to me,' and I say 'ALL RIGHT! That's what I wanted to know!'"

But then she started complaining again and rubbing her belly. She had had the hallways painted three times in the past two years, she said, and each time the kids had messed them up with their graffiti. I stopped myself from remarking that the paint job above the kids' reach in our hallway looked at least ten years old. Instead I asked her about the eviction that had been in progress the day before. Stern had hired Emilio Medina and several younger sidekicks to clear out a second-floor apartment above our office, leased to a woman with two young children. Stern was paying the boys a dollar an hour, and Emilio had simplified the task by first lowering the stuff out the window with a rope and finally just throwing it. Down it came, crashing around us: baby clothes, chairs, pots and pans. Mother Stern was now telling me that the tenant was a dirty woman, two months behind in her rent, who had abandoned the apartment and left it filthy. She went on to generalize about Puerto Ricans, interjecting into her remarks, lest I think her prejudiced, "There are bad apples in every nationality, including the Jews."

"But," she went on, "these are the worst. You should see the mess, you should see the clothes, the furniture, the garbage they leave behind." Which brought her round to the subject of Richie again, apparently increasing the bellyache. "They should get the electric chair," she said. "They should all get the electric chair, then they'd learn a lesson." I pointed out, mildly, that if they all got the electric chair there would be nobody left to learn a lesson. Tired of Mother Stern, I took my chair back across the street to the office.

When Stern's plumber, Jakub, finally arrived, he told me the eviction had been both cruel and illegal in his estimation. The tenant had indeed owed some rent, but she had been gone only a week, staying with her sister and children in Brooklyn because the sister's husband had been shot. His boss only wanted her moved out on a pretext because he wanted to let the apartment for a higher rent. Jakub had seen with his own eyes that she was a good "tenantka" and had kept the apartment very clean: She had even left her keys with him so that he could repair the pipes leaking into our office. He thought Stern should at least have put her belongings in storage. How was she going to take care of the kids without anything?

Jakub was a Polish Jew who had survived the Holocaust in forests as a fighting member of the Polish underground. There, he went under the pseudonym of "Jurek," which he asked me to call him. After the war he had emigrated to Israel, whose name he took as his surname, and finally to the United States, ending up in Brooklyn. But he often spent time on the Lower East Side, hobnobbing with Poles as a member of a Polish soccer team and working for Stern. He referred to me as *krakowianka*, a female from Crakow, where both of us had been born, and from time to time suggested we spend time over a glass of *wodeczka* (the diminutive of "vodka"), reminiscing over the good old days. He was a small, slender man, his face plowed with suffering and childhood deprivation. He thought the Sterns were greedy "Amerykanie," and now, referring to Mother Stern, told me, *ta stara to krzyz Panski* (that old woman is the Lord's cross).

Still, the Sterns' business had a serious downside. The tiny apartments were crammed with people, many of them relatives visiting or relocating from Puerto Rico, or victims of fires in the neighborhood; it was not uncommon for "visitors" to stay for prolonged periods. The families were large, with many young children. Under the best of circumstances children and teenagers in their exuberance are not careful of property, but especially so when neither they nor their parents have a stake in it. Even if the Sterns had wished to put some capital into major improvements, which was doubtful, the banks had long before redlined the area for improvement loans. The tenement was old, its electric and plumbing infrastructure inadequate and patched up, the old windows immobilized, the doors sagging in their jambs. The boiler, a giant locomotive circa 1950, guzzled oil—and the price of it was going up. Worst of all, the roof, already in need of tarring, had become the stomping ground for the boys. Well out of sight (and mind, they hoped) of the adults, the roof was an ideal hangout for telling ghost stories and teaching younger ones dirty ditties, smoking an occasional joint, and perfecting martial arts, but also a great place to raise *las palomas:* pigeons. The older boys bought and traded them, bred them, flew them, and constructed amazingly well-crafted coops to house them.

The birds represented freedom. Whenever a formation of pigeons flew up from one of the tenement roofs, people in the street, young and old, looked up, gazing, pointing, saying softly, almost reverently, "Mira, las palomas!" Nobody ever bothered to look up at ascending jets or hovering helicopters, although some years later, when the Lower East Side became a site for paramilitary action in the "war on drugs," the latter would acquire a dreaded significance. But now the pigeons flew elegantly, nimbly; an airborne ballet, rising above the currents of raunchy air, gleaming like silver, reflecting the sun, in flocked cooperation yet peaceful and free. That's why the boys went to the roof: to learn to be "mens" and to provide spectacles for the neighborhood.

Ranging in age from about eight to eighteen (with an occasional uncle giving a hand with the finer points of cabinet making or pigeon breeding), the boys learned and imparted manly roles on Stern's roof. There were lessons in kung-fu and karate, kite making and flying; morality tales were told and fantastic heists planned. Ballads were made up or transmitted and memorized. One ballad, loosely translated for me by Emilio, went like this:

> I have a chick who smokes grass
> And when she gets high she begins to dance
> She takes in coke and also heroin
> She looks for her dollars just for fun
> She hangs on the Fifth, she goes downtown
> And when she returns she asks for me
> And when she finds me she gives me a hug
> She gives me money, a happy pimp
> One day the chick grabs an overdose
> And in my arms she falls down dead
> And five days later after her death
> I'm on the Bowery—a poor bum

As far as I could tell, this was a cautionary tale, reflecting the boys' very imperfect observations of what to avoid in the drug-using subcultures of the Lower East Side. Other ditties, whose origins I didn't discover, included more straightforward songs that began, "I took out my hairy banana, I putted it in nice and sweet . . . ," or "One by one the show began, in the beeedroom, two by two I took off my shoe, in the beeeedroom," getting progressively more explicit, until the climactic "seven by seven I . . . . her to heaven, in the beeeedroom." After an educational session on the roof, the younger boys gleefully sang the songs whenever their mothers weren't around.

It was a tremendous pity that the subject matter prevented the boys from demonstrating their skills in school, where they were considered good-for-nothing students. Language acquisition, music appreciation, memory development, social critique, and preparation for adult roles—all were present in the rooftop sessions. In addition, math skills were developed as pennies and dimes were added and counted for a pizza or a joint, and their equitable consumption accomplished, to say nothing of the manual and physical skills and recycling awareness developed when beams and posts were lugged from abandoned and burned-out buildings to construct fine pigeon coops.

None of this, of course, improved Stern's roof. Eventually he paid Sam, the super, to demolish the coops, but this did not deter the boys. They just started over on Chino's roof. Later they moved back to Stern's and added another skill practice to their repertoire, leaping over the air shaft that went down six stories—as

Chulito would one day find out. But for now Stern's "roofa" remained the favorite hangout. In addition to its other attractions, it gave the boys an excellent vantage point for observing any unusual activity down in the street. And whenever some action was in the offing, they'd streak down like lightning.

Piddling around inside the office that day, I suddenly heard the squealing of brakes, a horrendous smashing sound, and then a prolonged blare of a horn. Glancing out the open door, I saw the boys streaking past the office in the direction of Avenue B. As Nilsa and I hurried out we saw a white Chevrolet that had plowed into a parked yellow Datsun across the intersection. Its occupants leapt out, ripped off the license plate, and scrammed down Avenue B. A running crowd followed them laughing, yelling, "Get them, catch them!" As Nilsa and I ran to the corner, we got a look at the car's occupants as they ran past. The man, in his late twenties, had cavernous eyes and a used-up, chalky face. Two women loped behind him, one with scraggy blond hair, the other with a tawny shag. Both wearing high heels and jeans, hanging on to their shoulder bags, hair flying—they looked like they were performing a sequence for *Charlie's Angels*. The young fair-haired cop who usually lounged on this corner was still lounging as Nilsa and I passed him. "There's been a crash," I called out, in case he had temporarily lost the use of his senses. He replied, "No kidding?" and continued lounging.

We approached the crash site, along with a growing crowd. Someone told us there had been about twelve people standing at the entrance to the schoolyard a few feet beyond the point of impact. Meanwhile, some men in the crowd were circling the Chevrolet like hunters would a dead gazelle. An older man led the way, got inside the driver's seat and, as some younger men began prying open the hood, ripped off the rearview mirror and handed it to a small boy. Then two younger boys jumped into the backseat and started rummaging behind it. Finally forcing the hood's latch, the two young men removed the battery, while the crowd began urging a man with a screwdriver to open the trunk. All around stood solemn housewives commenting quietly and little girls sucking on lollipops, watching with serious eyes. Everyone was tensely awaiting the opening of the trunk, including Nilsa and me. A treasure?

Suddenly, everyone fanned back onto the sidewalk as a squad car arrived. It paused momentarily, then went on. There was loud jeering for the two cops who'd driven away.

Soon a strong young man arrived with a jack and hammer. Cheered on by other young men, with their fists clenched on high, he knocked the trunk open to their chant. We all closed in tighter, anticipating. Drugs, gold, money? Nothing. Only a flat tire, a plastic bottle of motor oil, and spray window cleaner. The boys carried the items off. Richie took the spray and squirted a big *S* on the back window of the car. About twenty minutes after the incident, three squad cars arrived on the scene. The people surged, enfolding the windows of the first car, front and back. Meanwhile, two cops from the second car sauntered up and tried to form a screen for the cops inside. Their attention was focused on a tall Black man holding a paddle board who was giving an incoherent eye-witness account laced with reproaches for the late arrival of the city's finest. A pal by his side was urging, "Be cool man, be cool," sensing perhaps, in his lesser state of inebriation, that the paddle board might be construed as a weapon.

But the people surrounding the car were poised: Although not exactly hostile, they seemed to want some attention from the authorities. The third car, carrying "brass," backed up from Avenue B. The sergeant, chewing a cigar, like Kojak, stepped out, conferred with his men, looked over the crowd, and commanded his men, "Get rolling." The man with the paddle board boarded one of the squad cars, presumably as a witness, and the cars started. People smashed their fists into the cars and jeered, following their slow progress between human bodies. No cop had even bothered to look over the wrecked car. A few minutes after the cops left, jacks were up, lifting the Chevrolet, and several men were busy removing the tires, doors, seats, lights, and anything else that was usable. Soon, only a carcass was left. The boys carted off the pieces in different directions. Nilsa and I walked back to the office, not saying much. On the way we passed Señor Velasquez, one of the spiritist garage owners. He was resting on a chair in front of his shop, his arms crossed over his chest, something resembling a smile on his face, probably calculating how much he would offer for the spare parts.

Everybody went back to their tasks. The women went upstairs to cook the evening meal, the young men resumed their marijuana dealing on the corner of Avenue B, most of the adolescent boys returned to the roof. But not Richie and Heckie. They went off on another expedition.

Late in the evening they returned, and I could tell from the excited cluster of boys around them that they had made an important score. I snagged Richie's younger brother, Miguel, over to the side and asked him what the excitement was about. He said that the duo had raided a drug users' apartment and had discovered some silver dollars, a radio, and a cross. A minute later, Richie approached and asked me if I wanted to buy the cross, a small crucifix, hanging on a chain. I said, "Richie, first of all, you know that I think it's wrong to steal."

"Ah," he interrupted, sounding hurt, "that wasn't stealing, we were just taking. Anyway they're junkies, they're Americans."

"And number two," I said, cutting him off, with momentary thoughts of a discourse on the moral implications of his action abandoned in favor of a more directly understandable thrust, "You may get bad luck from trying to sell a cross."

Richie mumbled something about not caring, but suddenly it looked like the cross was beginning to take on the shape of a cobra. He turned round. "Who wants it, for nothing?"

Juan took it, while Emilio commented that he should give it to his sister: "She's the only one around here who respects God." Mona, a heavyset young woman of twenty, had recently converted to the Pentecostal church.

"Yeah," commented Rafael, a skinny fourteen-year-old, "maybe God can help her lose some fat."

"Don't let her hear you," said Juan, "or she'll sit on you and you'll never get up again."

That cross didn't bring anybody any luck, especially not poor Juan.

That Christmas I gave Richie the *Audubon Guide to Northeastern Birds*. Somehow, he managed to continue in school and attended fairly regularly. He'd give me a charming grin on his way home from school, knowing that I was watching. In the afternoons he flew his pigeons, and in the spring he graduated from the eighth grade. I helped pay for his graduation ring. But that was his last graduation. Unless you count parole.

4

A Gentle Young Man

One late November day I got a call from Emilio. "Juan is dead. They killed him. The supers Freddie and Sam killed him."

On the way downtown I was overcome with dread. Only the week before, Paul had interviewed Juan. The interviews included questions about how people earned a living. Had his talking to us endangered him?

Juan was a gentle person, known to the kids as Dodo. He smoked weed, so sometimes he wasn't all there, but he never did anybody any harm. According to what he had told Paul, and what we had heard and observed, he was a high school dropout and lived with his family in a fifth-floor walk-up apartment in our building. The family consisted of his old, ailing father; his mother; his sisters Mona, Clara, and Blondi II, and a younger brother, Alejandro. His mother received supplemental aid for the three youngest children, but the income was insufficient to support the entire family. His father, a now sober alcoholic who had ruined his liver through his drinking, obtained occasional low-paying work as a dishwasher. Juan contributed with odd jobs and physical help, but his mother was most instrumental in obtaining additional money.

In the mornings she took care of a baby in her home for pay and in the afternoons sold home-cooked food on a street corner a few blocks away. The daughters took over the baby-sitting in the afternoons and evenings, while Juan, sometimes with the aid of his father, helped set up and dismantle the street vending business. Every day we saw him carrying a shopping cart loaded with food, pots, a grill, and charcoal down the five flights of stairs and into the street. He then wheeled it to an empty lot a few blocks away and set up the makeshift stand. His mother sold hot food to men who played dice while waiting for some "business" connection in the lot. She had a brisk trade when the weather was nice, but she seldom earned more than $10 and sometimes returned home empty-handed. In the interview tape-recorded by Paul before Juan's death, Juan spoke a bit sadly about his mother's work:

We put it into a little carriage, and we bring it down from the fifth floor—all the way down it has to come, a heavy load, about ninety pounds, ninety pounds—oil, *ollas* [pots], we have to carry it to cook outside. She carries some rice, some chicken, pork chops, ribs . . . She cooks, you know. She goes out there on Eighth Street . . . she cooks. She makes *pasteles* [boiled vegetable and meat patties], she makes *alcapurria* [fried patties], *bacalao* [codfish]. Yeah, she cooks good. If it's a nice day they're playing dice, you know. Those people that play dice for big money? And they come to my mom's to buy her food, because you'd be playing dice and you get hungry. They get hungry. Yeah. When she goes up there, about four, five, she comes out about eleven, or twelve [P.M.] . . . one, sometimes. . . . Sometimes she sells nothing at all, and she has to be there most of the time, you know. Wasting time, be sitting down, you know, waiting for people to come, you see. But people come, once in a while, they come. Once in a while. Yeah.

Juan's contributions to the household during the year before his death were the following: a summer job as a street sweeper, occasional furniture-moving jobs with a friend, and a brief period delivering phone books. During the last few months of his life he was selling marijuana cigarettes on the street. This last job was the most lucrative, but after he paid off the man who advanced the product (on consignment, so to speak), he earned about $30 a week, and he gave most of it to his mother.

When Nilda and I first arrived at the office that day, we immediately began trying to find out what had caused Juan's death. Apparently the teenage witnesses were telling the detectives and other adults that the alleged murderers, Freddie and Sam, two adult brothers employed as superintendents in ours and an adjacent building, ostensibly killed him because he owed them $15. This was hard to believe, and my skepticism was confirmed as I sifted through what I heard.

The story varied somewhat in the telling. First Richie, visibly shaking, told us his version, which was essentially similar to what other teens would tell us, differing only about the people present and the activities preceding the murder. He said that he and Juan had gone to play pool with Sam and Freddie over on Avenue D and Fourth Street. The supers, angry at having lost some money, started bugging Juan on the way home to return a debt of $15 he owed them. Then, in front of our building, the brothers started a "play" fight. Richie ran to find his older brother Julio and his "stepfather," Sito, an expert in karate. When he returned, the kids told him that Freddie, Sam, and Juan had gone upstairs together with two other men, Mike and Victor. Just then Mona, returning from her Bible class, passed them, and Richie asked her to call down to them when she got to her apartment to let them know if Juan was there. (He did not tell her why this was urgent because Mona disapproved of all the teenage boys' activities.) Mona forgot to call down, and a few minutes later Richie ran up to the fifth floor to tell her to get downstairs because "they were going to hurt her brother." Mona said later that she didn't believe him, "he's such a liar," but her younger sister, Blondi II, did.

Richie and Blondi II ran downstairs to the lobby where they were joined by Blondi I, the former's fictive "sister," while Julio ran up to listen at the door of

Sam's second-floor apartment. To the group huddled in the street, which now included Miguel, he said he had heard the brothers and another man "abusing" Juan, and he told Blondi II to go get her brother out (lure him out, as a sister has a right to do without putting her life on the line). Blondi ran up and tried, knocking and knocking. Finally Freddie stuck his head out and told her that Juan wasn't there. When she insisted, sticking her foot in the door so he wouldn't slam it shut, he told her to go away because they were dealing with something. Soon, Mike and Victor came down, carrying a rug. They proceeded to the next block. Miguel, then eleven, casually followed them at a distance. They dumped the rug in a burned-out building across from the Mobilization for Youth building and left. When they had gone, Miguel tiptoed in for a closer inspection of the rug: It was full of blood.

Meanwhile, Mike and Victor had gone back upstairs. Now they came back down with Freddie and Sam, who told Blondi II that if her brother did not come down in ten minutes to go up and get him. Talking among themselves, the men went to Freddie's apartment, two doors down. Just then, Miguel came running up with the story of the bloody rug, and Sito, Julio, and Blondi II ran upstairs. Sito kicked in the door. There lay Juan's mutilated body in a pool of blood, with empty bottles of Colt 45 strewn all over. Richie shook as he recounted the scene. A few days later, Blondi I, equally shaken, would tell an even more shocking but also more revealing version of the story, which I tape-recorded and relate below.

After hearing Richie's story, not knowing that Señora Sanchez had gone with Blondi I to the morgue to identify the body, Nilda and I went to the Sanchez apartment to extend our condolences. The whole family was collected in the tidy, miserable place, with cockroaches running all over the walls. They were waiting for relatives to arrive from the Bronx. Blondi II was sleeping in a little room off the living room, and Mona was sitting with other female relatives on the torn sofa. She invited us to sit down, and we did. A young man helped Alejandro, Juan's eight-year-old brother, to serve us coffee. Mona, her face swollen from crying, was saying that if only she had believed Richie, maybe she could have prevented what happened. Nilda made small, comforting talk. One of the visiting relatives who had just arrived from Puerto Rico asked if I was part of the family from the Bronx because I looked like someone. It was an intentional, kind act of including me in the group. An older, very dark man came in, kissed Mona, and then went to sit in the kitchen with Alejandro and the young man. It occurred to me that I had never previously felt, even though I had seen it, how important the physical proximity of friends and kin is during traumatic events. I had been a part of groups crowding the bedsides of sick Puerto Rican friends, wondering how the patient could take it. Now, for the first time I saw the importance of "sitting with."

Presently Alejandro asked me if Paul was downstairs; he wanted to play chess with him. Mona gave him permission to go, but *only* to our office. Mona commented that after she, Juan, Clara, and Blondi II had been born, her mother had decided not to have any more children. But then Alejandro came along, in her older years, and it was a good thing, said Mona, because now he was the only *baron* left. Indeed, for the next few weeks I observed a protective aura surrounding Alejandro by all his relatives.

Later, in the office, I heard a lot of people talking in the corridor, and Blondi I came in to tell Alejandro to get back upstairs because his mother had returned. She looked terribly upset. That evening Paul and I went over to the Fernandez funeral parlor for the wake. Mr. Sanchez greeted us and showed us to the room where Juan's body was laid out. Several women and young children were sitting on folding chairs, chatting in low voices. One of the children asked an elderly woman where Juan had been stabbed, and she told him, "In the back, that's why his chest is all puffed out." I went up to stand close, to pay my last respects to Juan. He looked like a peaceful sleeping person, but not like Juan (Blondi I's later description of the murder would explain why).

After standing quietly and thinking, I went out into the antechamber. An adolescent girl was minding several older children playing quietly with the water cooler. Just then Señora Sanchez arrived with Mona. She was dressed all in black, with a black scarf covering her hair. Her face was distorted and she was crying. I kissed her, and we went back in and sat in the back. Other women arrived and came to sit with her and talk. She kept on crying. At some point Emilio arrived with Rocky, another teenager. They went directly to the coffin and stood over it staring at Juan for a good long time. Then they walked out with drawn faces. When Paul and I bid Señora Sanchez good-bye she walked us to the antechamber, thanked us, and gave each of us a small picture encased in plastic. On one side was a picture of Jesus, a very white, grown Jesus, wearing a halo and a serious look; on the other was Juan's name, the dates marking the short interval between his birth and death, and a prayer for his soul.

We drove to Seventh Street, where Count Augusto lived, to give him a loan of $25 that Paul had promised him. The streets were dark, empty. Paul went up to Gusto's as I watched. I couldn't leave the car. I locked all the doors. There were murderers lurking everywhere. Cold with fear, I slipped under the dashboard to hide.

The next day I had to face the music. Even if our interviewing and presence had not contributed in any way to this terrible event, it was obvious we were working in a perilous environment. Worried about the staff's safety, I was unsure of how to proceed. At the moment I felt like giving up. I went uptown to consult with Marvin Harris. As coprincipal investigator he was kept abreast of our progress, and I kept a duplicate set of our field notes secured in his office at Columbia University. His advice was to keep a light presence, to stop formal interviews with young men, and to continue concentrating on children. He was concerned but encouraging: The project's focus, how the neighborhood's people survive economically, could be shifted, for the time being, away from young men without undermining the purpose of our grant, if I decided it was necessary.

Reassured, I rode the subway back downtown. A few hours later we held a staff meeting in the storefront. I wanted to be sure that the team was committed to staying. After all, Juan had been murdered almost literally above our heads.

Would we have the courage to continue? The consensus was to keep on. Nilda thought it was crucial for the children's emotional health that they continue to carry out rehearsals for the Christmas play to be staged in our office. Twelve-year-old Paco, the play's author, and his sister Lisa, fifteen, its director, were in full swing recruiting, teaching, and mustering the small fry, insisting on private rehearsals so the play would be a surprise for the adults. Paul suggested that having a constructive project would help the children to see that life went on. Nilsa and I agreed. We decided to postpone formal interviews indefinitely and made a rule that no staff member should ever be alone in the office. I was most concerned about Nilsa, since she was youngest and our "early bird." We decided that she should take a few weeks off and work at home catching up on field notes and the project's account books.

We started to spread the word: Because the children needed the space for their rehearsals, there would be no more interviews for the time being. But people kept coming anyway. The teenagers needed this relatively safe place to talk out their fears and sorrows. Parents stopped by to discuss the murder. Neighbors were collecting money for the funeral expenses. Even the Dominicans in the bodega across the street prominently displayed a jar on the candy counter with Juan's name on it. Mr. Sanchez used our office to make phone calls to arrange for the headstone; the family had no telephone. After one of those calls he remarked to me how cold our office was. I told him that our main radiator was not working. Distracted as he was, he climbed the five flights to his apartment and came back carrying a wrench. Soon he had the radiator fixed. When I thanked him he waved it away. "When people be good to you, you be good to them," he said.

I didn't go to the funeral; I had my hands full. Nilda said that attending the wake if you're not close to the deceased fulfills the obligation. Richie and Rafael, who did attend, told me that the funeral began at St. Bridget's, over on Seventh Street, and then proceeded to New Jersey in six old cars that the family had borrowed. Richie was one of the pallbearers. He said, "Then they put Juan in the hole, they threw dirt on him, and that was it."

But of course it wasn't. The children were reacting very strongly to the murder. They were hitting each other, crying over minor slights, and walking out on the play. In several of the small, intimate conversations we had with children and teens during subsequent days, the theme of life and death was dominant. One evening Emilio, Rocky, Paul, and I were sitting around the table. Emilio wondered if he would live long enough to see the year 2000. I worked it out with him that he would probably live until at least 2050, at which time he would be eighty-nine. Since his grandmother was now 105 it didn't seem that impossible. He also asked me about having one's body frozen, and Rocky interjected that he had seen a movie about that (Woody Allen's *Sleeper*). Then he talked about transplants and a woman whose comatose body was being artificially supported to see if the doctors could grow her four-month fetus to term. As the conversation started to wind down Emilio said he was worried about not being able to live very long and repeated several times: "I love being alive" and "You don't know how I love being alive, but I don't know if I'm gonna make it. . . . " I said that obviously Juan's death was on his mind and that's why he had brought up the subject. "It's on all our minds," I said. Rocky nodded vigorously. This conversation was unusual because Emilio always danced and joked around the office, rarely talking about anything serious and never for any length of time. Up to then, his only comment on the murder had been that Juan had been "used like a woman" by the murderers. When I asked him what he meant, he said the men had "forced him to have sex" before killing him.

On the day of the indictment I came early to the office. Everyone was nervous in the Sanchez family, and the neighbors were looking out as the detectives arrived to take the family and witnesses to court. Sam and Freddie had been arrested the night of the murder and were now at Riker's Island. Mike and Victor had been arrested a few days later as "accessories" and were now out on bail, although not showing their faces.

For the trip to court, Señora Sanchez was wearing her best clothes, a tight skirt, high heels, and a baseball jacket. I watched the family leave, and then, because no one else was there to stay with me in the office, I made a detour to Mr. Stern's. I said, "You picked yourself some fine super" as I entered. Mother Stern started protesting that Sam hadn't really been the super, but Stern said, "Be quiet, Mother. He was *your* super." He went on to tell me he had planned to fire Sam anyway, that he was very sorry about the murder and had given Mrs. Sanchez $25 toward the burial, and that I shouldn't feel uneasy about remaining there because the murder wasn't committed in *his* building. He added that Sam and Freddie "must have cracked up."

I was stunned by Stern's denials but continued to listen, realizing how little I knew about the entanglements and connections in the neighborhood. He said that the Padrone had called him up to say he didn't even want to know those sons of his and that he was too afraid to return to the neighborhood, even though, Stern said, "he has a beautiful mistress here." Then he showed me receipts for all the supplies that Sam had supposedly bought—including an aluminum ladder, which had disappeared—and were certainly never used to maintain the building. But what seemed to annoy him most was that Sam had changed all the locks on the empty apartments: None of Stern's keys fit.

The inference was that Sam might have been "subleasing" the empty apartments to dealers and addicts and perhaps making a profit. It was hard to tell whether Stern was more pissed off about the misuse of his property or the fact that he was not cut in on the deal. It was all beginning to add up to an interesting story. We had observed the Padrone in Stern's office on several occasions. We had observed the Padrone sitting in Dolly Greenberg's car. We had also observed Dolly Greenberg sitting and chatting with a gangster *tipo* in a white Cadillac. I had once sent Dolly a woman with appropriate credentials who needed an apartment. Dolly told her she had no vacancies even though the tenants said the building was only half occupied—even though there was a constant movement of people going

J.: Mike and Victor?

B.: Mike, Victor, Sam, and Freddie, and they took it to Fourth Street, across the street from Mobilization, and they put it in one of the burnt buildings and they left him upstairs. So that's when one of the guys [who] had gone upstairs said Freddie and Sam had gone upstairs again, and one of the guys, before they closed the door, was standing there and listened, and they had said, "OK, Juan, we gonna give you one more chance tomorrow to pay us that $15. And we gonna leave it to five, five-thirty, for you to give us that $15." So the guy thought they gonna give him another chance. So he came back thinking nothing happened. So anyway, Mariel—they were waiting and Mariel told Julio, "There's trouble over there. Let's go check what it is." So they went in [into the burned building] and they checked [the rug] and it was full of blood. So when they came back and Julio's stepfather—you know, Sito—opened the door with his foot, he found him dead. He came downstairs and goes like this, "Mariel, your brother's dead." She goes, "Please don't tell me that, don't tell me that!" You know? She jumped him, you know, and she ran upstairs, and sure enough, he was dead. And when she turned around she punched her hand through the glass bathroom door. She didn't know it was glass though. Put her hand right through it.

But then, when I went down to identify him with the mother, you know, it was like, forget it! His face was all damaged up. They stabbed him a whole bunch of times, down the back of the neck, and the legs and the arms. And his head, his face was all black and blue, the hit marks on his face and everything. It was just the worst. I couldn't believe it, because you know, he never bothered nobody.

J.: You mentioned before that the guys used to be on heroin?

B.: Yeah, and they stuck a whole bunch of needles up his arm.

J.: Were they still on heroin now? Do you know?

B.: No, they sold it, they were selling it, but I don't know if they were still on it. But anyway, these guys, they just came out of jail, plus, they were still on probation, so they must have bumped probation, so.

J.: You said there is a warrant out for the father's arrest?

B.: Yeah, there's a warrant, but he went to Puerto Rico. But they know where he is, exactly the house he's staying at.

J.: Do you think the father was involved in heroin selling?

B.: I really couldn't tell you. I don't know. But I know they had everything planned, they had it all planned. I know.

J.: And you have no clue what possibly could have led them to this horrible thing?

B.: No. And when he was in the funeral [parlor], they had to—because they cracked his skull from here to here, they damaged him all over—and when he was in the funeral [parlor], it didn't even look like him, the bad things they did to him. 'Cause so much makeup they had to put on him, so much cotton they had to put in his mouth. He looked like he was still swolling up. It was the worst.

J.: God, these guys must be real perverts. Why do you think their father would plan such a thing?

B.: Their father—I couldn't stand their father anyway. He's been to jail too, for murder. This isn't the first time they killed somebody.

J.: Yeah? Were they living here in this area for a long time? Do people know them?

B.: I don't know.

J.: You didn't know them before?

B.: No, I didn't. I used to see him around though. But I never knew him.

J.: Well, listen, I'm going to finish because all this is heavy, heavy stuff. But I will do another interview with you in a few weeks. Okay?

Blondi I returned to our storefront a few times during the next few weeks. On one occasion she upbraided Gary, an African American seventeen-year-old from below Delancey Street whom we were training to become a census taker (she herself had refused the work). She said, "Gary, man, you should've come to Juan's funeral." She meant wake, but Gary misunderstood and said he had thought the family had no money so he hadn't known there was a funeral. I realized later that she had mentioned Gary's name as one of those present on the night of the murder. I also realized later that she was the only one to open up the scope for different interpretation of the causes for Juan's murder, by mentioning the alleged murderers' involvement in the heroin trade. But now she was rubbing it in for Gary's benefit with gory details, including how the makeup had come off poor Juan's face when his mother kissed him for a final good-bye just before the coffin was closed.

But life was taking over. Juan's little brother, Alejandro, kept coming over to play chess with Paul. It seemed to soothe him, and he seemed to enjoy a weekend uptown with the staff and a few other little boys. Within a few weeks the family moved to Third Street near Avenue D, and Alejandro's visits became less frequent. Señora Sanchez enrolled him in a school closer to their new home that made it easier for the family to keep a close watch over him. Paul visited the family and said the apartment was bigger, sunnier, and best of all, it was on the second floor. This made it possible for Mr. Sanchez to help his wife carry down the *ollas*, food, and charcoal to her little food stand.

One day two months later, Alejandro came in on one of his now rare visits, hoping to play chess with Paul. Paul wasn't there, and I was busy trying belatedly to coach Lisa for her admission test to the School of Performing Arts. Vibrant, competent Lisa, who had produced a magnificent Christmas play for us, engaging us and other parents to make costumes, collaborating with Paco on the sets, whipping the little rascals into an orderly crew of singing dwarfs (Christmas carols to a salsa beat), seemed overwhelmed by the upcoming test. Her school "advisor" had picked some dumb passage from a horror book (*Sybil?*), which she recited in a monotone. This passage was to be followed by a *recited* passage from "I Feel Pretty," of Bernstein's *West Side Story*. She had never seen the movie or heard the song, and the way she was reciting it now left very much doubt about how pretty she felt. I asked her if it was all right for Alejandro to sit in on the coaching. She agreed to make an exception for him—all afternoon we had been fending off curious small kids trying to bust in.

Alejandro told us he had a secret but we must not tell anyone about it. We promised. Proudly he told us that his sister Blondi II was pregnant. "I'm going to be an uncle!"

Lisa exclaimed, "That's crazy. Blondi is too young." But seeing his face, she quickly added, "What do you want, a boy or a girl?"

"A boy, of course."

Lisa said quietly, "You are the only boy left in the family, right?"

He hung his head. "Yes."

"You miss Juan?" I asked.

"Every time I walk into the house I see his picture there. . . . " He started crying. I put him on my lap, which is the right thing for a señora to do on the Lower East Side when an eight-year-old is desolate. We talked about how Juan was the only one in the family who had hazel eyes. Lisa offered that Alejandro looked like his mother. "And I have a gentle voice just like hers," he said, extending his thumb backward at me. In fact, his gentle voice was a younger echo of Juan's. Before leaving, Alejandro told us that he liked it better where they lived now. He said that in their old apartment, every time Mrs. Stern came knocking on the door for the rent "we all stayed real quiet, real quiet," to make her think no one was home. He said that they paid off the back rent after they moved. But I doubt it. They must have been broke from the funeral expenses, and the usual pattern on the Lower East Side, predictably followed by tenants with predictable choleric fits from landlords, was for the tenant to move out owing a couple of months' rent. The landlords seldom refunded "security" money that had been paid in advance, anyway. Mr. Stern told me he didn't have the heart to start looking for them. What he omitted to say was that there were new tenants in the wing eager to take the apartment for a much higher rent. No questions asked.

Juan's story was not unique. Most of the families we came to know well lost a young male relative in the drug commerce, and the homicides continued on a regular basis in the neighborhood. A few weeks after his death another neighborhood friend lost her two stepsons in a double murder/execution. The two young men had been high school dropouts and had performed a variety of jobs to help support themselves, their very young wives, their children, and their parents. They had become involved in the cocaine trade only a year before their death, earning a great deal of money by Lower East Side standards—approximately $30,000. For one year their family enjoyed a degree of material comfort they had never enjoyed before. Soon after the young mens' deaths, their father also died. Their mother, wives, and four young children moved to another state, again to subsist on welfare. The money had been spent on funeral expenses and on the move. Their stepmother, Janie, a former addict herself who was now not only "clean" but had channeled her newfound energy into creating and running a large program on St. Mark's Place that trained hundreds of women to become carpenters, electricians, cabinetmakers, and plumbers, was stunned by the event. She called me a couple of days after the murder, so Paul and I attended the wake.

About thirty people were standing around the two open coffins when we arrived. There were many more wreaths and flowers than at Juan's wake. Doña Mercedez was leading the rosary to Maria, and the assembled mourners repeated after her in unison. Two sisters of the dead brothers were standing in the center, dressed in black, leaning their heads on each other. I repeated the rosary with the crowd, but inside I felt rising anger, thinking about some of the local leaders in the area, what a friend called "the local-level elite," who participated in the use and dealing of cocaine. It was their younger, less privileged brothers who died in the fierce economic competition, I thought. Each time the local big wheels made a deal or threw a coke party they ensured that another boy would perish. But then, I thought, what about the dealers on the level above, and the level above that, and the banks that helpfully laundered the money? Soon enough we got a chance as a team to meet the local-level elite. Meanwhile, when I interviewed the victims' stepmother, Lady Carpenter, as everyone called her, she said:

> I guess one of the things, aside from the whole thing being such a tragedy that kept haunting me . . . you read the paper about their murder and it said that drugs were used [the *New York Times* had printed a short factual account of the murder, noting that drugs had been involved], and I know that if I read such a story in the paper I would be cold to the story, because the impression I would have [was] that these people weren't doing such a good thing anyway. . . .
>
> What was so difficult for me was to remember them as little boys, particularly J., he used to say to me . . . he was, ah . . . such a . . . interested in people, interested in things, and he would come to me and he would say to me, "Janie, the junkie—he doesn't love his mother." And he saw all the terrible things drugs did to people. I lived with them for two years, and they would visit me quite often afterwards, and then over the years I would constantly run into them. We had a very good relationship.
>
> But I really didn't pick up on the fact that they were really into dealing, and they had made a lot of money. I think it was after we'd seen the bodies, I hugged their mother and I said, "You know the *New York Times* should know about this, their lives, [since] they wrote about their death. . . . " And she looked very strange, and she pulled away from me, and she called the other children over and spoke in Spanish, and I realized, what I found out later, was that the parents had a key to the safe deposit box where the money was.
>
> See, when they grew up drugs were not so prevalent. I know in talking later on with people that they grew up with, people who are now young adults, their whole thing was just to get enough money to buy a house in Puerto Rico. . . . [Drugs] was

something that they did not approve of. They were kids who knew what went down and they did not like it. See, that was so hard for me to figure out—what happened to their heads that they would do this—unless it just was, after all their trying, it was the only thing that would give them any options. Well, I'm sure it is.

It's economic. It also is the fact that the neighborhood is so isolated, that the things can become so . . . I'm sure there are a million other things they could have done, but there was nobody there to connect with them. Do you know what I mean? I feel that if I had only known I could have turned them around. I believe that. I have a feeling, though, that their family, because of the great money they were making . . . that they were buying their family things and helping people out, paying doctors' bills. . . . When you're faced with that kind of misery and that kind of poverty . . . well, I don't know what else to say at this point. I found it terribly painful for a long time . . . and in my lifetime . . . I kind of had a feeling that if you work hard enough you can make things right. And that to me was the most tremendous unfairness, and I just couldn't come up with any kind of rationalization to make any of that all right. It's just . . . how terribly unfair this world is. And of course if you didn't know them as children, and didn't know them as people, just the newspaper article about their death, it would be just, you know, you know. . . . They were really fine young men. They were very gentle, very gentle. They were not, as children, messing with the gangs at all. In fact, their friends even said that's one reason they got killed. Because sometimes when you're mean, or you hang out with mean people. . . . They were known to be very gentle young men and they didn't have a lot of mean friends, so that as victims they were easier targets. I have such a cute little boy and that saved it, saved me. But I just worry so about his future, and part of what keeps me going here is to work for a better future.

Lady Carpenter then recalled the visit of President Kennedy to the Lower East Side. She said that he went down Avenue C shaking people's hands. He shook hands with the dead boys' father. When Kennedy was murdered, she said, grown men were weeping like babies. She said, and apparently she had given it a lot of thought, that the surge of hope building up among the poor in the 1960s was extinguished with the murders of the Kennedys, Martin Luther King, and Malcolm X. Particularly for young men, there was now no movement, no organizing principle that could embrace their energies and aspirations, unlike young women who did have new possibilities and new hope in feminism. She seemed a little remorseful about the fact that she was doing and had done so much for women, saying that boys were dying because they had nothing to live for.

The dead men's sisters told her that all of their male friends were dying. The only models for young men were the big-time dealers.

When Blondi II's son was born, the family named him Juan. But even this birth of a new innocent namesake could not erase the violent trauma that continued to haunt so many of the children's lives.

5

Chulito Flying

Our work as anthropologists helped the staff to retain some sense of perspective. During staff meetings we pooled information to try to make sense of incomprehensible events, to see them from different angles, to give each other courage. Sometimes we debated fiercely, and that too helped us to arrive at a closer approximation of truth, even when we were mainly aiming to deflect our depression at the misery around us. At a staff meeting following the brothers' murders, Nilda recounted her attendance at a rosario held at their mother's house. Again led by Doña Mercedez, the rosario consisted of nine nights of prayers conducted in relatives' homes, in the belief, said Nilda, that the prayers would give light to the dead person's soul to help it depart from the earthly life. With the combined prayers of family, kin, and friends, the troubled spirits of those who died violently would be induced to leave peacefully. Nilsa, who was raised in the Pentecostal tradition, fiercely contested these ideas as superstition. "We don't believe in that crap! Once you're dead, you're dead, that's it. You have to make it on your own into heaven. We sing at the wake and try to make the family happy so they can go ahead and get on with their lives." I pointed out that the differing religious orientations reflect two different strategies for life. The Catholic one depends on keeping shared kin obligations, the Pentacostal on shedding them and getting ahead. Who can tell what's a better adaptation for poor people?

My teammates weren't impressed with this bit of analysis. They'd heard it before. Paul wanted to discuss cocaine dealing and the rumors we had heard that Cecilia Montez, an organizer for Adopt-a-Building, a sweat-equity program to provide housing for poor families, was now involved with the Gatos gang, using them for protection and distribution of drugs. Nilda and Paul in the evenings floated around the local bars and social clubs and were much better informed on this topic than I. Referring to Belmonte's, a bar on Third Street, Paul said, "To my great surprise, Cecilia Montez is working at the bar there. First a communist, then a social worker to a gang, she has an apartment in an Adopt-a-Building and is now working at the bar there."

"People think there's a lot of cocaine dealing going on over there," I remarked, dubiously.

Nilda was adamant. "There is!"

"Well, how do you know?" I challenged.

"Well, because I was offered coke there. Everybody was offered coke there. They came up to Arturo [Fuentes] and me and asked."

I still didn't quite believe it. "What is this story about big cocaine dealing going on over there? If everybody's dealing, who's buying?"

Nilda said, "Well, maybe somebody has a big stash. . . . "

Paul shook his head. "I don't think Rico [the owner] would allow that. Maybe a little dealing, informally. The Fifth Street bar, they don't speak Spanish, they speak English, and that bar is very open, with the dealing going on over there. First time I went there, there was this envelope with cocaine being held by the bartender for his brother. It was coke, dope."

"How did you know it was dope?" I asked.

"This guy says, 'Here's the dope for your brother,' and the guy says, 'Tell him next time not to do that.' It was obvious."

I looked doubtful.

Paul went on, "Next day I came in the bar, went to the bathroom to take a pee, these two guys are sniffing coke, and the guy is offering me some and I say, 'No, I go crazy with this stuff, I can't take it no more.'" Paul made a pained face and we all laughed.

"I can estimate," he added. "I can't wait to ask the guy 'Is it coke or is it heroin?'"

"We are anthropologists, not journalists," I answered, as usual nagging about standards of proof and evidence.

We sifted through all this information as it poured in, tying names to faces, placing individuals in families and kin groups, discounting both exaggeration and "common sense" explanations. The "local-level elite" who had parlayed their better English skills and a certain amount of savoir faire, gleaned from their upwardly mobile experience, into wheeling and dealing were only one step up from the bottom financially of most of the rest of the population. But occasionally we got a glimpse of the bigger boys who directed the local drug trade. Shortly after Juan's death, we were invited to a party being given by a local, "Anglo," a "carpenter" on Second Street.

The invitation came courtesy of Paul, via a white block organizer (now a slumlord) who in the more innocent past had helped Paul to organize a rent strike in the building where he lived. The carpenter's building, ratty-looking on the outside, gave no clue to the slick elegance of the loft within, comprising the entire second floor, into which we were now ushered. The newly laid hardwood floors, antique furniture, and hangings were fresh out of *Better Homes and Gardens*. The side board groaned under roasts and platters of tropical fruit.

Tastefully displayed in crystal holders were bouquets of hand-rolled joints, vying with flowers for attention. The block organizer introduced us in a hearty voice to our host, Bob, modestly dressed in jeans and a T-shirt. The guests, especially the women, were dressed less modestly, some in antique dresses, others in very short or revealing costumes, but the overall effect, perhaps achieved through vampire-colored makeup, was "outrage." The men also looked like corpses—white, Latino, and African corpses. As the disco music beat its deafening martial tempo, as people partook of drugs in the rear part of the loft and lined up to strut like comatose robots or to chatter compulsively, I wondered if they were celebrating not only their ability to deal death but also a wish for their own.

As it turned out, or at least as we surmised the following day, putting all of our experiences together, each of us had been skillfully interrogated to appraise the extent of our knowledge of the drug business and the threat we might pose. Evidently we had come off as idiots, which in truth we sort of were—from their perspective.

But we would have occasion to see Bob and his boys in action, in the future, right on our front step. Meanwhile, as the weeks lengthened into months, we observed the mounting violence, official and unofficial, spawned by the drug trade and saw the wounds it was inflicting on the children. We redoubled our efforts to add normalcy to their daily lives.

One snowy Saturday in February I arrived at the office before 11:30 A.M., some twelve hours after leaving it the night before. I had promised to take the kids to see free films at "Someplace Nice" on St. Mark's Place. Paco and Jimmy Moreno were already waiting in front of the office when I arrived: Paco staid and solid; Jimmy quicksilver, jiggling the padlock, hyper as usual. They came in and were vague about who else was going. I sent Jimmy to ask Ginny and her brother Marco, and then Ginny to ask Lisa—the kid express, very complex. Although Lisa was Jimmy's older sister, she couldn't stand him and would be more likely to go if invited by Ginny.

While we waited and various kids drifted in, we amused ourselves with Play-Doh. I made a pig, and right away Jimmy asked me to make a wife and then a child for him (the pig). Meanwhile Paco was making a crocodile, and José Medina was fashioning a cobra. More children arrived, among them Isa Valiente, Lucita's sister, who set to work making a trough for the pigs, and with Lisa and Maribelle, little pellets to feed them. Paco caught the communal spirit and started making a fence, firing up José, who rolled out and curled into shape three little turds, which he placed behind the pigs' feet. Everybody was rolling with laughter, including Ginny's little brother, five-year-old Chulito. I made a *jibaro* (peasant boy) with a big hat, and the girls constructed a seat for him so that he could sit watching the pigs. It was so much fun that nobody, including me, wanted to go to the movies. But we set off anyway, sending Chulito home first to his mother. He was the apple of her eye. A wet snow was falling.

I walked down Avenue A with Maribelle and Ginny hanging on each of my arms, the older girls taking an alternate route (probably a wise thing, to avoid being seen with this motley crew), while the boys ran around and behind us, exercising their throwing skills with snowballs aimed at people distant enough not to catch them. Richie, Miguel, and Paco led the way, while Marco and Jimmy stuck to us. I should have stopped the expedition then and there; unfortunately I didn't. Because soon enough, the advance guard walked directly into the First Avenue traffic, daring the cars to hit them, Richie holding his hand up authoritatively to make them stop, which of course they didn't. The boys dodged the cars while we yelled at them from the curb. Once across the street I offered to take everybody straight back home, which produced moans and groans and had the intended effect of subduing the boys' high spirits. For about ten minutes.

An older Polish woman who was taking her grandchildren to see the free movies too showed us the way in. A movie was already on, being screened on a sixteen-millimeter projector against a sheet on the wall. This created interesting distortions. John D., an African American who lived in the place, invited us in. He was a one-man cultural institution. Without any grants or apparent means of support, he ran jazz sessions, art exhibits, and shows in his ground-floor apartment. He invited us to hang up our coats, but only Paco and I did. The rest kept theirs on, just in case (of what?). But the place was dark, and two skinny African American men with crocheted skullcaps and flowing robes were hovering around the projector. Carpets and pillows were scattered on the floor, and John laid out some pillows close to the "screen" for us. At first only I, Jimmy, and Marco sat down on them. Everybody else sat down primly on a built-in bench in the back. They looked and acted like a bunch of old ladies at a Quaker meeting. Alas, this was not to last.

Jimmy and Marco started in. Egged on by a gregarious eight-year-old who seemed to be related to John, they began frolicking and rolling, punching each other out, getting their various body parts into the projector's beam. John seemed to be tolerating this, so for a while I let them go on. But during the changing of the reels, first I and then their respective sisters gave them a talk about behaving in other people's houses. Marco listened politely to Ginny, and Jimmy screamed back at Lisa when she pulled his ear to emphasize her point. It didn't help much. Soon Miguel and Paco got into the act, with Miguel trying to mollify the elders by leaving every ten minutes to buy Starburst candy and distributing it liberally to all of us, including the projectionists, the Polish lady, and her two blonde granddaughters.

But the films were fairly boring "back-to-nature" and "Black heroes" type of stuff. No blood, no screams, no killing. The subject of the first film was Benjamin Banneker, the country's first important Black scientist of the eighteenth century, known as the "African astronomer." Although the children had no way of knowing that the film had mangled the facts, the patronizing, pompous voice of the narrator had already put them off. Paco squeezed his nostrils and gravely mimicked the adenoidal intonations. The next film showed the rather mild adventures of a white slum kid in New Jersey's Great Swamp. The last one, or at least the last one we could all endure, which brought initial applause for the title, was Walt Disney's *Bear Country*. By then everybody was down on the pillows, whispering, giggling, scuffling, and generally messing around. Most of the kids had their faces about a foot away from the screen; Ginny laid her head in my lap and complained about hunger pangs and eye strain. Oh well. As I was thanking John he tried to inveigle me into becoming a projectionist-program planner for the children's shows. Meanwhile, the Polish lady wondered aloud whether we wanted to accompany her to the next "cultural" event on her itinerary, a children's musical on Eleventh Street. I declined both.

The trip back resembled the trip there, with even more snowballs thrown, many of them aimed at the girls and me. Back on First Avenue, I popped into Kurowitsky's to get a couple of sticks of skinny dry winter sausage. Kurowitsky has the best *kielbasa* outside of Cracow, and I wanted to give the kids a treat and let them see the inside of this very clean store with its mouth-watering products. Paco and Marco gave each other meaningful, cross-eyed smiles when they heard me speaking Polish to the men at the counter. The only thing missing was index fingers turning crosswise at their temples to indicate their appraisal of my weirdness. The girls seemed more comfortable in this totally new environment with its strange smells and sounds. And nobody had any trouble either pronouncing the Polish name for the sausage, *kabanos*, or making it disappear on the way home. Back at the office, I promised the snowball boys not to take them anywhere next week.

But I was to be rewarded. Millie Cortez, the mother of Ginny, Marco, and Chulito, invited the staff upstairs to her apartment toward evening, a gesture she had never made before. By then we knew her children well, even Chulito, whom she seldom let out of her sight. We knew her and her common-law husband, Arturo Fuentes, somewhat from their occasional appearances in our office for the "parents' night." Nilda, Paul, and I climbed up to the second floor, accompanied by Bonnie, who had recently joined our team as a linguist. Upstairs, Millie, a pert, vivacious woman in her late twenties, wearing a flowery short-sleeved blouse, introduced us to her father-in-law and her brothers-in-law, who were sitting in the living room, sipping beer from four-ounce bottles. They were dignified men, wearing well-pressed shirts and trousers, who shook our hands politely. She then led us to the bedroom where Arturo's mother, sisters, and niece were sitting on a large bed covered with a red chenille spread. The windows sported matching red curtains; the walls were painted salmon pink, and the wood trim was red. The ladies were looking at an Avon catalogue, discussing the merits of the various products, and daintily sipping orange soda. Millie added our coats to the bed, and we all exchanged formal greetings in Spanish.

Then Marco dragged me off to the tiny bedroom he and Chulito shared to show me his mother's art. About eight young boys, some belonging to neighbors, others to the visiting family, were slipping and sliding and tumbling off the bunk beds. *Ay! Dios mio*, I thought to myself, can I take any more children today? But Marco pointed excitedly to a colorful guardian angel that his mother had painted, and saying "Watch, watch!" turned off the lights. We all oohed as the angel, now glowing, seemed to be floating in the air. This was repeated a few times until the children started tumbling again, and I gave them the slip. In the kitchen, Arturo was pouring rum from a half-gallon jug into shot glasses on a tray. He offered them to Nilda, Bonnie, Paul, Millie, and me and took the rest to the men in the living room. They drank it like vodka is drunk, in one gulp. As far as I could see, none of the other women were offered, or drank, beer or rum. Nor did they emerge from the bedroom, where the discussion now centered on a certain sister's-in-law failings, except to help out in the kitchen later. Nilda, Bonnie, and I joined the men in the parlor (female anthropologists seemed to be a third sex here), and a political discussion soon developed above and in between the sounds of salsa.

Throughout the evening, the men and women remained within their gender-segregated spaces, only the children connecting the groups by passing pretzels, Cheetos, and popcorn, lingering now with one group and then the other in between sorties to neighbors' apartments. Frustrated with the deeply conservative political views of Arturo, his father, and brothers-in-law, I wandered back into the kitchen. Ginny started showing me the family photo albums: pictures of Millie's mother's marriage at middle age to a younger man; Millie's grandmother, who had died recently; family outings to the Bronx; pictures chronicling Millie's children's infancy and childhood. Then Ginny came to a picture of a man in his early twenties, Millie's brother. "He's dead," she told me somberly. "He was shot." Pointing to her forehead, belly, and back, she said "they shot him here, here, and here."

I asked, "Why did they shoot him?"

She opened her hands in a gesture of explanation, "He owed them too much money."

"How terrible," I said.

Millie, who had joined us by then, gazed at the photo and said, "He was no angel, but he didn't deserve to die." She added that he used to send her a mug shot each time he was arrested so that she would know his new prisoner identity number, and she giggled. I didn't know her well enough yet to realize that Millie's giggling shrouded desperate memories.

The next morning while writing field notes, I waxed ponderously eloquent and wrote: "The incident set me to thinking that dead sons and brothers, whether literally or symbolically dead, represent a central theme in this study. Working with family albums and recollections will be a very important source of information. So far, every family we have met has in its immediate kinship network one or several casualties of the system (sacrificial lambs?)."

It was not until two weeks later that the full dimension of Millie's sorrow was revealed to me. Millie and Arturo came down to our office on a Friday night, and she stayed with me for several hours in the back office, talking about her life. She began by telling me that she had stayed "upstairs" for the past two weeks. She just hadn't felt like going out at all and sat home all day and night watching television, mainly novelas, *One Life to Live*, and *General Hospital*. She said, "My husband has enough respect for me not to turn the channel when he comes home," like some other men did. Then she said her mother had kept her "upstairs" throughout her childhood and adolescence. Her mother had been very cold and strict, unlike her father, who had been affectionate but seldom around. She got pregnant with Ginny at fifteen, in spite of (or because of) her mother's strictness. Her mother had never told her anything about getting pregnant or giving birth. She remained in her mother's house because the baby's father was too young, and three years later she had Marco by another steady boyfriend who had no skills or money either. If she could do it all over again, she would never start so young, but then again she wouldn't trade her children for any advantages she might have had. She was going to make sure that Ginny and the boys would at least graduate from high school. I asked her if she was planning to educate Ginny about sex. She said that Arturo and she had discussed it and he was opposed, but she herself firmly believed in informing her and perhaps helping her to obtain birth-control devices "when the time comes." She thought there was a very fine line between helping her daughter not get stuck with children prematurely and giving her license to become sexually active. She also said she had allowed her to watch a program on natural childbirth, something she had experience with, because her children were born fast. She did not believe in abortion.

The most painful part of our talk was about her brother. He was only a year older than she, and they had been very close in spite of the fact that "he was no angel"—stealing, dealing, and shooting dope. He'd come and spend the whole day sleeping in Millie's apartment even though Arturo objected. "But I couldn't tell my brother not to come. He was my brother. Right?"

When he was murdered, his girlfriend came and told her. She and the other people he had been hanging out with were very "beautiful" about the funeral. They took up a collection and paid for all the expenses. It was a terrible time. And then after Juan was murdered, she and Arturo had attended the wake, and it was like attending her brother's wake all over again. Arturo knew how she felt and said, "Come on," and took her drinking. She had not looked at her albums since her brother's death until two weeks ago, when we came. That night, after everybody left, she had "hysterics." She cried all night, Arturo holding her, trying to comfort her. So much for her giggling.

After this talk Millie and I began a friendship. As I got to know her and Arturo better, it became clear that they had the basis necessary for succeeding as a conventionally defined, upwardly mobile family. Arturo, a short, dark man built like a bull, had a solid background based on his father's persistence and luck in finding and keeping a union job. This job underwrote the stability of the family. They purchased a house in the Bronx and paid off the mortgage with his steady adequate wages, the children grew up well nourished and dressed, and there was space and peace to make each feel cherished since Arturo's mother could devote herself to family care on her husband's wages. The children all completed high school, and Arturo joined the army after graduation, where the conservatism and authoritarianism he had learned at home was (unfortunately) strengthened. Within a year of our acquaintance, he was asked by the owner of the dry-cleaning store in which he worked to become manager, and although he agonized over taking on so much responsibility, he accepted.

During our frequent discussions I was taken aback by Arturo's apparent dissociation between his beliefs and his actual life. He voted Republican, adored Nixon, and touted the usual conservative line about welfare cheats, crime in the streets, and the idea that anybody can succeed in the United States regardless of their original class or race. As we got to know him better, Paul and I, and often Bonnie, would challenge his arguments, pointing to what was going on around us: the undernourished, ill-housed, and poorly clad children; the lack of jobs, never mind unionized, for the adolescents and young men; the contemptuous (and in some cases, downright fascist) behavior of people in authority, like the police and welfare bureaucrats.

But there was no convincing him. He dismissed most of the local teenagers as active criminals, predestined either for prisons or the grave. He said, "Just watch—one of these days somebody is going to blow one of their heads off, and maybe that will teach them a lesson." He was already preparing a different lesson for his stepson Marco, a beautiful slender child of eleven, promising to take him up on the roof at fifteen to beat him into a pulp. "That will teach him to be a man, to understand that there are people stronger than he out there in the world. I'll do it for him so that he doesn't go out there and meet somebody who will kill him." And he recounted proudly how his mother's brother had done him the same favor at fifteen.

Millie never offered an opinion on political topics, but when Arturo previewed the beating to come, which he did frequently, she giggled. I still didn't know her well enough to understand that her laughter hid extreme anxiety, thinking only that she was planning to disarm Arturo when the time arrived by calling on the strong love he felt for her. It was not until years later, after they had separated, that she told me how much she had hated his pronouncements and was determined in spite of her fear never to allow the beating to happen. But back then she said nothing.

On one occasion, provoked once too often by his ranting against welfare cheats, I pointed out to him the hypocrisy of his words. "Here you are," I said, "living in a common-law union with Millie, and although it is true that you support Chulito, welfare pays rent for your apartment and helps support Millie and her other two children."

Oh, that was different, he said. His salary, although enough to support him and Chulito, would not pay for housing and food for five people. And, Millie piped up in his defense, if any of the children were to get sick, what would happen then? Even after becoming manager, Arturo had no medical benefits on his job; receiving welfare entitled Millie and the children to Medicaid.

This single item—worry about medical care for their children in an environment that made the probability of accidents, maiming, and ill health so high—made Millie and the other mothers reluctant to take a chance on marriage and the loss of these meanly dispensed and funded, but crucial, supports. Having been born and raised in New York, Millie was more "modern" and better aware of mainstream American aspirations than women who had spent their childhood or early adulthood in Puerto Rico. For instance, she fought hard to get Chulito into a Head Start program, and although it was located some distance away she faithfully walked him there and back, and often stayed for or attended the classes on nutrition and hygiene that the program offered to parents. She was very proud that Chulito had learned how to peel and cut up raw vegetables for his snacks and preferred them, unlike her older children, to candy. After several visits by the family to dine with us uptown, she started making fresh salads and buying fruit, at least for those occasions when we were invited back for reciprocal dinners.

She was also very aware of the disadvantages she faced as a result of the second-rate education she had received in New York City's public schools. As a child she had attended PS 63, down the block, which her older children now attended. Built around the turn of the century, the school was close to the bottom of physical neglect: crumbling ceilings, leaking toilets, and warped, monumental windows that could not be opened to admit a breath of fresh air in spring but seeped icy drafts in winter. It was also an educational swamp. The city-wide reading and math scores placed it near the bottom of Manhattan schools, even though it was so close geographically to Wall Street, the center of global corporate power. It might as well have been in a third world country, with its discouraged, moribund teachers and constant dearth of basic materials.

Discussing the school's deficiencies with me helped Millie to make up her mind to take some action, and one morning she dressed up in her best clothes and set off down the block to Immaculate Heart to see if she could enroll her children in its Catholic school. She was terribly disappointed. The school director told her that they could not give her a reduced fee even if all three children attended. She would still have to pay $45 a month for each child, which would take most of her rent or food money. She and Arturo discussed it over the next month but realized they would also need to have money for uniforms and books. Arturo's salary and her welfare allotment barely allowed them to live modestly without the extra expense. Entertaining their family several times a year (a necessity for maintaining their crucial network links, although they didn't conceptualize it that way) was one of just two luxuries: A bouquet of gladiolus that Arturo brought to Millie every Friday was the other. Realizing that Catholic school was out of reach, Millie decided to redouble her efforts to make sure her children did well at PS 63 and saw to it that the children used us as resources with homework that was beyond her capabilities.

She also opened herself up to new cultural influences and was one of the most enthusiastic mothers to accompany the staff and the children to museums and trips upstate and to Jones Beach during the two summer programs we organized. After the project ended, she formed a "summer club" with her sisters-in-law and a couple of friends to go on outings to these same places. This seemed to have a positive effect on all their lives, and she no longer complained about how boring her sisters-in-law were, how stuck they were in the bedroom and kitchen.

A year after the project ended, perhaps prodded by our challenges, Millie and Arturo decided to get married. This worried me because Arturo was losing weight and had developed a deep cough from the dry-cleaning chemicals he was breathing in ten hours a day. How were they going to manage if something happened to him? How could they live on his salary alone? However, they had thought it through. They had been together for seven years; Chulito was now six and would start going to school full-time, and Millie would take a job with Arturo in his dry-cleaning business. The Latino owner liked them both: He had already tried out Lisa as a helper but found her too flighty, so he was happy to take on Millie, although he wouldn't pay her as much as he paid Arturo. Best of all, she would be able to get off the hated welfare handout. Their combined income would be $11,000, with bonuses under the table. As for the care of the younger boys, Ginny could look after them after school and feed them by the time the parents returned home. After all, she was almost fourteen and had already been doing a lot of the cooking, which, unlike her mother, she enjoyed. Besides, she had been a good second mother from the time Marco was born, changing diapers, helping to bathe him, watching out for the boys on the street during all those years. It sounded good. Yet I was still worried.

When we arrived at our tenement on the big day, the wedding party was already forming. The previous day, Arturo and Millie had had a civil ceremony at City Hall. Now, standing in front of the house in preparation for the walk to St. Bridget's, all dressed up, were Millie's three children; her skinny younger brother, Chaco; and a couple of Arturo's male friends. Ginny informed me that her mother was upstairs getting ready and that Arturo had gone off on some mysterious errand. None of the other members of the family were coming, she said, because they were all busy. We were scheduled to arrive at the church at 3 P.M., which it now was. Presently Millie emerged, wearing a tea rose-colored gown and matching hat, followed by an excited retinue of small-fry. Mothers were sticking their heads out the windows, curious, and shouting well wishes. Nervous and fumbling, Millie pinned a corsage on Ginny, telling me that her gown and hat were rented from a store on Delancey. I asked her where her mother was, and she said that when her mother was not away at religious retreats she was running gambling games in her apartment. She used to sell jeans, door-to-door like an Avon lady, but found that running a gambling joint was not only less tiring but also brought in more income. Her mother had a nice apartment in the projects on Avenue D.

It was getting close to 4 P.M., everybody was fidgeting, and at last Arturo arrived. He had been waiting for a corsage of tea roses that he had ordered to surprise Millie. We walked the three blocks to St. Bridget's, where several more friends and a very irritated priest were waiting. The priest told them that they had thrown him off his schedule and hurriedly, in English, performed the ritual. It was over in fifteen minutes. We threw rice; my daughter, Jenny, took photographs; and we all repaired to Millie's and Arturo's to a feast of *pernil* (roast fresh ham), *arroz con gandules* (rice with pigeon peas), and a green salad prepared by Ginny. There was beer, there was rum, and there also was white wine, in deference to us. Ginny had made freshly squeezed lemonade for the children. We danced to salsa on the phonograph, we drank. Neighboring children and then adults, including Señora Ortega, Señora Madera, and Holly Peterson, drifted in or were sent for and were wined, dined, and asked to dance. It was a wonderful party. The children were ecstatic about their new status. Their mother was really married, "by church."

One afternoon a few months later, Chulito followed Marco up to the roof. Arturo and Millie were both at work. Ginny, who had been busy discussing boys with Maribelle, didn't even know he had given her the slip. The roof regulars, all older than Chulito, had invented an exciting new game, jump-the-shaft. The shaft, a four-foot-square opening in the center of the roof, was supposed to provide fresh air to the six floors below, a proposition whose obvious inadequacy even a hundred years earlier was noted by Jacob Riis (1890). Off the boys went, one by one, leaping over this new attraction and making it safely to the other side—except Chulito. Peering over the parapet, the children saw him lying motionless six floors below. Someone ran to tell Ginny, someone called the cops, and someone got the young men from the corner who came at a trot. Soon they were lowering a young man named Lefty down the six floors in an improvised alpine sling. He got to Chulito first, because the cops trying to enter from the basement level had found the steel door to the shaft sealed.

Lefty leaned down to start mouth-to-mouth resuscitation and was overjoyed to find soft breathing. Chulito was alive! Apparently the accumulated junk on the bottom of the shaft, which included mattresses pitched there by firemen during preceding fires, had cushioned his fall. When the police and paramedics finally broke through the basement door, they scolded Lefty and several other adolescents, who by then had also shinnied down a rope into the shaft and were cradling Chulito, saying they shouldn't have touched him. After they finally got him on a stretcher, Ginny was not allowed to accompany him to the hospital because she was too young. At last, someone had the sense—and the telephone—to call his parents, and the distraught family was finally reunited at Bellevue. After many hours, they were informed that Chulito had fractured both his legs and arms and had a mild concussion. "He is a very lucky kid, Mrs. Fuentes," the doctor told Millie.

His parents were not so lucky. Although overjoyed by Chulito's survival, they now learned that with their combined income they were no longer eligible for medical assistance. They agreed to pay the $10,000 bill in monthly installments. The financial stress increased because Millie had to take a few months off to care for Chulito, immobilized in casts like a mummy. She was reluctant to return to work, fearing that in her absence another accident would happen. But she had to return: She and Arturo owed the hospital almost a year's combined earnings, and as a married woman with an above-poverty-level income, she was now not only ineligible for Medicaid but also for welfare. However, shortly after that, one of the benefits that she had hoped to obtain by getting married came through: After ten years of waiting she got a sunny, roomy apartment in a housing project nearby. The Housing Authority preferred married couples.

The following year, disaster struck again. The dry-cleaning establishment burned down in a fire. Both Arturo and Millie lost their jobs, and in the recessionary business climate, with so many men clamoring for work, Arturo could only find part-time jobs, working for Koreans and getting paid less. By then Korean immigrants had taken over most of the dry-cleaning establishments in the area, using family members as managers and leaving the chemical part of the work to Latino part-time workers. He had three of those jobs, he was seldom home, his cough deepened. Millie hinted that he loved her less. I noticed that there were no more bouquets of gladiolus on Fridays.

Many things conspired to end their marriage. Unable to find work, struggling to make ends meet on Arturo's part-time jobs, Millie decided to go back on welfare. Knowing her own inability to lie, she knew that Arturo would have to be physically out of the apartment before she could make a convincing case about her failed marriage to the authorities. Also, by then, Marco was nearing fifteen, the age at which Arturo had promised to teach him a lesson. Millie asked Arturo to leave, which he did, sadly, getting a single room somewhere in the neighborhood.

When Marco cracked his skull riding on top of the project's elevator on a dare, Millie felt confirmed in her good judgment. They could have never afforded the lengthy hospital stays and operations that brought him back to (almost) normal. A few years later, at the end of Ginny's senior year of high school—with only one course to repeat—Ginny gave birth to a baby daughter, and Millie had her first grandchild at the age of thirty-eight. Millie insisted on marriage for Ginny and her seventeen-year-old drop-out boyfriend, to which they happily agreed. Marco also dropped out from school after the lengthy convalescence for his head injury. He thought he had been left too far behind by his age-mates, and he didn't want to appear stupid. But Chulito, like his father, finished high school. Her child-rearing responsibilities fulfilled, Millie found a new partner and moved to his place in the Bronx, leaving the apartment as "inheritance" to her children, with Ginny in charge.

Arturo remained in the neighborhood. The children said he stayed single and frequently dropped by to see if they needed anything, bearing sweets, sometimes clothes hangers, or unclaimed clean shirts. There was something very solid yet fragile about him. He had subscribed to the ideology that hard work would purchase success and family stability. He had played by the rules, but with disappearing jobs, decimated unions, and receding medical and pension plans, the nature of work itself had changed. Like many other working-class men with hardened conservative ideologies, he was left stranded, a dinosaur in a darkening landscape.

6

Victoria's Baptism

Although constrained by poverty, parents tried to provide special life passage celebrations for their children, to validate each child's significance to the social group. In deference to the cultural memory of high infant mortality in Puerto Rico's history, baptisms were celebrated after a child had safely reached one year of life. The child was then given his or her name formally and welcomed to the circle of the living. Until then, in a way similar to the belief systems of the poor Brazilians described by Nancy Scheper-Hughes (1992), the infants were considered to be little angels, capable, at a moment's notice, of returning to heaven. A baptism anchored them in the human community, just as a wake and a rosario allowed a person's soul to depart. Such was the celebration of Victoria's first birthday.

Victoria was the niece of Jojo and Delila, two children who participated in our after-school program. Jojo was a giant, overweight fourteen-year-old with an exceptionally dirty mouth. Delila, his eleven-year-old sister, was dainty. She wore pretty little dresses, always in the latest style, and her bedroom was rumored to contain a four-poster bed "with curtains that matched the duster on her dresser, that matched the window curtains—all in pink," said Ginny, whose own bedroom came nowhere close. Jojo was said to be taking classical guitar lessons, paid for by his parents, with whom he communicated in elegant, curse-free Spanish.

The reason for this affluence, we learned, was that the children's father, Señor Enriquez, was a local manager for la bolita. Apparently he was the direct employer of the man with the big nose who indefatigably collected numbers bets up and down our street. Señora Ines, the children's mother, was rumored to give her husband a hand with the accounts, but she had other pressing duties to attend to as well. For one, she was very religious and spent much time in St. Bridget's Church. For another, she was very partial to Bingo and would not miss the weekly game there. Her health was reported to be failing in a number of ways, exacerbated by the behavior of her drug-addicted twenty-year-old son from a former marriage. Bruno still frequently spent time with his mother's second family, but he created havoc when there. Señora Ines was said to have had it with him, particularly since she was raising his infant daughter, Victoria.

The baby's mother, *una americana*, had died shortly after terminating her second pregnancy, at eighteen. The dead girl's mother had kicked her out when she was pregnant with Victoria and had cut off all relations with her. She didn't even come to the funerario. So Señora Ines was raising the baby as her own. I first heard about the family on the day Miguel Valiente, with his knack for drama, rushed over to tell me that the bigger boys had just hunted down a rat across the street and were taking it to Jojo's house to feed to his snake. Ginny had roused me some minutes before from the back office to come and watch the hunt, but I had been content to go no further than the door. From where I stood, except for the backdrop, I might as well have been watching a group of Yanomamo youngsters, spears (in this case, broom handles) and all, cornering an agouti, a rodent with a probably superior flavor. Miguel was delighted with my disgusted face.

Following the doldrums of Juan's death and the passing of Christmas, our office had become a beehive of activity. We offered help with homework; crocheting classes in which the mothers, daughters, and even Paco participated; and in the evening, Scrabble, chess, and dominos. Soon after the rat hunt, Delila and Jojo started showing up in our office. We also had a few other additions. My youngest son, Matthew, then twelve, had graduated from the public elementary school uptown and for a year was attending the Friend's Seminary on East Fifteenth Street. At my suggestion, he took advantage of the Friends' volunteer community service program and was now assigned as a tutor to the younger children in our office. His advisor, who came by to visit us, also recommended it to a very pretty sixteen-year-old girl who very quickly became the tutor of choice for the older boys. It all worked out very well, even though the younger boys teased my son about his nickname, Maciu—"Hey, macho! Let's see how macho you are!" and so on, at which Maciu smiled philosophically. He was already inured, I think, from his older brother's variations on the theme ("Hey Machu!" "What?" "Machu Pinchu!" followed by an attempted pinch). In order to extend our math lessons into play activities and to give shape to the evening games, we organized a domino contest in which children were paired as teams. A big mistake. Here is an excerpt from my field notes on the contest:

> As the younger children arrived from school, only Ginny was doing her homework. The rest continued practicing dominos for the continuation of the tournament tomorrow. It began at five on Friday and was so tense with constant accusations of cheating that by seven we decided to postpone it. The major contentiousness was between Lisa and Isabel as a team against Jojo and Richie as a team. They were all screaming, but especially Lisa and Jojo, who seem to detest one another. He calls her filthy names in Spanish (*puta*, etc.) and she reciprocates with "fat bastard." The best team, surprisingly, is Ginny and Delila. I was surprised at Delila because she didn't seem so bright when I was tutoring her in math [at the time I didn't yet know about her mother's accounting skills]. Little Lucita is also good and she and Maciu make a fine team. . . .
>
> Anyway, while the younger kids were playing dominos, the boys, including Miguel and José, started a game called "open chest." The rules are simple. If your arms are not

crossed over your chest, you get a wallop. They ran around pounding each other's chests (if I didn't know better, I would have sworn they had read Napoleon Chagnon's book [*Yanomamo: The Fierce People,* 1968]). Maciu zipped a book inside his jacket. Maybe because it was so cold in the office. Finally I kicked everybody out at five. It was enough. They went out mumbling Spanish equivalents of "aw shucks" and "what a witch!" and threw chunks of snow at passing cars.

And the following day,

Later in the afternoon, the kids showed up for the continuation of the tournament. It didn't really get off the ground because Jojo and Delila were washing the family's clothes in the Laundromat. They are both in high-placing teams. Jojo finally showed up, and then Delila. She seemed very distraught, but the only thing she would tell me was that Paul was taking too long to get the game started, and she had to watch over the laundry. The reason Paul was slow was because he was searching for the score papers—somebody had apparently snatched them out of his desk. Later, Maribelle offered another reason for Delila's sour face. She said Delila's mother had told her that "she ain't no street girl to be playing dominos," dominos being apparently defined as a strictly male pursuit. By the time I heard that, Delila and Ginny had played against Maciu and Lucita and lost. It was the first game they had lost out of five.

It seemed to me high time that we met Señora Ines—to understand her objections to Delila's participation, for one, and to get some parental backup for controlling Jojo's mouth in the office. I asked Nilda to meet her the following day.

In the afternoon Nilda arrived all excited from her first meeting with Señora Ines. The kids had been procrastinating about the introduction. Each time Nilda proposed a visit, either Jojo or Delila would offer new twists to their mother's supposedly decrepit condition: going blind, swollen eye, diabetic, bad heart, and paralyzed from the waist down. I was really feeling for the poor lady. But Nilda got suspicious when she overheard that the kids had to go home to baby-sit because their mother was going out to play Bingo. So when Delila showed her face after school, Nilda just took her by the hand and said "Let's go!" Apparently the only item of truth about Señora Ines's condition is that she has a heart problem. She had heart surgery recently and has to take it easy. But she runs a large family. In addition to the two children, there is an older son who used to be a drug addict, the son's baby daughter, and another girl, eight years old, for whom she cares, all living in a four-room apartment.

Nilda says that the apartment is very clean—"you could eat out of any corner"— and that she was very warmly received. She said that she told the señora about the "bad" and the "good" things the children do in our office. The señora gave Nilda her telephone number and asked her to call anytime Jojo uses foul language in our office. Then she launched into a long story of her troubles and problems. These included a vivid description of how she got her son off drugs. She knew she was going to have an operation, so she decided to straighten him out before going (in case this was her last act on this earth). She did it by having a fight with him in the street [a public accusation is one of the ultimate tactical maneuvers available to a mother seeking to correct a recalcitrant relative]. She yelled at him about his ingratitude while holding a bottle and threatening to break it over his head so hard that "the police would have to carry him away." Then she brought him home and explained her situation to him, and he decided to give up drugs. It sounded a bit like a *miraglo* [miracle].

There is more to this story that is rather sad. The son had a girlfriend who was an "American" [generic white] and a glue sniffer. The girl's mother didn't care about her daughter. The girl got pregnant and gave birth to a baby girl, but the doctors discovered that she had a disease in which "the white cells are eating up all the red cells," so they kept her longer in the hospital and Señora Ines took the baby home. After she left the hospital, the girl came to live with the señora. She had been warned not to get pregnant again, but she did; she went to get an abortion in a different hospital where they didn't know about her condition and released her right after the operation. The señora tried to get the girl's mother to intervene, to get her back into the hospital, but she wasn't interested, and the girl got weaker and weaker. This was just before the señora's scheduled operation.

So one day, as she was sitting by the girl's bed, the girl said, "If either one of us has to die, I hope it's me, because so many people depend on you." Sure enough, the very next day, at the very same hour, the girl was dead. Her mother could not even be interested in suing the hospital. (This family is big on suing, by the way. Jojo had told me that they sued the landlord when Jojo slipped on a wet spot in the corridor, and they won. The father also sued on his own behalf in another accident, and supposedly won the suit.)

Then the señora took out the dead girl's album. It contained pictures of the girl as a child and young teenager, and finally pictures of her laid out in the funeral parlor. Nilda remarked to the señora that the girl "looked just like a virgin"—so innocent—and the señora agreed. She was so beautiful. Also contained in the album was a poem written by the girl entitled "My Glue Dreams." In it the girl describes how her twenty-five-cent high takes her out of reality into incredibly beautiful places and how she hates to get back. All her friends avoid her because she prefers her glue bag, but that bag is her only friend. Then, without a transition, the poem ends with a declaration that she decided to put her glue bag away. And so it goes. Nilda says that the girl's baby daughter, Victoria, is beautiful.

The following day was the final day of the tournament, but the air of tension and chaos only increased. For one thing, Richie had a visit from his cousin Heckie from Brooklyn, and together they spent the afternoon on acquisition forays. In the late afternoon they came in with three pairs of sweat socks.

Richie threw a fit when he dumped them out of the bag because he was sure he had taken four pairs, not three. He accused and then searched Heckie, patting him up and down expertly. He didn't find them but remained very indignant, suspiciously asking Heckie where he had hid them. Meanwhile, his older brother Julio and their cousin José were sitting around, playing dominos, now and then sending indulgent glances at the younger boys, and then smiling at me with a shrug as if to say "Boys will be boys." I was crocheting with Millie and her second-floor neighbor, Marta, and without looking up at him I asked, "Richie, have you considered the possibility that one of these days you gonna get caught?" He smiled and said, "Nah." They continued on their haunts, but the only additional item they picked up was a giant Doberman, which they tied up outside the office.

Another snag developed. Although Loopy had moved to the Bronx he still made frequent visits to the neighborhood, drawn by his pals and Lisa. Julio's partner in the tournament, he suddenly disappeared, and the final play-offs were being held up. Julio suggested that he play with his cousin, José, but since the guy hadn't played and was older, the kids said it wouldn't be fair. Meanwhile, Jojo, who was very eager to win, made a phone call and was supposedly informed that Loopy had split for Puerto Rico. All the kids started repeating this bit of news and almost had everybody convinced. Fortunately, Loopy's uncle was just passing down the street and told me that Loopy was with his mother in the Bronx. We finally decided not to wait and gave the trophies to the two top-placing teams—Ginny and Delila got second place, Richie and Jojo first. Richie wasn't even there when we announced the results. (He was at that moment in the process of acquiring the Doberman.) When he finally did arrive, everybody was eating donuts that Maciu and I had brought. Suddenly bedlam broke out. Someone blew the fuse, and as we opened the door, Max the Wolf got a scent of the Doberman—there were all sorts of murderous possibilities in the darkness—and everybody started to scream and yell and jump onto counters and chairs, just in case.

By then I'd had it. The kids didn't seem to like the donuts (they were sour-graped from not winning). It didn't help that Emilio was sitting at the table with the donuts in front of him saying grimly, "Get your donuts and you'll get diarrhea," while Miguel had been quieting Max by feeding him donuts in the bathroom. But as we started to clear out the office, the donuts suddenly acquired prize status. Everybody wanted to come back in for a donut. It took forty-five minutes to get the rascals out. Lucita was running around like a streak of lightening, hiding under the desks and slipping out of Paul's arms as he tried to carry her out. Everybody of course had to give us prolonged good-bye kisses. While we said our good-byes, the Doberman's rightful owner came to claim him and didn't seem to be too much put out. Apparently the deed fit into the "boyish pranks" category.

The following day, Nilda went earlier to the office to teach her Spanish class and called to tell me that the spiritist mechanic next door, Mr. Velasquez, said he would fix the ball joints of my car if I got there right away and bought the parts myself. I got them at the supply store on Houston and A and rushed over to the garage. When I got there, alas, Count Augusto, half drunk, had been negotiating on my behalf (come to think of it, maybe he got a cut later). Escorted by Gusto I went into the garage and was informed that the work couldn't possibly be done today, maybe tomorrow, they were up to their ears in work. One of the things they had to do so urgently was paint a yellow car black, something they had been messing with for the past few days. After long negotiations, Gusto finally persuaded them to work on my car (or pretended to persuade them).

While waiting I tried to type some field notes. I was continually interrupted by Emilio and Loopy, who had miraculously reappeared from Puerto Rico. He also continued the fiction of having been there. Practicing liars. At least they had the grace to finally smile in acknowledgment when they were sure I knew they were lying. Meanwhile, Nilda and Bonnie were using flash cards and trying to get the kids to pronounce the words properly, Bonnie winning points with the kids with her sense of humor. In attendance were Lisa, Maribelle, Ginny, and Coreen. The rest of the kids were excitedly running back and forth between our block and the grocery, getting supplies for Señora Ines's granddaughter's baptism party—Victoria had turned one year old that day.

The party was scheduled for the evening, and all the children and our staff had been invited to it by Señora Ines, via Nilda. But the day was still young, and Emilio was making phone calls to see if his mother's mechanic could find time to fix my car. He could, but in the interim the spiritists had decided to sacrifice their paint job and were already knocking one of the wheels off. Gusto asked me to come and observe the operation, then sotto voce but within the spiritists' hearing, inquired whether I had the cash to pay them. He knew I didn't. I had spent all my cash on the parts and had told the mechanic I would pay him on Monday. Now Gusto went into one of his pseudo-radical raps: "The man is making room for you! He's putting aside his other work to accommodate you. The man needs his cash for the weekend," and so forth. I told Gusto I'd see if I could raise some cash. Actually I felt like raising some cash to put a contract out on Gusto, because suddenly the price for labor had doubled and needed to be produced in cold cash on the spot, thanks to his negotiations.

While waiting for my car to be fixed I chatted with Emilio. The rest of the kids had scattered, many of them going to Señora Ines's apartment on Avenue B to decorate. He told me that Mr. Stern had come in earlier, furious because a city inspector had shown up (as a result of our and the tenants' complaints about the lack of heat). Mr. Stern wanted to know who had complained. Then Emilio went on to say how despite the current lack of heat, our building was the best between Avenues A and D. Like Señora Ines, he was determined to celebrate the positive: The building was frequently warm, and there had only been four fires since he and his family moved in. One of the fires had destroyed their walls and furniture, but they all pulled together, replastered and painted—with paint provided by Mr. Stern; and then his older brother, Pablo, bought a new washing machine for his mother. Every week after he got his paycheck from the bag factory, he bought her another present for her kitchen. "You name it, we've got it," said Emilio, detailing a blender, an automatic can opener, and a juicer. And perhaps to demonstrate this abundance, he later went upstairs and brought back two covered dishes of a thick soup of rice, potatoes, and chicken wings and thighs, flavored with *sofrito* (a blended mixture of pimentos, onions, garlic, and sweet pepper, *aji dulce*). He said Eti always made a big pot of it on Saturdays so there would be leftovers for Sunday.

When the mechanic finished, Gusto insisted we go for a trial ride to check their work. Emilio came along. He sat between us, trying hard to keep a straight face as Gusto, who didn't know anything about cars, even how to drive, told me what to do, and detailed how he had helped the mechanics. I drove very fast around the block—the snow piled high on the curbs, covering the cars, so we drove down white alleys—sliding around corners to give Gusto a bit of a scare. When we arrived back at the office he stepped out, unruffled, and said, "Well, darling, this is all I can do for you."

Emilio asked with incredulity, "*What* has he done for you?"

Annoyed and amused by Gusto's nagging machismo, I burst out, "Imagine being married to somebody like that! I'd die in the first week!"

Emilio laughed so hard that he collapsed backward into a snowdrift. Laughing just as hard, I followed.

Gusto returned to perform one final courtesy that evening: to walk us, the ladies, to Señora Ines's apartment. After all, it was a block and a half away from the office, and Paul had gone away; and so it was left to Gusto to perform this manly duty.

Arriving at the apartment, we were met by a group of very excited kids. They asked after Paul and led us in. The whole mob was there: Richie, wearing the latest style in heeled shoes, cheap, thin trousers with a sharp crease, and a newly acquired Timex watch; Daniel, wearing peach-colored trousers and a peach print shirt; José and his plump friend Choochie, squeezed into denims. Jimmy, Miguel, Adam, and two little boys from the Bronx who were Jojo's cousins were also there. The girls present included Lisa, dressed in a cowl-neck pullover, a printed shirt over it, and pants to match; Maribelle, in a black vest and trousers; Ginny; Isabel; Delila, in a pretty blouse and a miniskirt; and two tiny girls. Neither Evelyn, Coreen, nor any boys over fifteen were there.

We walked through a small kitchen, past the bathroom, and into the living room, where disco music was blasting. Most of the children were sitting politely, squashed onto the two small couches on the opposite sides of the nine-by-twelve-foot room. In one corner was a small round table topped by a huge, two-tiered birthday cake. The table was covered with a patterned paper cloth, and the cake was surrounded by small pink candy baskets. White and pink paper streamers were suspended above the table, framing it like a tent. One red lightbulb dangling from the ceiling lit the room. Red curtains separating this room from the next one were pulled back. Delila led us into it so we could put our coats on the edge of the giant white crib in which the birthday girl was standing. Victoria, a slender, big-eyed baby, was dressed in a white, two-tiered lace dress. Miguel introduced me to her, telling her to say hello. She said "Eillo" and "Bye bye." Two women were sitting in this room, one a heavyset woman of around fifty, and the other a very poorly dressed, emaciated woman wearing big glasses and a kerchief over graying hair and holding a baby in her lap. I said hello to them, and they nodded, but we were not introduced.

Bonnie asked me quietly who was the mother of the baby, and I whispered to her that the mother was dead. She didn't hear me—the music was blasting—but Miguel did. He went to the dresser and brought back a huge pin, a photograph of the dead mother holding Victoria when she was about two months old. She had had long black hair and a sweet smile.

Later I found out that neither of the women was Señora Ines. Both of them were neighbors, the heavy one a *comadre* (godmother) who had baptized Victoria earlier in the day at St. Bridget's. The thin woman, I found out, was very young but harrowed by some terrible disease (AIDS had not yet been formally classified). Having organized the evening's celebration, Señora Ines had gone to play Bingo.

As the evening wore on I half wished I had gone with her. Not that the children were wild. They were exceedingly polite and well mannered, compared to their exuberance in the office. It was the celebration of life, in the midst of death, that depressed me. I wondered if it had been too much for Señora Ines too. Maybe she was making room for the dead girl's spirit.

The comadre was in charge of the party. She brought us each a paper cup with soda; Gusto was given a four-ounce Miller's in the bottle. The thin woman shuffled around in slippers, tending to the toddlers. I realized she was pregnant. As the evening progressed, the children continued to "behave," although from time to time a small flock would put on their jackets, go out into the cold hallway, then return. I did not care to enquire what mayhem they might have been up to in the stairway. None of them really danced except Daniel, who showed off his virtuosity, using Adam as his straight man. Break dancing was already popular in the neighborhood, and Daniel did complicated motion routines, using his hands, turning trimly on his heels, then signaling to Adam, who tried to follow but invariably messed up. One particular movement required a fast spin and a vertical fall backward, which Daniel executed, catching his own fall with one hand, just inches off the floor.

A lot of whispering and intrigues seemed to be going on between the children, but these were confined to segregated sex groups. Lisa and Isabel stayed close, Isa holding Lisa's hand, stroking her hair, and sitting on her lap. Watching Maribelle, I recalled my own twelve-year-old longings: She frequently consulted with Ginny, then she'd take on a tragic pose; elbows on knees, holding her head in her hands, her face buried under the cascade of her black hair. At other times, she'd lean against a wall at the entrance to the room, looking melancholy. Meanwhile José was anxiously consulting with Miguel, but each time Maribelle went out to the kitchen, he'd follow. At some point he sat next to me and confessed that he had been crying because someone had told Maribelle that he wanted to go out with her. He had spoken to Lisa, and she had given him permission to court her younger sister, but he wasn't sure what Maribelle's reaction was. Later in the evening, after the cake had been cut and distributed, he wouldn't touch it, because he said he had a terrible stomachache. The poor boy is in love! I thought. I told him his stomach probably hurt from his emotions. He asked, "What's emotions?"

I answered, "You know, strong feelings, love, hate, happiness, sadness."

He went over to Maribelle and told her that his stomach hurt from emotions, and then asked me to explain it to her while he took a powder himself.

In preparation for the cake cutting, Jojo exchanged the red lightbulb with a white one in the bedroom. I offered to hold the ladder, but he said he didn't need me to, and he finished the job with a quivering jig up by the ceiling in time to the music.

The *comadre* brought Victoria from her crib and sat her behind the cake table, placing a silver and pink tiara on her brow. The tiara kept slipping down to Victoria's nose. Meanwhile, Jojo brought some candles, and the kids gathered around the table. Someone turned the music and lights off, and Victoria blew out the candles with all the kids' help. They sang "Happy Birthday" in English; when Nilda tried to get a round of "*Feliz Cumpleaños*" going, nobody followed. Then the lights and music were turned back on and the skinny neighbor took a photo of Victoria poised with a large butcher knife over the cake, the comadre holding the little girl's hand like a bride's.

After guiding Victoria's hand to cut the first slice and giving it to her, the comadre continued cutting while the neighbor added ice cream and Delila carried the plates to various guests, with paper napkins and forks. Meanwhile Nilda danced in the middle of the floor, popping candy from one of the pink containers from time to time. A huddle of kids in one of the corners imitated her movements and snickered, but circumspectly. The cake, a product of Valencia bakery, the Cadillac of Latino cakes, was doing its thing. The children were off the couches, and the birthday girl, liberated from the crib and high chair, was wobbling speedily between their legs. Nobody even noticed that she had wandered out into the hallway until a man suddenly emerged from a back bedroom, perhaps Señor Enriquez. But this was no time for introductions. He said a few angry words to Delila, who scooped up Victoria, and he returned to the bedroom, closing the door behind him. The comadre dragged Victoria back to her crib, scolding both her and Delila on the way.

At this point I made my excuses to Jojo and Delila, thanked the comadre for the party, and with Bonnie took several of the younger children home, as I had promised their mothers. Nilda went for a drink with Gusto, which turned out to be a mistake. As we got into the car, Emilio yelled good-bye to us from his window—he had been watching out for us. Ah, so many manly eyes looking out for us. On the corner of Fourth and B, stomping their feet in the snow, Rocky and his friends gave us a mild wave as we drove off. At Señora Ines's house the party was just starting; adults would begin to arrive now.

The following week Maciu left with his father for a five-month visit to Afghanistan. My former husband was worried that I was endangering our child's welfare by bringing him to the neighborhood. But one can never be certain: He and Maciu arrived in Afghanistan with little time to spare before the first Soviet invasion of Kabul.

I didn't write any field notes that week. Then I invited Miguel and José home for an overnight visit. It helped some. But when Nilda arrived uptown with Miguel and José at about 11:30 P.M., I didn't interact with them. She warmed up some spaghetti and meat sauce that my daughter, Jenny, had prepared earlier, and put them to sleep. Next morning they were up at the break of dawn, playing Ping-Pong. They asked me if they could take my dog, Puppy, out for a walk, and I asked them to buy some bread and milk in our local bodega. José reminded me that we had no toothpaste and they needed to "clean their mouths." They left with the dog and Maciu's skateboard. After enough time had passed for me to start worrying, they returned. Our bodega had still been closed, so they had to search for an open store in an unknown neighborhood. They had bought two French loaves, and José proceeded to eat a whole one by himself. Then he asked for two hard-boiled eggs with mayonnaise and drank his orange juice and both his and Miguel's hot chocolate. Miguel seemed shy and uneasy about asking for anything. He had some corn flakes and drank some juice. While I washed dishes, lost in thought, they opened up the trap door to the roof and went up "to fly a kite." In ten-degree weather, I told them to get their behinds right down. Their little clown faces, faking contrition, reminded me, like Victoria's baptism, that life must go on.

Soon after the party, Delila and Jojo stopped coming to the office. The last time I heard anything about Jojo was from Miguel, once again on the scene of a disaster. It was already summer, close to the Fourth of July. He came running into the office, shouting, "Jagna, Jagna, Jojo blew up his hand! There's meat and blood all over the ceiling!" (*Carne* translates as both "flesh" and "meat.") Jojo had been playing with a firecracker and blown off his right thumb, which according to Miguel they were at the moment trying to reattach at Bellevue. "How's he going to play his guitar?" asked Miguel sadly.

But for the time being, fortune was still smiling on this family. Jojo's thumb was successfully reattached, and I later heard that the family had moved to a spacious apartment in "the projects" by the East River. Señora Ines had had an application on file with the Housing Authority for over ten years, and she finally got a winning number. Now she had room for all of her children, and Señor Enriquez had an expanded sphere in which to increase his business. Still later, I heard he made the mistake of investing his accumulating earnings in the even more profitable cocaine business, which was the beginning of the downfall of the family. But for the present, the children were enrolled in Catholic school, they were well dressed and fed, and they enjoyed the other benefits of a middle-class childhood. It looked as if they might fulfill the conservative dream of the upward-bound, two-parent family. Little did we know.

Reflection 1:
Small Creatures

Sometimes, early in the mornings in springtime, maybe about six o'clock, you wouldn't know you were in Manhattan. At least until the crunching of garbage trucks tore the silence, the sounds were of a sleepy town. The first to be heard were the roosters. As in rural Puerto Rico, they announced the beginning of a new day. People who had grown up in the country would get up ready to go to their poor jobs, or start the day's work of raising children, not needing alarm clocks, their bodies attuned to the change in light, to their crowing helpers. But of course, like everything else in an urban ghetto, the function of roosters was different here: Their job was not to play machos to hens. They were gaming cocks, kept in cages, in apartments and basements, occasionally allowed into backyard pens where they furiously scratched at the dirt. At this time of day you'd also glimpse sight of homeless dog packs, beige generic New York City curs, with white paws, devil-may-care smiles, in hot friendly pursuit of a single bitch with hanging *tetas* (teats). Some of them had places they could call home, or at least a pad. But no one bothered to walk them, spay them, or heaven forbid, call the dogcatcher to send them to doggie heaven.

Miguel had one named Sweetie. When his family moved into public housing, he was not allowed to bring her because of the Housing Authority's regulations. Only the little chihuahua got smuggled in. Sweetie remained in the now almost abandoned building, running free with her pals, coming back to the block each day at the time Miguel got out of school nearby and returned to feed her. He was always able to scrounge up something for her, sometimes rice and beans, sometimes real dog food that he bought with money he earned sweeping out the *Cambiamos Cheques* (We Change Checks) store. One time he got a real haul of dog food during the raid on the Dominican's bodega.

The treatment of dogs was gender specific, resembling the way adults related to all smaller creatures, including children. "Good," or pure—or almost purebred—

female dogs were kept at home, given table food, cuddled and coddled, bathed, brushed, and mated. "Good" male dogs were pushed, teased, and annoyed into becoming attack dogs. Even Snowy, Loopy's little off-white terrier, was forever being challenged by Loopy and other kids to snarl, snap, charge, and if possible, bite, something he wasn't into. The boys went even further to turn their dogs into machos, using all sorts of experimental ideas. For example, one morning Richie came in with a Doberman puppy. While the little dog frisked around the office with Max, Richie asked if I would help him to trim the dog's ears and tail. "I'll do the ears, Teach, you do the tail." I was saying nothing doing, but someone else piped up that the best way to accomplish the task was with a burning cigar. Richie left, probably disgusted with my lack of cooperation or sense of humor. When I went into the back office to listen to Emilio read Spanish poetry, Daniel, who seemed to feel left out, apparently amused himself with Max the Wolf out in front. Gasping with laughter, he called out to Emilio from our front stoop to come see the results. Emilio dropped the book and ran out, and immediately collapsed laughing in the doorway. When I tried to get a peek, he barred the door, saying that this was not a sight for a lady. I finally saw poor Max, hunched over. I thought he was constipated but then I noticed his engorged penis hanging down practically to the ground. The poor dog couldn't get it back in. Daniel had used one of our office chairs for this masturbation session, and now both he and Emilio were calling Max a bad dog. Nilsa joined me and together we commiserated with Max, telling the boys never to do it again. At this point Richie returned and supported Daniel by saying he always did that to his own dog.

It was hard to know how to react. Our commitment to cultural relativism was continuously challenged. Another time, after we had been away from the office for a few days, Max in his loneliness had gnawed off half the fake paneling on the door. When we returned, Emilio said he had given Max a beating for it. We all swooped down on him like a horde of vultures, telling him never to beat Max again, but Emilio said he had already been punished by God for it—he had locked his keys in the office and couldn't get back in. Interestingly, the children were capable of switching their dog attitude when they came uptown. My male dog Puppy got walks and hugs, never smacks or teases. They seemed to think he didn't need to be a macho, to protect me or himself. A middle-class treatment for a middle-class dog—little did they know that at heart he was a street-corner dog, taking off to hang out with our street-corner men anytime he got the chance to escape.

Not a day went by on the Lower East Side without something animal-related, often hideous, happening. That very same day we had a live demonstration of what abused dogs will do. One of the spiritist mechanics, Señor Velasquez, came running in with his arm badly torn and bleeding, asking to use our phone, because the German shepherd guarding the garage had turned on him. He said he had tried to defend himself with a screwdriver. After getting the runaround from the ASPCA, we finally called the Ninth Police Precinct, because the dog could have been rabid.

Everybody, including Gusto, who had arrived in the meantime, got very excited at the prospect of a wild-game hunt by the city's Finest. But the two wild-game cops who turned up were pussycats. Nice guys, really. They lamented the fact that they had just used up all of their tranquilizers on a dog on Fifth Street, a medium-sized mutt who had suddenly ripped up his master and mistress that morning—they had to go to the hospital for stitches on their arms and legs. One of the two cops explained to the assembled throng that dogs were like people: "Suddenly they go crazy." Yeah, I thought, when provoked beyond endurance. Señor Velasquez tried to explain in English: He didn't know what had caused the attack, as the dog always had lots of water and food. Yet I had never seen the dog being let out or walked, and I knew for a fact that Mr. Stern had just discovered and severed the illegal electric line that provided the garage with heat and power, so the dog must have been very cold.

Armed with two nooses mounted on long sticks, the cops gingerly entered the garage while its owner hovered behind a double-parked car and Gusto hovered in our doorway, ready to split at a moment's notice—Nilda's sister's dog had attacked his trousers the previous week. Other people came out of their buildings to watch the show, among them Doña Mercedez, her three-quarter jacket only partially covering her long white priestly dress. As we exchanged *felicidades* (good wishes) for Easter with many of them, we saw the cops backpedal out of the garage with great alacrity. The dog had not bled to death, as they had hoped, from screwdriver wounds, but was just sitting there, staring at them. While the younger cop got back on the phone, trying to coax some more tranquilizers out of his superiors, the older one philosophized about the possibility that a cornered dog might suddenly come out fighting just like a man when cornered. Suddenly there were screams from the cop in the office. He had heard some scuffling noises made by the kids upstairs and had thought his partner had gone back alone into the garage and was now getting mauled. I went in to calm him down, and finally the duo took courage in their hands and went after the dog with their nooses. After the first pitiful sob from the dog I couldn't listen anymore, and I went into the back office. People were expressing pity for the dog—"*Ay, bendito,*" they said—as the dog got hauled into the police van.

Both children and adults in the neighborhood identified with the animal world. As fierce and swift as the passage of a smack given by an adult to a child, as quickly followed by a smack from the child to a dog, was the almost anthropomorphized identification with the life and sensibilities of animals. When Arturo Fuentes and Millie moved to their new apartment in the projects, he remarked wistfully that it felt almost too empty. He missed the sounds and drama of living with *cucarachas* and *ratones* (cockroaches and rats). And when we took a bunch of girls and some of their younger brothers for an outing on Bear Mountain, they weren't bored for one moment: They spent the time first observing, then collecting, ants, beetles, and crayfish, gently putting them into jars and cups, worrying about their safety, trying to feed them grass and other inappropriate comestibles.

When it was time to go home, Lisa insisted they set their collections free. To the younger kids' protests, she said, "What? You're crazy! They're gonna die on Fourth Street!" Then she said, "How would you like it if you got kidnapped from your family?" That clinched it. The children watched with deep satisfaction as their liberated captives crawled, slithered, and ran for cover.

In their most utilitarian aspect, animals—like people—could be used instrumentally by boys practicing the manly skills necessary for succeeding as machos in a market economy. I have already mentioned how Richie tended to show up at the office with different purebreds. Several of them were the temporary property of one of his violent uncles, or their dogs' progeny, given to Richie in the time-honored tradition of 4-H organizations and peasantries all over the world, to teach the young to care for and raise a young animal on their own. But in a neighborhood warped by poverty, the intent was bent by larcenous constraints. The dogs were acquired by dognapping, both dames and sires, and the progeny sold to people of better means who needed protectors but didn't care to pay for a paper pedigree.

The dogs also provided the basis for training in minor extortion. One such incident involved Florisol, the blue-eyed transvestite hairdresser whose shop was across the street. Florisol favored tight blouses with decolletage that exposed her considerable cleavage, and tight jeans. She let it be known that her husband, with whom she owned the beauty parlor (where one could also purchase modish lingerie and costume jewelry), liked to see her in sexy clothes. Florisol's prize possession was a miniature poodle, snow white, with a jeweled collar and a pink bow on top of her head. One day Florisol arrived, despairing, at our office. Someone had stolen her poodle. I told her we would all be on the lookout for the dog, trying to console her but not giving her much hope. Such hot dogs fetched a good price in nearby, more affluent areas. When the kids got home from school I passed on the word, and soon Florisol came back, all excited. A child had delivered a ransom note from the dognappers. She was to put $25 in an envelope and give it to the next messenger child, and her dog would be returned; otherwise her "eys" would never see it again. I advised her to put in $10, which she did, and within minutes the poodle reappeared at her storefront. Some time later I saw a contingent of our boys, Richie obviously in charge, setting off happily for the pizza store.

Because Florisol was an outsider to the boys and their kin, making a modest living but charging for her services, the boys apparently had no compunction about forcing her to share the wealth. If she minded, she kept it to herself, and her "cooperation" in this and in more legitimate community causes made good business sense in buying goodwill and customers. She would later be further rewarded for her generosity, and her ties with the neighborhood strengthened.

The ultimate neighborhood *animalito* story concerned a group of grown men connected by kinship ties. It was rumored, and maybe it was just wishful thinking, that they were raising a pig in a backyard. The pig was well fed from the leavings of the local restaurants and was slaughtered for Christmas, the story went, shares of meat going to all the families of the cooperating male group. Even if just a story, it was significant in that it connected local men to their rural past and showed all kinds of possibilities for cooperation and joint action. We were all fired up. Imagine, raising a pig in Manhattan!

It was not exactly what proponents of urban redevelopment had in mind when proposing capitalist solutions for urban "blight," but it certainly resonated with historical antecedents. Already in the 1630s erstwhile Amsterdamers were suing each other over injuries inflicted on their hogs and damage done to their produce by others' hogs (Hershkowitz 1965). We visualized trotters growing up in the world's most dazzling metropolis under the benevolent aegis of kinship-based corporate groups. Our dreaming was not as far out as it might seem. Charras, a group of young Puerto Rican men, had sponsored Spanish theater and film productions and were talking about economic enterprises that included the building of geodesic domes for housing. Other similarly dreamy ideas had already been put into action: a communal apartment house on East Eleventh Street heated with solar power, a portion of its electricity supplied by a sleek windmill; communal urban gardens that were beginning to take shape amidst the ruins of burned-out buildings, providing shade, beauty, and fragrance, and often vegetables to boot—many of them crowned with *casitas*. These were artful miniature houses, porch and all, built from recycled materials, decorated inside and out with "back home" details: a table covered with an oilcloth and a vase of plastic flowers, lounge chairs, perhaps a giant stuffed panda, slightly the worse for wear. People sat around them in the evenings, the women wearing housedresses and slippers, sipping sodas from plastic cups, the men in sportshirts and somber slacks, maybe over a domino board that had been set up on an upturned Con Edison wire spool, sipping beer from four-ounce bottles of Miller's High Life. As small children starting to yawn leaned into the solid laps of older women . . .

Like animalitos, small children were believed to lack the capacity to reason. Therefore they were protected and kept out of danger, swiftly snatched from the curbside, for example, a smack or spank reinforcing the lesson to keep away from the street, or simply providing a vent to the grown-up's fright. Up to the age of six or so, children—especially boys—were indulged and allowed to throw fits when thwarted. As the children grew older, however, they could and did receive serious hitting by a parent's hand, belt, or stick. Most adults were temperate about physical punishment—even the most furiously broom-wielding mom seldom left a welt on her son—but several parents abused their children. Among them was Ramon Caballero, former jazz musician and heroin user, now an alcoholic, who beat his daughter Evelyn severely twice, so that the welts up and down her arms and legs were visible. Her transgression, at the age of eleven, was "encouraging boys." The other case was hearsay, the children telling me that after Victoria's baptismal party Jojo and Delila's father gave both of them a big beating. They kept mum about Señor Enriquez's justification.

I personally witnessed Arturo Fuentes manhandling Marco, his skinny, wistful stepson, furious yet in control, and my impression was that although still cultur-

ally permitted, the hitting of children was disappearing from the mothers' disciplining repertoire but lingering in the men's. The women who told me stories
about being beaten with electric wires and brooms and tied up to beds by grandmothers and stepmothers on the island now averred that they would not allow
this kind of behavior to be inflicted on their own daughters. None of the team
members saw or heard of any abuse by the women of the neighborhood, so it was
reasonable to assume that a cultural shift was taking place toward a more middle-
class approach: Reason with your children, and if needed, use psychological
penalties. So, in the late 1970s, the trend was toward a closer, warmer relation, at
least between mother and children. There was no way then to predict that this
pattern of child raising is a luxury, predicated on having stable shelter, enough income for daily food and small treats, and above all, proximity and access to a
group of people—family and/or friends who can be converted to family—to give
you advice, loans, and a helping hand, especially with children, when the number
and intensity of stressful events and situations grow.

This is the kind of situation Carol Stack described for a group of poor African-
American families in 1974, and her portrait was, to some extent, still applicable to
what I was seeing on the Lower East Side in 1979. The safety net stretched between
the nodes of mother, mother's family, and comadres (godmothers), and her grown
children and grandchildren. It included coresidential men related by blood or marriage, and *their* mothers, ensuring collective strength for raising children through
vertical and horizontal lines of kinship. It replaced or added to simple husband-
wife units because those structures had become too unstable, as a result of declining jobs for men, to do the job. These cats-cradle configurations, mistaken by
Daniel Moynihan (1965) and his latter-day followers for simple, denuded, mother-
child dyads, connected large numbers of individuals through children, for the task
of rearing children. Young mothers lived with or next door to, or on the same block
with, mothers, aunts, and grandmothers from both sides of the family. At any time
some of these people might possess husbands, mates, extra food, money, and space
to share. Children would sleep or stay for prolonged periods at different relatives'
homes—sometimes for several years. Unlike a nuclear family, this family structure
was adapted to uncertain income and life on low wages.

Ironically, this ultimate safety net was blamed for producing structural conditions of poverty in the first place—as if the neighborhood's residents were making the decision to downsize IBM or relocate a lamp factory, say to the
Philippines, or move the Wonder Bread bakery to Cincinnati. Instead of praising,
cherishing, and helping to support the realistic and innovative ways people were
devising for bringing up relatively healthy and well-adjusted future citizens
against enormous and growing economic odds, the officialdom of the United
States society sought to destroy it, thwart it, and label it as deviant. And the time
finally did arrive when extended families were separated through the loss of housing, through attrition and gentrification (Susser 1993). When overcrowding and
the decreasing value of poor people's incomes overburdened formerly flexible

networks, and young inexperienced parents had to suddenly cope on their own, the official reaction to the resulting social anomie was surprise and finger pointing—in the wrong direction.

Outraged media printed stories about young dealers, female addicts, and abused children. Crack cocaine was blamed for young mothers' inability to raise children, as if all this had happened overnight, in a vacuum. In the stories the situation that was overwhelming some poor young women had nothing to do with having to spend nights in congregate shelters, of not having money for food, of not getting help because their mate was imprisoned and the community dispersed. It was all a matter of having been brought up in a culture of poverty, of having no future orientation, of not being interested in marriage or a nice nuclear family.

When the rabble was finally cleared out from big swaths of the Lower East Side and the neighborhood became safer for "urban pioneers," the gardens with their little casitas were left behind. But you could no longer wake up to a rooster's call. They had all been arrested. And except for the smart ones, who had the brains to take a hike to the South Bronx, the beige generic dogs had long ago been harvested by private vans supplying medical and cosmetic laboratories. The last time I talked to Miguel, he had no memory of having had a dog named Sweetie.

7

Blue Bayou

Maribelle Moreno said that Paco "dreamed with Juan," his dead friend. Sometimes they were just dreams, sometimes nightmares in which he was being haunted by a black flying spirit. Puerto Ricans don't dream "about" someone, they dream "with" them. The danger of dreaming with a dead friend is that you may follow.

Paco was a chubby, dignified twelve-year-old. He could join in the spirit of hilarity on the many occasions that arose, but he had a certain artistic talent that he himself respected, as did the other children. His mother, whom we knew as Señora Moreno, was also a very private person. Arriving from the island as a young adult, she had refused to venture into spoken English, although she understood it. She also kept herself "upstairs" as a good woman should, never joining gossip groups, never going dancing at the Spanish clubs like the more venturesome women, neither smoking or drinking nor actively looking for a partner. Our first contact with her was through Nilda, in whom she recognized another respectable woman, and through her children. She kept Paco, her eldest son, upstairs with her, only giving him permission to join our activities. She attempted to keep her daughters, Lisa and Maribelle, and her second son, Jimmy, home too.

When we first started our project, she lived with her children in the building owned by the German, around the corner on Avenue B. Because of her reserve, we didn't get to know her intimately. We knew that she spent her time *sufriendo* (suffering) because the father of the elder four children, to whom she was still legally married, had left her for a younger woman in New Jersey who already had three children and with whom he had two more. As a mechanic working for someone else, he had little money or time left for his first family. Señora Moreno's children were exposed to ridicule when he occasionally arrived in his old station wagon to take them for an outing. Her youngest son, Ricardo, then two, was the product of a short love affair, and because his father contributed money for his maintenance, Señora Moreno was proud that at least one of her children did not have to rely on welfare to stay alive. However, having no regular partner contributing to the family budget and care of the children made it difficult for her to keep body and soul together. Because her income was insufficient even to feed her growing children, Señora Moreno was one of the single mothers whose money and food stamps ran out about two weeks before the end of the month, and so she would resort to the rice-and-milk dinner plan, which may have been nourishing but was also indicative of rock bottom. When she moved into our building, we noticed that other mothers who had working elder sons or partners frequently helped to feed her children, as the group floated from one open-door apartment to another.

Housing was another source of deep anxiety. Her eldest child, Lisa, was a thin, very attractive fifteen-year-old, whose every venture downstairs, even to buy a loaf of bread, was magnetic to young males. She inspired graffiti on the walls and ceiling of her building's hallways, and breathless traffic jams that ended in other plans and activities when Lisa didn't appear. Both Richie and Rafael, just shy of fifteen, were in love with her and consequently, in her honor, defied the laws of gravity to etch their noms de plume in out-of-reach spots. Other undeclared young blades, like Daniel from below Delancey, and Lefty, officially from the Upper West Side (where his stepmother and half-siblings lived and where he was registered for school), paid extended visits or squatted in empty basements on the block, attracted by the attraction that Lisa generated in their peers. Nor were the prepubescents immune to the excitement. Whoever could get close enough to her might pull a hair, bump into her, or provoke her into verbal fury, watching the resulting torrent with shining eyes and a grin for an effort well rewarded. Neither the graffiti nor the assembled mobs sat well with the "lan'lo."

On top of that, Paco's younger sister, Maribelle, although only eleven and so off-limits to the sighs of adolescents, was a rounder version of Lisa and was starting to bud in her T-shirt, while developing a milder and more intelligent version of her sister's "mouth." Emilio's twelve-year old brother, José, could often be observed either annoying her or sending melancholy glances in her general direction. To top it all off, Paco refused to perform the eldest brother's role of playing the *dueña* for his sisters, and by default it fell to the next youngest brother, Jimmy, then ten years old, a total pain in the butt as far as everybody was concerned. When he wasn't letting forth a string of invectives, he was giving another kid a wallop in the chest. When he wasn't challenging bigger boys to a fight, he was doing bigger and better graffiti. When he wasn't balancing on the fire escape, he was waving a cheerful *adios* wreathed in the exhaust of the back bumper of an Avenue B bus.

One of the first missions of mercy that Bonnie performed after becoming acclimatized to our project was to go with Señora Moreno *y familia* to plead with their German landlord to forgo the eviction notice he had served on them. After the emotional but unsuccessful visit, in which both Lisa and Maribelle loudly took the landlord to task while Señora Moreno stood sadly by, Bonnie deduced that the landlord was using the two months' delayed rent as an act of divine providence to preserve his property. After all, delayed rent payments were the rule and not the exception on the Lower East Side. As often as not they were caused by the city's own delayed mailings of rent allowances, or temporary (and calculated) suspension of a family from welfare rolls, and just as frequently by the pressing need of families to spend the rent money on either food or warm clothing.

This was the spot Señora Moreno now found herself in, having spent the rent allowance on her children's Easter clothing, in anticipation of promised money from her husband, which had not materialized. Bonnie had been chosen by Señora Moreno for this particular unsuccessful intervention because of the growing influence that she was assuming in Paco's life. The family did move at the end of the month, to an apartment I had secured through my "special relationship" with the Sterns, and our office became an extension of the family's living room. Which, except for Jimmy's presence, was fine.

For Paco, the move began what must have been the most creative time of his life. We had already noticed his spectacular talent for being able to look at any picture and promptly produce a precisely exact miniature or blowup of it. For the Christmas play he had collaborated with Lisa on writing the story, and then patiently collected a pyramid of cardboard boxes being thrown out by Key Food, which he transformed, working secretly over a couple of days, into bold, imaginative sets. It was when Bonnie took on Paco's tutoring after school, however, that he began to blossom.

It started one day while he was watching her practice calligraphy. He asked her to teach him to do it, and in no time he was producing Gothic scripts that became *le dernier crie* for all the kids on the block. First they all wanted to have their own names inscribed in their notebooks; next, the names of their best friends or beloveds. This was followed by requests for "club insignia" inscribed on the jean jackets of a loosely coalescing junior gang. In this, however, Paco exercised discrimination, based on the supplicant's character. By then he was in a position to be choosy. Then Christmas came, and for a week before, we all slaved to produce fifty T-shirts for many of our young acquaintants, inscribed in Gothic with their nicknames from Paco's carefully cut stencils. Bonnie, Nilsa, Lisa, Maribelle, and Ginny rolled on the black paint and ironed, smearing up a number of the shirts that we had bought in bulk on Delancey Street for fifty cents apiece, while Paco designed, snipped, supervised, and subtly criticized. I got the best prize in the end: a navy shirt inscribed in white Gothic lettering that read Speak Truth to Power. Paco took my explanation of what it meant very seriously. Alas, it is not a message that poor children are supposed to absorb, as I was to find out later.

At the time I noted in my field notes:

A couple of junior gang members have drifted in and, using the "good" kids' materials, are trying to draw their gang insignia. The main problem seems to be that they don't know how to spell. I was asked to spell "young" for them and was eventually involved in spelling "dragons" and "gatos." The gatos customer looks about twelve, wears a green cap backwards over his dusty orange afro, and is incredibly dirty. While attempting to type on the broken-down typewriter in the back room, he informed me that his name is Cheetah, that he is the president of Young Gatos, and that he took up typing and ceramics in school, a place he no longer visits. The other, variously known as Eduardo or Lefty, apparently belongs to the Dragons. With another young sidekick, they got me to draw insignia. I attempted to recruit Paco but to no avail. He was obviously disapproving. Besides, he was having too much of a good time. Bonnie was giving him a compressed lecture that included history, geography, astronomy, chemistry, physics, and medieval art. At one point, as I passed through the office, she was standing, a globe in hand, representing the sun, while Paco, a Styrofoam cup in hand, circled around her, for earth. . . . Anyway, I think my services to the young gang cost me $14. At least that's how much had been taken from my wallet by the end of the spelling/drawing session.

It is surprising to me in rereading my field notes how seldom references to Paco appear. It is perhaps because he was so quiet. He observed the exploits of the more flamboyant children from the sidelines. We speculated on the difference of his behavior and upbringing, noting that Señora Moreno spoke to him in Spanish, confidentially, the way women do with daughters or female kin. Observations about people and events passed quietly between the two of them, often in glances, showing the closeness of their bond. The children didn't dare openly call him a "faggot," because of the dignity with which he eschewed involvement in physical fights and displays, but it was obvious that he was perceived as being "different" and special, not the macho that the other boys were seriously practicing to be.

It was their exploits that caught my attention. In the weeks following my first observations of the formation of a junior gang, we noticed a sudden influx of wealth to the boys evident in the appearance of three minibikes, miniature motorcycles illegal for use on city streets. Twelve-year-old José Medina acquired one, as did fourteen-year-old Rafael Ortega and Cheetah. By then I had discovered that Cheetah's mother lived in Boston and that he had escaped from the third foster home in which he had been placed. I also heard that his mother's brother was a functionary in the aging gang of senior Gatos and that he had formed a household in a basement on our block with Lefty. Señora Medina, Señora Ortega, and several younger women took turns feeding them and allowing them to bathe in their apartments, out of the goodness of their hearts, it was said. From various accounts of the sudden windfall, as told to Nilda and Nilsa by the mothers, and by the boys to me, a story emerged that was hard and unpleasant to believe.

In its bare-bones version, a woman whose husband had died placed the insurance money she received upon his demise in a paper bag that she stored under her widowed bed. Her son, a rotten nine-year-old, took the bag in a fit of vengeance, because his mother had publicly humiliated him "in the street," and distributed it by the hundreds to all the eager prepubescent and pubescent boys who happened to be standing by when the fit hit him. There were various embroideries on this theme, including a taxi chase to the Brooklyn Bridge, a supposed visit by the robbed señora to Señora Medina's, and a shifting of the cast of lucky recipients. Emilio avoided my eyes when I asked him for his version of the story. Millie Cortez giggled out loud in front of the other mothers when the "widow" story was told, one sultry spring evening, on the bench in front of our office.

I hated the implications of it, of the poor, knowing better, robbing the poor. The kids, including Emilio, took rides on one of the bikes, roaring off as far as Delancey Street. On his first trip Emilio came back fuming, leading the bike with its tires flat, outraged that a cop had stopped him and punched the holes with a knife, he said. Within a week, the minibikes disappeared, either confiscated or traded or returned for cash. Nilda, doubting the origin of the story, cited similar apocryphal stories from her childhood in East Harlem, where a miser's supposed buried treasure caused feverish gold-digging in junk-filled backyards. But here was real money.

In 1991, some twelve years later, Lefty reminded me of the event. Now a handsome man in his mid-twenties, dressed tastefully down to his shiny loafers, he was a teacher in an alternative high school and a born-again Christian. He was visiting me as a part of his search for his son, who would now be about eleven, whom he had fathered with one of the young mothers who had been particularly solicitous about his basement dwelling with Cheetah. At the time, fatherhood was not a burden she had wished to place on Lefty; neither could he have provided any kind of support. His son had grown up with a more mature stepfather. After I gave him the new number for Señora Medina, as the woman most likely to help in his search, we started to reminisce.

Lefty said, "Jagna, do you remember that heist we pulled on Fifth Street? When we got the minibikes?" Yes indeed. It turned out that the victim had not been a poor widow but a middle-level white drug dealer, and the visit to Señora Medina had not been made by any widow but by a burly go-between who had made it clear that all the money had better be returned forthwith. Lefty would tell me other corrective tales later, but this one in particular warmed my soul.

Attempting to channel the children's energy more constructively, we redoubled our efforts, perhaps naively, to provide a "safe house" where children could learn and work out their problems and focus on children's normal pursuits. Thus we engaged ourselves and them in the project of beautifying the front of our office. Like all our projects, it proceeded in fits and starts over the next two weeks, the tumultuousness of ongoing events constantly distracting us.

When we invited the children to help us paint the storefront, we were not yet conscious of adding to a tradition. Murals, some of them several stories high, were already an integral and expressive part of Lower East Side popular culture that went back to the early 1960s. The earliest were clearly political expressions calling for equality, racial justice, and the unity of the poor. Several, executed in brilliant colors and bold strokes, recorded the area's painful immigrant history; others included visions of an armed struggle against an oppressive militarist state; still others recorded and celebrated heroes of the Puerto Rican liberation movement. In the late 1970s more prosaic murals would begin to appear on doorways and storefronts, with themes expressing longing for a lost, tropical homeland. Palms, ocean views, people relaxing in light summer clothes—these invoked the longing that Bela Feldman Bianco (1990) terms "saudado," the mourning remembrance of a lost time and place she encountered among her Portuguese American informants. Increasingly the graffiti nicknames of pubescent boys would appear among the murals, sometimes defacing these works. In time, names and murals commemorating the death of young men, often accomplished with the passionate artistic zest of the earliest murals, would be added to similar, unofficial outdoor museums springing up in Brooklyn and the Bronx, the walls and even the sidewalks becoming monuments to the dead.

But back in 1978, daily life had not yet revealed such a grim level. Bonnie, having bought the paints with Paco on Canal Street, began. She laid out a scene from *The Lily Pond* by Monet and perched on a stool to paint it above our Max-eaten door. Meanwhile, to the left, Emilio was busy with a scene depicting a sad-looking prisoner behind bars, "good for the kids around here as a warning." At some point, when Richie tried to squeeze past him into the office, he said, "This is you, Richie. Next year!" The rest of us were playing musical chairs on the bench and chairs outside the office, half dazed by graying skies and high humidity. Mothers passed in and out of the building, some sitting down to chat, reprimanding children. Meanwhile Paco, in occasional whispered consultation with Bonnie, was sketching out a magnificent scene that would apparently cover the entire right side of the storefront. It was a downtown scene of huge skyscrapers, and clinging triumphantly to the tallest of them was King Kong. As he painted, the children and teens stood in awe. Nobody asked what it meant. It was apparently obvious. The mothers gazed solemnly and nodded, before sitting down to chat.

Among the mothers on the bench was Marta Cestero, who with her partner Ramon Caballero kept a constant eagle eye on her precocious eleven-year-old, Evelyn, and Marta's heroin-addicted sister's four-year-old, Tito. Marta—waiting for a nod from Florisol, visibly at work in her beauty parlor across the street—was wondering out loud what kind of a haircut to get. As she waited, consulting with Nilsa about hair length, she turned and asked me if I could lend $2 to Ramon, her husband—he would return it in a few minutes. I didn't believe the "few minutes," or the "return" part either. Once a promising jazz musician, Ramon had also been a heroin addict, and now he sold his methadone (distributed free to former addicts to keep them "safely addicted") on the street. The money paid for subsistence, while Ramon drowned his hopes in cheap wine. I handed her the money, and instantly Ramon materialized from behind a car, the two bucks passing from my hand to Marta's and into Ramon's. As he cheerfully set off for the corner, Tito in tow, Marta added, "He doesn't like to ask himself."

After Marta left to get her hair cut, Millie parked herself on the bench. She had just returned from picking up Chulito from Head Start and said she was tired from having stayed home all day. She had spent a boring weekend as well with her in-laws in the Bronx. Ginny, her eleven-year-old, amplified. They had had a "cheap" time. The uncles had gone fishing from midnight until 4:30 the following afternoon, and they hadn't even caught any fish. "They got scared of too many sharks." So they just bought some fish for dinner.

Also occupying the bench was Holly Peterson, an African American mother of five, in her late twenties, who lived on the top floor of our tenement. Holly now cheerfully commented that she was tired from jogging, adding, "I am grateful to you people for starting me off on this." Her regimen was inspired by Bonnie at one of our frequent Friday picnic excursions with children and parents to East River Park. Holly had been raised in North Carolina, where her mother still lived and where she sent her children for extended vacations during the summer. She was one of the best organized mothers I met. Each child, from the eldest, twelve-year-old Chet, down to four-year-old Tillie, had assigned, age-appropriate tasks to perform for the household. Holly shopped wisely, traveling on foot to distant sales, and juggled her heavy cooking, cleaning, and child-care responsibilities to make time for typing lessons.

She managed all this in addition to the special care and constant clinic visits required for her six-year-old, Tessy, mentally retarded and partially deaf from lead poisoning. But her style with her children was "short" and rough. "Get out of my face!" was her classic phrase for ending even the most timid requests. Now, as her eleven-year-old Coreen dawdled, sulking, unwilling to fetch the laundry because she hadn't gotten a ride in our car with Paul, Holly said, "Coreen, would you like me to beat your ass in front of all your friends? You go right ahead and see what happens!"

As the first in her family to move to the North, Holly led an insecure life. She was a pretty woman with button-shaped eyes and cute freckles that she would have gladly given away. She had married young, and all of her children were born of this initial romantic love, but her husband could not keep a job, he drank, and he strayed—and mostly stayed away. According to Pam, Holly's younger Black friend in the building, each time he did turn up he left her with another baby. Most of her children had inherited her looks, especially Coreen, who carried her delicate frame like a princess. Only Tessy seemed to favor her father, and the children teased her about her wide nose, calling her *el Nariz* (the Nose) behind her back and outside of their mothers' earshot.

Holly had finally given up on her husband and was now living with Jack, a handsome young man a few years younger than she. But the relationship was also young and fragile. There were constant flare-ups, ostensibly caused by Holly's jealousy, but often related to the nitty-gritty of Jack's sporadic employment. He tried different things: unloading trucks at the Hunt's Point Market in the middle of the night; demolition works and sealing up vacant buildings (a task frequently available in a neighborhood with so much arson); and eventually, when federal funds trickled down into the area, construction jobs to rehabilitate the housing stock, which didn't pay well but were prized by the men for their steadiness (and constructiveness?). When he was earning, Jack was generous; he bought winter jackets for the children, helped with buying groceries, paid some of the bills. When he was unemployed, however, he used the money he hustled up through little deals and spent it on vodka and smokes. Their fights invariably erupted after they did some of this "partying," because Holly was not averse to vodka either. And then the pathetic aftermath would begin.

After a few day's absence, Holly would come down and announce that she had "kicked his ass out" of her apartment. On each occasion she detailed the things she had thrown after him into the corridor: his clothes, his records, his shoes, and even the presents he had given her—a raincoat, Noxzema cream, the precious presents that poor lovers can buy to show their love to women who are seldom treasured. But then, in a couple of days, the reconciliation would start. Holly would say, "Last night he brought his shoes back in, but if he thinks he can. . . " And so bit by bit, Jack would bring back his things and move "his ass" from the sofa, to the edge of the bed. And once again they'd be standing together downstairs, side by side, ready to take the kids out to McDonald's, Holly wearing her beautiful beige raincoat even though the sun was out.

Holly's problem, like Meri's, was that she didn't have a mother nearby. As a recent immigrant from the South she didn't have the networks of help that a second- and third-generation New Yorker could lean on. Her mother's help was enormous in taking a child or two for the summer, but when it came to big city, day-to-day living, Holly was on her own. By contrast, Pam, whose mother lived three blocks away in a public housing apartment she'd occupied for the past twenty-six years, was privileged. She saw her mother daily, and often her four-year-old son, Errol, stayed with his grandmother overnight while Pam and Harry, her partner, went out. In addition, Pam could always count on her when she and Harry fought. When I asked her during an interview "Who do you spend the most time with?" it was her mother that she named right after Errol and Harry.

I couldn't understand her attraction to Harry. He was much older and washed out from several years at Sing Sing. But Errol was dashing. He'd say to me, "Jagna, get your coat, I'm taking you out!" If he had only been forty years older! Now, nineteen-year-old Pam, a high school dropout at fifteen, was generously sharing her extensive practical knowledge of finances and economics with Holly, ten years her senior. Pam bought meat in large quantities; she also shopped for her mother, for whom the long trip across town and on foot to the meat markets was no longer easy. Her food expenses were low because she and Errol often ate at her mother's house and brought generous portions back home. Holly, an avid learner, also went on foot to buy enough meat for the month for the seven people in her family, carrying it all back. The seemingly large amounts of meat she purchased when divided by seven people and thirty days of the month belied their mostly starchy diet, supplemented by large quantities of onions—until summer, the most affordable vegetable in the neighborhood.

Several of our conversations on the bench revolved lyrically around onions, following fond memories of home gardens. Holly liked to talk about her family's garden back home—they grew a large part of the food they ate. But her skills in the garden did her little good in New York City. The women who grew up in Puerto Rico listened with interest, but they had their own urgent memories of food to reminisce about: picking up free mangoes "from the floor"; twisting off a bunch of *platanos* (plantains) from a tree; foods that now appeared mainly on "festive" occasions, like *pasteles*, made of grated plantains with meat wrapped in banana leaves for Christmas. They did not shop in bulk for meat, because only a little piece of it was needed to embellish the basic rice and beans or soup (unless you had to settle for rice with milk). They bought rice in bulk, and also dried beans, which were cheaper than canned, and tastier. And then, with a little sofrito . . .

These conversations usually began around four o'clock, when we all started getting a little hungry and the women were getting ready to go upstairs to cook. Though the beans had been started in the morning, preparing dinner usually required about two hours of work, because everything including the sofrito was made from scratch.

Holly had to spend even more of her time preparing food that spring. Her old stove dropped dead (before, only the oven had been broken), and Mr. Stern was taking his time, probably looking for a cheap, secondhand replacement. So Holly, with five little mouths a-chirping, crossed over the fire escape from her fifth-floor window to an empty apartment in Chino's building, where the stove was in place, and the gas, miraculously, still turned on (thanks, no doubt, to Chino's socialist principle of not distinguishing between the sources of the tenants' energy and his own). There she cooked her heart out. While she cooked, twelve-year-old Chet ironed all the children's school clothes for the next day, hopefully supplied with clothing fresh out of the Laundromat by his sister Coreen. After dinner, Holly supervised homework and then braided all the little children's hair, finishing off with little caps so that their hair would be neat in the morning. The little ones had to find their shoes, line them up, and put fresh socks, ready for wear the next day, inside them. Holly said she was not going to start her day looking for shoes under pillows, when the children had to be on their way to school by 7:30 to take advantage of the school breakfast program. Chet took Tillie to Head Start before going on to his own school while Holly waited with Tessy on the street for the school bus to take her to a school for handicapped children. Coreen took her younger brother, Andy, to a nearby elementary school they both attended. It was like organizing Napoleon's campaigns.

Holly loved early mornings, something she shared with the first generation Latina women. She got up at 6 A.M. and had a peaceful cup of coffee, planning her work, enjoying the freshness of the new day. She had always wanted to get a job helping the elderly and wished that welfare, in its periodic fits of trying to make her "productive," would train her as a nurse's aide. But in spite of her earnestly and politely repeated requests, she was invariably shunted into typing classes, work she was not good at and didn't like. So that's where she spent several afternoons a week, going through the same routine, never making any progress, one of the ciphers whose characters were so casually maligned in Ken Auletta's *The Underclass* (1982). From his observations of people enrolled in a federal training program, he constructed a portrait of hopeless malingers, even though he never ventured beyond the safety of the work-training site to observe the conditions and events that held them back or made them drop out of the program. Ignoring nine-tenths of people's lives is not just bad journalism, but caricature. Auletta's one-dimensional account was tailor-made for politicians eager to cut spending for the poor—the majority of whom were like Holly.

What Holly did not share with most of the Puerto Rican women was her willingness to make do. Eagerly, she became Bonnie's student in finding secondhand bargains. Bonnie, an old hand at recycling, took her to neighborhoods where nice furniture could be picked off the street before the sanitation trucks arrived; to Goodwill and Salvation Army stores, where clothing, curtains, blankets, and bedclothes cost a fraction of new items; and to hardware stores that remaindered paint—and together they refashioned Holly's apartment into a pleasant space. Tired of waiting for the Sterns to replaster a ruined wall (the roof was leaking, and guess whose little feet had helped to finish off the ancient tar?), Holly did it herself, and then repainted the whole apartment with the help of Jack and the older children. Now, with that inspiring task accomplished, she was working on herself, jogging with Bonnie and happy. Later, during the summer, when we hired Holly and three of the Puerto Rican mothers to help run the children's summer program (a brilliant idea proposed by Señora Medina, or Eti—by then we were all addressing each other by our first names—that we financed with creative shifting of categories in our grant), the differences between Holly's adaptive pragmatism and the señoras' *dignidad* came into sharper focus.

The latter lived with borrowed and inherited furniture, but saved for the day when they could have their own mahogany-style suites. They bought bargain clothes, often from questionable sources, but always new. They used cheap coverlets, inferior to secondhand blankets, that fell apart after a few compulsive washings, but they were *new*—and that mattered most. They were willing to put up with certain forms of humiliation but not others, and secondhand anything was one of those. The Latina women also tended to give in to their children's pleas for objects that were heavily advertised—Converse sneakers, the expensive toys touted by television—almost as if equating their children's seduction by commodities with the achievement of upward mobility. But even more subtly, telling the child, I can't afford to raise you in that pretty home you see on the program, but at least I can buy you the Incredible Hulk.

Holly would have none of it. She had long-range, North American Protestant aspirations. Eventually, when all the younger children were in school full-time, she went to work with Millie and Arturo Fuentes in the dry-cleaning store where he was the nominal manager. She was paid off the books, so the store owner didn't have to contribute to social security. But it was a job nonetheless. When this establishment burned down she looked for other dry-cleaning work, but by then most dry cleaners were run by familial Korean labor. When I met her by chance on a bus some years later she had already been living in a public housing apartment in Harlem for five years. Chet had finished high school and had enlisted in the army. Coreen was attending college. Only Holly, poor Holly, had descended to cleaning apartments for the wealthy of the Upper East Side. Like her mother in North Carolina. But she said she didn't mind. Her children were making it. *And* she and Jack had made another baby. He was named John Jr., and his arrival gave Holly an even half dozen.

On that sultry gray afternoon, as we sat and chatted on the bench with the rumble of a storm in the distance, Holly drew my attention to Paco's painting. "Look at that ape!" Paco kept silent, an artistic prima donna, given awed space by the generally pesky younger children as he completed his mural of Wall Street dominated by King Kong. Maribelle had recently told me of Paco's nightmares. She thought he was having visits from the restless soul of Juan. It was well known in the neighborhood that the spirits of those who had died prematurely or violently, the intranquil spirits, hovered close to the earth's surface and might attach themselves to people, especially children who had little protection. This was believed even by people opposed to spiritist practice on religious grounds, and even children who as a result of their acculturation might have been a step removed from it still imbibed it from their elders like a brooding presentiment. And Paco was a sensitive child, gentle, abstracted, unmacho, a kindred spirit to the murdered young man.

Now he was painting King Kong, a gentle but terrifying giant eventually slaughtered by the technological arsenal commanded by the state. Looking at it that day, I had only the vague feeling that this was something important, something that Paco was working through. It was not until several years later, when the accumulated blows broke down Paco's mind, that I reconsidered the symbolism of the struggle and trauma staring at me through the art of a twelve-year-old. Then, I only got up and added a few fabulous fishes to the tranquil blue bayou that the girls and Nilda were painting on the other side of our storefront.

This was the year of "Blue Bayou," a popular song played incessantly on the radio, which the girls had learned by heart, word for word, and sang plaintively and constantly. Every trip uptown, every overnight stay or excursion was incomplete without "Blue Bayou." Perhaps it grabbed them so because of the contrast it provided between their own dingy environment and the possibilities inherent in the memories of their mothers and fathers of "back home," recounted in stories. Impoverished countryside, whether in North Carolina or Puerto Rico, still held memories of beauty. The eye could rest on blue water, the ear be soothed by the lapping of waves. They sang in sweet girl-voice harmonies, Evelyn, the former jazz musician's true daughter, taking the lead, powerful and poignant.

> *I feel so bad, I've got a worried mind, I'm so lonesome all the time*
> *Since I left my baby behind, on blue bayou.*
> *Saving nickels, saving dimes, working 'til the sun don't shine*
> *Looking forward to happier times on blue bayou.*
> *I'm going back someday, come what may, to blue bayou*
> *Where the folks are fine and the world is mine, on blue bayou*

Where the fishing boats with their sails afloat divide the lonely sea
At familiar sunrise too sleepy to see how happy I'll be.
Going to see my baby again, going to be with some of my friends
Maybe I'll feel better again, on blue bayou.
Saving nickels, saving dimes, working 'til the sun don't shine
Looking forward to happier times, on blue bayou. . . .
Oh, that boy of mine, by my side, the silver moon in the evening time
Oh, some sweet day going to take away this hurting inside.
Where I'll never be blue, my dreams come true, on blue bayou.

The last big deal of the season, as the steamy spring gave way to a steaming summer, was graduation from the sixth grade at PS 63 on Fourth Street. Miguel, Corrine, Evelyn, José, and Maribelle started acquiring the liminal air of children about to be honored in this rite of passage. This important function overshadowed the discordant notes that had been brewing between the neighborhood and the school system. For one thing, the local schools had been abusing their right to suspend unruly children, and by mandating lengthy suspensions for minor infractions, they almost guaranteed that children would get into additional trouble. Because very little effort was made to ensure that parents were informed of the punishment, and because three-quarters of the families at any given time had no telephone, the suspended children would hang around the streets until caught by their mothers or older siblings. Most of the miscreants slunk about in the vicinity of their schools, pretending not to care, and joined the returning gaggles on the way home. At the invitation of the Reverend Garcia, a caring man who ministered to the community from the venerable St. Mark's Church that was once home to the Stuyvesant family, Nilda, Paul, and I attended several workshops on how to become advocates for the children.

The others who attended the workshops were African Americans, the Civil Rights struggle having empowered them, it seemed, to be more active in resisting unreasonable authority on behalf of their children. The Puerto Rican mothers appeared still overawed by the learned status of teachers and principals. In any dispute they showed "respect" to the school personnel, siding with them against their own children regardless of the situation—their children were always in the wrong, and probably lying. Indeed, they probably *were* lying—the authoritarian child-raising practices were a great incentive. Any punishment the children received in school was sure to be followed by a walloping at home.

I tried out my newly acquired skills by intervening on behalf of Eti's son, José. He had been suspended for a week from PS 63 for "pushing" a teacher. According to José, he had been shoved first by the very same teacher and had only resisted by pushing the man's hand back. Whatever the truth was, the principal was now threatening a lengthy suspension from the school, and no graduation.

Eti was all set to do battle. She felt she had cooperated with the school wholeheartedly, via her broom-wielding forays, and the school was imposing an overly harsh punishment on José. A one- or two-day suspension, okay, but a whole week? And maybe no graduation? She could just see José sliding into hoodlum land, *criminalidad*. With a contrite José in tow, we set off for an appointment to see Señora Biencriado, the modish principal of the school. But as soon as we walked into the silk-flower decorated office, Eti melted away. She was so sorry, she said, her son had caused trouble, she would watch him like a hawk so that he would never be trouble again, and so on. José played his part by modestly down-casting his daredevil eyes, while I wondered if I'd get to play mine. The principal was magnanimous and gracious. She said, "We are attempting to maintain the atmosphere of home in this school, we are one big family, isn't that so? And disruptive behavior disrupts this atmosphere," and she added a few phrases in Spanish to show just how down-home the atmosphere was. I had been subtly forewarned by Reverend Garcia that the atmosphere was more plantation than home, but this was no time to point it out. The important thing was that José would be allowed to return to school after three days, and to graduate. The principal curved her talonlike fingernails over José's shoulders and prodded us out of the office.

Something we could not fix, and therefore even more maddening, was that Evelyn would not be singing with the glee club at graduation. Because she had scored 69 percent on her reading test, and the price of admission to the glee club was 70 percent, she was disqualified from participating. What better way, I thought, to make her want to learn than to let her sing her heart out, to excel in some way? But this was not the way New York City schools operated. Dull obedience, regimentation, endless, joyless repetition were the lot of poor children. One didn't need extensive research to understand why children who were so promising and highly motivated when they left the rich, intellectual environment of Head Start became dullards by the time they finished sixth grade.

Miguel Valiente was our one shining exception. He had been named "The Most Improved Student," and he was practicing a speech he was going to give. The other children gave him wider berth so that he could prepare properly, and his mother, Meri, bought him a three-piece suit for $39.95 on Orchard Street. On the day of the graduation, however, I was shocked to hear that she would not attend the ceremonies. She said that it would hurt her too much to go because the last time she went was to attend Richie's graduation, and look what happened to him—eight was the last grade he'd attended. I tried to persuade her, telling her how important it was for Miguel to have her there, but she was adamant. Later it occurred to me that perhaps she had had no money left to buy herself a presentable dress, but the thought came too late. Her daughters Millie and Lucita stood in for her.

The ceremony was already in progress when I arrived. Held in a depressing basement auditorium, it seemed much less formal than the ceremonies I had attended for my children. Although there were plenty of seats left, parents were standing around the aisles, some snapping pictures, some just supporting the peeling walls. There was no lighting system for the stage, in fact no stage at all; just a small, low dais on which the performers were squeezed together. To the enthusiastic piano accompaniment of a young, pony-tailed teacher, various musical numbers were performed—the same schlocky chestnuts performed at all graduations, with everybody off-key. Music teachers in the city seemed to be required to teach popular music that was forty years out of date, and not even catchy in its own heyday. In between such gems as "Doe a Deer, a Female Deer" and "Dream the Impossible Dream" (which a cynic might see as a very appropriate song for the fate of these children), there were various congratulatory and self-congratulatory speeches by a mistress of ceremonies, the principal, a "local merchant," and several children. The merchant awarded a prize in his dead wife's name to the best student, a Chinese boy. Finally Miguel made the farewell speech for the sixth-grade class. He looked very cute in his suit, hands on hips (he said later he always stood like that when he was nervous), looking like a small politician. He delivered his speech very rapidly, without stumbling, and seemingly without understanding what the words meant. I knew that a teacher had helped to write the speech, in flowery language, romanticizing the wonderful experience of PS 63. I had explained to Miguel what some of the words meant the week before.

We returned to Fourth Street, and while Paul took pictures of the graduates, Meri pointed to Miguel's "The Most Improved Student" gold button and said to Richie, "See, some people are not so stupid." Then she told me she had only expected to pay about $19 for Miguel's suit, but she didn't mind the cost because he did so well in school. Richie was furious. If looks could kill, Miguel's new suit would have served him at his funeral. It was all very sad. Not only because Meri's child-raising techniques didn't allow her to express her sorrow to Richie, dictating instead invidious comparison as a way of challenging him, but also because it was probable that a good half of today's graduates would end like Richie. I didn't tell her that I had cried through most of the graduation.

But we acted as if that day were a day of great promise. We partied outside, playing musical chairs in front of our two new magnificent murals: King Kong on one side, Blue Bayou on the other.

Reflection 2:
Slipknots and Lariats

A pause in the continuity of the stories is needed again for reflection on the patterns of reciprocity in the neighborhood. Within the seeming chaos of giving, taking, loaning, and "holding" that went on between neighborhood people, there was an order that marked the connections between them. There were also real gender differences in the way women and men connected in order to construct "social security" support that was not provided by decent jobs or government programs. Bank loans, credit cards, savings, equity, and bail-outs are simply not available to low-income people. They have to rely on each other.

One afternoon, manna fell from heaven. Actually, new bathing suits were getting thrown air express from the third-floor window of our building. Sauntering down Fourth Street toward the office, I saw an excited knot of women and children catching bright packages sailing out from the hands of Clara and Maria Medina. Clara yelled to her younger brother Emilio to bring me closer and then sailed one down to me, calling out that it was mine "*si te sirve*" (if it suits you). They continued throwing more suits for Bonnie, Paul, Nilda (who wasn't there, but I caught it for her), and Holly. Then they threw down some sweaters for Holly's children. While other women were unfolding their bathing suits, Florisol came to see what the excitement was all about, and a swimsuit was promptly sailed down to her too, a female one. Everybody was laughing happily. No one inquired about the provenance of this largesse, but Nilsa later told me that Pablo had returned from his factory job with a huge box.

Another time, Nilsa went on an all-night crabbing excursion with the Medina family and friends to Coney Island. They packed six-packs of beer for the men, soda for the women and children, blankets, and large garbage bags (to keep out the chilly ocean breezes), as well as plastic buckets, raw chicken backs, and crab traps. With two shopping carts loaded they left for the subway: Emilio, Clara and her husband, Myrna and her husband, and about six children, not all their own.

Crabbing is an exciting activity in Puerto Rico, but it is usually done by boys during dead time when the sugar cane is cut, and the prey are land crabs (Mintz 1956:353). This expedition was after sea crabs. The traps were baited with the chicken backs, lowered with a string off the pier into the water, then pulled up with dozens of crabs clinging to the chicken backs. The crabs were then pried off the meat, and the traps were lowered again. The crabbers returned smiling and jubilant the next morning with roiling buckets of crabs. Only the children had slept some, protected by blankets and garbage bags.

For the rest of the day, Eti, Dolores, and a new tenant, Señora Madera, cleaned and boiled the crabs and sent kids with tinfoil packages of boiled and seasoned crabs up and down the staircase and across the fire escapes. Everyone in the building, including Holly, got some. Seafood was a rare treat in the neighborhood, so although the crabs didn't have much meat on them, the eating was festive. The crabbers had had a great time—the kids had snuck under the turnstiles on the subway, making the trip inexpensive, and the expedition had been healthful, everyone breathing that good sea air—so the excursion was repeated with varying permutations of children and adults. But Nilsa, alas, was not among them. Her husband "caught a fit," she said, that she had been out all night within reach of adolescent Emilio.

Our crocheting club for mothers and daughters provided the basis for much giving and sharing as well. Nilsa was an expert, and she soon recruited Millie, who was so good she could duplicate patterns from books. The rest of us—Marta and her daughter Evelyn, Marta's friend, Señora Moreno, Paco, Ginny, Maribelle, Holly, Coreen, and a few others—just plugged along, using a basic stitch, a slipknot, to produce scarves and lots of hats for all the little heads.

The beauty of crocheting is that it induces tranquillity. You can sit and crochet with others and have good conversations without even looking at them, without putting them on the spot. The conversation flows, and sometimes there doesn't need to be any—silence is also nice. People come and go, and you keep doing your work. Because your eyes are on your work you can say things to people you might not have said otherwise. Things that need saying. While Holly was producing winter hats for all of her kids, Marta was making scarves for her husband and her addicted sister's son. "Nothing for myself," she said wryly. Paco was also struggling with a scarf, seemingly comfortable among the women's low-voiced chatter. Tomas, Dolores's mild older son, occasionally joined us to continue working on a baby quilt he was making upstairs for his younger brother Rafael's forthcoming baby. Millie was already moving on to *tapetes*, the ornamental doilies and antimacassars that accomplished nineteenth-century housewives all over the world put over the arms and backs of their sofas and easy chairs and on top of side tables. She was making them for her mother-in-law.

Another beauty of crocheting is that the simplicity of the slipknot, easily mastered by beginners, is built upon with loose chains that connect to succeeding chains, adding width and length with simple primary connections. This simplicity is deceptive, however. Simple variations can end up in very complex patterns, and even with the simplest ongoing chain, you can add a variety of colors and textures by attaching new yarns to your ongoing connected chains. Finally—and this is perhaps the most appealing part of crocheting—the nature of the slipknotted chain is such that you can unravel any part that's not turning out well; you can even unravel the whole thing, start again, and see quick progress.

As a graduate student, I used to make fun of the concept of the "warp and woof of the social fabric" and other similar analogies popular with sociologists and anthropologists, dismissing them as *shmata* (rag) theories of culture. To a certain extent the criticism was apt when applied to ethnographies that wove an illusion of a perfect social fabric, leaving no space for buckling, discontinuity, contestation, resistance, and rift. So the analogy I use here is but a loose one, applying only to the internal relations between kin and neighbors, and certainly not to the relations with superordinate institutions and their agents. Because usually, when women attempted to slipknot, let's say, a welfare worker into their needs by recounting personal stories, expressing concern for the worker's difficult job, or offering a little present, they were rebuffed with instant hostility or suspicion.

The women connected to each other and to their mates and friends in a style that had much similarity to crocheting. There was an ongoing reciprocity, and a woman's connections were compounded in symbolic slipknots, constructing relations in easily increased stitches, adding variability, texture, and color to their lives. Of course, much more was at stake in their daily struggle to survive and keep their children than there is in making a scarf. Yet the mode of adding people to their lives, unraveling false starts and starting over if necessary, had much in common with this craft. Maybe that's why this activity was so pleasing. In a simple, symbolic way it crystallized a mode of being and acting as a woman, of producing and reproducing with swiftly visible, tangible results.

Thus, in real life, women took from and gave to their connected comadres food, money, and services. Grandmothers and sisters took over the care of a woman's children for days, months, or years. Poorer mothers without mates could count on food and emergency loans from their neighbors without any worry that they might have to repay immediately, or with interest. Seemingly unorganized reciprocity flowed in the neighborhood, cushioning the constant crises and threats of disaster endemic to a poor area. The sharing held the community together, in spite of the lack of equity and the overarching violence from above and the competition and violence within. Women turned friends into kin and family, through matches and babies, through the links of fictive kinship, through the social bonds of co-parenthood.

Men had their own buddy networks, but these were usually not as strong and lasting unless and until women were added to the circle as mates. Young male cliques awkwardly worked on reciprocity within their own groups, but because of their inexperience in relating and the constant macho competition required of them, their networks were much smaller and more easily severed. What the boys had to learn eventually was how to lasso and bind, how to take and become the top dog. Males in general were much less connected than women. Even among the Puerto Ricans, where a man at least always belongs to his natal family, there were loners. Such men would not ordinarily ask for loans or gifts without posting security. If a young man approached Paul for five dollars, he would first ask Paul to "hold" his watch until the next day. Or his bike, or a pair of shoes. Women never had to hock; they asked each other directly. And when it came to feeding another woman's children, they didn't even need to be asked.

In the beginning, when we were not yet part of their reciprocity networks, the requests from women or children to us would come indirectly, through a social "broker." Thus José came running in one evening from a raging snowball battle to ask if I could lend my gloves to Paco. Paco's hands were frozen, said José. I gladly obliged, only to regret it an hour later when my gloves came back like two dead fish with holes for thumbs—until I saw the funny gray snowman in front of the office. Marta might ask for a $2 loan for her husband. Or Ginny would ask on behalf of her mother for the money we owed for the Avon products we had ordered through Millie, who was thus helping her sister-in-law. Another time, when Emilio and Richie had been invited to visit us uptown and part of the plan was to go swimming at the Columbia University swimming pool, both boys came tumbling into the office that morning, slamming the door behind them and yelling that they were being pursued by robbers. I swiftly wormed out of them that the only person pursuing them might have been a bus driver. They had gone shopping for a bathing suit for Richie and didn't have enough money either for the suit or for bus fare back. So they had ridden the bumper of the Avenue B bus until the irate driver had stopped and given a brief chase. Cutting through my admonitions, Emilio asked what color would suit Richie better, blue or yellow? I said blue, of course falling for the diversionary maneuver.

"See! I told you!" says Emilio. Then he takes me aside and asks if I can lend Richie $5. He only has $10. You can't go swimming at Columbia without a new blue bathing suit. And I suppose, for that momentous an occasion, it wouldn't have been seemly to snatch one either.

Another time, Maribelle asked me to ask Paul on behalf of Evelyn if Evelyn could sit next to Paul on the drive home from uptown. Going on twelve, Evelyn had a stirring young body and a terminal crush on Paul. We had already noted her father's watchfulness—Ramon chasing a supposed suitor down the street with a baseball bat was one of the first amazing sights we had been greeted with when we started our fieldwork. So on these sentimental drives back, as we neared Fourth Street, and Evelyn's head was listing to the side, about to rest on Paul's shoulder, Nilda would be sure to say darkly from the back seat, "Evelyn, you'd better sit up straight before your father sees you and gives you a beating!"

Men were expected to take advantage of girls. It was up to the girls to be always vigilant, and if their hormones were leaning toward being taken advantage of, the parents or older siblings had to take over. There were frequent flurries of accusations from girls worried that they were about to be molested, telling on the supposed culprit just in case someone else noticed and told the parents about the girl's lack of vigilance. There was at least one occurrence of molesting. This came from Sean, a man in his mid-twenties who had no kin in the neighborhood but started frequenting our office. He was a very bright man who enjoyed beating me at Scrabble, but he also seemed to enjoy supposedly "tutoring" pubescent girls. Fairly early on I noticed that he tried to provoke physical tussles with them, hitting them on the arm, provoking counterpunches. It was inappropriate, and we usually kept an eye on him and tried to keep him occupied elsewhere. Eventually he started talking about his major means of support, appearing in police line-ups at $5 a shot, and dropping hints about this cop he knew and another. It eventually occurred to us that this man was most likely a police informer. This, coupled with his provoking behavior toward the girls, caused us to tell him not to visit the office anymore. He stayed away for a while, looking angry and petulant whenever I saw him skulking nearby.

But one day when I was crocheting and talking with Millie and Marta, both their daughters, Ginny and Evelyn, came shouting into the back office that Sean had "touched" Ginny's barely evident breasts. He had also punched Evelyn. The two women burst out of the office in a fury. Sean self-righteously defended himself, saying that Evelyn had started the fight and that he was only helping Ginny write on the blackboard, so he might have accidentally touched her. Millie threatened to tell her husband, and that did it—he slunk out of the office. We had to leave it at that, otherwise the girls too would have gotten a beating from their fathers for leaving themselves open. In dealing with males, we had to invoke the threat of male violent repercussions from time to time because that was what the males respected as the ultimate arbiter of relations. Men related to each other and toward women differently than women did. Sean's attempt to, as Millie put it, "take advantage" of the girls appeared to be a warped variant of machismo, of taking without asking, of imposing oneself by force, and on a child, to boot.

Count Augusto's behavior, in contrast, was an example of a much more culturally appropriate, even if extreme, macho behavior. He related to people through symbolic lariats. Outwardly he had refined manners; he was helpful and generous, and on many occasions he donated "salvaged" spare parts to repair our forever broken toilet and faucets. He also cooked lovely Spanish meals, which he brought for potluck dinners or as a feast for the staff. Yet there was a subtle and profound difference between the way he made connections with us and others and the way the women did. His "gifts" to us, whether of services or food, seemed always to carry a heavy obligation, of becoming bound, of incurring debt. He also managed to insinuate an element of potential danger into whatever deal or transaction he tried to involve us, especially Nilda and me. I wondered whether this was a result of his long experience behind bars—an adaptive behavior acquired by prisoners—or if it was idiosyncratic, just essence of Gusto. His tossed his lariats at connections to rope them in and bind them. In one day of field notes I recorded the following examples:

Nothing much was happening in the office except for the renewed pleasure of Gusto's company. He tells it far and wide that he is "seeing" a psychiatrist (a woman) in order to quit drinking. This indulgent lady, whom he is supposedly free to call at all hours, day and night, has prescribed all sorts of "medication" for him, which in a fit of righteous anger last week he threw away in the garbage. The dosage was "too heavy," quoth Gusto. He only kept one medication of the batch: a bottle of Maalox. On the walk to the picnic on Sunday he was acting as if the Maalox were his family jewels (or a stash of heroin). He was trying to get first Nilda, then Bonnie, to "hold it" for him and finally got sucker me to put it in my bag, thereafter inquiring anxiously for the next three hours whether his "medication" was still there. I tried to figure out what it is about him that infuriates me so. I think it's his subtle way of exercising machismo, of getting women roped into some insignificant activity with him, which then grows out of proportion.

Like yesterday. Gusto had brought a birthday cake and the celebrant, a gruff guy named Cojo, to the office. They were sitting there when we came in. Gusto gets up, tells Nilda to sit in his seat, and she sits; at the same time he pats another chair, telling me, "Sit down, darlin'," and I lower my butt automatically, while Gusto suaves his way next door, returns with a chair for Bonnie, and tells her to sit down too. She sits. He has this way of ordering women around that is extremely annoying but difficult to catch in time or object to without seeming impolite. At one point I was objecting to the fact that he laid a large piece of cake on a small plastic coffee cover on the rug for Max. Gusto acted as if he didn't understand English, but after Nilda repeated my objection in Spanish, he replied that he didn't understand why I objected to his kindness to the dog [what I didn't realize then was that I was actually objecting to his taking over our office]. Then he picked up the dog-licked top and passed it to me, saying, "Here, darlin'," and I took it like a robot, and suddenly realized that there was no garbage can near me. I saw myself holding it, and said, "Here, what are you giving it to me for?" just as Bonnie cried out, "She doesn't want it!" I passed it back to Gusto: "You throw it out!" But this interaction was only a foretaste.

Soon Gusto stood up and in a formal, funereal voice intoned that we were gathered here together to celebrate Cojo's birthday, the observation of which, alas, was one day delayed. Since we didn't know Cojo from Adam—and in fact we had had no previous notice that we would be celebrating his birthday—Gusto now went on a discourse of Cojo's attributes. This man, his good buddy, was very involved in "community affairs" and contributing to the reconstruction of the neighborhood. Unfortunately, he had had too much to attend to on the previous evening, and it was thus that the birthday cake had had to spend a lonely night in Gusto's refrigerator. "Now we are gathered here to share in the celebration of Cojo's fortieth birthday." Gusto paused so we could clap, me with less enthusiasm than I might have otherwise displayed, because Nilda had filled me in on some details of Cojo's activities the night before. So while Gusto cut the cake and had Nilda distribute it and the coffee that he had also brought in individual plastic cups (all of which she did automatically, and with grace), I seethed. He was weaving a tale for Bonnie and me, the *gringas*.

According to Nilda, Cojo had a long history of using and dealing cocaine and had been imprisoned for it, and the reason he could not consume his cake the previous night was that while he had been at work, enforcers for a loan-sharking ring had paid a visit to his apartment and wrecked it, including a new loft bed that he had been building with Gusto's help—with money that he had borrowed and not paid back. He couldn't return home at all, in fact, because the enforcers had left a message that

there was now a contract out on him. So, Gusto had told Nilda yesterday, he had gone
to his own loan shark, borrowed the $600 that Cojo owed to *his* shark, with huge in-
terest accruing even as we spoke, and repaid his buddy's debt. So Cojo wasn't going to
get shot after all. Yet. Anyway, much of this may have been just Gusto's grandstand-
ing. Because, therapist notwithstanding, he smelled heavily of alcohol yesterday. He
may be hoping to rope Nilda in with promises of more fascinating information.

And he did try to rope her in. He knew how to arouse our interest in the esoter-
ica of "underground" information, but he was also very lonely and wanted Nilda
to become "his woman." It was hard to tell who was leading whom on more, but
whenever Nilda's interest flagged, he would drop dark hints about having been
connected to the Mafia. Nilda danced a pretty thin line keeping their connection
on just a friendly level. She liked Gusto; he was extremely handsome, but, she
sighed, if he were only less insane. . . .

She didn't mean it literally. Gusto's experience as the less-favored child in a
struggling, upwardly mobile family that had pinned its hope on his twin sister
may have contributed to his subsequent career as a drug addict and, later, alcoholic. But his behavior was idiosyncratic only up to a point; it was at the extreme
end of a normal range of machismo. For men who are constrained by their social
and economic position, machismo is dysfunctional in their relations with superordinate authorities such as the police. But their lack of social status also leaves
them less secure, positionless, vis-à-vis female mates. Perhaps to compensate,
men take stances that are extreme, fueled underneath by a kind of desperation,
talking up and occasionally demonstrating lurking violence as the main mode of
gaining and preserving self-worth. Although this attitude when aimed at agents of
the state or "enemy" males may give them temporary status, it almost always
eventually results in getting them either hauled off to prison, maimed, or killed.
And too, instrumental giving, engaged in only to secure relations with women,
and taking by force are not necessarily the surest ways to a woman's heart for the
long haul. Macho men are admired, and women fall in love with them, because of
the daring, protection, and resistance they offer against outside predators and the
authorities. But they cannot provide long-range economic stability unless they
are among the few who succeed in illicit occupations. The verdict is usually in
within a couple of years. Yet this way of life is functional for men, because there
are so few alternatives.

Contrary to beliefs expressed by conservatives, male children, even poor ones,
do not grow on trees. Like children of both sexes all over the world, they are raised
by women. When boys reach puberty, men become more active in their education
for manhood; but all throughout childhood, even in poor neighborhoods, fathers, stepfathers, older brothers, uncles, and grandfathers are in the background
and foreground, exhibiting through their behavior how a man should act.
Therefore, it cannot be said that the lack of male "models" turns the boys either
into "criminals" or, at the other extreme, "sissies." They grow up to fit precisely

into the niches of adult life that society makes available, through channels of class and race; through education, training, and opportunities the society provides. Unfortunately, the niches provided by this society were almost exclusively in illegal occupations, which so often meant a prison berth, at best, or worse, a cemetery plot.

But, of course, many boys got off the hook of having to fill prisons or suburban cemeteries. Perhaps a quarter were raised prepared to fill conventional, working-class jobs; another quarter were wasted through addiction to alcohol and drugs; and smaller groups survived variously through either assuming gay lifestyles (sort of "hypergamy" for men?), joining the armed forces and thus qualifying for higher education subsidies, or achieving some upward mobility through pure luck in either the illegal or legal sectors of the economy. A propensity to violence was not the only attribute that was developed if boys showed capacity in other directions. Nevertheless, the major mode of relating for growing boys, even when coupled with intelligence or guile, was learning to get, by hook or crook. Florisol and her missing poodle were a case in point.

For adults in the neighborhood, there were a few, more formal ways of obtaining lump sums of money for emergencies and needed items. One was a floating mother's club to which six to ten participants linked by kinship or fictive ties contributed $10 a week, to draw in turn larger sums at the end of each month. A more ambitious undertaking by the local level "elite," a credit union, was started after the Hanover Bank on Third Street closed down its last, still very bustling branch in the eastern section of the neighborhood. The credit union limped along for a couple of years, handicapped by undercapitalization, lack of experience, and consequently, complaints of irregularity. Eventually that folded too. Bolita, the numbers game in the neighborhood in which almost everyone invested according to their means, was another way of obtaining lump sums of cash that could be invested socially (treating buddies to drinks and other less legal substances by the men, and investing in durable goods or kinship ties by the women). Significantly, because of their frequency, funerals provided an occasion for including even distant neighbors and patrons in more diffuse, neighborhood-wide collectives. Even our landlord, Mr. Stern, was thought to be close enough to understand, be moved by, and therefore obliged to contribute to funeral expenses.

In a wider sense, one might want to ask if the social supports collected through government taxation and distributed by it as welfare, food stamps, Medicaid, housing, and aid to the disabled should also be seen as collective succor by the fortunate for the less fortunate. Were these policies generous in the sense of embracing the poor in the commonweal? The answer is, yes and no. On the one hand, social supports did make a difference in supplying a baseline onto which people could add through hard work and ingenuity. Without them, the Lower East Side would have been a Dickensian déjà vu. On the other hand, the qualifications and restrictions that turned these entitlements into a miserly dole tended to change the case workers into pressured and guilty satraps who, in turn, made the recipients feel both ashamed and angry. In addition, looking at the source and the eventual destination of the support money, it was obvious that the poor recipients were essentially conduits for transferring tax money from the middle class to the affluent class. Rent money went directly to landlords, often through two-party checks, for barely habitable, poorly maintained dwellings (when it didn't turn hotel owners who rented to the homeless into overnight millionaires). Food money provided some food for the poor, but also profits for agribusiness and supermarkets. Like the drug business, local off-the-books jobs provided uncertain, meager wages in the neighborhood while helping to enrich distant corporations. Both types of jobs guaranteed that the nation would not be liable for social security payments or unemployment compensation. Self-made rip-off artists from the outside, such as "talent scouts" and representatives from "career training" and "modeling" agencies, continually tempted the residents to invest money in their children's future and fame. Even as astute a mother as Holly paid a talent scout who promised to turn gorgeous Chet into a TV star. She never saw him again, or the photograph portfolio he promised.

Even the pattern of circulation of stolen goods among the neighborhood's residents, for much cheaper prices than they could have afforded to pay for new articles, was co-opted and used as a conduit for higher profits for the affluent class. A warehouse in the Bronx that bought from the poor and sold to the middle class stolen articles ranging from typewriters and computers to stereos and musical instruments was reputedly controlled and patronized by the cops. It offered in-house repairs for broken appliances and other durable products that could not have been fixed by reputable dealers and manufacturers, for lack of warranties. I never saw it, but one member of our team did. Thus when the boys stole something of value, they might make a few dollars by selling it to a connected middle-range fence, who in turn would sell it for a higher profit, but not close to the value it fetched at the "warehouse." Broken-down and antennaless TVs and cheap clothing and gadgets remained in the neighborhood, given as gifts to mothers, who used the items as circulating tokens for social connectedness.

In sum, reciprocity patterns in the neighborhood connected families to kin, to fictive kin, to neighbors, and to friendly co-residents in widening circles of slipknots produced by women. Items and services of high value were exchanged by closely related people, and easily or fortuitously acquired items and services connected wider groups. Abundant and frivolous items, such as discarded bathing suits and crabs, belonged to that wider category of generosity. Collections for funeral expenses included an even wider range of people. Male reciprocity, in contrast, was more restrictive and instrumental, although it overlapped with female patterns. But all of this reciprocal activity must be seen in the context of the business activity of the overarching society in which it occurred: to the larger society the people of the neighborhood served as conduits for the transfer of money from the middle to the more affluent class (Hamilton 1976), and as low-wage service workers or "clients" in both the licit and illicit sectors of the economy.

Truly cooperative activity in the neighborhood, what middle-class observers would call "civic" engagement, did occur, but, significantly, at a social level once removed from dire poverty. Men and women who had weathered the social upheavals of the 1960s and who once or still held community-organizing jobs, connected to each other and to "small is beautiful" ideas. One group was active in Adopt-a-Building and had installed a windmill and solar panels for self-sufficient energy in their cooperatively owned tenement in the neighborhood. Another group, El Teatro Ambulante, produced and promoted Spanish plays, music, and films in the neighborhood. All-Crafts, led by its dynamic woman leader, Lady Carpenter, extended its governing board and training to women of all races and ethnicities, producing hundreds of female carpenters, plumbers, cabinetmakers, and electricians, many of whom went on to get well-paying union jobs or to create cooperatives of their own. Finally, Miguel Algarin, the owner and patron of the Nuyorican Cafe, provided the venue where cultural expression and poetry of resistance could flow in English, Spanish, and Spanglish, creating ethnic self-consciousness and pride.

There were other community activities that to some extent might engage the poorer population as did the programs above. But it is my impression that being involved in those mainly raised the status and options of people who did not have to worry every minute about how they would feed and guard their children. As federal funds for some of these projects dried up, as competition for remaining sources of funds increased, even some of their most idealistic members either left or gave up, a few descending into dealing drugs and becoming addicted. By the mid-1980s the forces of military intervention in the neighborhood, combined with the scourges of a massive influx of crack cocaine and the AIDS epidemic, made it a very depressing place for any kind of civil undertaking.

It was at this point that Lady Carpenter stopped training journeywomen and turned her massive building on St. Marks Place into a round-the-clock Alcoholics and Narcotics Anonymous meeting space. She would also make room for sheltering about a hundred teenagers, now orphaned by AIDS.

But that was later. For the moment the Nuyorican Cafe was filled with cultural vigor, including Count Augusto's, that master of lariats. He often went there, after his stint of work at Adopt-a-Building, and occasionally performed. One of his poems published in an anthology (Algarin and Pinero 1975) reads in part,

> *Fierce curiosity, distorted mind*
> *But gratified at spectacle*
> *Sitting, drawing, fitting sections*
> *Used and new . . .*

8

A Dream-Come-True Apartment with a 1949 Stove

Meri had covered a lot of territory since she had first submitted her application for public housing in 1968. Among the agencies she asked for help (in addition to informal local advocates) were the Mobilization for Youth, the Commonwealth of Puerto Rico, Councilwoman Miriam Friedlander, and Adopt-a-Building, a local organization that took over dilapidated city-owned buildings and rehabilitated them using local human power. In order to have impeccable credentials, she had paid exorbitant Con Ed bills, even though I had presented her case to the Public Service Commission for investigation because it looked as if her landlord was hooked into her meter. Although the investigation would take a long time, she had to have a perfect record of paying in the meanwhile. She also kept all the receipts for her timely payments of rent, and she had obtained letters from her past landlords, testifying to her diligence. In addition she had obtained a letter from Bellevue Hospital attesting to her oldest son Julio's and her own severe asthmatic condition. But nothing seemed to work.

She had had her first interview at the Housing Authority office in 1972, four years after applying, and was told she would hear from them in a couple of months; she never heard from them again, in spite of repeated inquiries. She finally asked me to call a sympathetic señora at the Housing Authority with whom she had talked before. As a result, Meri landed a second interview in July 1978. But except for an unsigned form letter she once received, she never heard from them again. Meri lived on the second floor of a building on Fifth Street surrounded by the ruins of burned buildings on three sides. Rats and addicts also found shelter in the basement and lobby of this place. Meri shared her three-room apartment with her children, her father (when he wasn't with one of her other two sisters), a pregnant chihuahua, a mutt named Sweetie, and her now frequently absent common-law husband, Sito.

The latter, together with Count Augusto and several others, had at last obtained a job with Adopt-a-Building. Even though they had worked for the organization in the past, their jobs, entitled "construction" work, had been primarily short-term jobs of destruction, demolishing burned-out buildings, and occasionally sealing up structurally sound buildings to prevent the stripping and selling of pipes by addicts. Now they had been hired for actual construction work—insulation, carpentry, drywalling, installing electric lines, plumbing, the works. The pay was a little above minimum wage, but it promised to be steady and long-term. They could all look forward to paychecks, respect in the neighborhood and, what came with it, serious attention from women. Unfortunately for Meri, Sito saw this as an opportunity to break his dependence on her and her problematic family and to begin to move toward establishing a family with a woman who could have his children.

According to Meri, Sito had changed since he started working for Adopt-a-Building. He had stopped coming home to sleep, spent all his money on drinks (and possibly grass) with the crew, and either spent the night at his father's or at the "gay's" on Avenue B. When she confronted him about staying away, the main reason he gave was that he hated her brothers and father. "If he hates my brother then he doesn't love me. Right?" She was crying as she told me. "I have been good to him and now he turns his back on me."

But she was getting sick of her family too. Meri's demented brother, Pedro, lived on the first floor of her building, and she kept a constant eye on his whereabouts. Her other brother, Rogerio, had been a heroin addict and was now a raging alcoholic who picked bloody fights on the street. I had seen him in action outside our office as he drew a knife on a Gatos gang member and was fortunately distracted by Meri's shrieks, which sort of diffused the situation. I hadn't realized then that he was her sibling, the man who turned up at our office door with various Dobermans.

One weekend she bought a bottle of Bacardi, got very drunk, something she had never done before, and asked Sito please not to leave her in that condition. Very coldly he told her she'd be all right, and left. She ran out on the street and barely missed getting hit by a passing truck.

"I think I was trying to kill myself. Do you think so?" She looked at me, as we sat in the back room of the office, mulling over her love and housing problems. "I got to get out of Fifth Street."

Julio was another reason she had to leave. In fact, she said, would it be possible for me to give him a letter attesting to the fact that he had worked for us this summer? Julio had in fact worked for us, but only for several weeks, on the census. He hadn't done a bad job, so theoretically I could write a letter on his behalf. Meri informed me that he needed it for a court appearance because he had skipped seeing his parole officer all summer. And the reason for having to see a parole officer, she told me, was that during the big blackout the previous year, Julio had been wrongly accused of taking a pair of sneakers from a looted store. Apparently the whole family had jumped to the rescue, Meri claiming that she had bought the sneakers on the street, and Sito claiming that no, he had found them, confounding the record enough for Julio to get a suspended sentence.

But I knew from Paul that Julio's problems were even graver. He and two older guys had accosted a Chinese landlord with a knife just as he was emerging from a building holding a paper bag full of rent money. Ah, those paper bags! Julio, being the youngest and having no previous record, had the loot thrust upon him, and in the ensuing chase joined by cops, only Julio was caught. Meri either didn't know or didn't want me to know. But I had other fish to fry with Julio. The week before, I was pretty sure he had lifted $20 from my wallet. It would have been distracting to go into all of this now with Meri, so I just nodded and brought us back to the subject of housing.

The week before she had gone straight to City Hall, pitched her case, and been taken by the hand by a Spanish-speaking woman to Friedlander's office, where an assistant named Tomi, she said, wrote a letter to the Housing Authority, asking, in short, why the hell they had been stalling for ten years. A few days later, Meri got a letter stating that her application could not be located. Had she filed under her maiden name? Could she provide the name of her husband? Meri returned once again to the Housing Authority office, where one of the "civil" servants had yelled at her in front of the assembled crowds for having tried to cut the red tape via the councilwoman. She screamed that she didn't want to see any more such letters, and not to bother coming back. A woman friend who had gone with Meri for support was apparently also too stunned and embarrassed to be any help at all. She just stood there while Meri cried.

Meri's story had the intended effect of spurring me to help, and she and I set off in quest of justice. The first step was to find Friedlander's aide. But because I didn't want to patronize Meri with my geographic know-how, I followed her lead. This meant, unfortunately, that we had to repeat her previous itinerary step by step, starting literally at City Hall. Our quest was further prolonged by Meri's insistence that we were looking for a "Mr. Christian," the chairman of the Housing Authority, whose name was photocopied onto the bottom of her response letter. At City Hall they gave us the councilwoman's address, but Meri decided to follow the path she had taken with her advocate friend. She took me around to Chambers Street and started asking some loungers where "Mr. Christian from the Housing" could be found. One guy pointed over to Broadway, and Meri said no, it had to be here. Several people had by then collected around us and told her in Spanish to try next door. "This is only for rape," they advised. Reluctantly, we went next door, which advertised itself as being the "Mayor's Task Force Office." A thick young man invited us (actually only me) to sit down and attempted to ask Meri through me about her problem. Each time she told him something, he tried to engage me. Finally he gave up and told us we were in the wrong office. We should go to 250 Broadway. As a parting shot he asked Meri why she wasn't looking for apartments in Brooklyn or the Bronx.

Next we went to 250 Broadway, but as soon as we got close, Meri remembered it as the site of her humiliation, and we went back to Chambers Street, where in fact, Friedlander's office was located right next door to the "Task Force" on the other side of the "rape" office. I realized that Meri relied on visual memory, but also that visiting this "foreign land" of officialdom was a traumatic experience. So finally, after two hours, we were where we should have been in the first place.

Tommy L., the councilwoman's assistant, was very helpful. Speaking directly to Meri, he asked her about her husband's name because the application might have been misfiled, and also noted there should be six digits, not five, in her application number. He asked her to bring him the originals. He also advised her, with Miriam Friedlander looking on sympathetically, to always get the names of abusive public officials. We promised ourselves to make that the number-one item on the agenda for the next day.

The next morning Meri got copies of her applications from Mobilization for Youth, which had originally helped her file and had copies of documents that she had since lost. To ensure proof of her existence to officials, she also brought along her Medicaid card, her welfare card, her birth certificate from Puerto Rico, her children's birth certificates, and her father's social security card, all now reposing in a worn little paper bag. On several occasions her shoulder bags had been ripped off, and she wouldn't risk losing this documentation of her existence. Nobody would take a worn paper bag, she informed me. (I resisted pointing out that even her son considered them worthy of attention.) As we waited for the Avenue B bus, her brother Pedro scuttled over and she gave him a dollar, speaking low, whereupon he shuffled off to the liquor store, already open for business. I was a little surprised, but then I saw he was bringing back change, no bottle. She told me she needed it for our fare. I was touched by this gesture.

First we went to Friedlander's office and left the applications with Tommy. He seemed very confident that he could get the official wheels rolling, and he suggested Meri look over a new subsidized housing complex being completed on Clinton Street. Next we went to the Housing Authority, where a fairly pleasant woman promised to look for the lost application. We also asked her for the name of the uncivil servant we'd dealt with earlier and brought the name back to Tommy. Then we went to Blimpie's for a sandwich.

Meri had told me that when Julio had been hit by a speeding car two years earlier, they had come to the area to consult a lawyer. The lawyer had handled the suit successfully and only took $2,000 of the $4,000 settlement. The rest of the accident money was put in a trust account until Julio turned eighteen, because of the law prohibiting savings accounts for welfare recipients. On that occasion, Julio had invited her to lunch at Blimpie's. "He loves that food," she told me, indicating that she liked it too. She protested when I paid for both of our sandwiches, and she ate only half of hers, wrapping the other half in napkins and a paper bag "for Julio."

Unfortunately, the Blimpie bag turned out to be one too many. When we got off on Delancey, it got off with us while the little document bag rode on.

I called our office and asked Nilsa to intercept the bus on Fourth Street. She didn't understand the urgency and instead dispatched Lefty. On the next call, I asked her, bitterly, whether anyone in his right mind would give even a paper baggie to Lefty. It was not for nothing that he carried that nickname. Watching Meri's distressed face, I asked Nilsa to drive at top speed to Fourteenth Street and Union Square, the last stop of the B bus. Then, at Meri's suggestion, we rushed over to Allen Street, the return route for the bus. While we waited, she pointed to the furniture store on the corner and told me she had acquired over $1,000 worth of credit there, with $5 deposits over the past twenty years. She had also saved up another $1,000 at a furniture store in Brooklyn, but alas, the store had moved to somewhere in Long Island without advising its thrifty depositors. Could I find it? It was called either "Woubt" or "Wourld" Furniture. She had no receipts. "But the man knows me. He was always behind me, asking would I like this, would I like that." As Meri spoke, I wished I could introduce her to conservatives who relish pointing out how poor people have no "future orientation." Maybe they'd get motivated to take a look at some of the institutions to which poor people entrust their meager savings.

We held up three buses before the bus we had taken finally arrived. The driver said he didn't recognize us, but he did let us search, which we did to no avail. Nilsa had also missed the bus at Union Square. No bag. Over the next few days Meri went to her class in a depressed mood. But she did ask Paul to take her to the subsidized houses on Clinton. According to him, she did not have high hopes for getting in—the houses looked too elegant. (She was right. We found out later the policy was that only the elite poor need apply.) Afraid of heights, she was also worried she might be forced to live on a high floor. But most probably the basis of her excuses and ambivalence was her fear of separation from Sito.

That Friday she came into the office, holding a manila envelope and trying not to smile. Someone had mailed her back her little bag of documents, minus her food stamps, *and* she had been notified that there was an apartment available immediately in Smith Houses, by Chinatown. We all jumped around, kissing and yelling. That night she came after class to join what was supposed to have been a block party planning session but turned out to be the usual crowd: children, Millie, Holly and her man Jack, the more than ever obnoxious Count Augusto, who had resumed full-time drinking following a few weeks of restraint after obtaining the new job, and Gusto's construction crew, which included Sito, an African American named Lee, the foreman, and several others.

All evening, when not dancing or handing out quarters to the kids, Sito and Lee were on Gusto's back for getting drunk on the job and "spoiling things for everybody." Apparently he had downed a pint of Bacardi after cashing his check at noon and had come back just in time for a visit from the supervisor. He had called the supervisor "bourgeois" while throwing his helmet and assorted planks in the supervisor's general direction. From now on they would all be closely watched and wouldn't even be able to drink beer on the job. Even the two women construction workers who only drank coffee would be watched. From what Paul had observed I knew there were even more things they would not be able to do on the job: smoke marijuana and sell extra supplies for profit, for instance. The repetitious argument went on and on, Gusto holding forth on "worker's rights," "bourgeois bosses," and "low-wage exploitation," and Sito and Lee amplifying their accusations in an equally tedious vein: "This isn't you talking, Gusto man, this is Bacardi. Your *name* is Bacardi. Tomorrow you're gonna say you're sorry, but it isn't enough. . . . " I'd had enough and was glad when Meri arrived from her class and motioned me into the back office, where she asked me to ask Sito how he felt about her now that she was getting her new apartment.

I invited him out front and asked him. He told me he was very happy for her but that it wouldn't change anything. She had moved several times before and it hadn't stopped her brothers from following her. He was tired of Rogerio's psycho attacks on people, tired of feeling obliged to step in between. He was embellishing how much he hated Rogerio when Meri approached and heard him. She said nothing, and for the rest of the evening sat at the table as the other adults talked, quiet and subdued. Holly must have sensed that Meri was very sad, because she talked about how she often ended up crying after dealing with city officials. This led her man, Jack, to comment he wished she could deal with welfare people the way she dealt with him. After an hour or so of ignoring his pleas, that it was time to go upstairs, she finally left with him while Meri went home with her girls.

On Monday, Meri's big day for getting her new apartment, I came to the office bright and early, but she was still not there by ten o'clock, the time we should have arrived at Smith Houses. A few minutes later Miguel came in, puffy eyed, saying his mother would be right down. I asked him why he wasn't in school (my constant refrain), and he told me they had all slept too late. He wasn't going until the afternoon, he said. There was no point in going now because after nine o'clock they locked the school door and didn't let any children in. He would be allowed in after lunch. I made a note to check out this wonderful school policy later and found out he was right.

Meri showed up soon after, saying something was wrong with their alarm clock and she had had to write excuse notes for all the kids before leaving. She hadn't slept, she said, because Julio hadn't come home last night. She was unusually cross, and when a bummed-out young man who obviously knew her approached her for money, she ignored him. As we waited for the Avenue B bus, the man kept pleading, "Meri, don't be so hard!" Finally she relented and gave him a quarter.

Many people in the area had a kind, warm attitude toward derelicts, but Meri especially. The bums felt free to come close to her and speak with her even though they looked filthy and smelled bad. There was no recoil or revulsion in her nonverbal interaction with them. On the bus she told me she felt sorry for the young man because he was a "faggot" and an alcoholic. This led her to the topic of how Sito must be starting to use drugs—he was so skinny and had circles under his eyes. He had come over the night before and stayed for a while, saying he'd be back by eleven, but he hadn't returned. "I didn't even wait up for him." He needed to get up early for work, and she used to get him up; now she figured he was sleeping late, wherever it was that he slept. "I hope that he will lose his job," she said with uncharacteristic malice. "Then he will find out that he has no friends and no father. Before I didn't invite his father because I was ashamed of where we lived, and Sito told me not to be ashamed. Now that I'm getting my new apartment I told Sito his father would be able to visit, and he said, 'My father will never visit you.' He was cold, Jagna." And so on. She was dragging her feet to this final "dream-come-true" apartment, anticipating separations.

The dream turned out to be one cut above a federal slum. We were ushered into the inner sanctum of the Smith Houses rental office by a deceptively pleasant man of very short stature. He filled out Meri's application, got on his tiptoes to get the keys from a filing cabinet, and trotted beside us through the plaza, extolling the complex's high points. "There is an elementary school right behind your building," he said, pointing, "an afternoon center for the kids, Key Food, Laundromat, Shopwell," all, alas, which we were leaving behind on our way toward the East River. We turned the corner on South Street, in a desolate-looking pier area, and stumbling over ripped-up pavement, entered a grim, twenty-story building. Four of the lobby's six windows were broken, and the corridors smelled of urine, and worse. However, the elevator seemed to be working all right. As our guide stretched to reach the button for the sixteenth floor, I didn't dare make eye contact with Meri. A glimpse told me she was dying. The elevator door opened on a magnificent mural of a naked woman done up in scarlets and siennas covering the gray concrete wall. As I commented on its artistic merits, our guide eyed me severely and said, "This is one of the reasons we kicked out the family from the apartment you're getting." Why me? I wondered, but not for long, realizing that here was another civil servant loath to communicate with people he was supposed to serve.

We turned the corner of the dirty hallway and entered the prize of ten years' waiting. It was OK. The rooms were large and newly painted, there was light and a view of Chinatown, but the total effect was rather depressing: The glossy peach paint had been slopped on any old way, including all over the windows. The layout was updated railroad flat. Worst of all were the floors—grimy, gluey, dark brown tile that sucked up to our soles. Meri looked around politely, but I could see her heart was not in it. She looked at the doorless closets, simple nooks in the walls with wooden poles; and to the stove and the sink, circa 1949, which our guide explained was the date the housing was built. He kept asking me, and since I deferred to her, Meri, how she liked it. Finally she delicately mentioned the kitchen equipment and the floors. He said, "What did you expect?" implying "Don't look a gift horse in the mouth," but seeing my face, toned it down. He explained that all the state-funded housing was being taken over by the federal government, and sooner or later (leaning toward the later) all the projects would be renovated. Meri didn't seem to want to linger further in her prospective new abode, so we left. Going back, I made small talk with him to make up for Meri's silence. As we neared his office I asked him if it was OK with him if we came back in a little while. We needed time to think.

Once we were alone, I asked Meri what she wanted to do. She said she didn't know. She had seen much nicer public housing a few blocks away from her pres-

ent apartment, and she knew Julio wouldn't like this. She seemed very discouraged; she knew from other people's stories that if you didn't accept what was offered, your application got thrown in the dead-end file. I called Nilsa because she
knew about public housing, and she advised Meri to take the apartment. She confirmed the dead-end story. But she cautioned that if Meri really hated it, she
should not hope for an early transfer. "Once they get you in they don't move you."
Nilsa's mother had waited ten years—what seemed the magic number for the
Housing Authority.

After some more talking Meri said she was going to take it. I was surprised—it
would have been a very tough decision for me. But she had a few ideas up her
sleeve. On the way back to the office she suggested we try bribing the manager.
"You know, a little present of $100?" I told her she would have to do that herself. I
wouldn't, and he wouldn't accept it in my presence anyway. Then she said she was
too shy, but maybe I could ask him if he was sure that this was the only apartment. She had overheard someone in the office saying in Spanish that they had
five available.

When we returned, the manager asked, "What have you been doing? I was sure
you had run away." He gave us a big toothy smile, which he soon dropped as I
started exploring other options. No, there were no other vacancies. No, there was
no possibility of a transfer. No he couldn't hold Meri's application for another vacancy—it had to be returned to the Central Office. Just to show us he was telling
the God's-honest-truth, he got up, poked around the filing cabinet, seriously inspected some list and said, "Nope, no other vacancy at present." I wanted to ask
him if he had ever tried out for a role in Monty Python's Flying Circus, but the
timing was wrong. Next, he was telling Meri he didn't want to force her into taking an apartment she wouldn't be happy in—he didn't want to see her coming to
his office a week later to complain. Then he pointed out how lucky she was: five-
room apartments were rare. "And besides," he said, looking carefully over her application, "your priority is very low. In fact, no priority at all."

"I'm taking it!" Meri said. The papers she had to sign included a pledge to never
bring a pet into the apartment. "We allow a goldfish or a canary but nothing else."
He also gave her a letter to the welfare office requesting that they provide her with
a check for $147 for the first month's rent, and ditto for security.

As we waited for the Avenue B bus, Meri encountered a woman who attended
the same evening class with her and who had been living at Smith Houses for the
past four years. In response to our queries she told us the following: There were
two elementary schools in the area, one with a Chinese majority, the other a
Spanish one. The Chinese one was better and harder—children had to take exams
to be promoted from one grade to another. That's where she sent her son. Item
two: As soon as you got into Smith Houses "they fuck you over." The elevators often didn't work. She thought the management just turned them off for the weekends. She did her shopping on weekdays and stayed stuck upstairs on Saturdays
and Sundays. She supposedly had a "high priority" for a transfer because of a

heart condition, but she had been waiting for years. Item three: There was less crime in the Smith Houses than, say, at Riis and Wald, the two projects closer to our neighborhood.

Avoiding an argument about projects that were closer to her heart, Meri went on to a discussion of the merits of a plan she was hatching. "They are giving me five rooms, which is probably illegal from their own regulations. Only two people of the same sex, if they're not married, can share a bedroom. That puts Millie and Lucita in one, Richie and Miguel in another, and what—me and Julio in the third? They can't do that." I could see she had already considered this when making up her mind to accept the apartment.

Even so, she gave staying in our neighborhood one final try. After we got off on Fourth Street, she pointed to the apartment where Señora Moreno used to live and said she wished she could live there, but the landlord wouldn't take her because Richie used to visit Lisa there. ("Visit" is not the word I would have used.) She asked me to ask the landlord once more for her. Fortuitously, he was at the moment down in his basement, working with Con Ed people on something that stunk like hell. If not for the stink, I might have uncharitably jumped to the conclusion that he was preparing his boiler for the next "no heat, no hot water" season. One of the guys called down "Lan'lo!" and up he came, a tall Teutonic type with a pale mustache and a tight sardonic grin. No, he had absolutely no vacancies, he said, recognizing Meri. He would have nothing in the near future either.

"You see?" said Meri, as we dragged on toward the office. Holly and Nilsa were waiting for us, and together they told Meri of the advantages of living in public housing, foremost among them (from Holly, who dreamed of getting in), "You ain't got no Con Edison to worry about; you can use all the heat and electricity you want." Soon Millie joined us and confirmed the federal renewal plan, including such items in her mother's building as new tiles, newer kitchen appliances, kitchen cabinets, and maybe even rewiring for air conditioning. Hot dog! Plus, free repairs, no rats, and—the final clincher—no fires, or at least only itsy-bitsy ones. At this point Nilsa advised Meri (prophetically, as it turned out) to start complaining about the kitchen equipment as soon as she moved in. Millie also avowed that the nearer Wald Houses (as in Lillian Wald, the pioneering reformer of the Lower East Side a century before) were a criminal cesspool, with high turnover rates and even rats. So Meri was thus consoled and confirmed in her good judgment.

Within the next few days welfare gave her her rent and security checks—uncommon speed, but it meant savings for them. They also volunteered $180 for her moving expenses, but Meri said she planned to spend the money on cleaning supplies, maybe to have a go at the gluey floors. "I don't need to move any of that old shit," she said, "only my washing machine and the stereo." She had tracked down the missing furniture company in Brooklyn and discovered they had left a small office behind that would honor her savings. "Plus, I have all that credit on Allen [Street], and Julio said he's giving me his accident money for my new apartment."

The last item, mentioned within Sito's hearing, was perhaps meant to sting. Because Sito indeed had another woman all lined up.

As for the accident money, Julio did receive it on his eighteenth birthday, when he was supposed to no longer live with Meri but to strike out on a career and a home of his own. They hid it carefully inside the 1949 kitchen stove. She only cooked on top of it, and the reasoning went that no self-respecting macho robber would stoop to search a woman's oven.

Alas, sometimes even the Housing Authority didn't give no heat or hot water, and so one cold day the old stove was put into action. That is how Meri and I made our acquaintance with the United States Treasury on Wall Street. I must say that they tried to be fair. Whatever bills had not been burned to a crisp were refunded, about $350 all told. Meri's attitude was, "That's how it goes." It was perhaps the least regrettable of the misfortunes that would befall her in her dream-come-true apartment.

Summertime

Although it may seem as if our team spent most of our time "hanging out," my research method was strongly influenced by the epistemology of cultural materialism. In practice this meant that the team of researchers would be observing, counting, using scientific instruments uniformly to collect data, and reaching approximate concordance on what had been observed. My research assistants were keen observers, familiar with the area and endowed with a cultural insider's point of view, yet capable of detaching themselves from their backgrounds, a skill they worked hard to develop. From the outset, I brought in ethnographic articles and books that the team read and discussed, and during our second summer of research Nilsa and Paul participated as regular students in a seminar entitled Street Ethnography that I taught in the summer session at Columbia University. At our staff meetings members reported on events and occurrences from their various perspectives, and we sought to reach concurrence on what had been observed before interpreting the implications. I believe this provided a fuller approximation of reality than what could have been reached by a single scientific observer.

This strategy was supported by a collection of reliable quantified information on housing conditions; the ethnic and racial distribution of the neighborhood; its commercial, educational, and religious resources and institutions; and the patterns of dealing in illegal drugs. We completed a massive census of 168 blocks in 1976, followed by a smaller random census of the same area in 1978 to ascertain trends in physical and social conditions and to document the visible deterioration in them.

In 1979, the last stage of the research, we gathered data on the household and kinship level. We used a standardized interview schedule with heads of households, which provided us with uniform information on 150 individuals. In addition, throughout the research period, each member of the team performed regular observational tasks: Nilda attended the local community board meetings and those of other community organizations. Nilsa went to courts, welfare offices, police stations, and other institutions with the mothers. Paul walked the neighborhood during randomly chosen hours with a small grocery counter in his pocket, counting drug dealers on street corners. And I interviewed officials in various institutions including the schools, the churches, the police department, and City Hall. Everyone was available to accompany another researcher, and we joined or substituted for each other as needed or as time permitted.

Time often did not permit. I also expected everyone to produce field notes, the daily bread of ethnographic work, in which a detailed description of daily events provides a basis for the reworking of ideas that will direct the additional gathering of empirical data. But only Bonnie, who joined the research in its last year, and I consistently wrote field notes. Paul wrote notes in a telegraphic style, reducing extended interactions to short, terse messages; Nilsa wrote extensively, but on very few occasions; and Nilda, almost never. It became necessary therefore to hold frequent, lengthy tape-recorded staff meetings so that the vital information we were collecting and needed for modifying our paradigm would not disappear with fading memories.

Research alone in this dangerous, emotionally debilitating environment would have stretched our energies to the limit. But given the degree of need, of the misery we saw in the lives of the people, and especially their children, we were driven by an added sense of urgency, by the belief that if we tried hard enough we could make a difference. So we organized Friday afternoon picnics in the East River Park; took the children camping on Bear Mountain; organized excursions to Jones Beach, where neither the children nor the mothers had ever been before, and expeditions to museums, galleries, and cultural events that had similarly been terra incognita to the poor people of the neighborhood. We drove the children to dental appointments on the Floating Hospital in the harbor; accompanied them to art and dance classes at the Third Street Music School (actually located on Eleventh Street and Second Avenue, already out of their range), where Nilda had won a bunch of free scholarships for them; and dragged mothers, often accompanied by children, to community meetings, and even up to Albany, so they could begin experiencing the sound of their own public voices.

I tried to combine "bread and roses" in our approach to service in the neighborhood. Nilda, who during her adolescence had been influenced by the presence of the East Harlem settlement house staffed by volunteers of the American Friends Service Committee, was convinced that the children needed exposure to "culture" that was lacking in this isolated neighborhood. Her aim was not of the "multicultural" kind (which the local schools today give only lip service anyway, while pressing assimilation), but a more complex, bicultural proposition: to help the children learn the important aspects of their Hispanic background while becoming literate in mainstream culture. It was a tall order, given our other commitments. My own primary concern was to help provide the mothers and children with skills that would help them to achieve better living conditions and a modicum of economic security. The other members of the team saw both priorities as important. Eventually, my proclivity for giving each researcher the freedom to focus on what suited her or his talents and convictions resulted in a constructive and innovative expense of energy, helping to stave off burnout.

But there were frequent occasions when I had strong doubts about what we were doing. What kind of social science were we engaged in when we were actively helping to change our informants' lives? When we befriended them and grew to be concerned about the safety and well-being of their children, were we not becoming a part of their networks, a relationship even closer than what we had already assumed as amateur social workers, psychologists, teachers, and housing and legal advisors? If I used my status and middle-class knowledge to help Meri move from her terrible apartment in the neighborhood to a better one far away on the outskirts of Chinatown, where she knew no one and would live in anonymity behind locked doors on the sixteenth floor of a housing project, was I doing her a favor? Worse, by using my skills to get favors from a politician to help a single individual and her family, was I not contributing to the abandonment of the principle that all human beings are entitled to decent housing within the neighborhood where they have social ties? In Rome even stray cats have a feline right, guaranteed by law, to remain in the neighborhood of their kith. Applied anthropology texts had not yet even considered the dilemmas of human rights; there was no guidance.

I spent sleepless nights worrying about even more basic concerns. What if a child was hurt during one of our excursions? We were not licensed or insured as a social agency, and if anything happened, there would be hell to pay from Columbia University, which was administering our grant. I took the basic precaution of making sure that each child had a parent's written permission for any trip outside the neighborhood, and we encouraged parents to come along to help us. But this was not enough, given the liveliness of the children and their lack of experience in the outside world, and our enthusiastic but inexperienced staff.

Aside from Nilsa's used car, which she lent freely to mothers, we had a succession of several old vehicles for transportation. At first we used my ten-year-old Dodge Dart. When that fell apart, I was persuaded to buy an old Ford van from a couple of visiting graduate students. Each time Paul took off with the vehicle loaded with children, my soul perched on my shoulder. And with good reason. After their trips the children would regale me with hair-raising stories:

> Oh yeah, after we left Fourth Street in the Dodge, we saw Lefty on his skateboard. He wanted to go to the museum too but there was no room in the car. So he hunged on to the car window and rode his board. All the way up Madison Avenue. And oh yeah, when we parked the car, you know, they had these tall clean buildings, with no gates on the first floor? So Lefty and Richie climbed up the window to show how easy it was, you know, to rob? And everybody was laughing. And then the girls had to go to the bathroom, and then we couldn't find them until it was time to go home.

Another time, on a visit to the respected uptown Latino gallery Tallier Boricua to view collage art, Paco, our own artist-in-residence, said: "Yeah, it was all junk. Old pieces of junk pasted on boards, it was cheap." So of course they all had to run around and explore the building inside and out, giving Bonnie and Nilda heart attacks. Coming back from a camping trip to Bear Mountain, a group of young adolescent boys chorused, "Hey, Paul, you faggot, how come you didn't stop and let us take that bike we saw in the driveway?" complaining that not only didn't they get to see no bears, but also "Paul, why you made us stop smoking?" around the evening's campfire. The smoke in question was a marijuana joint, possession of which would have landed them all in a local upstate jail, since even alcoholic beverages were not permitted in the campground. It must be noted in their defense that all this complaining was good-natured ribbing, outside their mothers' earshot; otherwise the brooms would have been busy that night. But the reports only deepened my anxiety. It was therefore a great relief to me, an act of providence, when one day late in the spring, Eti Medina cornered me in the office and demanded that during the upcoming summer vacation we do something to engage the kids constructively right there in the neighborhood. Apparently she had already given the question considerable thought: She proposed that I hire her and several other mothers to run a summer program from our office.

There were several programs in the neighborhood, but none of them was full-time, or free, or not oversubscribed. City-wide programs such as the Fresh-Air Fund had been filled by the beginning of the year, and the federally funded summer jobs program was so limited that none of the young teenagers (including those who had falsified their birth dates to appear to be fourteen, in order to qualify) had been accepted. So, after some preliminary meetings of the staff with Eti, where various ideas were explored, and after Nilsa and I did some fast calculations as to how we could shift around various grant categories, Eti, Millie Cortez, Holly Peterson, Dolores Ortega, and Count Augusto joined our team for the summer.

The anchor for the program would be the summer lunch program funded by the federal government. The program provided poor children with lunches they would not otherwise receive because the schools were not in session. Communities deemed to meet the federal guidelines for poverty, based on census tract information, were invited to propose sites for lunch distribution. These had to meet several criteria: They had to have clean space and seating for a number of children, contain a refrigerator because deliveries might be made early in the morning, and have staff on hand to accept the delivery, distribute the lunches, and supervise the lunch hour(s). The supervisors had to make sure that no child, regardless of age (infant to eighteen), received more than one sandwich, one piece of fruit, and one drink, either milk or juice. They also had to make sure that no lunches or parts thereof were carried off the premises, that no adult was given any of the food, and, in initial directives, that leftover sandwiches be thrown out, to insure adherence to this rule. Surprise inspections throughout the summer would be carried out to insure compliance with all regulations.

Our office was contacted as a potential site by a community organizer because, three years before, I had sponsored an apparently successful lunch program from my research office on Seventh Street. No inspector had ever appeared on the scene then, when poor Latina mothers with children, taking away leftover sandwiches for their evening meal, would stop at the door and give some away to poor, elderly Ukrainian and Polish women waiting to see if there were any leftovers. Several women had told me it was a heartbreaking sight to see these old, worn-out ladies rummaging for food in corner garbage bins. No sandwich or container of milk had ever seen the inside of a trash barrel, I proudly reported to our enlarged team, whose members were seething with indignation at the mean rules.

"Imagine!" said Eti, shooting out the words in bilingual salvos, "the same size sandwich for a *nene* [child] as for a *hombre* [man]! These people are *loco* [crazy]!" More people jumped in, assailing one or the other rule, advancing objections that had apparently not occurred to federal planners, such as the fact that small children would need more time to eat, so how could we do two or three seatings in an office that only accommodated twenty children at a time without either having the lunch hour and our supervisory and clean-up time stretch to three hours, or having some children be able to take at least part of their lunch outside, breaking the rules. I added fuel to the fire by reporting that at least three years ago, the lunches had hardly been worth the trouble: The sandwiches consisted of two pieces of soggy white bread interspersed with either a slice of discolored baloney or a piece of sweaty processed cheese; the fruit, if a peach or plum, hard as a stone, or if last year's apple, battered and mushy inside its waxed skin.

I could see that I had gone too far. The team was ready to tell the government to go and stick its lunch program. And I hadn't even mentioned the newspaper articles reporting that a number of food vendors had been investigated for "an absolutely criminal misappropriation of funds" by the state comptroller (*New York Post* 9/8/76). It was a complex issue, because in the politically heart-hardening climate, the conservatives threatened to do away with lunch "hand-outs" to undernourished children. The liberals, conversely, on the defensive about the so-called failed anti-poverty programs, were loath to turn any investigative or corrective attention where it was required—on the agribusiness lobbyists, contractors, and vendors getting fat profits off the substandard food they pawned off on poor children—for fear the entire program would collapse.

To the newest members of the team the issues appeared as a series of affronts to their backgrounds, their intelligence, and their *dignidad*. Eti wanted to know why the federal government did not establish a food preparation site in the neighborhood where mothers could make delicious, fresh Spanish food at a fraction of the cost the government spent preparing and shipping food in from remote areas. Nutrition had been her profession in Puerto Rico. She knew. Dolores assented, having when younger raised eight strong sons on the wages of a migrant farmworker. She knew how to stretch money to feed all those mouths. She also remarked that most mothers preferred to have their children eat at home, which was cleaner (perhaps not exactly true in her particular case, as several eyebrows swiftly raised and dropped signified). Millie, who hated cooking and left it to her daughter Ginny, offered from her experience with Chulito's Head Start Program that fresh raw vegetables and salads would be far superior to what was being described. Holly suggested that as experienced mothers, we didn't need spies and overseers to teach us how to distribute food equitably.

This brought forth nodding assents and landed the conversational ball in the lap of Count Augusto, who sat up straighter, gathered the fierce eyebrows that formed a straight line over his nose, and embarked on a disquisition of the issues in full courtly Black English. Harking back to his cooking experience not only in prisons but in the finest restaurants, he now condemned the condescending attitude of the agents of capitalist imperialism who had transformed his pearly isle of Puerto Rico from a self-sustaining economy into a vast plain of sugar, sending its sons and daughters into exile for sustenance. He summarized the various arguments made so far and then sketched out the ways in which the lunch program was an indignity, an insult to the pride, the race, and the sensibilities of the community.

Well, I thought. That's that. Good-bye summer program. Without lunches we could not keep the children engaged all day, nor justify hiring the mothers to help. There was no money for food in the grant—in fact, there was no money for wages. Nilsa and I had figured out that if we expended all the funds from the "gifts to informants" and "fees to informants" categories and sacrificed our travel funds, we would have enough to pay modest salaries for part-time work to five people for six weeks.

But Eti, practical as ever, now jumped in again. Bad lunch was better than no lunch. Teenagers will eat anything, they're hungry all day anyway, she said: *"Pueden comer los clavos de esa mesa"* (they could even eat the nails off this table), emphatically rapping on Paul's sturdy table (which was, in fact, overfortified by nails). We could make schedules for two mothers to be in charge every day, and we could post teens to alert us when inspectors were coming (clearly the lessons she had learned while dwelling with her criminally inclined sister-in-law had not been forgotten), already arranging for us how to make the program more flexible and equitable.

Everyone agreed to her fine solution, the regular staff members with a bit less enthusiasm than the newcomers, and the meeting went on to discuss who would contact whom to get instructional materials, supplies, and space for an arts and crafts program, what sports to offer, and what kind of excursions the mothers wanted. Everyone left the meeting beaming. But the arguments about the lunch program would surface over and over again, first when the community organizers came to visit our site and were assailed about the stupidity of the rules (although the mothers, polite as ever, accused "them," the distant bureaucrats in Washington), and later as the actual food began to arrive (and sometimes not arrive), and was often worse than expected.

During June, organizing proceeded at full tilt. Nilda, with the longest Catholic school experience, dispatched herself to an appointment with the principal of Immaculate Heart to ask for space for our arts and crafts and sports programs. Father Flaherty, she reported at our next meeting, was less than sanguine about the proposal. No, there was no way they could let us use the interior of the school, they were not insured. The playground, he would have to think about.

"Do you know a youngster named Richie?" he asked her innocently.

Well, yes, she allowed, there was such a boy in the neighborhood. "Why do you ask, Father?"

"Well," he replied, "if this kid is to take part in your program, I don't think we would agree to have you use our yard. You see, we think he has been climbing over the wall to play basketball at night, and we can't permit that, and we think that's his name, because after the janitor caught him, someone sprayed his name all over the walls." With a sweeping gesture, he invited Nilda toward a window to take a gander at the severely decorated walls of the interior court. Suppressing her argumentative instincts, which under other circumstances would have led her to point out that the names Cheetah, Lefty, and Kid (the nom de plume of Dolores's oldest scion, Rafael) also figured in the mural, Nilda assured Father Flaherty that Richie would not be participating in the program. He had other preoccupations.

In that case, Father Flaherty said, he would consider our request.

Needless to say, as the summer progressed, the boys who had decorated the court were occasionally to be seen tossing baskets in the Immaculate Heart hoops, and not precisely at the hours appointed for our sports program. As Richie confided to me, it wasn't as much fun when the gates were open. Besides, among the young blades, the program fairly quickly acquired a reputation for being for little kids and *bobos*, so they avoided it. But Nilda needn't have worried about getting caught in her sin of omission. To the Irish Fathers, privy to long institutional memories, every swarthy boy looked alike, and every one had similar proclivities ("youngster" = gangster) going back to the Italian "Roccos" of a hundred years before.

The next coup was getting the elementary school that occupied the Sterns' former landholding to give us space for the arts and crafts program. I was surprised at my own ability to bully the two assistant principals in charge to allow us to use two classrooms with sinks, four days a week. Their initial reluctance to allow anything constructive to occur in the school was worn down by my apparent surprise at encountering not one but two assistant principals in a school with such a decimated enrollment, followed by hints at how disappointed Councilwoman Friedlander would be if this school were not available to accommodate some community activity, and so on. Gross forms of blackmail, but desperation lent me strength. The research part of our work needed respite from flour paste, water, scissors, and brushes wielded and flung in tune to childish shrieks against the backdrop of adolescent taunts. We needed a modicum of peace to fit in an interview, now and then.

Nilsa and Bonnie also got marvelous instructions for making puppets and other projects from the art teacher at the Third Street Music School. In addition, the teacher donated some materials. There was no doubt that she was a very kind person, but the alacrity of her offerings was suspicious.

I recalled, with a touch of jaundice, the last time I had picked up the kids from their Saturday class, Nilda having decided to take a dance class herself. I had found them all clustered at the window of the studio, providing unflattering commentary on the movements of the dancers, with Paco beginning a pantomime that mimicked the gait of both an elephant and one of the dancers. A very gifted boy. The rest of the gang was bent double in convulsive laughter. It took all the self-command I had to control my face and tell them to stop at once—which they did because I followed by asking, in a deceptively mild voice, why they were out of their art class so early. Because they had finished, Paco said, trying to distract me by showing me a lovely green worm finger puppet, which he immediately began to walk through Coreen's corn-rows, whispering in a sinister, wormy hiss, "Ugh, this flower stinks!"

His taunts understandably brought shrieks of fury and tears from Coreen, which brought the dance class to a halt, which brought the dance teacher to the door, with Nilda stomping out behind her, promising never, ever again to bring the kids to the school. "I went through all this trouble to get you kids scholarships, and this is how you disgrace me," she scolded, insulting their dignidad; but that was not enough to stop some of the children from punching every floor button on the elevator when we left, and a number from running home ahead of me to get their side of the story to their mothers first. I had collected the last stragglers from outside a basement music room where they had been dancing in tune to the conga drum session like a bunch of crazed chickens, their heads moving in and out from their stooped shoulders, led by massive Jojo, whose older brother was playing inside. Coreen let me hold her hand on the way home, as I explained that Paco was probably teasing her because she was so pretty. She wasn't buying it though. Relaying my experiences to the staff later, I was informed that Bonnie and Nilda had had similar experiences in the past but hadn't bothered to burden me with tales. But now we knew why the art teacher was so eager to pass on her skills and materials to us.

The wrinkles in the program were smoothed out by the time summer began. Three mornings a week Count Augusto, now suddenly as sober as a deacon (at least in daytime), took about twenty children swimming at the Twelfth Street swimming pool, accompanied by two older teenagers from a different neighborhood who had qualified for summer jobs. On the other two weekdays, Paul and the Count took whoever wanted to play baseball, jog, race, or play other games to the East River Park. On Friday afternoons the entire team joined them with fresh hamburgers or hot dogs, which we had managed to extract from the lunch program instead of the usual disgusting sandwiches. Even on rainy days, Paul, a seasoned camper, would make a fire in the two heavy hibachis we dragged in a shopping cart, hanging large plastic sheets on ropes sailor-knotted to trees, providing a cozy, if smoky, interior for our repast. Thirty to forty kids would partake, politely waiting to be offered the food; the only scramble would occur at the end of the day, when I'd offer extra cookies to the child who could pick up the biggest pile of trash. I had little remorse over this environmental bribery. Most of the children had ingrained habits of cleanliness from their homes—it was only a question of translating them to public spaces. I also knew they had been made to feel over the years that public spaces were not theirs to occupy. The litter pickup helped change that perception.

In the afternoons, a smaller group worked with Bonnie and Nilsa in the arts and crafts program. They were joined by another summer job teenager, a young Latina, Elena, who turned out to be a talented, interested aide. In theory, the teenagers were hired by the city for a six-week summer job for which they were paid minimum wage to work six hours under the mentorship of an adult in a nonprofit or city agency. This was supposed to provide them with skills and experience leading to future jobs upon graduation, because, the rationale went, inner-city youths had almost no access to apprentice jobs in ghetto neighborhoods, unlike their working-class age-mates in the outer boroughs.[1] The theory was fine, but the practice failed in a number of ways. First, the teens hired already had some advantages; at the very least, contacts to people in schools or community agencies who knew when the hiring began and how to ensure an applicant's acceptance. Second, mentors, either through excess of work or a preference for spending their work time in more urgent endeavors, generally did not provide goals or job specifications, leaving the teens to their own devices, which turned out to be flirting, listening to music, and playing paddleball, if not worse. On any day they could be seen lounging and playing in the elementary school yard, and the two male teens who came to work with us very quickly fell into the general pattern of lassitude of the local teens who had been unable to get jobs. They showed up late, disappeared, left early, and gave lip to the mothers. After all, this was not their neighborhood—they had no fear of word getting back to their parents.

I warned Carlos, a saucy, good-looking Cuban kid of middle-class background, several times to mend his ways. He mended them temporarily, but a few weeks later he began to throw his weight around the office, conspiring with some of our teens, and finally showed up with a menacing older man who introduced himself to me as Commander Garcia. Mr. Garcia informed me that the older teens were requesting he open a chapter of "junior cadets" in the neighborhood, and that our office would be most suitable to his purpose. To my inquiries as to the precise nature of his organization, he replied that it was purely educational and recreational. Despite some misgivings, I decided to let him use our office for two weeks.

The fever that gripped our boys when the word went out was amazing to behold. Apparently they were instructed at the first meeting to forthwith buy, borrow, or otherwise acquire whatever military garb they could. At the next meeting, when Commander Garcia reverently unrolled a giant flag and hung it above our blue, Max-tattered settees and the ragtag group got up to pledge allegiance, it was a toss-up whether to laugh or cry. Eti's youngest, José, was wearing an army jacket. Dolores's oldest, Rafael-the-Kid, sported army boots. Myrna's ten-year-old, Adam, had a water canteen tied to his waist with string, and so forth. But for an hour, I witnessed unusual quiet, concentration, and obedience, as Commander Garcia laid out authoritarian rules and regulations. That weekend, he informed me after the meeting, the boys from our chapter would join boys from all over the city for an overnight lesson in "survival skills" in Van Cortland Park in the Bronx. Questioning the boys later, I realized they were being inveigled into a simulation of paramilitary maneuvers, and that the commander had let it be known in the neighborhood that the exercise was being cosponsored by us. But although I sent out urgent notices via the children's telegraph denying our collaboration, a number of mothers and fathers had already given permission to their war-fevered progeny. The boys strutted, conversed, gathered up provisions of baked beans in cans, and boasted that they were going to "beat the shit" out of their fellow cadets, preferably under the cover of darkness.

Tearful farewells delayed the young warriors' departure for their mission. Adam's father, a former Marine, the very person who had given his wife Myrna a black eye for Christmas and who was presently three sails to the wind, kept changing his mind about letting his son go. *"Ay, papito!"* he'd cry, gathering his son into his bosom with his left arm, because the right was engaged with a Miller's High Life, "How could I let you go? It's gonna be dark there, you know, no *mami*, no *papi*, you sure you're ready for this?" Adam tried to weasel out of his father's embrace, saying: "Papi, I'm sure. I ain't scared. You'll see, you gonna be proud of me!" I hissed on the other side to Myrna, "Don't let him go, this is dangerous!" and Myrna answered, "There's nothing more I can do. I tried, but he says this is business for the mens." I was also furious with Paul, who had been persuaded to give the boys a ride in the van to the subway, where they were going to rendezvous with cadets from Brooklyn. I thought the gesture put a false stamp of our approval on the expedition. Fortunately, that night there was a big storm. The young army was back home by the following noon, wet, hungry, and bedraggled. They had eaten the beans cold, and there had been no significant engagements with the enemy. Except for a few scratches, everyone was fine. Carlos, who had not joined the ill-fated bivouac, was presently seen smoking a joint in front of the Salvation Army store at a time when he was supposed to be minding the kids with Count Augusto at the swimming pool. He protested when I told him he was fired, and when Commander Garcia showed up to ask me what the problem was, I told him to find another place for his activities. And that was that, except that various chapters of cadets kept popping up in the neighborhood, parading with wooden guns and assorted military paraphernalia.

Meanwhile, our summer program bloomed. Having already produced decorated paper plates and clay ashtrays, Bonnie and Nilsa's art class developed into a full-scale puppet production. Paco wrote a play with "help" from Coreen and Miguel, and Paul's editorial assistance. It was enough to melt your heart. An evil count, named Garbanzo, turned children into dogs by offering them poisoned candy. Two winsome youngsters, a boy and a girl (the latter predictably a *rubia*, a blond, like all the heroines they saw on TV), were produced from papier-mâché in our public school atelier, along with the ugly count, a policeman, a mother, and the unfortunate dogs. The story line started with the innocent but stupid acceptance of the candy by the children, followed by the mother's desolate search for them and the (naturally) unhelpful actions of the policeman; in the climactic final act, the mother takes the two mangy critters home and through this loving gesture restores them to human form.

As the production proceeded, showbiz fever gripped the children and the entire staff. Paul not only built a magnificent puppet theater, with my favorite pillowcase for a curtain, but also enthusiastically acceded to being the voice of Count Garbanzo on the tape recording we made in hopes of making the production run more smoothly. He produced richly descending octaves of maniacally greedy laughter, to Paco's annoyance inflating the count into something resembling a crazed-out landlord. "Hew, hew, hew, hew, now all of this will be mine, ALL MINE!" he intoned, presumably indicating the burned-out landscape that Paco was in the process of painting as background scenery. The mothers and the staff cut and sewed costumes, the mothers hectoring and disciplining. Before we went into recording, Nilda taught a motley crew of children a Mexican song, "Pimpom," which to the accompaniment of Paul's slightly off-tune guitar, began and ended the show:

> *Y cuando las estrellas comiencan a lucir*
> *Pimpom se pone a cama, Pimpon se va dormir. . .*

Reflecting, perhaps a nostalgic wish on Nilda's part, because our children certainly didn't go to sleep when the stars began to shine.

The show was a tremendous success and had to be repeated on several succeeding days as the word got around, even though minor production difficulties surfaced. For one, the crowded space inside the puppet theater, which presents obstacles to puppet handlers under any circumstances, tended to exacerbate Paco and Coreen's stormy relations. For another, the operation of the tape player activated by Miguel was at times out of sync with the action. Thus, just as the mother's voice (Nilda) was wailing "*Niños*! My niños! Oh where could you be?" the policeman's head might be popping out. Or, as the maniacal laughter of Count Garbanzo rose to a pitch of greed, only two dogs could be seen skulking through a ruined city landscape. I thought the mismatches lent the production a macabre, eerie touch. But not Paco. He was a perfectionist. We'd hear "I'm quitting!" followed by a crash, followed by Paco elbowing his way through the crowd with a hideous pout on his face—the height of each performance. At first the drama might be extended by an adult, grasping after Paco, entreating "Paco, Pacito, please come back, it's OK, baby!" but if this was followed by a wild harangue between Paco and Coreen—"I'm not working with *her* around!" "Well, then *I'm* quitting!"—someone always jumped in as a substitute, and the show went on.

The mothers' lunch program flowed smoothly enough. Eti arranged their schedule, and each was assigned in turn to be present when the food arrived, to count it, sign for it, and store it in the refrigerator. Then another mother or two would arrive at noon, clean the tables, set out the lunches, and sit talking with the children as they ate, discarding the trash, tucking fruits into little hands. Then the routine was repeated for a second or third seating. We were feeding about fifty children on a daily basis, but even when attendance slacked off on some days, no food ever remained in the refrigerator, except maybe a few juices, and our garbage pail contained only discarded containers and napkins. After a final cleanup each day, a thorough affair involving sponges, lots of detergent, and the mop, the mothers rested, chatting or telling stories, or just hugging kids and correcting their behavior from the bench in front. I didn't inquire too closely as to how the food was shared, except to notice that teens were leisurely posted outside of our office during lunch times and that they were the last ones to be fed. But I didn't think they were subsisting on one sandwich each. In fact, the children were looking stronger and healthier. Golden brown from their excursions to the pool. Full, happier.

Only Holly approached me with a grievance. She said the Latina women were excluding her. They spoke Spanish in front of her and, she thought, were criticizing her. We held a meeting to discuss it, a novel experience for Eti and Dolores. Having been raised on the island, they had been taught that direct confrontations must be avoided. They were more uncomfortable about the meeting than they had been about Holly's displaced unhappiness. Millie, a Nuyorican, was more flexible, and since she and Holly were close in age and Millie was truly bilingual, the meeting began what was to become a good buddy relationship. Equilibrium thus achieved, the women went on to plan a block party that would cap the summer program.

It was getting toward the close of the summer; there was a nostalgic sense of ending in the air. As the city program ran out of funds, the summer workers were prematurely terminated. Elena hung on, out of general interest and good will, but even the younger children started worrying about the beginning of the school year. And our van dropped dead.

It was a scenario from one of my nightmares. We had spent the day at Jones Beach, Holly, Millie, Paul, and I, and about fifteen younger children. We had stayed late, cooking an evening meal on the charcoal grill, and the children were tired. On the BQE, a highway from hell that has no space on the sides for a pull-off, the engine started choking up, and Paul was barely able to get two wheels off the highway onto a curb before it sputtered out. We were sitting ducks for a fatal crash from the speeding, horn-blasting traffic. I jumped out into the narrow space between our van and the wall that contained the BQE, with the mothers and children bailing out behind me, all of us hugging the wall, single file, all with minimal shouting and shoving, the children suddenly very awake and cooperative. We dissuaded Paul from attempting to get into the motor, and left him standing against the wall, with the van's lights flashing, while the rest of us started a goose file toward a distant ramp. When we finally emerged in the wilds of Queens, cars swerving around us, their horns wailing long after they had passed, we were at a loss. It was late; it was a weekend and no mechanics were on duty; mothers were waiting for us at home, worried, and the few passersby were not particularly eager to give directions or help to our multiethnic, partially deshabille crew. Fortunately we found a phone and called Bonnie, who went through the neighborhood and spread the message. And then, after what seemed like endless walking through apparently deserted blocks, we found a subway entrance. We left Paul to his wits and fate.

Once on the train the children miraculously recovered their stamina, and there was no end of wheeling round the poles like gerbils on a treadmill, as well as chin-ups suspended from the straps, the mothers and I beaming with indulgence at our snatched-from-the-jaws charges, the Queens riders regarding us with a great deal less approval. You just can't please everyone.

Back on the block, we were greeted with a prodigal's welcome as mothers snatched up their beloveds for baths. As it turned out, Paul got a push up the ramp from someone, and finding no mechanic, left the van on the street. By Monday, when he returned, the van had been stripped down to its basics. I was overjoyed.

My research accomplishment of the summer was to have completed household budget interviews with thirty-six women in the neighborhood. Several years of participant observation in their homes and the efficient way the women ran the summer lunch program demonstrated their good management and planning skills. I wanted to test my impressions by collecting uniform data that could be quantified. The data coming in indicated that even the younger women allocated their limited funds with care and wisdom. Here, as an example, is a portion of an interview with Holly's young friend (and mentor!) nineteen-year-old Pam, who also lived in our building. As a teenage mother and high school dropout, Pam might have been considered as inadequately prepared for adult roles even by sympathetic policy makers.

J.: How much money do you spend on food? You can tell me each month or every week.

P.: A month? I could spend about $80, about $80 to $90.

J.: For a month?

P.: Yeah. That's because my food stamps, when I get them the first of the month, that's $63. I spend all of that on food.

J.: Sixty-three dollars?

P.: Right. And when Harry gets his check, or I get mine, I go and buy more meat and stuff. So mostly at the end of the month, I'll buy more food. So, about $80.

J.: All together? For the three of you?

P.: Yes, yes.

J.: That seems low to me. Eighty in addition?

P.: No, no. Sixty-three plus whatever makes up to eighty.

J.: Oh, yeah? That's all?

P.: Yeah, yeah. Because I know how to stretch it. We eat off a meal for two days. That's right. And I don't do, like cooking, if they [don't] eat it, put it in the refrigerator and cook something else—and have all that—I'll make sure they're all finished and then I'll go cook something else.

J.: When you go and buy your meat and everything, when you get your food stamps, do you go and look for sales?

P.: Yes, I go to a lot of sales. Like, I get the paper every Sunday, and I'll look in the Sunday paper, I'll see what supermarkets have sales. Mostly I go to Key Food or Met Food, or wherever they're from [sales coupons]. But I go to buy my meats on Ninth Avenue because it's kind of cheap.

J.: You go with Holly over there?

P.: No, I told Holly where to go! We don't never go the same day. I go when I get my check and she goes when she gets her check.

J.: When you go, what do you buy? To Ninth Avenue?

P.: Yeah. When I go, I'll buy, like, a chicken, I'll buy steak, I'll buy pork chops. I'll buy beef ribs and sausages, liver, I'll buy chopped meat, you know. Sometimes, if I have a little extra, I'll buy ham. I can make ham and cheese sandwiches, you know. And I'll go on the other side, where they have their little canned goods, tuna fish. . . . It's not just a meat store, you know, you can get other stuff there. You can get seasoning with food stamps, you can get aluminum foil.

J.: Yeah? It's on Ninth Avenue and where?

P.: Fourteenth Street. Fourteenth Street and Ninth Avenue.

J.: What's the name of that place? I'd like to go myself.

P.: Oh, I don't really know the name. But when you get in front of it, it has this yellow sign. You can't miss it. It's all meat areas there.

J.: Like wholesale meat?

P.: Yeah. But the one has big sales and stuff on it. You can't miss it. When you get inside you go through this big freezer department, it has a plastic door. It's kind of cold there and it's kind of cheap there.

J.: Do they let you buy two pounds of something, or do you have to buy five pounds?

P.: You can buy anything you want, any quantity you want.

J.: Yeah? That's good to know. You told Holly about that?

P.: Yeah! My mother told ME about it! My mother used to go there, and I think I was telling Holly's old man about it, he had heard about it, and the next thing I know, Holly started going there.

J.: Yeah? That's terrific. So you really know how to stretch it?

P.: Yeah. (*Laughs*) Yup!

We finished the summer off with a block party, which I thought would never end. It was too loud, too contentious, Holly and Pam getting angry with the Muslims who lived at the end of the block, the Muslims acting insulted, everyone vying to make money from home-cooked foods, and Eti's money getting stolen sometime during the night. Count Augusto, who with the help of the older boys earlier in the day had rigged up a platform for a raucous salsa band, using recycled wood from torched buildings, had also rigged up electrical sources by cutting into streetlight wiring. He was drunk by nightfall and started a fight with a male community organizer who he claimed was trying to get credit for the party and interloping at the mike as an emcee. The word "bourgeois" was heard, even above the beat of the conga drums, until Gusto's pals, assisted by Paul, dragged the count off.

But a few days later, the younger women and the children were pronouncing the block party a great success, a fitting end to a wonderful summer. Millie said she hadn't danced so much in ages.

After the whirl of energy required to send the children off to school in spiffy clean clothes, as the days grew cooler and shorter, the women who had worked with us grew wistful. Their comments indicated how much confidence they had gained by working and how much they missed the work, not just because of the sense of purpose it had given them but because of the contribution they had made to the neighborhood. The sense of community we had fostered was disappearing, along with community based jobs. The cold air moving in from the north carried a scent of foreboding.

10

Sometimes the War Close to Home Is the Most Difficult to See

When my brother Andrei was seven and I was ten, we spent many a night in shallow trenches dug by our East European fellow prisoners on the grounds of a German labor camp, while Allied bombers flew overhead and dropped their cargo. Being already a grown-up girl I took political comfort from the fact that the Germans were getting theirs. Not so my brother. Emaciated, dwarfed by the rations we got, chicken-chested and bow-legged, he was already beyond comforting. Each time a bomb exploded, quaking the earth of our shelter-grave, each time the night sky lit up with flares, exposing the ghostly landscape, followed by the vicious rattling of Wermacht artillery and the roaring hiss of missiles, Andrei moaned and trembled and tried to escape from the tight body grip my mother had on him.

Now I was witnessing a similar scene—only this was not supposed to be wartime. Black smoke was billowing from the house next door. Fire engine sirens engulfed the airspace like the roaring moans of rabid dragons, and barking bullhorn commands dwarfed the screams of panicked people. Dolores Ortega, sitting well away from the window of her apartment, had a tight grip on her four-year-old, Francisco. He was trembling and moaning, trying to escape her, as she rocked her body back and forth on the bare mattress that was her bed. His eyes were huge and unfocused. There was tremendous strength in those sticks he had for limbs. She said simply, "He gets like that when he hears sirens."

Ronna Berezin and I sat quietly, waiting for Francisco to subside. The fire next door in Chino's building was only a small one, caused perhaps by an overloaded extension, and only a foretaste of the building's eventual fate. In the fall of 1979, all around us the Lower East Side was still burning. Not as flagrantly as it had in

1976, but burning nonetheless. The census we did in 1976 of the 168 blocks of the neighborhood, and a subsequent random census of forty blocks we completed in 1978, supported our initial impression that at least a third of the housing stock had been lost through fire, a process of "slum clearance" that was now slowing.

I had brought Ronna up to introduce her to Dolores, who had agreed to partic-ipate in the nutrition study I had asked Ronna to do. A nutritionist with a mas-ter's degree from the Minnesota School of Public Health, Ronna was taking a short professional break from her job for the Papago Tribe of Arizona. During her four years on the reservation, she had officially provided supervision and in-service training to seven community service workers implementing the WIC (Women, Infants, and Children) Supplemental Food Program. Unofficially she worked with people of all ages, providing contacts and aid in a situation of des-perate poverty. She thought that working with us would give her a new perspec-tive on the situation back home, and perhaps a breather.

Now, as we sat in Dolores's rather bare, but neater than usual, apartment, Ronna began to work with Dolores on her shopping, cooking, and dietary knowl-edge. She planned to spend at least two days with Dolores, observing and inter-viewing a couple of her six boys, using the *24 Hour Dietary Recall* and *Food Frequency Recall* schedules. By then I had strong empirical evidence that the chil-dren in the neighborhood were undernourished and that their status was due not to their mothers' ignorance of diet or lack of thrift, but to the lack of money for food. Judging by the budgets we were collecting, the food stamps to which the mothers and children were entitled to provide adequate diet were insufficient, be-cause the cost of food was higher in New York City than anywhere else in the country, yet the program made no allowance for the difference. Moreover, be-cause of negligent or deliberate administrative mistakes, all the women were get-ting less food stamp money than they were entitled to. This was even aside from the perennial problems of entitlements arriving late and of families being cut off from all forms of support payments for capricious reasons. I asked Ronna for a scientific assessment of the children's nutritional status and its implications.

In the short time she spent with us as a consultant, Ronna was able to complete work with only four mothers and seven of the children with whom we were inti-mate, four girls and three boys. The sample was small, derived from about 10 per-cent each of the mothers and children we knew, and although not random, it was fairly representative. In addition, Ronna spent a number of days in the local pub-lic school, sitting with children during breakfast and lunch, observing what the children ate, how the food was presented and served, the environment in which it was served, and its nutritional value. Among her many findings, I cite the follow-ing from her final report:

1. The women are already shopping according to the guidelines set up by USDA
    [United States Department of Agriculture]. . . . Rice, beans, potatoes seem to
    be the staples; canned and dry milk is used to cut down on the cost of fresh

milk. Two women use 75 pounds of rice/month, one woman uses 40 pounds of potatoes/month. Holly purchases more nutrient-dense vegetables than the others: spinach, broccoli, collard greens, more fresh vegetables.

2. None of the women spends money on unnecessary "convenience" or junk foods.

3. All of the women shop at more than one store to purchase better quality food at lower prices. Holly is the most motivated and gets the most out of her limited food money.

4. There are seasonal changes in the diet. During summer, more fresh fruits are bought, more fish is eaten.

5. The women need more money in order to buy adequate amounts of food for a nutritious diet. They also need more consumer information and accurate nutritional information. (Berezin 1979:4)

Ronna's report also points out that the food stamp allotment in effect in 1979 was based on the 1975 Thrifty Food Plan, the cheapest of USDA's budgets, which "many authorities believe . . . fails to meet human needs. . . . In addition, rising food costs have made it impossible to buy adequate amounts of food to meet even the nutritional needs outlined in the Thrifty Food Plan"(page 8). In addition, the report shows that of the mothers interviewed, Eti received only 54 percent of the recommended amount in food stamps, Delores 58 percent, Millie 82 percent, and Holly 77.6 percent (pages 8–9). Ronna also notes that the children did not take full advantage of the free school breakfast and lunch programs because of the food's poor quality, thereby straining the family budgets even further. In addition, "guests" needed to be taken into account: "There is a kind of food network among these families; a constant sharing back and forth—whoever is around or is hungry, is fed. I made no adjustments for 'guests'"(page 8).

Her conclusions about the children's nutritional status are as follows:

The children's nutrition is inadequate. Aside from the universal high-sugar teenage diet, these children are at nutritional risk for all the essential nutrients—protein, iron, calcium, vitamins A and C. The problems with the school program . . . prevent that program from making a significant contribution to the children's daily caloric intake. (page 22)

Ronna had also accompanied several children to dental appointments and, noting the generally poor state of their teeth, commented on this specific index of poverty and poor nutrition. "The children's teeth were in very bad condition. . . . Dental disease is probably the most clear-cut example of the relation of diet to health. A well-balanced diet is essential for the proper structure and composition of the tooth and its supporting structure" (page 18). She indicts media promotion of poor eating habits as one of the factors involved: "The selection of a nutritious diet on a tight budget is a difficult task. Nutritional confusion abounds due to this advertising. The messages are unfair to all consumers but they place a special burden on people who must spend limited food dollars very carefully to provide an adequate diet" (page 19). And she concludes: "An inadequate diet contributes to poor health; it is not healthy to be poor. Where the structure of society limits the capability of members to obtain adequate and enough food, malnutrition is not only a consequence of inequality, but also becomes a mechanism for maintaining it, as malnutrition produces physiological and behavioral stress" (page 22).

Ronna's study documented what we had already observed: that the children as individuals were at risk because of their poor nutritional status. We had also already obtained documentation showing that both the children and the people in the neighborhood, as a collective, were in addition experiencing high environmental stress because of the fear of fire and the increasing scarcity of places to live; the deteriorated condition of the buildings leading to neglect and abandonment by landlords, and in the end to homelessness.

In searching for causes of this evidently "scorched earth" situation, we interviewed a number of officials, community workers, and residents who had been "burned out." One of the more eloquent and dedicated women that Paul and I interviewed was Clara Valiente Barksdale, director of the Sloan Center for Children, on Sixth Street. She said, in part:

> Well, I've been here for two years, and in the two years that I've worked here eleven buildings on this block were destroyed. And of the eleven, some of them are not even there anymore. As you can see, some of them are just vacant lots, some are sealed off, and some of them are just open to the garbage, or whatever, and hopefully they will be demolished. But demolishing is going very slowly. It's the sense of devastation, of destruction, I imagine what it must do to everybody. But of course, when I think of the children, it's . . . we lose about thirty percent of the population in the center in one year because they disappear. I mean, one day they're here, and three days later they're gone because the fire took over. And some of them go with the Red Cross [or] Department of Social Services. But others go with relatives. And some of them call and say, "I'm in Brooklyn," "I'm in Rockaways," and some of them are just gone. But I think that, emotionally, the sense that they are here, they are playing with their friends on the block, and the next day they're not there anymore . . . the sense of fear . . .
>
> I remember a year and a half ago we were having a party at the end of the school year for one of the programs for children that have reading problems. And they fixed it up in a very nice classroom, there was a clown, the kids were having a marvelous time playing. And all of a sudden, this black smoke came from the building next door—the building is not there anymore, but at that point it was a hazard, the last time they had a fire there the city decided to demolish it. But what it did to that party! The teachers were like, paralyzed. It was not so much the fear, but almost the sense of futility of anything you do. Well, you see, you're doing all this, what for? Tomorrow will you be around? It constantly reminds you that all human endeavors will end up, someday, in death. But you don't want to have that around you all the time, you know? I've sensed that. I felt like, "What is this? Is this the death of the community?" It's a sense of death. I mean, you strive to create services, or maintain services, but it doesn't mean anything. People are leaving. . . .

> There are so many people [here], on various levels, who have vested interests, for a variety of reasons. On the other hand, I think the authorities watch it happen without intervening because it's convenient. It's a way of bulldozing without bulldozing it. If you want to get rid of the people, all you have to do is watch it happen. And eventually nothing will be left.

Clara indicated that arson, either directly by landlords or by young men or addicts they hired to do it, was the most frequent cause of fires in the neighborhood. Caught in the downward spiral of redlining, higher taxes, and steeper costs, many landlords were choosing to torch their buildings and collect insurance rather then see their profits dwindle. There was never any serious investigation of this in our neighborhood, but many people who would not have testified to official authorities, for various reasons, led us to believe that this was so, adding that young arsonists usually warned the remaining residents in buildings about to be torched. Lives were saved, but insecurity and stress mounted. By 1976, the number of fires had increased by 170 percent over the preceding five years (Sharff 1976); thereafter, the fires slowly decreased. During our research they were still endemic, part of a consolidation process whereby real estate combines collected and traded parcels of sufficient size for future "development." Landlords, whose gold-rush fever had risen during the early 1970s in response to the city's plans for construction of a new subway line on Second Avenue, were still hopeful, in spite of the city's abandonment of its plans during the fiscal crisis of 1973–1975. The proximity of the Lower East Side to the Wall Street area provided recurring visions of sugar plums: high-priced condo developments where tenements once stood.

Meanwhile, ordinary residents, the victims, seemed to accept the fires as a way of life. Some hoped that getting "burned out" would make them eligible for better housing, which usually did not happen. Most were too fearful to inform on the arsonists, if they knew them, or had simply given up. Most also assumed that the firefighters, like so many other city employees, simply didn't care about them and allowed the fires to destroy the buildings before controlling them.

The truth of this was difficult to gauge. Collecting statistics on response time and speaking to people from Adopt-a-Building, who were putting pressure on the fire department, persuaded me that the response time on the Lower East Side was officially as prompt as that in other sections of the city. However, this information contrasted with a fire in progress I witnessed around the corner from our office, in 1978, as recorded in my field notes:

> As we were getting ready to leave today, I heard fire sirens, and I looked out to see smoke all over the block. It seemed to be pouring out from the building on the southwest corner of Fourth and B. All the kids ran out (Nilda scaring Lisa by saying that it was Lisa's building that was on fire). Two fire engines and a squad car were blocking the intersection, and about a hundred people were collected on the southeast corner, looking up and across. I went over with Emilio first, then Millie and Bonnie joined us. On our way over, Emilio told me that he wanted to point out to me the cop who

had slashed the tires of his minibike. And he did. Officer Stoney was leaning against the squad car—a nasty type, with a fashionable hairdo and sideburns. Next to him, also leaning, was a lady cop with bleached blond long hair, her open jacket and open shirt revealing her cleavage (the temperature was about 17 degrees). They were looking at the fire and laughing. As we passed, I gave Stoney a dead fish look.

Firemen in a cherry picker from another engine company were breaking the windows in a third-floor apartment, and soon huge flames came roaring out of the window. I haven't seen anything like this since Warsaw. The flames seemed to go on for ages and yet we didn't see any water being poured. A gaunt Puerto Rican lady standing in back of me commented in a loud voice, "If it was their neighborhood they'd've already put it out! They think we're not human, so they wait until it's all burned down." Several people around her assented, nodding their heads. Meanwhile Stoney and his partner were chatting and laughing. People were looking at them with hatred. Also standing there and watching were Rocky and his dealing friends, their business temporarily interrupted. Finally, we saw water being sprayed inside the apartment, and after about fifteen more minutes, all the flames subsided. But not before the windows had been broken above and beside the burning apartment. Meanwhile, people had started descending down the fire escape, carrying children and small possessions. They had to jump the last flight down, because the last part of the emergency ladder, which is supposed to slide down, was frozen in place. So was I. As we slowly walked back we saw an elderly woman leaning against the wall of the building, sobbing.

A Red Cross vehicle had arrived, and a middle-class white woman was distributing coffee and sandwiches to the firemen, not to the victims. In an earlier interview with a Red Cross official, Paul had been amazed by her description of the "usual" Puerto Rican victims' reaction to disaster as "apathetic." Her description echoed the official, stereotypic view of Puerto Ricans by city agencies. Perhaps it was merely defensive: If you can't help them, dehumanize them. The gaunt lady had been right. But so was the Red Cross lady, had she bothered to analyze what she was witnessing. Shock, which may appear to an unsympathetic official as "apathy," is one response to overwhelming trauma. Weeping is another, not usually done in front of officials. Uncontrollable trembling and moaning are two responses of children, as is raging by adults and teenagers. Depression, abuse of analgesics and drugs, and mental health problems may follow, and have been documented cross-culturally (Figley 1985). We would have plenty of opportunities in the future to observe the whole range of responses as state-sanctioned violence increased the already high stress level of people's lives in the neighborhood.

Violent and corrupt cops worried me most. The national policy of the War on Poverty had ended, bringing with it increasing unemployment and underemployment, deepening the poverty of the people of the neighborhood. Low-level drug dealing by young men in all urban areas of the nation seemed to be the only alternative means of earning a living, which in turn began the national political response of the "war on drugs." In practice, on the local level, this new policy meant a new permissiveness for the police to suspend all respect for civil liberties. Not only did the police department form new undercover narcotics teams, largely unanswerable to civilian oversight, but ordinary policemen were given free reign to brutalize the population, and extraordinary temptations in the form of large sums of money or drugs were placed before them by the cartels who controlled the drug traffic from outside the neighborhood. The Ninth Precinct, on Fifth Street between First and Second Avenues, already had a poor reputation for its propensity for violence, and several policemen were said to be working hand in glove with the drug dealers. More concerned about the danger to our safety of rogue cops than of dealers, I followed up a news story about a policeman who had been effectively demoted by being transferred to a precinct in Brooklyn after allegedly fighting to expose corruption in the Ninth. I wrote him a letter asking for an interview and went out to Brooklyn when he answered affirmatively.

Officer O'Donnell seemed a brave and hardworking man. He lived on Long Island, where his two daughters attended parochial school; the tuition payments coupled with a high mortgage on his house compelled his wife to work also. Because they couldn't afford the Long Island Railroad fares, his wife took a bus and two subways to work. He told me several interesting things. First was his disapproval of the heavy reliance on informers, who were paid according to what the police thought their information was worth. They informed for three reasons: They needed the money; they were facing time and thought the district attorney would be lenient if he heard what he needed to hear; or they wanted to rub out the competition. Big sums of money had been allotted to the "war on drugs" and fed this parasitic class of informers.

Second, Officer O'Donnell told me that one of the reasons he had been transferred was because he had been pressing for a policy of going after drug buyers rather than dealers. He had been doing that by noting and tracing out-of-town license plates and going after suburban drug users, but he was promptly stopped. When I expressed enthusiasm for continuing this practice he cooled me down. He said you needed contacts in the police department to trace license numbers, and that I should stay as far away as possible from the Ninth Precinct, and be wary. There were some serious leaks there. His advice confirmed my suspicions. Reviewing the interview in my mind as I rode back on the subway, I felt very paranoid. A number of cops had seen me going to meet him at the Brooklyn stationhouse. Cops have good memories for faces. Cops carry guns.

Nevertheless, as summer gave way to autumn, and Indian summer prolonged the sentimental memory of relative plenty, I continued my habit of taking my chair across the street to catch up on my tan and observe the action. Only now I was mentally counting the out-of-town license plates that stopped near the corner of Avenue B for short tête-à-têtes with the young men who dealt.

Mothers on their way to and from errands stopped to chew the fat with me, including Mother Stern. One day Eti stopped to discuss her two new charges, a chihuahua with a broken leg, and Cheetah, the twelve-year-old boy with the dusty orange afro who had run away from the third foster home in which he had been placed. According to him, his addicted mother was living with her new husband in Boston, and the children had all been placed in separate foster homes. With the permission of the super, he was temporarily living in a basement room across the street from our office, together with Lefty, who had once again absconded from his stepmother uptown. The room had no bath or cooking facilities. While Eti tended to the feeding and bathing of Cheetah, her girlfriend and dancing buddy, "we go for sisters" Cuckie, was taking similar care of Lefty. As the days grew colder, so did the basement room—which by then had acquired the status of a clubhouse for the teenagers in the area—and the boys became permanent charges of the two women, without any support from the city. In spite of our advocacy, even after Cheetah had been living with her family for a year, Eti was unable to establish a legal foster-parent status and hence receive money for his care.

She had even more to worry about. Her younger daughter Maria had returned from Puerto Rico with her even younger and more irresponsible partner, Oliverio. Olie had no visible means of support. After being pressured for weeks, he commuted for two days with Cisco, Dolores's man, to a factory in distant Connecticut, then declared it was not worth the trouble.

At present, Eti worried about establishing a welfare claim for her daughter so that the young couple, who had a new baby girl, could live on their own until Olie found something to do, as his elder brothers had. They owned several stores, having wisely invested their variously earned savings, and had good reputations in the neighborhood, especially Rocky, the owner of the hole-in-the-wall smoke shop on the corner. Olie's brothers all thought Olie was too wild, and they were waiting to see if he would come to his senses before they offered him help.

In the meanwhile, Olie consorted with younger teenagers, giving them special education classes on the roof of our tenement, or in the basement. Very soon it turned out that he was both inept and unacculturated. He planned an elaborate "geesing trip" to Saks Fifth Avenue, dragging with him Cheetah, Lefty, Rafael-the-Kid, and Eti's youngest, José. The boys were spotted by the store's detectives as soon as they sauntered in, given the opportunity to swipe several "gold" chains, and immediately arrested. There was no end to the extra hours we had to put in in police precincts, with Legal Aid lawyers, and in Family Court. Nilsa and Bonnie were busy for several months, and Eti's broom got an extra workout. There was no end of jeering by the more moral or more sophisticated boys. The latter practiced their skills close to home, staging several "geesings" of the neighbors via fire escapes, where, if discovered, there was a high chance that only restitution would be required.

As Eti and I chatted, I mentioned idly that I had noticed José wearing some fancy new clothes. I did not add that he also suddenly seemed very generous with pizza money and had proudly revealed in the office a chest covered with hickeys that made him look as if he had been attacked by a bunch of leeches.

At that point, fixated on her dog, whose leg was in a cast, Eti didn't comment. (Sometime later, after I had also shared my wonderment in full detail with José's older brother, Emilio, he discreetly followed José to a gay man's retreat, where young boys were treated to money and "smoke" in exchange for sex. In the aftermath of being publicly dragged away by the ear, with an occasional kick and punch, José was imprisoned at home for several weeks, looking down sadly on the street action, while Eti paid a visit to the man and told him that the next time he invited any boys to his apartment, she would personally see him to prison.)

After Eti left, I saw Richie sauntering up the street with Olie. As they got closer I asked him why he wasn't in school. He mumbled something about being out on lunch. I thought, out to lunch more likely. Olie laughed. "When he saw you sitting there he said, 'You watch, she's gonna ask how come I'm not in school.'" Later that night I wrote in my field notes, "Well, at least he knows I'm watching. He's been hanging around too much with Olie, and Olie has been hanging around too much with the new drug dealers."

Indeed, a week or two earlier, a drug operation had moved into the top floor of our building. Holly's children, among others, were telling me they were afraid to go up to their apartment. The center of the activity seemed to be the two late-teenage sons of Señora Marta Madera, who with her husband, two younger teenage daughters, and younger retarded son had recently moved into the building. I don't think the señora or her husband, who both worked, or the younger children were aware of the older boys' activity, which took place during school hours, at the top of Mr. Stern's filthy, unpainted staircase. Coreen said the men were "injecting theirselves," showing me the motion of a syringe going in and out of her skinny arm. Fine doings, I thought to myself, trying to put two and two together, because at the same time, incidents of violent treatment of the children by the bodega owners began.

First it was David, Dolores's twelve-year-old, who got slapped around for allegedly putting a hole in a loaf of bread. Next Miguel was confronted by the mailman, off duty, who lived in the same building as the bodega. Miguel said he had only asked the man for a quarter, when the man started cursing him and his brother Richie and then pulled a gun on him. Miguel ran into the bodega for protection, whereupon the owners slapped him around, and for good measure, also cuffed Coreen when she started protesting. The bodega owners were then visited by Richie and David's older brother, Rafael-the-Kid. As self-appointed hector-protectors of their younger siblings in particular and of the children on the block in general, they were reported to have threatened to burn down the store in the event of further child hitting. Olie was said to have been a passive backup during the exchange, only modestly striking matches against a box he held in his hand. The bodega owners were said to have replied that if they ever caught any of the present boys in their store they would blow their heads off. A fateful prognostication. But the owners' anger was not about holes in a loaf of bread. The neighborhood was entering a higher and more deadly escalation of competition in the drug trade, and the children were sitting ducks.

All this was going on almost outside of our consciousness, like a deadly twister gathering force to level an already eroded land. The daily life of the neighborhood continued. At Christmastime Nilda, Paul, and I made the rounds, visiting, bringing modest presents, and staying for parties. We visited Meri in her new Chinatown home, where she was suffering from "nerves" because now she had to travel to Fourth Street every day to try to keep her eye on her boys who, in trying to avoid the fiercely reputed Chinese gangs, stuck to their old friends and old ways. She served us a big dinner of pernil and arroz con gandules. Her apartment was beautifully furnished with the fruits of her "investments," the sofa and easy chairs encased in plastic to preserve them. At Millie's we had to eat another meal, as Arturo's extended family drank sagely and engaged in conservative talk. Millie told me that a new drug operation had moved into the first floor, right behind our office.

While playing with the kids on the stairwell later, I confirmed her story. Just as we tumbled down, laughing and chasing each other with Max the Wolf in happy pursuit, I observed a man taking something from a hole in the door where the peephole should have been. The man looked as if he would have liked to stab me were it not for Max and the kids.

From there we proceeded to the top floor to visit Señora Madera, who with her bus driver husband had been enlivening Millie's dignified party and had invited us up. The corridor heroin operation or shooting gallery reported earlier by the children had either been discontinued or was taking a Christmas break. The Madera apartment was barely furnished, but the *coquitos* (rum with pineapple juice and coconut) soon flowed, even the seven-year-old retarded son finding them tasty. Although the father, Roberto, had his foot in a cast (ironically, it had been run over by a bus), he insisted on giving me a twirl, which is sort of okay when you're doing *merengue*, as the dance requires a bit of limping on one leg. So we danced a little to recorded music, with Holly's brood in attendance, and then left some presents for them, admonishing the children not to open them before Christmas. Holly and Jack were out doing their Christmas shopping. We next proceeded to Eti's apartment.

We found the whole family engaged in making pasteles. While Emilio was cutting up lean pork butt pieces (a man's work), Eti's daughters Clara and Maria and some other girls were washing tons of green bananas in a tub of water, peeling the hard skin off the plantains, and grating yuca by hand. Nilsa was there also, chopping olives. She had been firmly pulled into the clan. I think Eti was hoping that Nilsa would once again divorce her husband, which she did periodically (always promptly remarrying him), and for a change marry one of her boys. We were promised a large shipment of pasteles when we returned to pick up some of the children for a visit uptown.

Our last visit that day was to Señora Moreno, who appeared very sad. Not only did she not have any money for presents for her children, but something else weighed heavily on her mind. Millie had informed me that the señora's eldest daughter, Lisa, was pregnant. Millie said she herself had cried all night when she found out. "Now her life is ruined, like mine. Just like the rest of the women around here. We had so much hope for her. She looked like she was going to make it." Lisa had tried out for the High School of Performing Arts but, due either to the heavy competition or poor preparation, had not made it. Her brother, Paco, had also not won a slot at the High School for Music and Art. Lisa had started missing school and hanging around the "clubhouse," finding solace in the arms of Dolores's son Rafael-the-Kid.

The two prospective grandmothers, neither one of them yet forty and living next door to each other, had had it out earlier in the day in the hallway, Señora Moreno accusing Dolores of ruining her daughter's life by running a slatternly house, and Dolores responding that Lisa knew what she was doing. She didn't know what all the fuss was about, she said, she had had her first child at fourteen, and Lisa was already fifteen, a little older than Rafael. According to Nilsa, who had heard the fight and had dissected the implications with Dolores's friend, Eti, Dolores was wildly happy. She had only boys and was hoping that Lisa would not only become a daughter to her but also give her a baby girl. She said she hoped Señora Moreno would come around once the baby was born. Meanwhile she had proposed to Lisa that she attend Lamaze childbirthing classes as her "partner." The Kid, even though he was her son, could not be relied on for such an important responsibility.

During the next few weeks I tried, very gingerly, to find out whether abortion was being considered as an option. Lisa was one of the children identified as "at risk" by Ronna. So far in the pregnancy she had gained fifteen pounds, "probably due to the great amount of empty calories she is eating" (cakes, candy, soda) (Berezin 1979:38), while rejecting her mother's rice-and-beans and rice-with-milk combinations. Once a day she did eat one of Dolores's nourishing soups. Nevertheless, in Ronna's opinion, "Lisa's diet was at risk for all nutrients" (page 38), which was not a good starting point for bringing a healthy baby to term. But each of the major players in this situation, for different reasons, would not even entertain the thought of abortion. Señora Moreno, though she never attended church, seemed to really believe it would be a sin, whereas Dolores used the church's teaching pragmatically, as a justification for her desire for girl children. Lisa knew that becoming a mother would give her the status of a señora, and although this would mean in practice that she would no longer be allowed to play with virginal señoritas, she would be freed from her mother's vigilance *and* be able to engage in sex. As for the Kid, he would also gain some status as a "father," but no one took seriously any possibility that he could provide for Lisa and their baby, nor that the union would last.

It shortly became clear that the Kid and Olie (and sometimes Richie) were becoming useful to the new operation on the first floor. One of the boys hinted that they were getting paid to steer potential customers to the drugomatic behind our office. They were ranging within several blocks of our location, swaggering, chatting up girls, and acting cocky. Meri, very upset, showed me a note from school stating that Richie had been absent for ninety days. Like most of the mothers, however, she was reluctant to press her son for information as to his whereabouts or the source of his money. Unable to adequately clothe and feed their boys, especially as they got bigger, the mothers were in a bind and did not seem to admit to themselves the probable source of their sons' incomes.

The drug operation flourished. Now two beefy guards dressed in army camouflage uniforms, their "pieces" suggestively bulging in their pockets, stood at either side of our building's entrance, day and night. Now I had no problem in counting the out-of-state license plates, from New Jersey, Connecticut, Pennsylvania, Massachusetts. Among the New Jersey cars was a silver Porsche, apparently owned, or at least driven by, a young guy whose Polish parents, it was said, had grown up in the area. When he'd arrive, the guards sort of snapped to attention. Sometimes he brought cartons. One time, in the midst of a delivery, as Paul kept his ground, staring, the man challenged him. "What are you looking at?"

Paul answered, "At the pile of garbage over here," which brought one of the guards sauntering over, cool-like, idly flicking a switchblade on and off.

I was very worried. But local reactions were confusing. On the one hand, Nilsa told me that Eti had called the cops twice, from a street phone so that her number wouldn't be traced. The cops staged two dramatic raids, arrested several men, and then let them go because they had found no drugs. Obviously some leak, some warning system was operating. On the other hand, Eti's son, our own Emilio, told me, when I gave him a ride to school, that he had had a talk with those guys, that they knew all about us, and that we had nothing to fear. "Anyway," he said, "I know these guys from Twelfth street." Similarly, Millie's upright husband, Arturo, dismissed my worries with, "I know these guys. They wouldn't hurt nobody." Yet the mothers were getting worried. Delores warned the Kid publicly in our office that he had only a few days left to start behaving. She was going to have him "sent up to Spofford" (a jail for minors).

We watched helplessly as the chaos mounted. On the national level Lyndon Johnson's War on Poverty had been subtly and swiftly transmuted into its opposite, a war on the poor, but this war was undeclared. The children of the Lower East Side couldn't get the kind of social support that a named, declared war provides for the victim society. They were trying to survive in an endemic situation of an insidious, undeclared war, and they could not name the ultimate causes of their misery. Any other sector of the population in the United States enduring such long-term trauma would have had teams providing psychological support and federal emergency aid. How would the children, if they could not even name the enemy, deal with their unhealed wounds?

11

The Day of the Big Gun

I was on the office phone talking to Reverend Garcia about Dolores's younger son, Mateo, who was being forced to repeat the third grade on account of his small size. I got as far as the first sentence, when suddenly I heard a lot of screaming in the street and saw people running past the door. Eti poked her head in, shouting, "Call the cops! They've got a gun to his head!"

I excused myself to the reverend and quickly dialed 911. The woman on the other end wanted the description and ethnic identity of the victim and perpetrator. I simply repeated the address and told her to move it.

No sooner was I off the phone than Eti ran in, holding the biggest gun I have ever seen. She thrust it at me. "Here! Keep it! Hide it! Don't let them get it!" Seeing I was transfixed, she shoved it on the shelf of the counter that divided the front from the back office, threw her cloth bag over it, and pushed me against it for additional camouflage.

There I stood, on buckling knees, hiding a Magnum, but whose? The dealers' perchance? Might they not possess several matching ones and come calling for this particular one?

A few seconds later, Paul rushed in, pushing in front of him a fragile-looking Asian man, Chino-the-socialist's new partner. Paul turned around, shoved back the crowd pressing behind, slammed the door, and bolted it. Pale as a whisper, the man asked Eti, "Where is my gun?"

"We have it and we're saving it for the cops!"

The man started asking for his gun, and she started screaming, jabbing him with her index finger, "That was a twelve-year-old boy you put that gun to—that's a kid! I was there; all they were doing was throwing a ball in the garbage can!"

The man tried to interrupt, saying the kids were always harassing him, breaking down his property.

"YOU DO NOT PUT A GUN TO A KID'S HEAD!" screamed Eti.

There was a banging on the door. "Open up! Police officers!" Paul let them in, four of them, ready for action. Emilio sneaked in behind them.

They took us into different corners to get our stories. I showed one of them where the gun was. He took off his sunglasses and stared at Emilio, and only then did I realize I was talking to Officer Stoney. He lifted the gun, and pointing it at me, asked: "Is this the gun we're talking about?" I nodded, while sliding out of range. The gun followed my movement. Then, with a smile, Officer Stoney put it away. Meanwhile, the other two cops were handcuffing the culprit. I asked them if that was necessary. The man was so slender, and judging from the smell filling the office, so scared he had defecated in his pants. Officer Stoney tilted his head. "What if he has another gun and shoots you? Then I'd have a lot of paperwork to do." He smiled. A great sense of humor to boot.

They marched the man out, through people crowding the street to watch him get hauled off. All except the dealers, who were nowhere in sight. I slid to the stoop, trembling, laughing, and sobbing. Ronna was supporting the doorway, in pale, wide-eyed wonder, while Paul, Eti, and Emilio were giving a dramatic replay of the event.

Rafael-the-Kid, Cheetah, and Daniel had been playing "garbage basketball" outside of Chino's by now half-empty building. After several fires, Chino had hired or gone into partnership with the thin Asian, whom the kids called "Chino Two," stationing him to guard not only the building but also perhaps a heroin operation on the top floor. He had already brandished his gun at the kids once on the roof when they were simply flying their pigeons—or had they been paid by the first-floor drugomatic to disrupt that operation? In any event, his reaction to the ballplaying seemed excessive. He had rushed out of the building, yelling at them to move. When they didn't, he grabbed the Kid (who was fourteen, not twelve, but Eti deserved some dramatic license) and put the gun to his temple.

Everyone froze, Olie pointing to the frozen tableau, Eti silently screaming. Meanwhile, José slithered down the fire escape, grabbed an empty garbage can, and shoved it over Chino Two's head, knocking the gun from his hand. José had still been grounded "upstairs" for allowing himself to be "used by the faggots" but had in fact been hanging out the window, watching all the fun he was missing. Now he grabbed the gun and crouched, holding it with both hands and pointing it at the man. Paul mildly ordered José to hand the gun to his mother. After some tense consideration—and stronger requests from Paul and Eti—José did, and she ran with it into the office while Paul marched the man in, shielding him from the angry boys with his body.

"Our" dealers' guards had sat through the whole event without blinking an eye. They now had a customized van, in addition to a jeep, in which they sat across the street. Before the cops arrived they had driven off, but after the cops left they were back again at their posts. An hour or so later, Bob the carpenter, whom we hadn't seen since he was our host at his party, drove up in the van and had a conference with the guards. He didn't seem to be in the mood for renewing our acquaintance. His eyes went right over and past us.

People had various responses to the event. Arturo Fuentes said, "He should have blown the heads off a couple of them, then they would learn something."

"It's a little tough to learn something when you don't have a head," I said.

"No, I meant the rest of them. They must be doing something to drive a man to such desperation."

Overhearing this exchange, Emilio began arguing that the cops didn't do anything. "Look at that [drug] traffic, two hundred people a day!"

"That's nothing new," Arturo responded. "There's been dealing in the building for a long time."

But so *big*?" demanded Emilio. "Where you can't pass by it's so crowded, they start at seven in the morning, and keep coming as late as eleven, twelve, one? How would you like it if during a shoot-out one of your kids got killed—say she's just coming down the stairs and the cops are raiding? Or other dealers?"

"I know these people," Arturo said. "I grew up with them, I went to school with them. They won't do nothing."

As Paul, Ronna, and I left, the dealing activity was back in full swing, people entering our building only to exit a minute later—all colors, both sexes, well dressed, poorly dressed. It's a democratic country. No cops in sight, undercover or otherwise.

For a few days after, the boys teased Paul. "Hey, Paul, man, how come you didn't let us shoot him? Why you didn't let us beat him up?" Apparently Paul had graduated to the status of a "man."

This is what Eti attempted to accomplish for Olie and the Kid the following day in our office, assembling a number of people for this trial cum rite of passage. The theme seemed to be "On Becoming a Man." Eti played the role of prosecutor and judge, with Dolores as silent partner, Ronna and I as witnesses, and several teenage boys as audience (in need of a lesson), among them Richie and Miguel, along with Sosicho, David, and Johnny, other neighborhood boys. Locking the office door, she placed the two "defendants," Olie and the Kid, in two chairs in the center of the room. The audience, with Dolores, sat on the benches; Ronna and I stood behind the counter; and Eti paced and accused. I was stunned to hear that the problem, as she defined it, had to do with the accused's lack of respect for their women: Olie had been observed flirting with a girl two blocks away, and so had the Kid, although this was not as big a transgression, because he was not yet a father. "My daughter is your woman! She is my flesh and blood and she is the mother of your child, also my flesh and blood. You have to show her respect, otherwise get out! If you have to fool with other women, do it outside the neighborhood. And that goes for you, Rafael! Lisa is going to be the mother of your child!" And on she went, for about a half hour, all unfortunately in speed Spanish, so I didn't catch some of the finer points, which made everybody, including Eti herself, laugh. But I could guess from the movements accompanying them: a finger going in and out of a hole made by the other hand.

The two boys sat meekly, sheepish grins on their faces. When Olie tried to get in a word in English, she cut him down with a Spanish salvo. For once, they had to work on their native tongue. From time to time Eti glanced our way, to include us, but we were clearly the outsiders. When she was finished and the boys were allowed to escape, she told me to hurry up and write another grant to start an after-school program. I should also ask the Quakers to pay for the utilities. She was on a roll.

I was tired and wanted to go out to catch up on the dealing activity. But I didn't get to go until the end of the second episode Eti staged, which concerned her actions of the day before.

She was adamant that she had been right in disarming Chino Two. Arturo had an opposing view. He said that if the man had wanted to kill the Kid he would have done so instead of just putting a gun to his head. Without her interference, the Kid and the rest of them would have learned a lesson. Nilda tried to mediate: Yes, what Eti had done was correct, but the boys should still be disciplined; otherwise, if they kept annoying people, they might run into someone who would kill one of them. Somebody cynical, who had no ties to them.

Eti was livid. She felt they were censuring her instead of praising her courage. She left the office in a fury, saying, "*Ese pendejo!*" (that dangling piece of excrement) about Arturo.

Later I suggested to Nilda and Arturo that they give Eti a few days to recover from yesterday's trauma before offering sage advice. Nilda agreed; Arturo did not. He invited us to eat upstairs—or rather, as it turned out, to listen further to his point of view.

After serving us from a big pot of rice with gandules and pork ribs, he recounted some stories. He began with a complaint about his stepson Marco's behavior. At 3 P.M. he had told Marco to go upstairs and eat. Marco replied that it was too early, so Arturo repeated that he should go upstairs and eat and then he could come back down again. Marco went, but with an "attitude." He kicked the door open and threw himself on the bed. Then Arturo picked him up, slammed him into a chair, and told him, "Eat!" He analyzed the situation quite correctly, from an authoritarian point of view. Marco had been influenced by Jimmy Moreno, who never listened to his ineffectual mother, went in and out as he chose, and told her to "fuck off" when she tried to correct him—her native Spanish shielding her from understanding the depth of his insolence.

Arturo said that at that age (eleven), he had done everything his father told him to, there was no questioning, and his father was very strict. He had to show his father respect and never show he was angry. His mother and her brother were the indulgent ones. His mother's brother took him out to baseball games and bought him presents. But when he was sixteen, this indulgent uncle had taken him up for a bloody rooftop beating, the same rite-of-passage he was planning for Marco. "It's better if I do it to show him that he can't take on the world, than somebody else who might kill him." I asked if he would do the same thing for Chulito (his own son). He seemed puzzled by this question and finally said, "I guess I would, if he deserves it."

"It's all so messed up," I wrote in my field notes that night. "Welfare insures that mothers have no legal husbands living with them. Adult male presence is missing in a third of these homes—some are dead, some in prison, some dead to the world, addicted. The women overprotect. Naturally, given the circumstances, the boys begin to feel invulnerable, courting danger. But instead of what? Becoming authoritarian-trained drones? Great choices."

But I didn't have any answers. And the violence kept escalating.

One morning before entering the office, I went across to the bodega to buy cigarettes, wondering why there were two police cars on the block. When I tried to enter the store, I realized the door was locked, although several people were inside. One of the three men standing outside told me that somebody "got sick" inside. Then I noticed that the lower part of the glass on the door was broken. As my gaze continued downward, I realized I was standing in a puddle of blood and melting snow. Sick, all right.

I joined Rene, a fourteen-year-old who was watching from the other side of the street, and he told me in the prophetic tone he had that a man had been shot in a holdup. "He wanted money, but the owner liked that money. He stays open all hours, late at night, because he wants that money. . . . So they shot him—first one shot at him and then the other ran in and shot him. This neighborhood is getting bad again."

Harry, Pam's partner, explained further. A veteran of the Vietnam War, he had been treated for combat shock after his discharge and was very alert to the sound of gunshots. He was always the first one on the scene, passionately reconstructing an event. He told me that two men with guns had held up the Dominican owner the night before. The Dominican fought them off with his machete, and his sister helped by knocking the holdup man's arm upward. But he was shot by the second man in the arm and leg. He was recovering in the hospital.

Inside the office, no one seemed to have been aware of the holdup. Nilsa was hassling on the phone with Stern because the temperature inside the office was below freezing. The building had had no heat or hot water for the past three days. Stern was claiming he had ordered 2,000 gallons of oil last Friday and that only 500 gallons had been delivered. He had been "robbed," he said. It seemed to be warmer outside, so everybody went out to see what had happened, joining the people collecting in small groups in front of the store and across the street.

I took myself on a mission to find Stern and came across him sunning himself in front of his office (maybe he gave himself no heat or hot water also). He was unshaven, had a sweater on, and held a monkey wrench in his hand. I asked him politely about the heat, and he launched into a lament of how the oil company insisted they had put 2,000 gallons of oil into the tank and that something must be wrong with his gauge. I suggested that perhaps the delivery man had helped himself to 1,500 gallons, and Stern earnestly responded that this was not possible on two counts. "Number one, steal they may," he said, "but only a hundred, two hundred gallons tops, because they can claim it's in the pipes. Number two, the man who made the delivery is the brother-in-law of the owner of the company, and I have known him for twenty years." Then he gave me a long story of how this morning the oil truck had gotten stalled on Houston Street, how another one would come as soon as the old one returned, and so on. All of this punctuated with little jabs at my arms and stomach with the monkey wrench.

I told him I hoped the oil would come soon, and then asked if he had heard about the holdup. He had, but that was nothing. He launched into another holdup story, about the Upper East Side. "And the rents there are $450, $500, $1,500, even $2,000!"

Tired of getting poked, I said good-bye and returned to the office. Although the truck did arrive within an hour of our conversation, the heat did not come on until five o'clock because the super said he was waiting for a mechanic to bring a clean oil filter. It was very painful to sit in the office, even with two electric heaters on. I was feeling deeply for the tenants upstairs who had had no heat for three days. Ginny told me her mother had to spend the whole day in bed, covered with every blanket in the house. Delila, who lived on Avenue B, said there was no heat in her building either. They were trying to keep the place warm with a stove. Johnny said it was the same story in his house. All over the Lower East Side, children went to school to keep warm. "I guess the schools *do* perform a function," I wrote in my notes.

Nobody, at least nobody we knew, was arrested for the holdup attempt and the shooting of the Dominican grocer. But things were getting seriously out of hand. Olie had been arrested and then released as a suspect in the mugging of a woman. The Kid had been arrested and kept at Spofford over the weekend on suspicion of mugging as well. (Dolores had no money for bail, even had she been inclined to bail him out.) When he returned I inquired what the experience had been like. "Oh, it was OK. They gave good food, and I fought off fifteen guys who tried to jump me." The younger kids, especially Johnny and Jimmy, listened to his tale, totally absorbed, their eyes shining. Then Rene piped in, adding a warning for the benefit of the younger kids from his own experience: "When they put you in, it ain't gonna be no picnic. You gonna cry all night for your mother." He knew. He had been convicted of stealing a bassoon from his junior high school. He was musical.

Then one evening as we were getting ready to leave and Emilio was trying to learn how to roller skate in old lace-up girl's skates someone had lent him, a squad car drove up and stopped in front of our office.

Two large cops got out, grabbed Olie, who had been combing his hair in a car mirror, and rammed him against the car. Emilio staggered up on his skates and asked the cops, "Why you did that?" Whereupon they grabbed him too, still on his skates, frisked and handcuffed both of them, and shoved them into the back of the squad car. Since several of us were now asking why they did that, one of the cops rudely told us to come to the Ninth and find out. After informing Eti, we trotted over. But at the precinct house we were told we couldn't see the boys— they were being questioned upstairs in connection with a robbery. Nilda and Eti stayed there until 1 A.M., demanding to see them, or at least to learn what they were charged with. The rest of us went back.

At 3 A.M., Emilio returned, barefoot, carrying his skates. He was bloody and bruised all over and said the cops kept slugging him between each other, as he rolled between them and kept falling on his skates. Eti and Nilda took him to Bellevue, where he was diagnosed as having an injured kidney. There was blood in his pee, said Eti.

With Nilsa, Maria went from one precinct to another trying to find Olie, who had disappeared.

We got started on a letter complaining about police brutality.

Next day we held an emergency meeting, trying to assess what was going on. We began by trying to analyze Olie's situation:

Nilsa: His family doesn't want to do anything. His mother does not want to get involved. . . .

Jagna: So how come Señora Medina wants to get involved so badly?

Nilda and Nilsa (*in unison*): Because of Maria.

Jagna: For Maria it would be much better if he stayed in jail.

Nilsa: Yes, but Maria is madly in love with this guy.

Jagna: He's a hoodlum.

Bonnie: People fall in love with hoodlums.

Nilda: He is not a hoodlum, he is just a mixed-up kid.

Jagna: He holds people up, he takes small kids stealing; what kind of bullshit is that?

Nilsa: I had spoken to his mother during the week. She told me she is tired of his bullshit, she won't do anything until she speaks with her older son. This isn't something that's just been happening lately. He's been getting in trouble since he was a kid, since he was thirteen years old. She's about had it. . . . But Señora Medina still doesn't give up, and it is because of Maria, she wants to get Olie out [of jail downtown where he is detained].

A discussion of Olie's culpability disclosed that even his court-appointed attorney believed he'd have to go to prison.

Paul: Maybe Señora Medina is just making a big effort, and she knows it can't be done, but [wants to show] she did her utmost?

An exchange followed about how Olie lied to Señora Medina and how the boys all supported him.

Nilda: The thing is that Emilio is taken in by him [believes in Olie's innocence]; you know, they really stand by him.

Nilsa: He swore that his daughter should die if he was the person that mugged.

Nilda: He knows his daughter is not going to die!

Bonnie: The point is that the kids all believe him.

Jagna: He'll swear to anything now.

Nilda: Señora Medina feels like a big mother.

Nilsa: I don't think she's still given up—she's hoping that tomorrow they're going to lower the bail.

Jagna: This is just so strange.

Nilsa: Señora Medina told Maria that if he gets out she'd better straighten his ass . . . but then, Maria, she really let's him have his way. She says trying to keep him home would make him a sissy. And she says, "He's a *hombre* [man], he's a macho, and you can't hold him too tight, and a macho never loses." You know—that kind of bullshit talk. If she really put some more effort in sitting down to talk to him and say, "Look, you're staying out? Fine. Goodbye and forget about me and about the baby."

Jagna: I think she's afraid of that.

Nilda: It takes a lot of nerve to do that.

Nilsa: The thing is, I could get rid of him easier than she. I could get rid of him easy (*smacks her hands*) just like that! (*All laugh*) I'd put his clothes out the window!

The issue of bail money exposed divisions of opinion even within the Medina family. Although Maria was his sister, Pablo told Nilsa that he felt guilty and depressed because he didn't want to contribute to the bail for Olie's release. He complained that his mother appropriated all his wages so he couldn't even save enough to move out, but that nevertheless he was treated with disrespect, like a bobo, by his family. Further discussion disclosed that neither Eti's oldest daughter, Clara, nor her husband were willing to contribute to the bail either. The staff concluded that even though jail was not the best place to learn one's lesson we would not contribute to the bail.

But Eti did not give up. Since Nilsa and I were the only staff members with sufficient bank accounts, we made ourselves scarce all day Friday, feeling the pull of our social obligation so strongly that we drove to the end of Long Island to become totally unreachable. Driving three hours each way, we spent another hour morosely freezing at the stormy tip of Montauk Point. We hoped that at the very least Olie would have to spend a weekend at Riker's Island (the city's mammoth jail). He did. But we got roped in anyway. Eti inveigled a friend to put up her small savings for bail, so Nilsa and I became obliged to contribute too. When Olie was released, his greetings to his mother and wife were, "It's about time."

Still idealists, we drafted a letter to the police about police brutality. We also visited Bellevue to see Emilio, who was quickly improving. The doctors were drafting a report of their findings of his injuries. By a coincidence, Lisa was also in Bellevue. She had developed a serious kidney infection due to her pregnancy and poor physical state. Now we could visit both at the same time.

Meanwhile the dealing in our building continued relentlessly. One day the two guards showed up wearing black suits. They had attended a funeral and hadn't had time to change. Their immediate boss, the Polish man with the gray Porsche, had been gunned down while walking with his Puerto Rican girlfriend on Avenue D. A pregnant woman had also been killed in the crossfire. But the business continued.

Because the upstairs pipe was leaking sewage all over my desk again, I had a good reason to visit Stern again. When I arrived he was leaning back in his old leather chair, bulging more than ever, in the midst of explaining to a dark young couple that if they didn't have a month's security *and* a month's rent together they were wasting their time trying to get one of his apartments. The couple was standing on the entrance side of the counter, and he let them ponder his words while turning a welcoming smile in my direction. "Yes, sweetheart, what can I do for you?" Ma Stern, perching on an old wooden chair in the back, piped in, "How are you? Haven't seen you in a long time. I didn't recognize you." I told them about the pipe dripping onto my desk. Stern was fatherly. "Just move the desk and your papers out of the way, dear. I have the plumber coming in, maybe today, maybe tomorrow. Tell the super he should come around to see you." Then he returned to the pondering couple and repeated what he had told them a minute ago. When they left, I told him there was another problem.

The people to whom he had rented the apartment behind our office were dealing drugs. I said I believed that three mothers from the building had already come in to complain to him about it. "It's really important that something be done—we have many children living in the building."

Mother Stern interrupted, "And I bet half of those kids are using those drugs!"

I said patiently, "No, this is, you know . . ." and I started sticking an imaginary needle in my arm.

Mr. Stern took a deep, thoughtful puff on his unlit cigar. "Well, the people who signed the lease were a lovely couple. He has a steady job. It's just him, his wife, and the child. It's all in the lease." Mother Stern said, "Show her the lease, Ronald!"

"I don't have to show her the lease. Where is my coffee, Mother?!"

As she retreated to the hot plate, he told me, "My friend Irving, where they used to live, recommended them as good tenants. And the super, he is a lovely man, told me they are good tenants. He can usually sniff them out. And if they"—here he makes a drinking and then an injecting motion—"he tells them he already has a deposit on the apartment. I rely on him, because I can't tell even if they're falling off their feet. I mean, if they fall off their feet in front of me, I can tell."

After I told him we saw a procession of people going in and out of the building all day, he admitted that he had sent a "hand delivered" note to the tenant, asking to see him, but the tenant had not responded. Mother Stern wanted to know how I knew there was a procession of people going into the building.

"They're out there *observing*, Mother!" Stern moaned. "Well, that's funny," she sniffed, "because just the other day I stood in that corridor for two hours and I didn't see anybody." While I doubted that she had spent two hours in that freezing corridor, I reminded her that the look-outs posted outside would hardly let anyone come in while she was present. I left, in no way reassured.

Despite our good reputation we were kept intentionally confounded; people wanted to keep us from looking too deep, to keep us confused about the resistance that smoldered beneath the surface, where every rule of the, well yes, bourgeois world was meant to be broken. I was allowed a peek, now and then, but I think even Nilda kept things from me that she didn't think I would understand. And we were continuously tested.

For example, Count Augusto walked in one afternoon wearing a serious look that telegrammed he was on a mission. A sort of diplomatic mission, it turned out. There had been a fatal stabbing on Avenue B for which one of the Gatos had been arrested. The Gatos were a feared gang, rumored to be providing protection to one of the former Adopt-a-Building female officials who now dealt cocaine. Cheetah claimed that one of the members of the gang was his older brother. Rocky, Olie's brother, seemed to know them well too. Now Gusto proposed to me that I receive a delegation of three Gatos for "some serious dealing" (prison talk for negotiating), on the condition that no one else be present in the office. Paul was very opposed to this, but he contented himself with staying posted outside the door, his hammer literally up his sleeve. I couldn't resist it. I was too hungry for any information that might help me unravel what was happening in the neighborhood.

But I blanched when the three beleathered, chain-clanking, boot-stomping specimens entered the office and Gusto bolted the door. The spokesman told me that this here "brother" wanted to give himself up in the stabbing "because they got the wrong man." The cops, that is. They wanted me to accompany the brother to the police station so he could safely give himself up "before the cops jump all over him." I gazed into the brother's eyes. Up to now, he had kept them occupied elsewhere. But now I got him. Acting cooler than I felt, I asked, "Did you do it?"

"No," he mumbled, maybe out of practice of lying.

"Well then, I can't do it," I said.

The speaker tried to save the situation by telling me that while both the arrested and the real killer had families to support, this brother didn't, and he was willing to take "the fall."

"You have to understand," I said, "that I have a responsibility for all the children here. I can't afford to get arrested for perjury," pulling the old-woman-who-lived-in-a-shoe routine, but believing it fervently as I spoke. They accepted my excuse gallantly, thanking me for my time. Count Gusto left last, telling me sotto voce that not a word of this must pass beyond these walls. I was left bewildered by what Gusto had hoped to accomplish for himself with this deal. Maybe to show how well connected to us he was, or maybe to demonstrate that we wouldn't inform the police about local confidences, so his hanging out with us was all right?

Yet I also felt we had passed some sort of test, but of what? I knew something about these guys from way back, when I had been temporarily detained by their brothers-in-arms, the Hell's Angels, while doing student research for Margaret Mead's field methods course. Afterward, she had sternly warned me not to get into any agreements with them because they tended to break them—with untoward results. Later our team had become well acquainted with a member of another motorcycle club—the *Moto Nuevos*, related to both the Gatos and Angels—who was intelligent and trustworthy. He had described for us how the FBI had tried to either buy or bully information about the Young Lords during the Civil Rights protests on the Lower East Side, from him and other gang members, and how several of the guys, brutal and conservative by nurture, had turned into police informers. He recounted being held in a basement prison by the FBI, "asked" to identify photograph after photograph of men who had been his childhood buddies. He didn't recognize a single one, he said, even though he was beaten to improve his memory. Now he was sweet on Nilda. He gave children rides around the block on his motorcycle.

So what did I know? At the time, I thought that no one did what they said they did. No one reported what they really saw. Only my team members could be trusted, up to a point, to search for "truth" and to try to disentangle it from ideology. The state through its media mouthpieces was embroidering upon its cloth of ideology. Slogans did not mean what they said.

When the nation's leaders paid lip service to the well-being of children but instituted de facto policies that militarized their communities, they created a climate of a lack of respect for poor children's rights and lives. Being devalued by policy and default led adults and children to place negative evaluations on their own and their peers' lives, leading to abuse and neglect and, eventually, involuted fratricide. The national indifference to the well-being of its smallest citizens trickled down locally and brutalized daily life.

I was paranoid after the incident with the gun. It didn't really matter what its provenance may have been. Having read about and heard of secret government Cointelpro actions, sting operations, and other provocateur activities in the neighborhood, and having seen some of the mid-range dealers in action, there was a good reason for us to at least feel as if we were tiptoeing through quicksand.

12

A Death Foretold

One fine day in April I was leaving Bellevue, where I had been visiting Lisa, now Rafael-the-Kid's "woman" by virtue of her six months' pregnancy. Although malnutrition, in addition to a kidney infection, had landed her in the hospital, Lisa refused to eat both the hospital food and the nutritious *delicias* her mother brought her: corn soup, rice pudding, gandules, avocados, pears, apples, all items faithfully recorded by Ronna from Lisa's bedside. So taking a turn, and using my recently acquired Ph.D. title to call myself "doctor," I penetrated the inner chambers of Bellevue and traced the interns in charge of Lisa to a staff room where they were busy telling a hilarious story. Trying to speak with the voice of authority, I requested that Lisa be given fortified milk shakes. The interns quickly saw through my ruse and belittled my dietary credentials, but since theirs were also rudimentary, the conversation became fairly friendly when I explained Lisa's situation as that of an acculturating teenager. By the following day, she got not only her milk shakes but also a lot more attention. She started improving rapidly.

Just as I emerged from Bellevue's gates, self-satisfied with my mission's success, I noticed our "new" old car pulling in, driven by Paul and crammed with the boys. They all looked pathetic, their eyes red. They told me that Olie had been shot, that they were coming to see what they could do. Both the Medinas and the Rojos, Olie's family, were already at the hospital, accompanied by Nilda and Nilsa. Olie and Maria had arrived by ambulance.

Within a few hours we learned that Olie had died. In shocked small groups we returned to our office, where the staff reconstructed the day's events:

Nilda: I was sitting upstairs with Maria. I had bought a pair of shoes for her baby, Sally. All of a sudden this guy bangs on the door, comes in, and says, "Maria, Maria, *tiraron a Olie!*" [They have just shot Olie!] So she just ran out, and I think Clara's husband also ran out, and by the time I went down the police wasn't there [yet]. Maria was there, and they wouldn't open the [bodega's] door for her. And she started cursing, saying, "He's in there

shot, and they won't open the door! *Maricones, hijos de una gran puta!*"
[Faggots, sons of a great whore!] The kids meanwhile, I saw Miguel
[Valiente], he was very upset, I mean, he's into discovering every dead
body around, and so he was crying, and I tried to hold him, and he says,
"Oh, those motherfuckers!" and he let me hold him a bit. But then, the
one who was really upset was José. Daniel was crying, Richie was crying,
and they were just buzzing around like bees. And three or four of them
had sticks, very strong sticks, so I was just around them [holding them
back]. Maria was running around like crazy, and I felt like it was already
ugly, ugly, ugly.

He was lying where the counter is, where they have the potato chips,
and you could see him. So the kids were really wild, they wanted to tear
down the window, so I say, "Look, you kids, you are only going to get into
more trouble, and he doesn't need a broken window. He's already
sprawled out there." Then José, he was really very, very upset, and he just
clung to me and he said, "Nilda, make it stop! Do something, do something! Tell me it's not true. Do something." Well, there was nothing that I
could say so I said, "José, he's shot in the head. He's not dead yet."

Paul: When I came out I saw all the kids crying. All the kids were crying, the
girls, everybody had tears streaming down their faces, and some of the
women were crying.

Paul went on to describe Richie and Daniel's version of events: They had been
ordered out of the store by the owners. José ran to get Olie, who ran down from
the roof with Rafael. An argument with the owners ensued. When Rafael pulled
out a box of matches and threatened to burn the place down, the owners grabbed
Olie, and one of the Dominicans came charging out from the back of the store
with a gun. The boys scattered as the man started shooting. Olie was shot four
times. But somehow one of the Dominicans was shot in the stomach during the
struggle, by someone, *not* his brother, who wrestled the gun from the owner, according to the boys; and, as I was later to find out, another Dominican was
wounded with a machete.

Nilda: So then the ambulances came. They took one of them out in a patrol
car. But I went in with Maria, because the cops weren't going to let her in.
. . . The cops didn't know what was happening, they just saw all these people around that were ready to . . . Maria was still crying, she didn't know
what she was going to do, so I says, "Well, Maria, maybe I have to ask one
of the cops." So I told them, "Look, that's his wife, she should be in there
with him." So the man took me to the second police, so then the second
police didn't pay much attention, so he took me to the third. So I says,
"Look, I was just sent over because that's his wife, and she has to be at his
side. They won't let her in." So I went in with her. . . .

Two ambulances arrived, the first taking the wounded Dominican away. The crowd that had collected by then was urging the ambulance drivers to hurry up and take Olie. At this point in our meeting, Emilio entered the office and now answered my question about the location of the wounds:

Emilio: They shot him in the head.
Nilda: His eye was out.
Emilio: That's why he didn't have much chance to live.
Nilda: His eye was out. You know his eyes were big. Now they were bigger.
Emilio: One of the bullets must have—
Nilda: —gone through his eye. Because his eye was out and his face was swollen, he was green, ah—you know, I mean, when you get shot in the head—
Emilio: —that's the first thing that goes, is your brain—
Nilda: —You know? So I saw this, and Maria, Maria, did they give her any sedatives or anything?
Emilio: Yeah, they did.
Nilda: Maria was just, I mean, Maria just screamed and screamed, she just cried and screamed, and the policeman, he was very nice, he says, "I can't leave you in here because there's too many people."
So I says, "Okay, as long as his wife is here."
Emilio: Olie didn't do nothing. They thought that he was going to jump in, so when they think that Olie'd jump them, they figure, "Hey, we gotta do something!" They run to the back of the store, they got their piece, and they gave him . . . and you only need just *one* person. You don't have any *one* Dominican out there, you had *seven* of them, seven grab him. Then, you know, I mean, *once*, in the leg, is enough, just to wound him—not to *kill* him. They held him, and the other guy shot him.
Paul: José was very angry. I saw him with a stick at a certain moment. They were all very angry. There were a lot of people around the ambulances, and everyone was shouting "Hurry up! Hurry up!" Then I met Rafael and Cheetah, Cheetah was crying too. They wanted to burn the store, they were angry, they wanted revenge, you know. They came into the store's building, and they mumbled they wanted revenge.
Nilda: *This killing has got to stop!* You know they could very easily kill somebody, and that's not right! It has to be stopped because everybody on the fucking block that didn't like Olie, that was always talking about Olie or something, now, all of a sudden they're getting into a lynch mob [against the bodega owners]. And that's bad. The man there was saying, "Well, we shouldn't burn it because there's people upstairs," but Joe was saying, "Oh, we're gonna burn it!" I know that fucking Joe, that Joe is crazy—you know, that Polish guy [Basia Plotek's son]? What the hell did he do with Olie? [What was his connection to Olie?] He's drugged up to his ass right

now. [And *that* probably was his connection to Olie and to the drug dealers in our building.]

People in the neighborhood were very upset. Pam's partner, Harry, vigilant as ever to the sound of gunshots following his Vietnam experience, vividly replayed the events for me, commenting that it took four adult men to hold Olie down and kill him. "They're not men, they're mices," concluded Harry. As an immediate measure, the staff decided to "invite" the boys to stay at our apartments in different parts of the city. The parents eagerly accepted our offer. Daniel, who lived below Delancey Street, had never received permission to go on trips with us, but I called his mother and explained the situation. She thanked me, but said she would send him to his grandmother's house in Harlem, which she did.

We kept the boys away from the neighborhood until the last day of the wake. The three boys who were staying at my house slept for fourteen hours at a stretch, refusing to listen to music or to watch TV out of respect, they said, for Olie. But they did manage to smoke a joint in my basement. They were constantly calling home, and it was obvious that they were chafing to get back, even though on previous occasions a visit to my house had been a treat for them. Back in the neighborhood on the day of the funeral, they ran upstairs to their homes and then just as quickly flocked to the roof. Paul joined them there and reported that all of them had gathered together and were flying the pigeons. "They look fantastic, you know. I was looking up at their wings, and the sun was pouring through them. And the boys were saying, 'This is Olie, the white one. That's Olie flying.'" No matter what his actual misdeeds had been, in death Olie was acquiring a status even nobler than his former Robin Hood "rep." His allure for the boys probably lay in his disobedience to adults, but maybe even more in his flaunting of the rules of American society to which his own family subscribed enthusiastically.

The wake and the funeral revived the tensions between the Rojos and Medina families, and between them and the boys. According to Nilsa, even before the doctors had pronounced Olie dead at Bellevue, the Medinas were swearing vengeance, whereas the Rojos, who were Pentecostal, favored Higher Judgment. The Medinas had said, "We're gonna get him! We're gonna get vengeance!" Olie's family had said, "Look, leave it in the hands of God. Why should you get yourself in trouble? He's the true judge, and He's gonna judge them—leave it in the hands of God." But Maria had said, "Whaddya mean, leave it in the hands of God? *I am*, I swear I'm gonna kill them!"

Nilsa also said that Dolores was advising the Medinas to wait: "Let it cool down, and when it cools down, we're gonna get them." The animosity and different socioreligious orientations of the two families continued throughout the week of the funeral. The Medinas complained that the Rojos did not even let them know at what time Olie would be buried. The Rojos were paying for all the funeral expenses and unilaterally decided to hold a Pentecostal service. Underlying their aloofness was their disdain for Maria for being only Olie's "woman," not his legal wife. It turned out that Olie's mother had been paying the couple's rent, even though she considered Olie the black sheep of the family. Now it came out that Maria had used that rent money to get Olie out of prison, giving his family another point of blame to pin on her. There was blaming all around.

In the Fernandez's funeral parlor the differences continued. Olie lay peacefully in an open casket, his face heavily covered by makeup, his folded hands stiff with a cross inserted between them. The Medinas did most of the wailing. Maria, thin and haggard in spite of the small rise of her pregnant belly, stood by the casket sobbing, *"Tan sola, tan sola"* (So alone, so alone), while her sister Clara alternated between bodily supporting her and hissing out in the foyer that she was going to "kill that Richie, because he always gets other people in trouble." The two families sat on separate sides of the funeral chapel. I went out and found Richie, Daniel, Rafael, and José standing outside on the street, looking downcast and guilty. Eti, who had started to slip Valiums into Emilio's coffee when he was younger to keep him peaceful and studious, was now distributing them openly to all her children, like vitamins.

The service was conducted in an uplifting, almost cheerful tone by the Rojos's minister. Just before the casket was to be closed, people started crowding around it to touch Olie for the last time, their caresses disturbing the careful layer of makeup to reveal the purplish trauma beneath. Then Maria and Clara sent up a tremendous wail, and their fifteen-year-old brother, Jorge, ran vomiting to the men's room.

After the coffin was closed, the women went outside and watched as the boys bore it out to the waiting hearse. A Puerto Rican flag, on loan from the Gatos, was draped over it. The hearse and the flower car started up slowly, followed by ten cars, including our own. Earlier I had tried to discover from the driver of the hearse where we were going, but he could not point out the destination on my map and had only told me to follow the car in front. The procession went slowly through the neighborhood, around the blocks where Olie had grown up and lived. Some Medina family friends riding in our car said it was his last opportunity to say good-bye. On Avenue B, a van driven by Vincent Finelli joined the procession, and several boys jumped into it. Finelli, who with his wife had formed a Lower East Side branch of an organization called the Fourth World Movement, had taken Olie and several other boys camping when they were younger. As one of the boys now recalled it, "Vince drove us to this big forest in Vermont, unloaded the gear, got back in the van and said, 'So long fellows, see ya in two days,' and took off." Now the procession stopped for a light on our block, and about ten members of the Gatos gang—wearing their formal duds of black leather, chains, red bandannas, and cowboy hats—jumped into several of the waiting cars. By their cheerful *holas* passed from car to car, it looked as if they had already started the ceremony with spirits and such. Their attendance imparted a bizarrely carnivalesque air to the rest of the funeral proceedings.

By the time we got to the Holland Tunnel, we had already lost the hearse. We emerged in New Jersey, steered by a stopped car with Gatos hanging out, waving their bandannas to point the way. Cars were passing us on either side, their horns blaring. Up ahead, the hearse was traveling at about seventy miles an hour as we all tried to catch up with it, passing cars on the wrong side, weaving in and out of traffic, speeding. The Fernandez family had a lot of business to attend to; the hearse had to get back to handle the next customer.

As Nilsa later pointed out, it was a good thing that the New Jersey state troopers had apparently taken the day off. As she described her trip the following day,

Oh my God! We were racing! . . . I think I hit ninety-five to reach Julio [who was driving in the car ahead of her]; I didn't want to get lost. It was like flying. I told everyone, "Close the windows" so we could go faster, because the air pushes, and I finally caught up. I was behind a white van that had all the kids. All of a sudden, the tire, it started losing air, there was too much weight on the van. I see a flat so I decide Julio is going to stay with him, I'm gonna go in the left lane, catch up to all the cars, and stop them and tell them what happened. Well, I almost went under a truck. I raced like you wouldn't believe, and I was honking and honking my horn, and I finally caught up to the limousine that had the casket and the one that had the flowers. And I told them, "Wait, wait, the kids are lost back there!" and he didn't want to stop. I forced the guy with the coffin to stop by stopping right in front of him. He couldn't go on top of me. So anyway, I made them stop. Everybody pulled over to the right. You should have seen those racers!

When we finally arrived at the Rosedale cemetery, the hearse and some of the other cars had yet to arrive. We milled around, wondering whether we had come to the wrong cemetery or if the service was already over. It was said later, among the boys and the Gatos, that Olie didn't really want to be buried. It had been his spirit that caused the flat tire and other uncommon events. Paul and Bonnie construed the events as something out of a strange film. In different ways we were all producing distancing narratives for coming to grips with a young person's death:

Paul: It was like a Mexican movie. . . .
Bonnie: It was a Fellini movie. . . . Going out there I thought, "Why is everyone in such a hurry? I've never seen a funeral like this." Robbie, who was driving [the car she was in], must have thought that since this was a funeral procession we all had the right of way.
Nilsa: We didn't see one cop car. If we did we'd all be in jail. I decided never to go to anybody's funeral.

At the graveside—a raw gash in the red earth—the minister said a few words and the coffin was lowered. For a second it looked as if Maria would jump in after it—she swayed over the grave, seemingly half conscious, but her mother and brothers grabbed her and held her back. Olie's mother had remained in the car, unable to face her son's burial. Her sister was standing in for her, surrounded by Olie's brothers and their wives, in silence. Tearing flowers from the massed wreaths, first the women then the children and the Gatos threw them into the hole in the ground, finally covering the coffin. I walked away toward a more heavily wooded part of the cemetery. Here the monuments were more intricate, some with angels, moss covered, many decorated with fading turn-of-the-century photographs encased in glass, with inscriptions of Italian names. Walking back to the car I noticed that the newer section contained mostly Spanish names, many recently engraved, showing short life spans. The stones were straight slabs. The Latinos had followed the Italians into the old neighborhoods, they filled the old Italian funeral parlors, and now they were transported into the Italian sections of suburban cemeteries. Here was material evidence of ethnic succession.

The two families were finally reconciled during the rosario held at the Medinas' apartment for nine consecutive days after the funeral. Doña Mercedes led prayers and chanting that Nilda said would help Olie's spirit finally rest. The fact that members of the Rojos family attended, even though attending a rosario conflicted with Pentecostal teachings, added an otherworldly insurance for Olie's spirit, not to mention reestablishing harmony between the living. Friends on both sides attended, including Nilda and Bonnie.

And so Olie's spirit was temporarily put to rest. But the Medinas' need for justice, for compensation, was not quenched.

13
Settling a Blood Feud

I didn't go to the rosario for Olie's soul. I was busy collecting and analyzing information about the potential fallout from the growing hostility toward the Dominicans in the neighborhood. Even though one of the owners was still in serious condition at Bellevue, the store opened for business on the day of the funeral. Echoing Harry's verdict, people were saying that not only were the Dominicans murderers—with no style because it took so many men to kill one boy—but they were also so greedy that they couldn't even show some respect for the dead. I heard Rene repeating the magic number seven, the number of Dominicans who had purportedly subdued Olie while an eighth one shot him. As the story acquired fairy-tale dimensions, the Gatos increasingly congregated in Eti's apartment, and the boys conspired darkly in the corridors of the building, going mute whenever one of the staff passed by. On a visit to the family to pay my respects, I noticed several cans of gasoline in Eti's bathroom. Our endless homilies to anyone who cared to listen that setting the bodega on fire would endanger innocent lives in the upper apartments seemed to fall on deaf ears. Fires had been set throughout the neighborhood for far less noble reasons.

At staff meetings we discussed the increasingly dangerous situation. Blame, which the Medinas had displaced onto the Rojos and the boys during the funeral, was once again clearly flowing across the street in the direction of the bodega. A Mexican woman who was the new super in the Dominicans' building was suspected of spying for them. She had chatted up Eti in a friendly way, supposedly trying to pump her for information about the Puerto Rican intentions. Rumors flew among the kids that Dominicans from below Delancey Street were arming themselves and massing for a preemptive onslaught. This in turn prompted paranoid preparations for a "first strike" by the residents. Even the guards in front of our building looked nervous, fingering the bulges in their pockets. I suspected that the entire affair had been triggered by their competition for drug turf with the bodega—that our boys and the Gatos had been inveigled to harass the Dominican operation.

My professional mandate was not to intervene but to be neutral, to observe. In addition, although police intervention at this point was clearly called for, I had strong reservations about calling the Ninth Precinct. We will never know to what degree some of the cops were involved then as bribe takers, dealers, and informers/enforcers, but what we did see and hear then has been supported by the findings of the Mollen Commission investigating police corruption. Nonetheless, further loss of life, including ours, was a strong possibility. Nilda suggested a way out of our dilemma. At one of her perpetual community meetings she had met a Puerto Rican policeman whose new job title was "community outreach officer." She liked and trusted him. Hoping he would pass the message upward, I asked her to give him a general outline of our fears, without mentioning names.

The precinct got the message. And so did the Dominicans. The next week they closed the store, sold the stock to a new owner, they said, and announced that on the following Friday the stock would be moved to a new location downtown. Whatever remained would be given as a gift (implying settlement of a blood feud) to the neighborhood.

These messages were transmitted through the Mexican super, now transformed into an ethnic intermediary who understood Latino cultural norms, in the form of *bochinches* (gossip) with Eti. In effect, the two women were performing the work of mediators, but lacked the acknowledgment, and hence the public authority, for performing the role.

The night before the removal of the merchandise was to take place, the police sent an armored car and officers in riot gear to protect the store. They spent the night and remained on hand the next morning while four truckloads of groceries were removed from it. Meanwhile people started gathering across the street. By three o'clock, the time set by the Dominicans and supposedly confirmed by the police as the deadline for the removal, the growing crowd started getting restive.

The boys began harassing the police, darting into the store, then creating a fight near the corner, getting the cops to chase them first in one direction, then another. With the cops out of sight, other boys leaped in and spray-painted "Olie" on the squad car, while Maria hung out the window, cheering them on. As the cops raced around, other people started snatching groceries, the Mexican super first among them. Emilio tried to stop her, and she pulled a knife on him, whereupon Señora Madera threw herself in front of him, protecting him with her body, as Dolores screamed *puneta!* (whore) at the Mexican from her upstairs window. Dolores was besides herself with anxiety because Eti, delayed by a "face-to-face"[1] meeting at the Human Resources Administration, was not there to help control the situation. Then someone threw a bottle from the roof. By then the crowd was close to five hundred and the cops were clearly outnumbered. Some drew their guns, and others charged with their nightsticks, hitting right and left. People scattered sideways, falling into doorways and into our office, retreating.

At about 5 P.M., it looked as if the owner was finally leaving. The truck pulled away to chanted yells of the crowd. Captain Maloney, who had just arrived on the scene, conferred with his men, and they all drew aside. For a few minutes they watched, laughing, as the crowd surged into the store; then they got into their squad cars and left.

The newspaper accounts would prepare the ground for how this event was to be understood by the general public. Although the news of Olie's death was given a mention in *El Diario*, the Puerto Rican daily, the English dailies only became interested after the bodega riot. And even then the reportage was offhand and inaccurate. For example, this is how the *New York Post* covered the story:

> A Lower East Side feud that has been smoldering between Dominicans and Puerto Ricans for the past 2 1/2 weeks burst into the open last night as looters stripped a small store to the bare walls. "Let them have it," said one of the Dominican owners of the store as he walked off. "I'm leaving." Cops from the nearby East Fifth Street station house stood idly by and watched as the law of the street took over and some 250 neighbors picked the place clean. . . . (Norman and Fagen 1979a:3)

After the local ABC affiliate broadcast footage of the riot that night, New York City's high police officials and Mayor Ed Koch were said to be outraged by the local commander's lack of action in the face of looting. Upon being presented with a report that "blasted" Captain Maloney's "extremely poor judgment in removing the police detail from the scene," Koch was quoted as demanding "an investigation and a full explanation" (Federici and Meskil 1979:17).

But the media had already prepared the ground by framing the issue as "looting." Under the headline "Cops Rip 'Hands-off' Order During Deli Riot," police officers were quoted as being stunned by Captain Maloney's order to retreat. "We had tears in our eyes," said one Ninth Precinct cop. "We couldn't believe the order when it came down over the radio . . . ," said another. "I'm furious and I don't give a damn who gave that order—none of the men could believe it. We were made to look like fools and idiots. *How can you maintain respect when the people take over as bosses?*" a third was quoted as saying (Norman and Fagen 1979b:4; italics mine). The *Daily News* reported a week later that as a result of the incident, Captain Maloney was facing departmental charges and disciplinary action.

Poor Captain Maloney. If the bodega stripping was an act of looting, the police should indeed have stopped it. The "community leaders" interviewed by the newsmen had gone along with this official view, at least publicly. The residents, in contrast, saw their actions as righteous retribution, material compensation for the taking of a life; to some extent, the Dominican owners shared this view. In fact, the local cops were shedding crocodile tears, ex post facto, because Captain Maloney had read the situation correctly. He was closer to the everyday life of the neighborhood than high police officials, and he seemed to understand that differences in class position and resources between the poor Puerto Rican population and the slightly better off Dominican store owners did not necessarily create cultural divides, that instead a blood feud was being settled. We didn't stick our necks out, however, to offer eyewitness accounts or culturally sensitive lectures. It was already bad enough that nine-tenths of what we felt called upon to do didn't fit a traditional ethnographic research job description.

But observing did. During the two hours following the police withdrawal, Paul and I watched as the crowds carried out groceries, stashed them or gave them away, and went in for more. There was joking, laughing, and sharing. A Chinese lady who had only obtained a package of toilet paper was handed many items by Señora Madera, who with her wild sons was making repeated forays into the store. The Chinese lady was saying, "Thank you, thank you!" Even Mr. Cintron, the bus driver driven over by a bus, had thrown his cane away and was hopping into the bodega with everybody else. Leading the mad scramble were Maria, her brothers, and the boys. I watched all this action from the open doorway of our office, phone in hand, describing to Nilsa at home what was happening. Nilda had left with Count Augusto, the count saying that the block was "too hot" for him. I guess he needed some liquid coolant, and Nilda herself was close to the breaking point. Only Paul was in the street observing the events, dropping in from time to time to update me on the latest inside the bodega.

For the first hour or so I refused to allow people to stash in the office what they were carting away. But then I decided that because even the cops had given up and there was a full-scale riot in progress, I might as well forget about moralizing. Anyway, the pickings were pretty meager: Ajax, Tide, toilet paper, dog food. Emilio, wearing a football helmet, brought in a case of food for Max the Wolf. Miguel had dragged in another for his homeless pet, Sweetie. Millie, who had said at first she wasn't going in there, did, flitting in and out with her kids, bringing me a present of two boxes of cake mix. "Here, take it, you're the only one I know that bakes." Spoiled milk, which the kids were pouring out all over the street, soda, and a few crates of beer were the beverages left behind by the Dominicans. Harry Belmont came in saying he'd tried to sell a crate of soda to the pizza store around the corner (another drug retail place, I was pretty sure). He calculated the price they usually charged against the price they offered him: "They were trying to cheat me, they think I'm a dummy. . . . That guy should be crazy! Ain't that some shit? I said no. . . . I said I'd rather throw it in the street first."

Holly, who was watching the scene from the office, finally gave up trying to keep Coreen and Chet out of the fray and went across the street to watch them, returning with a roll of paper towels appropriately named Bounty. Señora Moreno watched from her upstairs window, trying to keep an eye out for her wide-ranging Jimmy. Paco kept a dignified stance by her side, and Maribelle was also stuck upstairs. Because Maribelle was becoming visibly nubile, her mother was keeping a very sharp eye on her. One pregnant daughter was enough. Toward the end of the action, Meri came into the office. Looking distraught, she smacked her two daughters, Lucita and Isabel, for being around at all. She was the only mother who smacked anybody for it. She was shaking like crazy, like a leaf. I held her, and said, "Look, the cops said it was all right, so don't smack them."

Eti, who in the midst of the action had finally arrived on the Avenue B bus, was now being escorted by her sons Emilio and Jorge toward the bodega. Leaning heavily on their arms, she walked like a woman ready to faint, and from the way the crowd parted for her, possible loss of consciousness was part of the expected behavior for a woman playing a major role in this drama. As she entered the nearly gutted store, Maria jumped up high on some crates and urged the crowd to strip everything away. "Do it for me!" she cried. "Do it for Olie!"

The crowd obliged. To the sound of cheering and laughter, some Gatos backed up a car, and with chains attached, ripped off first the outside gates, then the telephone, and then pulled out the meat case. Boys were tearing off the wooden shelves and hauling the wood across the street, no doubt to build more pigeon coops. As I watched I saw Daniel climb the wall up to the *Bodega* sign and swing from it like an acrobat until the sign started collapsing downward under his weight. He fell into the waiting arms of the crowd. Bleeding all over and smiling, he stumbled over to me for first aid.

At her window, Dolores stood watching, holding her youngest, Francisco. Ronna sat with her, to give comfort and be comforted.

As evening fell, Doug Johnson of ABC's Eyewitness News arrived with his crew. Lighting up the spectral landscape of the former bodega, he interviewed Marta, the pretty community organizer who had magically materialized on the scene for the cameras. She told Johnson that the cops should have exercised better crowd control and prevented the "looting." Mobs should not be allowed to destroy private property.

Just then the police arrived, at a trot, to get into the picture too, as Johnson commented for the camera on the hopelessness of ghetto existence, how a young life could be snuffed out as a result of the theft of two cupcakes. After first attempting to be interviewed, to set the record straight, Emilio watched Marta's performance with rising fury. He stalked into the office, fuming, but he could not articulate precisely why. For one thing, he said, Marta wasn't telling the truth about the real reasons for the wrecking of the bodega. For another, she wasn't one of the people affected by Olie's death, it was none of her business, she should not have stepped forward to be interviewed.

Other tired children joined me in the office. The crowd outside had grown to about a thousand people, jeering and shouting and making faces into the TV cameras. I asked Millie's six-year-old son, Chulito, who was leaning into my lap while his mother stood near the door, why the bodega had been destroyed.

Chulito: Because they kilt him. They wanted to do that for Olie.
Jagna: Yeah? They messed up the store for Olie. Why did they do that?
Chulito: Because they didn't want nobody to go to that store no more, because they thought those two, um, um, bank robbers were hiding, so they went into that store to capture them.
Jagna: They wanted to capture the people who killed Olie?
Chulito: Uhm.
Jagna: You think that's good?
Chulito: It's good for them.

Jagna: Good for who?

Chulito: Good for them. The people that kilt Olie.

Jagna: You mean?

Chulito: It was good for the man who shot Olie. It was good for him because he got arrested. That's good for him.

Jagna: It's good that they messed up his store too?

Chulito: Uhm. Good for Olie.

Jagna: But you used to go and buy food there, didn't you?

Chulito: Every time I used to go to the store—I always feel—I always go to the bathroom. . . . I got places to hide out. Under my bed, on my bed, on the bureau, even in the bathroom I could hide. They won't find me.

Jagna: Are you scared, now, of everything that happened?

Chulito: When they shot Olie? When he was in the hospital my sister told me she was crying.

Jagna: Were you crying too?

Chulito: I could hardly listen. I closed my ears.

Jagna: Oh. . . . Did you see Olie getting killed?

Chulito: I saw him in the store. They shot him right here and right here, in the eye [*correctly pointing to the wounds*].

Jagna: Yeah? You saw that?

[*Other children who had drifted closer now joined the conversation, adding details about shot wounds, "and they shot him here and here and here, in the head, on the leg."*]

Chulito: I saw the man with the gun sticking out, and the thing went *phliing!* I heard that too.

Jagna: You heard that? Were you scared?

Chulito: Oh, I ran under my mother's bed. And then I got this gun.

Jagna: Well, that you did not do. I know.

Paul: Fantasy Island.

Chulito [*to Millie, now leaning close by on a counter*]: Momi, I know why they messed up that store. For Olie.

Millie: He's already dead and there's nothing in the world that's gonna help him come back. And they're gonna keep it up all their lives, "doing it for Olie." And it makes me sick. Maria was telling this guy, "Get the gates for my sake, do it for me, don't do it for me, do it for Olie," you know?

Jagna: Gatos. They wanted to burn the place down.

Millie: And my brother died. They shot him down too.

Jagna: Over here?!

Millie: No, over there on Sixth Street. Well, fine. And he was looking for it too. I mean, he was no angel, you know. He was my brother and everything, but he did it. He did what he did. And I feel bad, I feel terrible. That guy is loose [the man who killed her brother is not in prison]. But I'm not gonna go after him and kill him. Or take revenge on his family. What the hell. You let things go. Bye. Let the guy rest in peace.

Jagna: How long has it been since your brother got killed?

Millie: Three years. Three years until tomorrow. But I can't do nothing. I can't go and take revenge. It's not gonna bring him back. It never will.

Jagna: Daniel, come here. Let me see that leg. See? Why did you pull down that sign?

Daniel: I was mad.

Jagna: You were mad. Why?

Daniel: I don't know.

Jagna: You were mad about Olie?

Daniel: That wasn't the only thing I did. I broke up things inside. I wasn't using a hammer. I was using my hands.

As I later replayed the tape on which these conversations are recorded, I had a sense of profound sadness. There is Chulito, my Little Porkchop, only six years old and already like my brother and me at his age in the midst of a vortex of violence, magically thinking of all the places he could hide. In his tiny slum apartment he invents cubbyholes and a make-believe gun that will make-believe protect him. And Daniel, the brave and loyal friend across ethnic divides, who couldn't prevent his friend's death, like an adult war veteran now eases his helplessness by inflicting wounds on his own body. Even the adults are snatched back, in a fast rewind, to face the face of death. Millie slides back three years to the murder of her brother, as if he is being murdered here and now; and Meri, trembling as she smacks her daughters, returns to the moment when her partner died in police custody. Upstairs, Dolores gazes on the street with her downward slanting *Dolorosa* eyes, holding fast onto her trembling baby boy.

The effects of these violent traumas would play themselves out in the lives of the children in subsequent years. Commitments to mental hospitals and prisons, accidents, unfulfilled promise, bouts of anger, and self-medication along with addiction and the loss of self in careless sex would mar so many of their lives as young adults.

Two years later Paco was committed to the mental unit of Albert Einstein Hospital by his mother. He was suffering from hallucinations. At approximately the same time, Marco cracked his skull riding the top of the elevator. And about then, Miguel walked in front of a speeding car and spent the next four years "upstairs" on the fifteenth floor of the Smith Houses, isolated and imprisoned with his mother just as surely as his older brothers Julio and Richie were doing time in upstate New York penitentiaries. As was Jimmy Moreno.

As was Rafael-the-Kid. Except that the Kid was doing big time, in partnership with his stepfather, Cisco, for big-time dealing, in a federal prison. Lisa, after getting several minor parts in plays, would go from one street-dealing boyfriend to another after each one's imprisonment, leaving her baby girl to be raised by her mother.

Analyzing these events some years later, many puzzles remain, not the least of which is what Olie and the boys were doing to earn such murderous retaliation by

inicans. A connection to the Gatos in their extortion/protection activities
ibility. More likely, the boys were encouraged or maybe paid by the drugomatic's operatives to harass the bodega's own drug operation. Large amounts of
money were at stake, and male Latino life was cheap. The drug operators may not
have imagined that the bodega owners would go so far, but interestingly enough,
the day before the riot they packed up their goods, carted them into the gray van,
and moved. Not too far, mind you—only to Third Street. The timely move made
us realize that the information hotline was going full blast, maybe directly from
the precinct house.

The puzzle of Eti Medina's excessive concern for her son-in-law Olie is, I think,
amenable to an etic interpretation. As the head of a female-based kin group, it was
in her interest to bind a risk-taking macho to it. Her own more or less law-abiding
sons would eventually be moving into their wives' female networks and switch
their allegiance and economic assistance to their respective mothers-in-law. The
fact that the Rojos were a family doing well by Lower East Side standards would
have increased her interest in an alignment with them through her daughter. Even
though Olie had been a young bungler, with maturity he might have advanced
into higher ranks of illegal/legal occupations with his family's influence and name
behind him. Similarly, his growing ties to the Gatos, an easily mobilized group,
would provide Eti and her family with security and some measure of power in the
neighborhood. Furthermore, Olie was a role model (alas) and a protector for her
youngest macho, José. Her other sons, like her second, Pablo, were following a
path that led mostly to hard, dead-end jobs, and even those jobs were disappearing. In the context of discouraging economic prospects, a start in an illegal occupation promised the only certain path to upward mobility. She had gambled on
Olie, and she lost.

A few months later Eti found an apartment in the Bronx. She moved with her
boys, Cheetah, Maria, and Maria's daughters. In the interim Maria had given birth
to a baby girl. Had the baby been born a boy they would have named it Olie. But it
was wonderful to have another girl, said Eti. Girls don't break your heart. Cuckie
soon followed to the same apartment building in the Bronx, with all her children,
including the latest, supposedly fathered by Eti's son Pablo. Relying on other
women, especially turning them into kin, was a much sounder strategy than relying on men.

The media and the local and higher city officials refrained from analyzing the
reasons for Olie's murder, and they framed the storming of the bodega as an act of
"looting," although the first reports had hinted at vengeance. As the story was now
transmuted, the murder had been caused by the stealing of two cupcakes and a
grocery owner who "flaked out." Once again the curtain of silence descended on
the larger, socioeconomic forces that had led not only to this particular death, but
to the widespread dying of young Latino men *as a class*. Already, by 1978, the
Hispanic Research Center had published statistics showing that a quarter of male
Latino deaths were caused by homicide (Oscar Alers, 1978). The media's curtain

of silence shrouded the fact that a segment of the population was being denied meaningful work and the social status that comes with training for and performing that work. Pundits such as Ken Auletta popularized the label of "underclass" and indiscriminately applied it to young men whom society had abandoned as prey for recruitment by warped, sociopathic drug combines and incarceration by the "law."

The residents, about whom the agents of the state—its police force—didn't really care, reached back into their cultural repertoire to reduce the social chaos that follows the murder of a young person. For them, the storming and dismantling of the bodega was an anachronistic act of settling a blood feud, which temporarily restored a semblance of order.

Yet, at the deepest level a mystery surrounds the events, and depending on who tells the story, there are different versions of "truth." As close as we were to the events, I am convinced that in the brutal environment a certain degree of solidarity between the very poor and the less poor Latinos in maintaining resistance to prying eyes made us not privy to some of the facts, sweet as we were.

But at least, temporary peace had come to East Fourth Street.

14

King Kong on 4th Street

In 1980 the project was officially over. I wrote a final report to the funding agency, started analyzing the data and presented it in a series of papers to fellow anthropologists, and wrote an article for a popular journal. Some of my colleagues and students encouraged me to publish the data. In the public arena, my analysis pointing to street-dealing in drugs as an alternate avenue for earning a living in a situation of diminishing jobs was useful and was widely quoted by social scientists. Privately, Puerto Rican students in the courses I taught throughout the metropolitan area told me that I was describing the lives of their families very accurately.

But the early 1980s recession and the advent of neoconservatism created a hostile climate for such points of view; even my minority students were not immune to the conservative "law and order" propaganda. They were often the only upwardly mobile members of their families, in effect sponsored by their kinship units to achieve; in class discussions they invoked "culture of poverty" truisms that implicated their kin as the primary cause for the conditions of poverty and violence in which they lived. The whole edifice of conservative thought that laid the blame of structural poverty on the victims, as crystallized in the single phrase "underclass values," had taken an iron grip even on the thinking of the people implicated in its judgment. Even liberal Puerto Ricans, whose island had been colonized by the United States since 1898 and who were very sensitive to what they perceived as an imperialistic social science, proclaimed only truncated criticism of how the poor were being maligned.

For example, Oscar Lewis's *La Vida* (1965), in which several of the women were described as engaging in prostitution, was criticized as insulting and misleading. Which it was: Prostitution is not a representative occupation of Puerto Rican womanhood. But that was not the book's worst fault. One of its central tenets, the speculation that for about 20 percent of poor Puerto Ricans the "culture of poverty," not poverty itself, is passed down from one generation to another, independent of socioeconomic conditions, had the merit of being fatally attractive to opinion molders because it so easily absolved the economic and political elites from any responsibility for human misery. It was handy. Its simplicity obviated the need to analyze and attempt to change structural causes. When it was bodily lifted by Daniel Moynihan into his report on African American families—and coupled with his ethnocentric belief that only a nuclear family makes a family—it became a potent concept for neglecting the need for engaging in complex thinking about complex problems that might have led to the exposure of fundamental injustices within the U.S. socioeconomic system.

I had made my findings available to local community organizations, who used them for successful grant applications. But a "public" washing of what was considered the community's dirty linen, and any creative resistance to what appeared to be a death warrant for its poor majority, was seen as unseemly. Too strong a spotlight on what was going on—and on some of the leaders themselves—would disturb the status quo, and especially the leaders' own upwardly mobile paths. As far as pushing harder for exposure for myself was concerned, I also had to think of the poor residents themselves. Even though I had changed all the names—and some of the occupations and circumstances—in my report, the people remaining in the neighborhood might be recognizable and consequently harassed by government agencies. For the time being, I put thoughts of further publication aside.

In 1983 I was hired to teach a college course at the Greenhaven Correctional Facility. My inquiries into prison life had been tentative during the official research period, and I wanted to get closer to the experience of some of the fathers and husbands of the people I had worked with. As an anthropologist, I was concerned that there would be no way for me to corroborate prison narratives; as a middle-class person I did not want to intrude into experiences I thought the men would wish to forget. Only two men had referred to their prison life: Count Augusto, but rather vaguely and when under the weather, and Harry Belmont, when recounting his story to Paul. In 1980, when Harry was hauled back to prison for not reporting to his parole officer in time, Paul visited him in Sing Sing and heard more.

My teaching experience at Greenhaven, a maximum-security prison in Dutchess County, New York State, was disappointing on one count: Out of a class of twenty-eight, there was only one Latino man, a drug dealer from Colombia. With the exception of a young white drug dealer from upstate New York, the rest of the class was solidly African American. It appeared that the Latino prisoners, who were younger, had neither the high school education nor yet the motivation of the older Black prisoners. The advantage of the course was that I was interacting with the prison's crème de la crème—several former members of the Black Panther Party, who considered themselves political prisoners, and a group of highly politicized Muslims. Though the course, entitled Social Problems, was being taught by me, I learned as much from them about the prison system and the structure of society as they did from me. Several became friends with whom I corresponded, and one was to advise me on how to help one of my Lower East Side young men when his life was endangered after he went to prison.

I next took a job as coprincipal investigator in a study of a working-class neighborhood in Queens. Though the new site was less dangerous than East Fourth

Street, I soon noticed that drug trafficking connected to Central American cartels was expanding in an adjacent community and had drawn at least one of the families I knew from the old neighborhood. I spent most of my work days in Queens, but my schedule was flexible, and some evenings or weekends I helped my old friends with letters to officials, personal intervention, money, loans, and advice. This is one of the little-noted complications of doing urban ethnography. Unlike ethnographers who go to a faraway society, spend a year or two gathering data, and then return home to analyze it and get on with their careers, an urban ethnographer is much more likely to remain immersed in obligations. But even had I wanted to disentangle myself, conditions in the old neighborhood were becoming so bad that I felt bound to do what I could.

With the increasing profits and expansion of the drug trade in cocaine in the early 1980s, the neighborhood became ever more dangerous, its growing impoverishment and fragmentation increasing the ferocity of the competition. Knifings and gun battles endangered not only the drug sellers but often children and women caught in the crossfire. The police continued to arrest mainly street dealers or uninvolved bystanders, often employing excessive force in the act. The brutalization of life had become commonplace, and it seemed irreversible. The drug commerce had become so firmly entrenched in the neighborhood through patronage, favors, crisscrossing loyalties, and fear of retaliation that a number of families left on their own for the outer boroughs in a vain attempt to escape the unbearable conditions. Their flight, after the decade of arson, helped reduce the Lower East Side population to one fifth its 1960 number. A further boost to the growing exodus was provided by landlords hoping to rent their ratty apartments to drug dealers and displaced artists able to pay higher rents than the original residents, though still low by Manhattan standards. Increasingly common were evictions for falling behind in rent, and on other pretexts, of families who were now being churned off from transfer payments or could no longer afford to pay more than half their meager monthly allowance for housing.

During this period the entire island of Manhattan was experiencing profound changes. Decisions in corporate investment priorities and new job opportunities for young white professionals created a new demand for commercial and living space. Older and ethnic neighborhoods were co-oped and condo-ed, sending thousands more of the city's most vulnerable residents into a frantic search for affordable shelter. On the southwest side of the area, The Soho district, a formerly Italian neighborhood that had also provided living and working space in its abandoned manufacturing lofts, was now invaded by affluent newcomers. To the southeast, Chinatown, with its growing population and sweatshops, was also pushing into the area. Artists, students, venturous Midwesterners, began to move from the mostly western sector of the area into what had been the Latino section.

With their arrival, real estate prices and rents started to climb and displaced most of the remaining poor Puerto Rican families. Galleries, expensive coffee shops, "hot" new nightclubs, and high-fashion punk clothes and gift shops re-

placed the remaining small service and goods stores in the area. Real estate operators began a feverish speculation in the building stock that remained and in the
land that had been razed by arson. From the real estate point of view, one of the
most successful "slum clearance" operations had been quietly accomplished.

But there were still two major obstacles to full-scale gentrification of the area.
The first was political, composed of local multi-ethnic coalitions that struggled to
salvage part of the area for rehabilitated low-income housing. The second, and
more important, was the existence of the drug market. Some of the young men
whose families had been pushed out either remained in the area or traveled there
daily to work. The loss of familial and neighborhood restraints, such as they were,
escalated the risks, the profits, and the extent of the operations. Drawn by their
friendship and kinship to each other and their past on the turf where they had
grown up, younger boys were now replacing their older brothers and uncles, who
had been incarcerated or killed, and they were less worried about using the product they handled, or of the sanctions of their scattered community. With few
adult monitors to rein them in or disarm them, the area became a free-for-all
drug frontier. As the pressures from the cartels and the police mounted, as the
stress and competition increased, so did the ownership of firearms and the addiction of the street sellers. By 1983, the media began their coverage of what they
termed "the most open heroin market in the nation." And with an election only a
year away, the mayor ordered a dramatic "sweep" of the Lower East Side.

In December 1983, Mayor Koch named Benjamin Ward as the first Black police
commissioner of New York City. Within a month of his appointment, at dawn on
January 19, 1984, two hundred and forty police officers supported by undercover
agents, transit, and housing authority police moved into action in the neighborhood. They were backed up by mounted police to disperse crowds, and by canine
units to sniff out people in abandoned buildings. The operation, code-named
Operation Pressure Point, was directed from air by helicopter units. In the words
of one report, "The police became in effect an occupying army, determined to re-
capture the streets from the drug traffickers and return them to the community"
(Zimmer 1985). But where was, who was "the community"?

Within a month the police made two thousand drug-related arrests. Within a
year and a half, seventeen thousand. According to police sources, 60 to 65 percent
of those arrested had lived in the area. An overwhelming majority were street sellers or merely bystanders, because the commissioner had made the physical "appearance" of the streets a priority. Top- and middle-range distribution rings were,
as the police conceded, virtually unaffected. And retail distribution of drugs
moved directly into the projects on the boundaries of the neighborhood, where
the drug sellers could find cover, or moved one step ahead of the police with innovative tactics and equipment. The actions against drug buyers consisted mainly
of the issuance of parking tickets!

For the drug cartels, the challenge by Operation Pressure Point apparently led
to geographic expansion directly to the more affluent customers in Manhattan,

Queens, Long Island, New Jersey, and Connecticut. The forces of "law and order," a good few paces behind, tried to pursue this expansion with a repeat of the tactics employed on the Lower East Side into the outer boroughs, the effort now code-named TNT(!).

The intended detonation was a bust, doing nothing to contain the demand for illicit drugs; on the contrary, it only stimulated James Bondian innovations from cartels and provided new jobs for poor white men—as prison guards in expanding upstate prisons. The real losers were the young men of the neighborhood and their families. Even for those not convicted of any crime, the effects of Operation Pressure Point and TNT resulted in their involvement in the process of the "revolving doors of justice." An arrest, even as a bystander, was often the first step that tied them permanently to the criminal justice system. Even though not eventually convicted of any crime, most of them would spend time in jail because they could not "make bail." Their families' resources were too stretched to help them. A conviction, even if suspended, remained on their records, putting them in the category of repeat offenders, which meant longer prison terms if convicted again. The most unlucky ones would face almost automatic convictions and a guaranteed long stretch in a federal penitentiary if they happened to have been arrested on a day when the city police were deputized by the federal district attorney as "federal marshals"—an innovative "get tough" measure devised by then district attorney Rudolph Guiliani.

The perception of "law and order" on the Lower East Side encouraged the movement of "urban pioneers" into the area, increasing the rents the landlords could charge and sending more families into the streets. To accommodate the growing numbers of homeless families whom strained kin networks could no longer absorb, the city began to rent space in welfare hotels. In 1980 Nilda and I visited Myrna and her family at the Hotel Martinique, the hideous hostel for homeless families on Thirty-second Street in Manhattan. A number of other families had been scattered throughout the homeless hotels of the city from the fire-damaged house of Chino-the-socialist. Myrna was not in touch with any of them, but she had attended a wake for one of the mothers, who had died of a heart attack while moving her mattress down the street on a dolly with her two young boys. Dead also was Señora Madera. Having moved with her "bad" boys, daughters, and retarded son to a public housing project in Harlem, she had stepped between her son and a dagger intended for him by a member of the housing's gang. She was stabbed in the heart.

By 1982, Mr. Stern started serious evictions from our former building, while renting our former office to a drug dealing operation. Paco's King Kong was now all but obscured by scribbly black graffiti, his magnificent symbol descending into psychotic scrawl that reached up to engulf him with insectlike appendages. Paco himself, now sixteen, had taken to his bed and for three months lay facing the wall, not responding to entreaties or threats. His younger sister, Maribelle, speculated that the immediate cause of Paco's collapse was their father's belated filing for divorce. She also thought that Paco had spent too much time at the marijuana dealer Ismael's storefront, smoking grass and participating in the latter's experimentation with espiritismo. She thought that together they had been inexpertly raising "intranquil spirits" of the dead that attached themselves to Paco.

Señora Moreno was pragmatic. City agencies were not about to help cure a ghostly infestation. But a medically certified status of mental illness would at least provide psychiatric care for Paco and make him eligible for Supplemental Security Income (SSI) support payments to help her take care of him. She signed him into the Beth Israel Psychiatric Center.

She was sorry as soon as she did it. When I visited him there, he was reduced to a swollen robot, taking stiff miniscule steps, his drug-thickened tongue making him unable to speak but only dribble saliva. He had been overmedicated with Haldol. My conversation with his Egyptian doctor, whose English was better than his knowledge of Puerto Ricans but whose faith in classical psychiatric theory was firm, resulted only in a lowering of the drug dosage. Though bolstered by anthropological descriptions of espiritismo and its possibilities as an alternative psychiatric folk method, my arguments for a different treatment approach fell on deaf ears. It was known by then from the writings of Vivian Garrison (1973) and Alan Harwood (1977) that competent, trained practitioners of espiritismo could be successful adjuncts in the psychiatric treatment of some culture-specific manifestations of mental illness. Paco's activities with Ismael had in effect been attempts at self-medication, which any competent espiritista could have corrected. One of the first principles of the practice is that you cannot effect spiritual growth when under the influence of mind-altering drugs. It is said that "intranquil spirits" of those who have died prematurely may attach themselves to the living. A spiritist practitioner can cure the infestation by providing the spirit with light to move on and the infested person with spiritual cleaning.

After a few months of conventional, mind-altering drug treatment, Paco was released from Beth Israel. But Paco didn't get better. His new SSI status required constant outpatient connection to psychiatrists and continuing high dosages of these licit drugs. Even though he seemed to walk around in a fog, I helped him get involved in a therapeutic community and a G.E.D. program at the American Friends Service Committee (AFSC). But though he came close to getting his high school equivalency, other events intervened.

First, Mr. Stern evicted the family from their home on the pretext that Jimmy, Paco's younger brother and a macho, was scribbling graffiti. He probably was—he had been for years—but it was perhaps not coincidental that Lisa, the family advocate, who could use her big mouth to stand up to authority, had decamped for Brooklyn with her new boyfriend, leaving her mother to raise her baby daughter while Lisa pursued her fledgling acting career. But by then Mr. Stern had better candidates for the apartments; one of them, not famous yet but typical of the people moving into the neighborhood, was Madonna.

The marshals evicted Señora Moreno and her family on a rainy day, putting all of their earthly belongings on the street to soak. The furniture was later moved to storage, but the family was never able to redeem any of it; it was too expensive to pay the storage for the two years they had nowhere to put it. After a few nights in an emergency shelter and a short stay at the Hotel Martinique, they were placed in a "transient" hotel for the homeless in Brooklyn, where they remained. The younger children started attending Brooklyn schools; Maribelle commuted to her junior high school on the Lower East Side, and Paco, to the AFSC program on East Fifteenth Street. Jimmy stopped attending anything, but daily found his way to the Lower East Side anyway.

One morning, Paco forgot his subway pass and jumped over the turnstile. Two undercover cops grabbed him, and when he resisted, confused and unsure of what was happening, he was punched and dragged into the men's toilet, where uniformed cops joined in and beat him to a bloody pulp. He had a concussion and lost several teeth when he was hit across the mouth with a blackjack. At Maribelle's urging, Señora Moreno filed a complaint, but nothing ever came of it. Paco was left an inarticulate young man, stunned by prescribed drugs and now also given to sudden inexplicable rages.

Not long before the eviction, Maribelle, in her fourteenth year, had fallen in love with Kid's younger brother Tico. Unlike their older siblings, Lisa and Kid, who hadn't been able to make a go of it and deprived Dolores of remaining a close grandmother to their baby daughter, Maribelle and Tico proved a devoted couple; in 1985 they provided her with a baby girl whom they named Maridel. Other events had occurred that made Dolores apprehensive. Her husband, Cisco, dropped his unrewarding work at the factory in Connecticut and applied his talents to drug selling. He was mature, hardworking, and urbane, and he could count on his stepson Kid's loyalty. He advanced quickly to a local mid-level position, then quit and with the money saved bought land and a house in Puerto Rico. For a while, even though it meant leaving her new granddaughter, Dolores's whole family moved to Puerto Rico, except for Tico, who wouldn't leave Maribelle, who wouldn't leave her mother. But there were few straight jobs in Puerto Rico, and when the money ran out, Cisco renewed his work connections and the family rented a whole floor of a private house in Queens.

After their return, Maribelle visited her mother-in-law frequently, staying for as long as a week at a time, relieving the crush in the two hotel rooms that her family occupied. Paul and I interviewed her at the time, in Dolores and Cisco's very comfortable living room, which boasted a four-by-six-foot television projection screen.

During the interview, Maribelle confirmed many of the impressions that Paul had gathered in a previous visit to her family in the hotel. For two small rooms, the city [from combined federal, state, and municipal funds] was paying $2,200 *every two weeks* to the corporation that owned the hotel. (The AFDC housing allowance at that time was $258 for a family of four, with small increments for each additional child.) Mattresses and a small refrigerator were the only household items the hotel provided. Maribelle had brought a crib, bought by her mother-in-law, but did not dare leave Maridel in it at night because the rooms swarmed with rats. A hot plate, a radio, and a television set, also gifts from Dolores, had to be replaced three times after robbers broke the door and the management did not repair it. The robbers also took the iron and ironing board, clothing, money, and their last few remaining possessions. Lisa, who arrived one day bearing gifts to replace some of these items and to shop for clothes for her daughter and youngest brother, was attacked in the doorway of the hotel, her necklace grazing her throat as the muggers dragged her backward and ripped it off. No one made a move to help her. Such an incident as this could not have happened with this impunity in the impoverished yet socially responsive community where they had lived. Here, the hotel's anomie was compounded by the management's disdain for the residents through whom they reaped such huge profits. The hotel's regulations were aimed at creating a prisonlike atmosphere without providing any comfort or safety. This was the very same hotel where armed guards, who stood around doing nothing as Lisa was robbed, had confiscated Paul's camera a few weeks earlier, because taking pictures was against regulations.

Either from the rat fur or the dust embedded in the filthy carpets, Señora Moreno started suffering from severe bouts of asthma that required prolonged hospitalization. (It didn't help that she had to climb up and down the stairs to her eighth-floor apartment—the hotel's one elevator never worked.) During her mother's absences, Maribelle had to be mother not only to her own infant but to her little brother, Richard, and her niece, Crystal (Lisa's daughter), both toddlers; unmanageable Jimmy; and withdrawn Paco. She was on call and anxious all the time, even when taking a break at Dolores's apartment. But she was looking for an apartment of her own. Though Dolores and Cisco would have helped them more, Maribelle and Tico did not want to be beholden to them. It was a complicated situation, made more so by the fact that it could never be openly discussed. Maribelle and Tico resisted taking too much because that would make Tico vulnerable to Cisco's requests for help with his drug dealing. From time to time, when Tico was laid off from the construction jobs he worked for the $3.25 minimum wage, he'd do a little selling for Cisco on Manhattan's fashionable Upper East Side or in the Wall Street area. He was a presentable young man. He was levelheaded and knew how to take public transportation to anywhere in the city. But unlike Kid, his heart was not in it. Both he and Maribelle had aspirations for a conventional life.

Maribelle also said that in between her hospital stays, Señora Moreno had gone on two city-sponsored trips to inspect available permanent apartments. Everything she had seen was even smaller than the hotel space, and even more dilapidated and dangerous. Her mother was holding out for something better, but her chances were limited. The city was instituting a policy of taking shelter residents on only three trips—if they didn't take what was being offered they would be thrown out of the hotel as well. There was no question of finding an apartment they could afford in the private market. As it was, their AFDC food allowance was barely enough to feed them, and it was further depleted during periods when their hot plate was stolen and they tried to get by on one hot meal a day at fast-food restaurants. Often they subsisted on cold cereal and bread and margarine.

Though at nineteen still a very young woman, Maribelle did not complain about her many responsibilities or the anxieties her brothers caused her. Musing about Paco's illness, she said, "I don't know. He turned crazy somehow. But he never told us what he really took or what happened to him. He just said that his mind was just like running, drifting. He's still a little bit crazy, like if you talk to him you don't know what you're talking about. He talks about everything."

"Maybe everything was too much for him?" I asked.

Generally smiling, now Maribelle gave me a serious look. "Right after you left [the Lower East Side], the cops hit him, you know? All that together makes somebody go crazy."

"And then, not having a real home. Makes it even worse?" I suggested.

She nodded emphatically.

During the 1980s, life went downhill for other families we knew, although not all families, and not all their members, were equally affected. After her marriage to Arturo and a move to public housing within the Lower East Side, Millie was doing well, and all her children were in school. But after paying the hospital bill following Chulito's fall down six floors in Stern's building, she had given up working so that she could keep her children out of trouble. Happily, Ginny was still in high school and, unlike the other girls in the projects, still a señorita (virgin). That warmed Millie's heart. Millie and Ginny had kept in touch with some other families—it was interesting to see how news of each other continued to connect them. But much of what they told me I didn't really want to hear. One after another the boys were getting either shot, addicted, or imprisoned. The girls were doing somewhat better, but they were already saddled with responsibilities.

For example, Evelyn, my Blue Bayou girl, had been forced into a marriage to an older man by her father, Ramon, after she got pregnant. The husband was a heroin dealer who supplied Ramon with the goods, they said. Evelyn already had a baby and had quit school. Lucita ("Luz") was still in high school but also worked after school and on Saturdays in a local supply store. She had to, to earn money to help her two older brothers survive in jail. Her sister Isabel, in contrast, had become the second common-law wife of a manager she met as she bagged groceries at the Key Food supermarket. She had two children, lived in New Jersey, and refused to help her brothers. She had only finished her junior year in high school.

Millie's stories about the girls were confirmed during my visits and calls to Meri. (One *nice* thing about urban research is that you can telephone your informants—*if* they have a phone.) By 1983 life was also unraveling for Meri. She called me in tears one day; the Housing Authority had sent her a letter of eviction because of her little chihuahua. "They got four apartments here in this building dealing drugs, but they go after my little dog!" But later, by staging a creative asthma attack in the manager's office, she persuaded the staff to let her keep both the dog and the apartment. Furious at having to resort to subterfuge, like a child, to lead a normal adult life, she commented: "You got to be scared of these people all your life like they're your mother and father."

Yet the threatened eviction was only the tip of the iceberg. Her older sons, Julio and Richie, had been recruited into drug dealing on Fourth Street, a fact she at first refused to acknowledge even to herself. Julio, less drawn in than Richie, lent a hand to friends when needed, but mugging had become his specialty. Richie had become addicted to heroin, both using it and selling it. Both of them had been arrested several times and were busy trying to support themselves (and their lawyers) between jail time and court appearances. In the fevered, helter-skelter atmosphere of mass arrests, no one's case was being properly pursued by law enforcement, and on occasion, when arrested, they would give false names, including that of Miguel, their youngest brother. Miguel, meanwhile, was staying "upstairs." He had walked into the path of a speeding car and sustained severe injuries to his body and head. He underwent four operations in nine months. Afterward, he remained home, quiet and isolated, for several years, while his brothers got into deeper waters. Meri had no time for him. She was too busy visiting her older sons at Riker's Island. Meri was beside herself with anxiety and scrounged around to give her sons money. By then AIDS was spreading like wildfire through the Lower East Side, and one of the factors in its spread was infections contracted in prisons—through homosexual contact, including rape, and shared needles—because drugs were available and used. Having money to buy favors and consideration was crucial for men interested in surviving.

Meri called me in November 1985 after having had three asthma attacks in one night. She had used four pumps in the past four days and been taken to Beth Israel by ambulance. She was getting hospitalized more and more often, this time for five days. She complained, "They come and take my blood every morning—I'm scared. I don't want to be in the hospital, my [blood] pressure goes up, real up."

But back home, the situation was not so rosy either. Meri's sister had been burned out of her apartment in Brooklyn and, after a short stint in a welfare hotel, had moved in with Meri at her invitation. (She and her four children would spend two years camped with them.) Julio was now serving time at Woodburne Prison in the former "borscht circuit" of the Catskills, rapidly being transformed into "the prison circuit." Richie had returned home from Riker's, cured cold turkey from his heroin addiction and assigned to a methadone "maintenance" program. But he had fallen straight into the arms of his former buddies—except that now they didn't allow him to work with them. Meri made an oblique reference to this by telling me that drug dealing was going on not only in the projects where they lived, but also on Fourth street. "On Avenue B there are still white people going there to buy drugs, with the police right there, and the people going back and forth. They give those kids forty, fifty dollars—that happened to Julio and Richie (not to Miguel, thank God)—and when their minds get confused, they let them go."

Meri was upset because her boys had first been encouraged to become users and then were laid off after becoming debilitated by the effects of the drugs; also, the drug cartel provided no legal assistance for low-level dealers. She summed up: "Now, all they've got to do is drugs. They go to jail, jail, all your life jail."

Meri realized that Miguel was neglected in the midst of his older brothers' drama. Yet she didn't have enough energy or know-how to really help him. She told me in a low voice that while she was hospitalized, Miguel "drank" all the Valiums she had stashed, to commit suicide. Thank God she had gotten home in time and called the ambulance; they saved him by pumping his stomach at Bellevue. "A little more [time], and I almost lost my son," she whispered, adding, "They took some meat from his leg [during reconstructive surgery after the accident], and he thinks he is different. He thinks he can't look at a girl because she'll feel the same way."

Yet, in the same conversation she told me, within Miguel's earshot, "Julio [now in prison] looks like a real man. He doesn't look like a kid. He looks like a marriage man, not a kid. He is going to school, he writes good English. He writes me to tell Richie not to do nothing wrong. He's the best one in the house—he came out like his father."

I called Miguel a few days later and suggested he check out a program for young people in the neighborhood. He told me, "The walls, like, be caving in on me. I got nothing to do." But he was cautious about promising to check out the program. The Most Improved Student in his sixth-grade class had dropped out of high school in his sophomore year and was afraid of being among his peers. He said they would stare at him. He shifted the focus to Richie's problems. "He broke the habit at Riker's. He came out pretty healthy and big" and was put on a 10-milligram dosage of methadone. "But then his friends, the people he *calls* his 'friends,' got him back on. He dropped all those pounds." And then, speaking about his mother, he said: "She be too soft with Richie. He could do anything and she won't throw him out." He said that Richie was taking heroin and free-basing cocaine. For that he needed money, and because he wasn't trusted by drug dealers to deal, he had taken to mugging. Miguel was worried about his mother. He said, "She don't like anything that's good for her," commenting about her coffee drinking, which he himself avoided. "When she can't sleep at night, I can't sleep. . . . I be thinking that she's going to die. Yeah, when she can't breathe like that." I told him she'd said she wanted to move out from Smith Houses because Richie had access to drugs there. Miguel hesitated. "Yeah, but there's going to be drugs wherever we move."

Indeed, the drugs were radiating everywhere, into the outer boroughs, into suburbia. They also followed the routes to rural prisons in the borscht belt. As rural communities upstate vied with each other to get prison contracts to replace those jobs lost in the declining resort and light manufacturing trades, their own children, faced with small prospects and parents juggling low-paying jobs, were being seduced by the drug trade. The young men of these areas had one new major job opportunity, as prison guards, where they were guaranteed low, steady salaries, health benefits, and a lifetime spent in overcrowded prisons, just as surely, if only half-time, as their captives (Bowles, Gordon, and Weisskopf 1990). It was a sure bet that some would increase their earnings by bringing in contraband and selling it. And it was also a sure bet that the stresses of the job—the prisons were chronically understaffed—would lead some of them to addictions, licit or illicit. The chickens were coming home to roost all over the heartland.

Nevertheless, as I would discover, a certain empathy sometimes sprung up between the jailers and the jailed, in spite of frequent transfers of both guards and inmates, racial and ethnic differences, and the increasingly brutal and brutalizing political climate and economic depression. Yet it flowed like a subtle subtext: Urban prisoners contributed their music and language, and their captors brought Standard American English and slower-paced rural ways to the common prison culture they made together. I'd like to think that the possibility of confluence was a legacy of Woodstock, whose former site in Bethel lay within miles of several prisons.

Each time I visited Meri over the next year, Richie was in worse shape. His feet became deformed and swollen from injecting, so he couldn't walk very far. He was also running a continuous high fever. Then, late in 1986, Meri called me, sobbing, to tell me that Richie had been arrested at home the day before and was again at Riker's. Her story was that Richie had gone downstairs [in her building] to get some "shit" [heroin] with $25 she gave him, and had come right back up. A few hours after he injected, there was a loud knocking. Richie ran into Meri's bedroom and hid under the bed. Fresh out of a bath, clad only in her robe, Meri went to the door and said, "Who?" Two voices answered, "Police! We want to talk to you about the loud music." She opened the door, keeping the chain on, and told the two housing cops she saw that the music came from the apartment next door. The two cops then told her they wanted to talk to her about Richie. (According to her, the reason Richie was hiding was because he had not been reporting to his parole officer.) She opened the door wide, and ten cops materialized from hiding places in the hallway, knocking her out of the way as they rushed in—"They had no warrant, nothing!"—searching and overturning things. They dragged Richie from under the bed and started hitting him, and as she screamed "Don't hit my son!" they yelled for her to shut up or they'd arrest her too. They dragged Richie out, shoving her crazy brother, Pedro, out of the way, and didn't give her a chance to get dressed, or come along. In the elevator, she said, they "hit his balls, busted his mouth, and fucked up his neck." She was furious, all the more so because they hadn't given Richie a chance to put on his underpants.

According to Meri, the dealer from whom Richie had bought the drug had been arrested first, "with ten decks of heroin and other 'shit' [cocaine]." The cops had offered the dealer a deal, saying he wouldn't be charged with possession of the drugs with intent to sell if he informed on whoever had robbed a dealer in the lobby of the building. Eager to be cooperative, the dealer gave the cops Richie's name and apartment number. Ignoring the question of Richie's guilt or innocence, Meri said disgustedly that the dealer "ratted to keep his own ass out of jail."

At the arraignment, although the lawyer (referred to by Meri as "the legal aid") pointed out the lack of a warrant, the judge insisted on a $2,500 bail. Because bail bondsmen were no longer willing to take chances on poor suspects, Meri offered to sell some of her and Miguel's things if the judge would lower the bail to something she could raise. But the judge refused, and off to Riker's Richie went.

Meri wanted me to go to the indictment so that I could speak to the legal aid and to the judge to persuade them that Richie didn't belong in jail, but in detox and a therapeutic community. Miguel told me, separately, that Richie had threatened to kill himself if sent to prison. He couldn't face another cold turkey withdrawal. So at 9:30 A.M. on the appointed day, the coldest day in the past eighteen years, I arrived at 100 Centre Street, the site of the New York State Criminal Court. I waited near the newsstand, then walked to the wall where lists were posted with names of that day's cases. The lists had forty to sixty names, and there were four of them. But none with Richie's name.

At 10:00, I went up and started casing the courtrooms. In all of them, the clientele was about 60 percent Latino and 40 percent black, with only a few white and Asian teenagers in evidence. In front of each courtroom were white court officers, white aides, and white lawyers, male and female. Hanging outside in the corridors were assorted Latinos ill prepared for the cold; frail, thinly clad girls, slight men wearing double sweatshirts, some smoking, conversing hyperactively in Spanish, others mutely trying to understand what the lawyers were telling them.

I went downstairs, roaming the once majestic, now grungy lobby space, asking questions of the armed guards. They were neither hostile nor friendly—they just didn't know anything. Finally one told me to go to the "computer room" and ask for Richie's name. The computer man told me that if I wasn't sure of the spelling of the first name (Richie's formal first name was that of an obscure ancient Greek hero), he doubted if he could help me. I asked him to try anyway. He left for a few minutes, time enough to spit, and came back with a false smile saying there was no such name. I resumed inspecting lists, stuck my head into an indoor cafe that was belching hamburger grease, and finally at about 11:15 spotted Miguel just as he noticed me in the lobby. He gave me his beautiful smile and led me to his mother, already upstairs. He had found out from one of the clerks the precise courtroom where Richie's "papers" already were, although his name had not appeared on the lists. I was amazed at how these formerly "parochial" people were now capable of navigating this swamp.

Meri was already seated on a back bench, seemingly calm, monumental in a mauve down jacket. She gave me her cheek to kiss and made room for me next to her, pointing out a guy, a few benches ahead, as the one who had "ratted" on Richie. He was out on bail—as an active dealer he could afford it; that's why he wasn't back "in the cage" with Richie. Perhaps sensing that we had our *ojos* [eyes] on him, the dealer kept shooting troubled glances back in our direction. Meanwhile, people wandered in and out of the courtroom as lawyers called out the Hispanic names of their assignees, previously sight unseen, and if they connected, beckoned them out for a "conference" in the corridor. You couldn't hear what was going on up front, and from time to time, a uniformed clerk warned everyone to do their talking outside. But most people just buzzed on in low voices. Meri said she hoped Richie's parole officer would show up and recommend detox. Their legal aid wasn't there either, and Miguel went up to one of the clerks to find out who would defend Richie that day. The clerk gave him the name of a new lawyer and estimated that Richie's case would not be heard until after lunch. Just before the noon recess, the "rat" went before the judge. His case was either postponed or dismissed, because he was walking out on his own two feet. Meri stopped him and inquired in solicitous tones how his case had been disposed. He answered pleasantly in Spanish that the case had been continued. Meri gave me a fish eye after he left.

I had to leave for a doctor's appointment at 3 P.M., so I discussed with Meri what I could do. She asked me to get her the names of some therapeutic centers. Miguel, too, said he needed to leave—he wanted to go get his hair trimmed. His hair looked trim enough to me, unlike his future. So I suggested he come with me so I could introduce him to the American Friends Service Committee's G.E.D. program. They both okayed this last idea, Meri affirming her hopes for her youngest son.

I felt optimistic for Miguel, too, based on a conversation we had in a Greek diner where we stopped while waiting for the two women who administered the program to return from lunch. Over hamburgers, Miguel told me what a nightmare Richie's addiction had become. Unlike Julio, Richie no longer cared about his family, and although Miguel didn't articulate Richie's behavior as manipulation, his narrative described it. He said that Richie had sold his winter coat, his graduation ring, and Miguel's music tapes, and then everything else in the house, to buy crack cocaine, which he smoked in a little pipe. Getting as close to anger as I had ever seen him, Miguel said that when they visited him at Riker's, Richie mimed hanging himself, for Meri's benefit, so she would be reminded of her husband's death. Miguel said that Meri believed Richie would hang himself if he was left in jail or without drugs. On several occasions Miguel had tried to stop Richie from extorting money from their mother, but he could not raise his hand against his older bother, even though he felt an obligation to protect Meri. Even so, Richie had once threatened Miguel with a knife and on another occasion slapped Lucita around.

"She's such a good kid. She goes to school and she's working," Miguel said. "She's doing better than I," he added ruefully.

When I presented to him my ideas as to why females were encouraged to do better by the system, he understood intellectually, but his emotional distress was stronger. "We tried to tell our mother about us—the good kids." He looked close to tears. "But she's only interested in our older brothers."

At the AFSC office I introduced him to Beatriz, a sweet young college girl from South America. She talked to Miguel in soft Spanish phrases. Maybe he'll go, I thought, as we parted on Third Avenue and Fifteenth Street, where he was catching the bus back to the courthouse. Just before I lost sight of him he turned around, grinning, and waved.

Over the next few days I learned that Richie had been indicted on a second-degree robbery charge and was returned to Riker's Island. Meri still couldn't post bail, and she didn't even ask me for help. As she cried over the telephone I reminded her about all the trouble Richie was causing. She countered, yes, but he had bought her that nice snow jacket, and he had been helpful with the cooking. She said she couldn't count on help from Lucita, who was always going downstairs to see her boyfriend; Isabel had forgotten about her, living her own life in New Jersey; and Miguel was useless, just sitting at home.

But in the next few days Miguel moved. He went to the welfare office to open up his case for disability and started seeing a psychiatrist in order to obtain SSI. He needed to have some money to help out his mother and to have "a dollar in my pocket" when he started school, he told me.

The evening after my return from Richie's hearing, thinking about Miguel's eagerness to leave the courthouse and our conversation in the diner, I had written: "Miguel is really eager to get out from the gloom and doom of his kinship's fate, even though he may be convinced that only a loser merits his mother's full focus."

Miguel was struggling toward manhood, a babe in the woods. All around him boys his own age were entering adulthood as innocent and as naive as he was. Some, like Paco, seemed already to have lost the fight, sunk into obscurity like the King Kong he had painted. Others, like Richie, were already forming the next wave of street dealers and muggers who would replace their older brothers as grist for the mills of justice.

I had high hopes that neither fate would claim Miguel.

15

I, Miguel Valiente

In December 1990 I received a narrative from Miguel. He was writing from Attica, one of New York State's fiercest and most remote maximum-security prisons. For the past sixteen months he had been confined to a SHU, a Special Housing Unit—in prison parlance "the box" or "solitary"—designed for the most violent inmates. He lived in a small cell, unable to communicate with anyone except the guards, confined twenty-three hours a day with one hour for exercise, in a small, also isolated yard. He wrote out of extreme loneliness, rethinking and reconstructing his life story, in order to attempt to give continuing meaning to his life. He had said he wanted to send me something for Christmas, but was also cut off from the privilege of commissary shopping, so I had suggested he write his story for my book. I was hoping that it would help him retain his sanity. The spelling, punctuation, and spacing are retained exactly as they were in the original handwritten letter.

Part 1

On 5/3/86 I was arrested and charged with Robbery 1st. I can remember it well. The robberies started when I got addicted to crack-cocaine. At first I started selling heroin just to buy myself clothes and to have money to buy things and to go out to places. When I was selling the heroin I started to use my own product. I didn't like it. So I gave up the heroin. But a few months later I was introduced to crack. I was still selling heroin but only a short time after I started using crack. I was fired off my heroin sales because the owners noticed that I was strongly addicted to crack so for [that] reason I was fired. They didn't want to trust me with their money. So I took on a different way to make money—robbery. At first when the thought of robbing a person came to my mind, I was afraid because I never in my life robbed anybody. So it was scary. I needed the money for my addiction so my need superseded my fears so I went out to rob Chinese people. On my first mission I was nervous, very nervous but it wasn't as scary as it had felt to me as when I first thought of robbing a person. The money was easy to get. I didn't have to stand in a corner eight hours of the day selling drugs. Robbing people, to my eyes, was very easy. So after the first robbery I did another one and another one. I started to get paranoid for the reason that the police were aware of the robberies that were taking place. I had to slow down and I tried, but my addiction of crack was too strong. So I didn't care if the police were on the look out. Things were starting to get worser. I started out smoking one vile of crack, but before I knew it I was smoking five and seven viles of crack. I was stronged out. I had no conscious, whatsoever. I sold my disc jockey equipment. I sold my clothes and I stole from my girlfriend. I was even starting to demand money from my mother. Everyday I wished to die. I just wanted to die. One day I borrowed my sister's [Lucita's] bike and I sold it. When my head was cleared from the crack I had smoked with the money I got for my sister's bike. I took a walk over to the East River and I was going to drown myself. I sold my little sister's bike. I wanted to die because the bike meant a lot to my sister. She worked hard to get that bike. I didn't drown myself. I just didn't go home. I was too embarrased to see my sister. She found out that I stole her bike and she was furious, but she forgave me. All she said was—Miguel please stop the use of crack. I tried, I tried and I stopped for three days and I stood at home. I decided to go out and get some fresh air and a walk. Before I knew it I was smoking crack again. I didn't start robbing people. What I did I started selling drugs again. This time I had a little control of my habit. I was not using crack like I was before. I was selling drugs—heroin— to support my addiction, which was not as big as the beginning of my addiction. So here I was pushing drugs for a little money.

One day as I was moving the business I was robbed. A black man in a brand new lincoln Continental approached me and asked me where can he find some heroin. I told him that I had the best. He parked his car and got out while his companions sat in the car. I asked him how much did he wanted. He said that he wanted two bags of the Tragic Magic. So we exchanged the money for the drugs. He took the bags and he snorted it. I paid no attention to him because I was waiting on my supplier to bring more stuff. As I was waiting for my supplier my customer, the one who bought the two bags off me, tapped me on the shoulder and when I turned around he had his gun on my stomach. I panicked. I tried to knock the gun off his hand but to no avail. He had a grip on his gun. So I ran for my life. When I was 15 feet away from the assailant he shot his gun and the bullet enter the back pocket of my pants and entering my pelvis and destroying my hip. I was rushed to the hospital where I was taken into the emergency room. The Dr. examined my hip and he explained to me that my hip was terribly fructured by the bullet. I was taken to the operating room. I awoke 4 $1/2$ hours later and to my surprise I was buried in a body cast. I mean I was covered with a cast from my toes to my chest. It was terrible. I had the cast on for three months. I was released from the hospital. I still had a court date to attend for the robbery charges I got in 5/3/86. Of course it was postponed because of my incident.

On 1/15/87 I was sentenced to 5 years probation. I was doing well at the time. During my stay at the hospital I broke my crack addiction. I didn't go back into drugs. I was too busy with my doctor's appointments and my physical therapy appointments. I had no time to use any drugs. I was feeling great in spite of the large piece of cast I had on my waist. The cast was being partially taken off piece by piece. I must tell you that people started to look and notice me again. I was clean and drug free. It was the best thing that happen to me. I was doing well but I started to feel alone. I have always felt alone. I never had a real group of friends. I started to walk around again. I healed nicely. But only I didn't stay clean. Again, I was over by that damn park where I was purchasing the viles of crack when I was first stronged out. Before I knew it I was smoking crack, again and I was robbing people again.

Part 2

October 18th, 1987

On October 18th, 1987, I, Miguel Valiente was arrested again for Attempt Robbery in the 1st degree. Again I found myself under the control of crack. On 1/15/87 I was sentenced to 5 years probation. Maybe if I was sent to prison on my first robbery charge I wouldn't have robbed another person. The day I was sentenced to 5 years probation by Judge C.—on that same day as I stood in front of Judge C. I was intoxicated on crack—right at the same time I was being sentenced for probation. Only if the judge would've given me prison time. I would've not robbed anybody. Well it wasn't too long before I was arrested for an attempt to rob somebody. On October 18th, 1987, I Mr. Miguel Valiente attempt to rob a Chinese man. I followed him into his building and into the elevator where I then displayed a two and 1/2 [inch] camping knife and I demanded money. The Chinese man told me that he had no money. I then padded his pants pockets to see if he did have no money. He didn't. So I didn't push it any further. I made my attempt to leave him when he called me back and asked me why do I rob people. I told him that I was strongly addicted to crack and that I desperately need money. I apologized and went on my way to nowhere. The incident took place on October 18 at approximately 7:A.M. At 9:A.M. of that same day I was arrested. This same man I had tried to rob two hours earlier was looking for me in the police car. As I was coming out of [Hester Street Park]—the park where all the drugs are sold I was approached by two police cars and in one of the cars was the Chinese man. I was told by the police to lay on the sidewalk as they pointed their guns on me. I did as I was told. The officers then stomped me to the ground and put their guns to my head. They searched my back pockets and found the knife they were told I had displayed during the time I tried to rob Mr. S. W. The police grabbed me through the collar of my jacket and took me over to one of the cars where the Chinese man waited to identify me. And he did identify me. I was handcuffed and put in the police car and to the police precinct they took me. As the result of this robbery, I got 2 $^1/_2$ to 5 years for it. And on top of that I received 1 to 3 years for violation of probation. Now I'm in prison doing a total of 3 $^1/_2$ to 8 years. The good part about it is that I'm no longer on drugs and I'm not robbing anyone. I just pray to God that I find good friends to help me fight my weakness to drugs. I really don't have a weakness to drugs but sometimes I can find myself with no meaning to life. It is then when I drown my sorrows in drugs. I need attention and careness. I need friends. I have always lived a solitary life. I need friends to help me through the darkness. I will find the light with or without friends. I had enough time to see things more clearly. I have more knowledge of my errors and I'm aware of my problems. With my friends I can make it. (Would you help me).

Part 3

Why Chinese People

I robbed Chinese people because they don't give a hard time. They just give you what you ask for with out a fight. Which it is better. That way no one gets hurt. They also don't call the police, at least most of the time they don't. But most of all they carry a lot of cash money. The Chinese people are into gambling money so they always have a big bag on their posession. I know that any money that is taken from them is easily replaced. So for that reason I did not feel guilty when I took their money. I know for sure that I was not taking their only money. I'm not saying that taking their money was a fun thing to do. I didn't enjoy robbing them. I needed money because I was on drugs. Now that I'm here in prison with a clear mind, I'm devastedly shocked at the things I was doing when I was in the street, and using drugs. It is something that I wouldn't do right now. When I think of the ways I approached and took these people's money. I look at it and say to myself I must've been mad. That what it was, I was mad. Insanely mad. I hope that those who are aware of the things I did will forgive me and try to understand why I did what I did. I will prove myself. I will show people that my reason for robbing people was for my addiction not my pleasure. I don't enjoy taking things from people. If I was ever to become a rich person I would pay double as much to these people of what I took from them. I have to clear myself. I want to be trusted again. Would you help me?

Part 4

What Motivated Me. How Did I Feel.

During the time I was robbing these Chinese people what motivated me was the urge to smoke crack. Again I say it. I wouldn't have robbed anyone if I was not on drugs. How I felt about robbing people? At the time I didn't feel much. When a person is on drugs. He feels no hunger, no worries, no responsibility and no caring. I stole from my girlfriend. I bothered my mother for money. I sold my disc jockey equipment and I sold my sister's bike. All that hurts me all the time I think about it. Sure, it does hurt me. And that is why I felt like dying at the time. I wasn't enjoying none of it. I was only feeding drugs to my needs with no conscious whatsoever. I'm paying for it right now. And I don't feel so bad. I'm being punished and I'm accepting it. It bothers me sometimes when I think about the time I'm doing for an attempt to rob a person. I didn't take anything from him—Mr. S. W. that is. At least I'm no longer a crack addict and I will never again be one. Would you help me?

Part 5

Me and my brothers have caused a lot of heartache and pain to my mother. She is the one who suffered through all the things that me and my brothers did. It will always hurt me and it will hurt me worse when she will no longer be with us on earth. She never let us down. My mother had to raise us by herself. My father wasn't around to help. Of course he too had his problems. My father always had a problem with alcohol. And that cause to be a [failure?]. Things always have been rough for my mother. She raised five children all by herself. That is why I feel guilty. I feel guilty because I have caused her so much sorrow and so much pain. She took care of us. She brought us up by herself. She fed us and put us through school. She never walked out on us. Because of her strength and devotion to take care of us I love her dearly. She never put us in no foster home and she never walked out on us. She stood and took care of us. This is why I'll always feel guilty, guilty because I caused her so much pain when she didn't deserve it.

When she comes to visit me. She tells me that she forgives me and that the only thing she wants from me is that I never do the things that I was doing. I promised her that I won't. I will never live like I lived on drugs and violence. I made it clear that at the time I had no knowledge of what I was doing. I also truthfully told her that the pain that I caused her were not intentional and that I will regret what I did for the rest of my life. She is the most caring, devoted and the most loving mother anyone can have. I'm truly proud to be her son. I love you mother!!!

She has always cared. Every time my brothers would get arrested she would always try to bail them out. She always use to visit my brothers at rickers Island. As I was growing into a teenager I remeber my mother not being in the house in the weekends. She was always visiting someone in the prison. She use to go visit my uncle at Green Haven and my brothers at ricker Island. She has been visiting jails and prisons from the years 1975 to 1990. She always did good deeds for everyone. She even use to take care of my uncles. When they had nowhere to turn to my mother would bring them home and feed them dress them and give them a bed to sleep in. She has done wonderful things for everyone. She deserves to be granted what she asks for and that is for us to correct ourselves and to never use drugs or steal. And that is a wish that will be granted by me. I Love Ye so Mother!!! You are a Special Lady, and I love you. Please forgive me. I Love You Mother.

Part 6

December 16, 1990

Here I am in my cell. I've been continued in solitary confinment since July 21st, 1989 to right now December 16 1990 and I still have 9 months till I be released from a 23 hours a day, 7 days a week solitary confinment. I do and I have spent my days reading books, writing letters and listening to music. It helps to speed up time. I get one hour in the day for daley excercise. I get out to the yard. I usually excercise or just walk around in the yard for a whole hour. The days can become so long sometimes. Sometimes I feel that I will loose my mind. It is horrible. That is why I read a lot. I write a lot and I listen to music because if I don't I can loose my mind. I have 16 months in solitary but I'm still strong mentally and physically. I won't deny it. That sometimes I become scared and nervous when I leave my cell. I guess that is because I have been in solitary for so long. Sometimes I feel very driery [dreary] when I'm near people. It's kind of weird because of such a long time of not being around people and socializing. It scares me but I remain strong. There have been people who have gone insane during the time I've been in solitary and I've seen people hang themselves in their cells. Being in solitary can make a person mad. Being in solitary can make a person mad, or it can make a person wiser. It has made me wiser and more understandable of the suffering people experience. I'm glad to be still alive through I have been through. Me and my family are known for being strong. We take after my mother. She has shown us how to live through difficult times. Anyway I have only 9 months to do in solitary. Hopefully I will be release from solitary before the 9 months are due. I prayerfully hope so. As long as I continue to receive letters from my love ones and friends. That will keep me going. I want to say that I'm truly grateful to those who have taken their time to write me and remind me that I'm not forgotten but I'm truly loved. That is what keeps me going. Thank you Mother, Julio, Richie, Isa, Lucita, Jagna and Paul. Carmen. You all helped me survive this ordeal. I Love You All with ALL MY "HEART".

Sincerely Miguel xxFINAL

I was touched and very perturbed when I received this letter. It was the first time I had ever heard of Miguel's use of drugs. For a long time I rejected this part of the story as just a part of reformulation of events to parallel what the media represented as a typical "criminal career." The Miguel I knew as a child, a clean, hardworking boy who didn't even drink coffee because it would mess up his body, was not congruent with a crack-cocaine user, the hollow-eyed, emaciated crazed freak of mediadom. I knew about one mugging and the attempted second one because I had been involved in helping his lawyer to prepare his defense on the first charge that resulted in the first five-year suspended sentence. I was also greatly disappointed when he was arrested the second time (as was Judge C. apparently, since he walloped Miguel with consecutive rather than concurrent time in prison), because several people including myself had expended a lot of effort to try to get him on the "straight and narrow."

But when I thought about it I realized that I too had been conned into stereotypical thinking about "typical" behavior of drug users, and Miguel's story helped me to examine the stereotype. Through his eyes and memories he was demonstrating that the magical quest for anesthesia through chemical substances can take varied paths. At the beginning of his document he says that at first he sold heroin as a job, tried it as a drug and didn't like it. But crack cocaine "stronged" him out. As a "good boy" he did not fit the typical profile of a deviant whose "gateway" drug is either alcohol or marijuana. His gateway was the need of a job to help his struggling family. As with other drugs historically proscribed and demonized by the popular press, starting with "marijuana madness" and continuing with heroin, angel dust, and so on, cocaine's impact on young, poor white and minority populations was again taken out of its socioeconomic context.

Few articles and no newscasts ever mentioned that it was poverty that sent drug users like Miguel to prison. Rampant middle-class and upper-class drug use and addiction remained largely unexamined and unpunished because the users had the means both to buy and to conceal their use and its effects. As companies hid theft and embezzlement for public-relations reasons, white-collar crime committed to supply middle-class cravings was often dealt with out of court. A trip to "rehab" was more likely than one to prison. And, as Patricia Adler documented (1993), trying and becoming dependent on the "product" one handles was almost always as much a part of the middle-range dealer's life as it was seller's.

Miguel's relationship to his parents and siblings and to his peers and society as a young man coming of age also needed to be taken into account as a factor in his transformation from "good" to "bad." Both Meri and Miguel had voiced the insight that Meri's focusing of her energy and concern on her imprisoned kin left her younger children dangling in an emotional void. The only way for Miguel to shift the focus to himself had been to become "bad." Despite their perception, Meri and Miguel seemed powerless to change their ongoing interactions, enmeshed as they were in the structural situation of their lives. The older boys, by engaging in criminal activities the way they did, were always able to "support" themselves, as paradoxical as that may sound. Dealing in heroin, even if using the product, meant that Richie often had money to contribute to Meri's household budget, to buy her some things she needed. After he was cut off from dealing, robbing became a substitute income-generating activity. When he got too close to the end of these cycles, through overuse of drugs, when he was not even capable of stealing, he would become a true "ward of the state," fully supported in prison, with the caveat that Lucita's earnings and a portion of Meri's small support payments would provide him with the "luxuries" he needed in prison to ensure his security.

A similar pattern operated for Julio, who seemed less vulnerable to drugs. During one of his years on parole, he established a union with a young woman who bore him a daughter. From Meri's partially articulated perspective, both older sons were trying, albeit imperfectly, to act like adults: contributing some income for their room and board, or at least removing the burden of upkeep when imprisoned (although it is questionable what the balance of mutual giving was, because even such items as the warm jackets needed in upstate New York's cold climate were purchased by Meri), and in Julio's case, bringing forth descendants. Grandchildren, especially the first produced by a son, were not a matter of indifference to Meri. They were her future. She went to great lengths to try to retain visiting rights over Julio's daughter after he went back to prison and the girl's mother decided she didn't want her daughter to have a jailbird for a father.

With both brothers incarcerated, Miguel was next in line to be man of the family. Up to this point, he had been stuck at home, not contributing any income, incapable even of venturing out to establish a claim for disability. He was afraid to interact with people; his childhood experiences had left him with an unexamined depression; he was maimed and at the same time too proud to ask for help from people in power. Economically, to Meri, he had been a total deficit, draining her meager resources. It should not have been surprising that when he did move, regardless of his aspirations, he moved first into occupational areas that he knew about secondhand from his brothers, in which he could use their names and kin connections. No matter what his eventual hopes, he needed to obtain some initial money for presentable clothes before applying to educational programs, and also some to give to his mother to show her he, too, was a man. Not having any means to meet and treat a young woman must also have been a powerful incentive. When he did move he was momentarily successful on all counts.

The secretary of the psychiatrist he went to consult, a single mother of two young children who was attending college and served on weekends in the army reserves, promptly fell in love with him. Carmen encouraged him to get his G.E.D. and to go on to college. He enrolled in a class, but at the same time enrolled through Jimmy, Señora Moreno's pain-in-the-neck son, as a lookout for the heroin operation on Fourth Street. He needed "money in his pocket" for taking Carmen out and buying gifts for her children, to contribute to his room and board at his mother's, and to look respectable for his class and his future college career—at one point he showed me a pair of nonprescription glasses and a plastic "briefcase" he had bought to make him look more serious. In his mind, he was not fearful of being attracted to drugs; on that score he felt strong, having seen their impact on people all around him.

There's many a slip 'twixt the cup and the lip, however. Whether it was the fact that he was handling drugs, that he needed to try the "product" in front of his buddies, to know it, to praise it to customers, to take the edge off fear (see for example Adler's 1993 discussion of upper-class dealers' seduction into addiction), or the family background of alcoholism, what is certain is that Miguel became dependent on what crack did for him. Looking at his narrative, his changed use of the verb "strung out" to read "stronged out" implies that the drugs won the struggle, that crack, even in small doses, was something he could not resist, or was at least something he needed as the admission price to the drug dealing world of his more sophisticated and controlled peers.

Miguel's letter was framed by the knowledge that all letters posted in prison, especially those from "the box," were subject to "monitoring." When he was writing he had to be aware that not only warders but also trustees might read it; to a certain extent the tone and contents of the narrative were shaped by this understanding. In addition, what he was composing already had a foretaste of the kind of "life story" an inmate composes for the benefit of a parole board. Events, circumstances, and motivations are selected to suit what the prisoner thinks will impress the authorities to set him free. Miguel was aware that the status of being addicted was one of the few excuses a felon may offer for his past actions that a middle-class parole board may understand. The subtleties of an economy that lacks decent jobs and pitches its young people into indecent ones seems to escape them. But not all of them: One of the most merciful outcomes of a parole hearing is to remand the prisoner to a "halfway house" where he can either work at a "normal" job on the outside and return at night for group sessions, or attend group sessions and work "in-house" all day, if he had been addicted. But given the infinitesimal number of such halfway house slots, it is only the luck of the draw that gets a parolee placed in one. I think Miguel was expanding his options with his "addiction" passages. Lastly, Miguel was also consciously composing his own self-presentation, an autobiography for my book, which might outlive his own life.

Even though Miguel was trying to put his actions in what he thought was their best light, I was annoyed at the cavalier way he explained his victimization of Chinese people. Because so many of Chinatown's people are exploited and poor, working long hours in sweatshops and restaurants for substandard wages and living in even more crowded conditions than Puerto Ricans, I was outraged by Miguel's ignorant statement that they always had money from gambling. But I was expecting too much from him. When mainstream media perpetuate the myth of a "model minority," when most middle-class adults don't care that some of the affordable clothing they wear and the deliciously cheap food they consume in the Silver Palace is subsidized by lack of "quality of life" and the shortened life spans of Chinese workers (Kwong 1987), what could I expect from my parochial friend?

All he knew about the Chinese from the stories of his older brothers and every other older brother on the Lower East Side was that you had to avoid their gangs. Even as upwardly oriented a boy as Emilio Medina had scars on his arm from a defensive engagement with a Chinese gang after a group of boys attempted to see a kung-fu movie on the outskirts of Chinatown. In the heart of Loisida, which the gangs still left alone, the only Chinese presence was the landlords, who might very well have had piles of either rent or gambling money. And the Housing Authority, which ran Smith Houses and in its official publications trumpeted its "democratic" achievement of "integration," in reality did nothing to promote ethnic understanding.

None of which excuses Miguel's robberies and attempted robberies of Chinese people (though I do believe he was polite with Mr. S. W., who apparently felt secure enough to pull rank in age and ask Miguel why he tried to rob him— Miguel's *respeto* for his elders ensuring that he would stop to answer). Nevertheless, in spite of the crimes he admitted to, Miguel was patching together a story about a valiant man, loyal not only to his mother, his siblings, his woman, and me but also to his buddies. This last was evident from the way he lied to protect them. I knew he had not been shot by a "black heroin customer" but by one of Jimmy's associates, for intruding onto an already overfull and competitive heroin distribution network and for doing it ineptly. I had visited him at St. Vincent's Hospital after he was shot, and at that time he was worried that the cops were trying to make him "rat" on his former pals. I also knew that some of those pals thought his inexperience and basic honesty endangered them. Maribelle had also told me that he had tried, without success, to get a job through her man, Tico. She said Tico wouldn't even talk to him.

Miguel's document felt like an "official" autobiography because he was attempting to reconcile the competing values clamoring for ascendance in his life, to shape them into a fitting portrait—the good boy, the bad boy, the macho, the scholar. Despite the picture he drew of serving his sentence with fortitude, I knew from his frequent collect calls and letters, which began almost from the moment he was incarcerated, that unlike his older brothers, he was not "good prison material." Indeed, his inability to negotiate the prison networks and to navigate within the virulent prison subculture would have serious consequences. (For a valorizing description of prison violence see Fleisher 1989.)

From the moment he began serving his term, it seemed, Miguel was out of place. First incarcerated with older prisoners because of a mix-up between his and his brothers' arrest records, Miguel was transferred with his mother's help to a minimum-security prison in Orange County on the dubious assumption that he would be safer in a younger prisoner population close to the city. But because of overcrowding, he was sent on to a prison with older prisoners in Greene County, where his brother Richie was also incarcerated. They seldom saw each other. When Meri visited them and they requested to be seated together for her visit, it apparently dawned on the prison management that they were brothers. Miguel was informed shortly thereafter that he was getting transferred elsewhere. Paul and I visited him shortly after he attempted suicide, by hanging, and almost succeeded. He was despondent about leaving his brother and moving again to another prison. For a short period he was placed in "protective custody"—the "box"—while awaiting transfer to a prison where he would presumably receive supportive psychiatric help. Neither he nor his mother knew where that would be.

Miguel called me the day after he arrived in Sullivan (Sullivan County), to which he had been transferred after being temporarily detained in Shawgunk (Ulster County). That morning he'd been told by a guard, "Valiente, you got to pack up. You're leaving." He was very depressed. "My brother was there—just as I was settling down, they do that to you, they just send you away. I feel very sad that I left Richie there. Jagna, can you call my house and tell them what happened to me? They didn't tell me nothing. It's just so messed up."

Prisoners are only allowed to make collect calls, at specific times, which are very expensive for the recipient. Meri needed a phone for emergencies, for which Lucita paid, but they could not afford the calls from prisons. When I called her she was wheezing with asthma. "Damn!" she said, "they split them because they're brothers. Last time they asked to sit at the same table I knew it was gonna happen. I feel so sorry for Miguel. Richie is stronger than him. How did he sound, Jagna? *Bendito*! [poor boy]. Richie is strong, but I'm worried about Miguel now. I know how he's feeling. I'm scared for him."

Richie called me the next day and said he had spoken with a counselor who had been Miguel's counselor too. Richie was trying to get a transfer to be with his brother but said it was hard. He said he had told the counselor that Miguel's safety would be better assured by Richie's being closer to him, and the man agreed but said, "It says in his record that he needs to be seeing a psychiatrist. The authorities didn't want to take a chance" and wanted Miguel in a prison where one was available.

Sullivan, not far from Bethel, New York, turned out indeed to be a place that handled psychiatric cases, but on the order of the Son of Sam and the Amityville mass murderer. On our way to visit Miguel in February 1989 with Paul and Lucita, Meri expressed her reservations about the place. "Miguel shouldn't be there. That place is for killers. Julio had a lot of cases and he's at Woodburne [a minimum-security unit close to Sullivan] and this is Miguel's first case. Right, Jagna?"

I sort of agreed with her, though I also thought Miguel needed help. But what he needed and what he would get were very different things.

As we drove up Route 17, the old route to the borsht circuit, Meri and Lucita reminisced about other prisons they had visited in the area. Meri remembered one time when Lucita and Isabel were still small and she had taken them along to visit her brother at Greenhaven. During the visit a snowstorm began, and somehow they missed the bus returning to the city. They got kicked out of the prison's waiting room at about 10:30 P.M., and the only place to go was a bar in Stormville frequented by prison guards, about a ten-minute walk in the deepening snow. I knew the place, a dangerous macho hangout; I had once made the mistake of going in to ask for directions, and walked right out. But Meri stayed there, hoping to get help. They were not dressed for snow. Meri said the men were drunk, playing with their guns, and she was afraid one of the girls would get killed. One helpful young corrections officer made phone calls to try to find them a motel or transportation, but he had no luck. At 1:30 A.M., the barmaid told them she was closing up and they had to leave. The officer drove them to a police station in Fishkill, where they sat until morning in a drafty room, all wet and freezing from walking in the snow. "Up to my thighs in snow," Lucita added. Meri said she never went back to Greenhaven after that.

But they also remembered some good times. Lucita remembered Walkill, the place where they could see cows. Meri's husband used to be there, and she would bring food and cook it for him when he got a family visit assignment. They had even spent a New Year's there. "But now he's in Comstock," Meri said. "That's a bad place. That's where they have the guy [Robert Chambers] who killed the girl in Central Park. Ooh, I wouldn't want to meet him. He *used* her and then he killed her. He's a bad man."

But even with a knowledge of other prisons, one is never quite prepared for a visit to a new one. Even Meri, a seasoned prison visitor, was panicking. We passed through the town of Fallsburg, a transformed shtetl bustling with Hasidic Jews, its main street lined with poorly maintained little shops. As we arrived in Sullivan, the snow bleakly falling, we were informed that only three of us would be allowed to go up. New rules for the weekend. Paul elected to wait while Meri, Lucita, and I passed through the security gate, set its alarm bells clanging, and had to return over and over, removing items one by one, glasses, earrings, belts, boots, shoes, emptying pockets, feeling more and more undressed.

Passing through the inner gate and the courtyard, Meri seemed tense. "I don't like this place. It looks like a place for people who did something really bad." It really did—like a futuristic bunker, carved into the hill and shored up by cinder block, buff colored against the falling snow. Our cold-eyed escort marched us upstairs past a futuristic, James Bondian decor, into a shiny, blue-padded elevator. Meri was giving the place a wary eye. She didn't like the silently sliding doors, the skylights that gave it the feeling of a fish tank. I supposed that it was superbly secure and controllable. Only three years old, it was on the cutting edge of prison architecture.

Upstairs in the modern visitor's room, we were assigned a table at which to wait for Miguel. The prisoners started filing in, all looking older and harder than Miguel. Meri kept repeating that Miguel shouldn't be here, this was a place for killers. She was very anxious. So was Lucita. She put her beautiful little face on her arms on the table. A pathetic rest after so many prison visits.

When Miguel finally did arrive, he looked as if he was fighting back tears. He hugged Meri for a long time, then Lucita, then me. Meri had forgotten a sweater she had bought for him, but she had brought two large shopping bags full of tins and boxes: potato chips, cereal, Spam, salmon, rice, cookies. These had been left, labeled with Miguel's name, at the entrance. They would be inspected, and offending items removed (the rules for forbidden articles changed from week to week) before he got the bags—*if* he got them. But right after she told him what she had brought, she started picking on him. How come he had a cold sore, how come he was licking it, why was he here, in a place for killers? Miguel wanted to know how Julio was; though incarcerated only a ten-minute walk away, Julio might have been on the other side of the world. He said he had received the photo of Isabel's newborn son, and he listened with interest as Lucita described the physical fight she had had with Julio's wife to avenge the stories the latter was telling in court about the family in her suit for sole custody of their daughter. She was being so heartless in spite of the fact that she had spent two years living with Meri and her family after her own mother put her out. Lucita was doing a lot of talking to deflect their mother's pecking.

Miguel pointed out the man a few tables away whose life story had provided the narrative for the Amityville horror movie, a skinny, bearded, rat-faced, shifty-eyed man, his long, wiry hair in a ponytail. A fat, toothless woman was fondling him. Meri said, "Ooh, that guy looks crazy!" Lucita added, "If he killed my whole family I wouldn't go to visit him. He should kill himself."

The conversation shifted to moral distinctions, Meri saying how different the Colombian mafia was from the Italian and Jewish ones. "The Colombians are the worst. They kill the whole family." The Chinese mafia were almost as bad as the Colombians, she said. Near her project by the waterfront, all the mafia and the cops hung out together. Every day, she said, by the *New York Post* building there were bodies with bullets in their heads.

Miguel interrupted to tell us he had been assigned to the "pre-G.E.D." class, because there was no room in the G.E.D. program. He had also requested a work assignment, but these were rare and contingent on a sixty-day probation of "good behavior," after which time they were not guaranteed either. In the three weeks he had been there he had seen a psychiatrist once, for fifteen minutes.

Before coming upstairs I had had to leave all my personal belongings in a locker. Now I asked a guard if I could go down for my heart medication. He said,

"Once you come here you can't get out." Seeing my incredulous look, he added, "I mean you could go out, but you can't come back." Meri, Lucita, and Miguel urged me to speak to a sergeant. "There he is now! Speak to him, tell him you need your heart medication. You have to stand up for your rights!" Meri tried to imbue me with her own spirit of resistance, honed as it was right in the "belly of the beast" and along its extensive slimy entrails.

But they wouldn't bend the rule. I was escorted down with a woman of means, wearing furs. She had been visiting an old fat man with whom she had had words. He told her to get out. Meri wandered if this was Son of Sam, but Miguel said, no, Sam was younger, and the other prisoners barked at him.

After I came down, Paul went up. They practically had to strip him because he kept tripping off the security system with all the loose change in his pockets. They finally went over him with a hand-held scanner.

During the next few months Meri alternated her visits to her sons and her husband, taking early-morning buses with Lucita, lugging food. On one visit to Julio, the bus stopped first to let out visitors at the Katonah and Walkill prisons, and during one of those stops someone stole the packages she had for him. "To steal something that is for a poor prisoner . . . I wanted to stay and find the mother-fucker who took it. 'Let me go to jail too!' I spend my welfare on food for my boys, and that's what happens. My boys committed crimes, and they're paying for it, but I'm paying too."

Miguel, meanwhile, seemed to be all right. At first he joined Latinos Unidos, a Latin gang, then he was taken under the wing of an articulate white jailhouse lawyer, who was doing a long stretch but raised Miguel's hopes for an early parole. However, Miguel was not able to get into any programs that counted toward parole, including work assignments or educational programs. He spent his time exercising in the yard, and for a short time keeping a diary that he sent me in installments. It reflected in painful detail the deadly passage of time frittered away. I sent him books and kept writing.

In May he was finally placed in school. He was ecstatic. "Jagna," he wrote, "I learn something new every day." But by July he was in the hospital with a fractured jaw and soon after placed in solitary confinement, where he would spend the next two and a half years.

16
Jail, Jail, All Your Life Jail

Meri and Lucita were visiting Julio in Woodburne Prison when he told them he had a feeling that something bad was happening to Miguel (the prison grapevine?) and that they should go over to check. Sullivan was a ten-minute walk away, and when they arrived they were told Miguel was in the hospital. Over the phone, Meri told me:

> We didn't know nothing. We got there and he was already in the hospital, there was no one there to help him. The guy [who did it] is a drug dealer, he's a big man over there. He pays the police [correctional officers] with the drugs. This man paid a person to do it, somebody from the 'avenue' [B?]. He's the man who put a contract on Julio's uncle. I don't dare to tell them because Miguel said that if he's not careful, they'll harm Lucita. He can't say who did it because then the rest of them think you're a "rat." Nobody in jail talks, Jagna, nobody, because they know they're gonna get killed—not even the person [who] got hurt, because they're gonna say "he's selling tickets" [informing]. How long has Richie been in jail? How many years, how many years has Julio? But they never got hurt because they're already used to doing time, but Miguel, he doesn't know how to defend himself. They wanted to damage his face—he looks like a Frankenstein. The CO [correctional officer] said he got this because he wasn't looking. They [prison officials] told Miguel they made a mistake. He belongs in a medium- not a maximum-security prison. They found out that Miguel wasn't supposed to even be there. It's a big criminal place.

But Miguel apparently did talk. He named his assailants—a big mistake. Two weeks after he was released from the infirmary and placed in "protective custody," his jaw was broken again, this time by guards, and Lucita got an anonymous letter, written in fine curlicued handwriting, suggesting that the best way out for him (and her) was for Miguel to hang himself in solitary.

Meri went into feverish activity, screaming at the prison entrance to see her son (she was denied), then fainting and having an asthma attack right there. In the meantime, I wrote to the prison superintendent (on City College stationery), enclosing a copy of the threatening letter and politely hoping that Miguel's safety would be assured. I also called the Prisoner's Aid Society in Poughkeepsie, New

York, and urged them to immediately send someone to photograph Miguel's wounds and talk to him. Most of these moves were made on the advice of my former-prisoner friends from Greenhaven. The situation was urgent. From my conversations with counselors, hostile nurses, and the chaplain, it didn't look as if Miguel would survive.

From the most sympathetic civilian, a Roman Catholic priest who was not an official chaplain and who seemed sick to death of what he was witnessing, I got the most depressing news. Miguel had been given hundreds of "violations" for protesting his treatment on the "mental health" unit. He was now in a SHU— "solitary"—a very dangerous place. He said that a Filipino psychiatrist who had tried to see Miguel had been denied access.

> He's in Class A danger. He's marked now. They'll send him to another prison, and they'll get him right there. I can't get any information out of SHU, there's no grapevine there. They have a back door to his cell where they can get in without any- body seeing them. Or they'll transfer him to some place in the boondocks where they will kill him. I wrote him a letter—through internal mail—telling him to shut up. He slipped through my fingers. He really did. Not too many people can slip through my fingers, but he dug himself further and further in, he wouldn't listen to counsel. I gave him communion on Sunday. They opened up a little patch in the plastic [where the food is passed through] to give him communion and shake hands. My hands were shaking. He said, "Calm down"—he was telling *me* to calm down. I said, "Look who's talking!" But of course he is too young to know I fear for his life, that's why my hands were shaking. Now I have no access to him. Boy, this has been the hardest case in a year, I can't stand this place anymore.

He spoke as if Miguel were already dead. But, perhaps to humor me, he said he thought some of my actions might help. During my second phone call he said he would talk to the head chaplain but cautioned me that even chaplains had very little freedom. "They do what they are told. That's why I would never want to work for the state." He himself was a volunteer, supported by his own order.

Meanwhile Meri had gone again to see Miguel. She told me she had had to fight her way in, finally convincing them after two days of pleading that he was only vi- olent because he was afraid, and that if they let her see him he would calm down. "I didn't even want to look at him—he has no teeth. His teeth, Jagna, he took such good care of his teeth, always brushing them, buying toothpaste. The COs beat him up even more than the prisoners. They broke his jaw the second time, outside the hospital, and knocked out his teeth. They broke the other side of his jaw. He has to have another operation."

While she was there, the CO was watching through the window the whole time. Miguel was crying from shame because a Cuban CO threw kisses at him every time he passed his cell. The other prisoners were laughing; it made Miguel appear "like a woman." She told him to ignore the insults and said loudly so the CO could hear, "'If that bastard throws you kisses just ignore him. He knows as a CO he shouldn't be doing this. He's trying to make you mad so you'll start fighting again and they'll beat you up. You know you're a man, so please, Miguel, just ignore him.' So Miguel said, 'OK Ma,' but I could see he was almost crying."

The "box" was a tiny room with no window to the outside. "I was two hours there and I thought it was a year," Meri told me. Pretending he was hot, Miguel pulled up his shirt quickly to let her see his bruises. He told her they had put a rope inside his cell. He said, "Ma, don't leave me here too long, they're gonna kill me—they put a rope inside my cell to kill me." As Meri told me this, she was crying. "They're killing my son, Jagna. This is killing me. I can't do nothing for my son—sometimes when I go to sleep I don't want to wake up again."

But of course she was doing a lot. When Lucita got another anonymous letter, with ugly sexual innuendoes, we decided to photocopy it too, for certified mail to the superintendent. But even as I was running around in New York's July heat, underneath I felt that Miguel was slipping through all our fingers. At the time, there was no official death penalty in New York State, only an unofficial one, for being poor and naive.

The only letter I received in response to my letter and phone barrage to the prison read as follows:

Dear Mr.[sic] Sharff,

. . . Mr. Valiente's custodial adjustment has been very poor. He has shown disrespect for Correctional authority and with other inmates. We are continually working with him through his Counselor as well as our Mental Health Unit personnel. His safety at this facility is not jeopardized nor is his health. Any incident of unprofessionalism among staff would be investigated immediately and handled according to our Department procedures.

We thank you for your concern in this matter.

"Bet your life!" I thought when I got this letter. But in fact our actions did have an impact, as did the intercession of the Prisoner's Aid Society. Toward the end of Miguel's incarceration, the number of "violations" he had earned in Sullivan's version of the "cuckoo's nest" were reduced through an administrative hearing, and the legal aid who helped him urged Miguel to pursue a lawsuit against the state. This, unfortunately, he could not do. After his subsequent transfers to Attica and then Bare Hill, near the Canadian border, he was kept in the "box" most of the time, for his own "protection," unable to get counsel or use the library. At least he survived.

Later, after he was let out of solitary at Bare Hill, he told me in his calls about the difficulties he had getting used to living in an open dormitory; after several years of isolation it was hard for him to socialize with people. He walked in the snow-covered yard and sometimes went to see the movies, but the movies were invariably violent. "It's always cops and robbers, cops and robbers," he said, "only once in a while a love story. I guess they're trying to give us ideas," he laughed. He was unable to get "programmed"; that is, to obtain work or attend a G.E.D. class or a drug treatment program. After years on waiting lists, and only two months before his release at the age of 22, he was finally given a job cleaning tables, from which he was soon promoted to washing dishes. He sounded very happy about it.

When Miguel was finally paroled in March 1992, I was invited by his family to meet him at the Port Authority Bus Terminal. He stepped off the bus with a radiant smile, wearing a pair of horn-rimmed nonprescription glasses that made him look like any other Greyhound traveler. He hugged his mother for a long time.

A few days later he agreed to come to my house on the Upper West Side for an interview. Traveling by subway, he called me from Grand Central Station, the halfway point, and said he couldn't go any further. He said people were staring at him and, sensing his discomfort, either giving him a wide berth or getting off the train. I asked him to try to continue the journey, pointing out that people get off when they come to their stop, and he made it.

He spent the afternoon telling me prison stories, repeating them word for word as if he had memorized them. This is his story, told as he wants to remember it, though perhaps imbued with more bravado than was evident at the time. He did not give a definitive reason for the savagery he experienced, first at the hands of the prisoners, then at those of the guards. Maybe it was too dangerous for him to reveal it even now that he was "back on the street." But something I learned from the prisoners at Greenhaven serves me as a powerful reminder and an analogy. At the time I taught there, a young woman guard was murdered and stuffed in a garbage barrel. The prisoners told me that she was about to publicly reveal the extent of drug dealing by the wardens and prisoners, so a lifer was hired to shut her up. Similarly Miguel, with his big uncensored mouth, might have been perceived as a potential threat and therefore taught a lesson. He might also have bragged that he was collaborating with me on a book that would "tell all." When prisoners call home, not only does the prison staff sometimes "monitor" their calls, but other prisoners, waiting in line, may also listen in. In his calls to me before he was injured, Miguel presented a valiant, I'm-not-afraid-of-anybody front. This was congruent with his basic honesty and bravery. I had written him a letter, intended not only for his but also for prison censors' eyes, saying that I was not interested in other people, or accusations, but only in his daily life. The subtext of the letter was, "Shut up." But Miguel was a young man now, one grown from the same child who, as Nilda had said, "was into discovering every dead body in the neighborhood." He would not be suppressed.

Because Miguel was nervous at first, I began the interview with open-ended questions about prison life and then got down to particulars. Miguel said he had first befriended an acquaintance from the Lower East Side, but then stayed away from him because the guy was doing a long stretch and was therefore "on the wild side"—that is, he didn't care how much trouble he got into.

J.: "On the wild side" means that he likes—

M.: Fighting. Stuff like that, violent stuff, you know. And being he had as much time as he did, and I wanted to get home, I had to, slowly but surely, get away from him, you know. And he started disliking me. He started noticing that I didn't want to participate in any of his activities. So that started to make him furious. He started disliking me. He stopped talking to me.

J.: What can they do in prison, you know, when they're going wild? That gets them into trouble?

M.: Well, there's a lot of fighting, knife fights, extortion—well, it's mostly extortion and knife fights. . . . They make them from any piece of metal. They can make them from a stool—a stool has four pieces of metal on the bottom—they just break one off. To sharpen it you just take it in the yard, or in your cell, and you just scrape it, scrape it on the floor, file it, and you make a knife.

J.: Yeah? And extortion is like—getting money out of people?

M.: Yeah. As far as extortion, when guys go to the commissary they try to take their commissary [goods], and, I don't know, have their family, the victim family, to send money to the guy's account.

J.: Oh really?

M.: You know, put pressure on what we call a "weak" person that comes into the jail for the first time and that is scared, you know, and that would give up his money just to stay alive. Well, they'll pick on small guys like that, have them call his mother, whatever, and have her send money, and put that in somebody's name account. Stuff like that. It's extortion. And commissary. Whenever they go to the commissary, they make sure that the person gives his bags to this other guy. This guy has nothing for himself.

J.: How do guys show they're strong? So that they don't get taken advantage of?

M.: You got to walk with an attitude, an attitude that says, "I'm not taking your bullshit," and the attitude is one thing, but the time comes when you have to prove yourself. Like when you bump into somebody that's ready to *test* you. So, he might come around to you and you bump shoulders, purposely, you bump his shoulder into yours, see how he's reacted, if you would ask him why he did that, he'd say—

J.: Just challenge?

M.: Right. The guy might tell him, "Because I felt like it." Then the guy that got pushed must come out and say, "No, I don't like it." Eventually, there will have to be a fight, so if this guy fights and does pretty well, he'll be respected after that. But if the guy backs off, stays pushed without saying a word, he'll become a victim. He'll be a victim of extortion, anything.

J.: Do they fight in the yard with people watching them?

M.: Yeah, they fight in the yard, in the cells, anywhere.

J.: In the cells? I thought—isn't everyone in separate cells?

M.: Yeah, they have separate cells, but when they open the cells, whenever, to go out in the yard, to chow, if there was an argument before they go to chow, these guys will run right into the guy's cell, and they'll fight in the cell.

J.: Really? And do the guards permit that to happen?

M.: No. But the guards are too far away, so by the time they get there, the fight's over. Either someone got knocked out or stabbed.

J.: So it's fair to use weapons in those fights?

M.: Is it *fair?*

J.: Yeah.

M.: Nah. There's never a "fair" way in prison. All right. Suppose somebody wanted to stab somebody up, he might know that with his hands he would beat this other guy [but] he wouldn't want to go through the trouble of just fighting with his hands. He would just want to hit him once and get rid of him.

J.: So let's say a guy wants to test you, let's say you're coming in, right? The guy wants to test you, he pokes you in your arm on purpose. The first time he does that you have to react?

M.: Yes, yes.

J.: And what do you say? "What did you do that for?"

M.: You say, "What's your problem?" You've got to ask, "What's your problem?" On the outside, in the streets here, you'd ask why did he do it. While you're in prison you have to come out a little stronger, that's part of the attitude to survive, you know. So I'd have to ask, "What is your problem?" So, the guy, he'll tell me that he has a problem, that we have to settle it, so I would have to make him a "call out." We'd have to go into the yard, or into the cell, wherever, where the police don't see us. There are certain areas in the yard where they can settle that, you know? And you go into the yard, or the cell, and he'll be worrying about whether I have a knife, and I'll be worrying whether he has a knife, or whether this guy is going to come clean, whatever.

J.: "Come clean" means without a knife?

M.: "Come clean" means without a knife. You know most of the fights are clean, with your hands. But most of these guys tell you they'll fight you with their hands, and while you're fighting, they just pull out, they grab you unarmed, they just . . .

J.: So is this like a test of how far they can push you?

M.: Right. Sometimes it's just a test to see how well you'll defend yourself. Sometimes, just by giving this test it will go further than that, into a bigger fight, into a major problem, you know.

J.: But they wouldn't necessarily stab you at that point?

M.: Not really. Most of the time, no. But sometimes you have these guys that have no control, which at the beginning they feel they do have, that they'll control the situation, make sure it doesn't go too far. But it winds up going out of control, turns into a big thing, a major fight, fistfight, to a stabbing. Some guys will just back off. They'll test you, they'll see that you're the kind of guy that won't take no crap, that you will defend yourself, and they

ready in my room, hospital room, and I wasn't feeling no pain or anything. The corrections officer said, "We have to leave now." So he asked me to get dressed and stuff, get ready to leave. So I went to the bathroom, I looked at the mirror; I looked like a toad frog. This was swollen like a balloon.

J.: Oh my God.

M.: And when they took me back to the facility. . . they put me in the hospital ward there in the dormitory. . . .

J. : And your mother didn't know anything about it yet, right?

M.: No, my mother—I don't remember clearly—but I think my mother was trying to visit me. . . . And I think they wouldn't let her come in and stuff. As a matter of fact I requested, I mean I asked them not to let my mother come and see me. They came back to me and said, "Your mother is very worried" and that we have to let her in. So she came to see me. They brought her over to the hospital, not the visiting room, the hospital, the morgue. She'd seen me, and she'd seen the way my face was all swollen, and she broke down. She started crying and stuff. I told her not to worry about it, it was only swollen, it would go down. Yeah, I told her it wasn't that bad. And it went down. It took a month before it healed completely, before they pulled the wires out.

J.: Did you stay in that hospital ward throughout that time, or did they put you somewhere else?

M.: Oh, they put me in a SHU, the box.

J.: That's right. That was, how long were you in the hospital ward first, after you were wired?

M.: Four days.

J.: Right. Then they took you to SHU, S-H-U, right?

M.: S-H-U. It's a special housing unit for people who are confined for misbehaving. I was taken there because in the hospital they had me in an isolation room, by myself, and they kept the door locked there. I needed to get out of the room and stuff, and they kept me there all the time. I was getting upset.

J.: This was over the three to four days that you were there?

M.: Right, right.

J.: They kept you isolated?

M.: Right. In the isolation room, door locked and everything. I wanted to get out of there, and I was getting pretty upset about that. And really, nobody was paying any mind to me. You know, any time I felt the pain, the pain in my jaw, I wanted to get the nurses there to give me the medication they prescribed for the pain. And they would get me very upset when they would ignore me and not give me my medication, and I was pretty tired of the room and stuff. So I started making too much noise, you know. I started creating a disturbance, I started—

J.: What did you do? Did you kick the door? (*We both laugh.*)

M.: Yeah. I started kicking in the door.

J.: What else? Did you scream?

M.: Yeah, I was yelling a bit, yeah, and kicking the door and stuff, and I was warned to stop that.

J.: Who warned you? The nurses?

M.: The nurses and the corrections officer who was there.

J.: On the other side of the door? Did they stick their head in the door to say that, or—

M.: No. They kept the door closed. They just said, "Shut up."

J.: "Shut up, Valiente, or we're gonna get you"?

M.: Right. So you know, they felt like I was becoming unstable, whatever. So I told them I didn't want that, I didn't need that, I just wanted to get out of there, get out of that room. I said, "Could you please just put me in a dormitory instead of that room?" But they kept me in the isolation room because they had different inmates coming in there, and they didn't trust anyone trying to harm me again. They were keeping me—

J.: Supposedly for your protection—

M.: For my protection. Right. But—and I appreciated that at the time—but I became, I just wanted out of that room. And after I kept asking that for a while, they started ignoring me, and that's when I started getting upset. Anyway, they came one night, the correction officers, the nurse, they wanted to sedate me, give me a shot, calm me down. I told them I didn't want it. I refused. They said, "You gonna get the shot." I said I didn't want it. So they put the key in the door, they were going to open the door, so I took my bed (*laughs*), I pulled my bed, pulled it right in front of the door, so I could keep them from coming in. (*We both laugh.*) Because I didn't want the shot. I didn't want to get shot [!], and I knew they were, in order to restrain me, they were going to physically—

J.: Put you out.

M.: Yeah, put me out so the nurse could give me a shot. So I put the bed in front of the door. They warned me a few times that if I don't move the bed from in front of the door, they were gonna have to rush in there, and once they do, they would beat me up. So after thinking it over I took the bed out the door, let them come in. But they still rushed me.

J.: Oh, they did?

M.: Yeah, both of them [the COs]. They pulled me into the corner, pulled my hands up, and twisted them. The nurse came behind me, pulled my pants down, and gave me a shot in the back.

J.: In your butt.

M.: Yeah. And boom! They gave me the shot and stuff, the nurse left the room, one of the COs left the room, the other one had me still up against the wall. He said, "I'm gonna back off out of the room, I'm gonna go out. I want you to keep your hands on the wall. Don't turn around. If you do I'm gonna drop you" [shoot you]. I kept my hands on the wall. I started to feel the medication, the stuff they shot me with. So I felt pretty worn out. So I didn't bother to try to turn around and grab him for what they did to me. So I just let them go. They shut the door, and I was still angry, I was still making a little noise. But after a little while I started feeling drowsy and I just went over to the bed. I became quiet and I fell asleep. Because you know that medication puts you to sleep. But the next day I was even more upset. So I started doing the same thing over again. I started making noise.

J.: So what were you doing? Kicking the door?

M.: Kicking the door.

J.: Yelling? Did you bang anything into the door too?

M.: Yeah, they had what they call—what is it that they have? These trays that they have in the hospital that you could lower them?

J.: A cart? (*Laughs.*)

M.: A cart, yeah (*laughing*). I was hitting one of the carts against the wall. I kept banging the cart against the door. They came again. This time they didn't warn me, or to get back. They just opened the door again and just rushed me.

J.: Two guys?

M.: No. Three correctional officers and one sergeant.

J.: Oh, so there were four of them.

M.: They just rushed into the room and put me against the wall. They didn't hit me or anything. They just restrained me but kept me very close into the wall. And the sergeant put some handcuffs on me and said that I would have to be taken to a—I think it's called 101 Observation—it's, they put you in a strip cell, with just your underwear. They strip you from your clothes . . . to teach you a lesson.

J.: Oh. So, observation cell they call it—it's supposed to be like a psychiatric cell?

M.: OK, no, no. They used it for that, but sometimes they used it to punish you. They took all my clothes off and left me in my underwear. In the room there's a bed frame there but there's no bed [mattress], stuff like that. So I had to stay there overnight. I slept on the floor.

J.: On the floor?

M.: Yeah, on the floor. I slept on the floor because the bed frame was cold. It's cold on that floor. Being that I had no clothes on. . . . What made it worse is that they had blowers that shoot cold air. Being that I was in there and I was giving them a hard time, they gave me a hard time and they turned on the blower. Kept it on all night, you know.

J.: So you were freezing.

M.: Yeah.

J.: With your jaw still wired?

M.: Yes.

J.: It was, like, a few days after you were injured?

M.: Yes, yes. So they kept me there overnight, and the next day they were taking me back to the infirmary, into the isolation room, you know. I told them again I didn't want to be in there. They just put me in there again. I was in there for a couple of hours before I started.

J.: You started *again*?

M.: Yes. . . . When they put me back there and didn't put me back in the infirmary, I started making noise again, and I knew they were going to come in and rush me again, it's like I had no control, you know, I was very upset. And so when they rushed in, I knew they were going to beat me pretty bad this time because I had been bothering them too much. So when they were coming into the room they said, "Valiente, we're gonna come in again, and the nurse is going to give you a shot." I didn't want another shot.

J.: Why were you afraid of the shot, by the way?

M.: I didn't want it, I didn't want medication, I didn't want any of that stuff. . . . They said, "We're coming in! Back up against the wall!" I said, "I'm not!" and I put my hands up. I put my hands up, and they said, "Valiente, we gonna come in, we gonna have to use full resistance"—how do you say?—"full restraint," full restraint. Which means, "We're gonna use the night sticks," and stuff like that. So I told them, "Come on in then!" I told them because I was pretty upset about that, after spending a night at that station, in the cold, and I told them, "Come in then!" and I put my hands up, fighting position, you know.

J.: They could see you through the window?

M.: Yeah, they have a, like, window, ten by fifteen [inches], so they can look right in and see my whole body. So I stood there, my hands up, in a fighting position. They just opened the door, they rushed me. I didn't swing, even though . . . I didn't fight with them. And they pushed me against the wall, I mean, slammed me against the wall, and threw me on the floor. Officers put their shoes in my back, just to hold me down—

Miguel was taken to the box next, because he was now charged with an assault. But he made noise in the box, in the same way, and was warned, rushed, and once again taken to the "observation" room. This time he was handcuffed and led by two COs, one of whom was stepping on Miguel's bare feet as they walked. When he protested he was lifted up by the guards, into the air, and had his underwear pulled up, to reveal his buttocks:

M.: And so I, once they did that, they pulled my underwear up in the back, I tried to struggle with them, and I tried to struggle and didn't get anywhere, so they kept carrying me back to that little room, that observation room, and they just dropped me there on the steel bed. On the steel frame. They dropped me there on my face, my face, my face hit first, hit the bed frame first.

J.: Yeah. Because your arms were in the back.

M.: Yeah.

J.: Were you handcuffed at this point?

M.: Yes, I was handcuffed. Every time they take you out of a SHU cell they handcuff you.

J.: And that was behind your back?

M.: (*Nods.*) So they took me to that little room, they body-slammed me, and my face hit first.

J.: You say "body-slam"?

M.: Yes. They picked up my body and slammed me, and my face hit first. From that my lip was swollen and stuff, and they sat me up a couple of times, they hit me in the body and in my face. And then they had the nurse come in so she could clean up the mess they did, the scars [cuts, abrasions] on my foot. The nurse came in with the gauze pads and alcohol, tried to clean it up so it doesn't show much, just in case I tried to report them. . . . So while she was doing that I tried to push her off with my foot, so she would leave it like that, in case anyone came to see me. I wanted them to see what these guys did to me. While I tried to do that they kept pressing on my face, punching me on my leg, so I wouldn't move while she was cleaning it up. So they did that, and she took off after she did her job, and they left me there. The officers walked out, they closed the door, they left one officer there in front of the door, and they kept me there overnight again. This was Saturday. Sunday morning I got a visit. And they said, "Valiente, you got a visit. We're gonna take you to the shower—get your shower, put your clothes on," stuff like that. The visit, ah, I think it was my mother and my sister. They came to see me.

J.: Your mother was going crazy at that time.

M.: So they finally did let her in, they finally did let her in, and when she came in she could see why they were keeping her from seeing me.

Miguel went on to describe (circumspectly) how he also had scars around his genital area, because as a final act of humiliation, the guards had ripped off his underwear before leaving him in the observation room. So far he had earned twenty-seven "tickets"; but at the same time, following Meri's visit, my calls to the Prisoner's Legal Aid, and a visit from them, when his wounds were photographed, he was able to file for a hearing. As a result of these actions—his mother's dogged persistence, my help, and the intercession of the outside agency—the prison authorities made sure he remained alive. This, however, did not mean an end to the provocations, chicanery, and violence.

Miguel said he stopped provoking the guards at this point; he was all worn out. They, in contrast, "dissed" his food, provoked him verbally, and when he reacted, piled on more "tickets" claiming assault. For example, with his jaw injured and reinjured, he was supposed to get soft cereal with milk. One day he would get cereal, but no milk; the next day, the opposite. Sometimes the missing item would be thrown at him. When he threw it back (through the small opening through which the food tray was passed), he would be charged with assault. "They kept saying, 'You punk, you got your jaw broken. It's a good thing you got your jaw broken.' They were disrespecting me. Doing that to me personally."

When I asked why that bothered him so much he said, "Well, it hurted me from the very beginning, just to get my jaw broken. You know, any man that puts a hand on another man, that's a big disrespect, especially in jail. And being teased about it by police is even worse, because I dislike them more than the prisoners. So I would let it get me upset. So I would argue with them and start banging the door again, and that's how I continued getting tickets."

Going back to these events now in the interview, I was surprised that even though he had been under such severe stress, Miguel was still able to distinguish and appreciate kindness from some guards. He told me he thought that the men on the morning shift were nicer because they came to work when "the sun was shining." What he did not say, and I didn't want to press him on, was that with fewer supervisors and administrators around in the evenings, the guards on the late shift might have been tougher, more sadistic, and more likely to be involved in drug dealing networks.

Nevertheless, a certain empathy sometimes sprung up between the jailers and the jailed, in spite of frequent transfers of both guards and inmates, racial and ethnic differences, and the increasingly brutal and brutalizing political climate and economic depression.

We talked some more about his subsequent transfer to Attica, which occurred soon after these events. There he continued to be held in solitary until his two and a half years of the violations he earned in Sullivan were completed. Finally freed from solitary, he was assigned gardening work in the elaborate flower displays that grace prison entrances outside of the prisoners' view. Able at last to interact with other inmates, he received some grass-roots political education that younger prisoners get in Attica, Sing Sing, and Greenhaven from older politicized or political prisoners. Two months later, when he was transferred to Bare Hill, he seemed to have improved, perhaps as a result of this resocialization, and was less self-involved and more capable of feeling empathy for others. He described in detail and with feeling the sadistic treatment meted out by the guards to an African American prisoner who had been transferred with him from Attica. He concluded, "Bare Hill was the first place that I've seen such racism." But in fact, this was the first place where he was not in solitary and where his eyes were at last open.

During the months following our interview, I was in touch with Miguel and his family by phone, although he seldom called me. He had promised to call when his life was going well. It wasn't going well. He said he was attending a drug program mandated by his parole three times a week, but he was not encouraged by his parole officer to seek work, another condition. Instead she helped him obtain public assistance, which together with food stamps provided him with an annual income of $2,724. This he turned over to his mother, since she needed it, and didn't spend money on going out. His social life would in any case have been limited by the other conditions of his parole: He had to be home by ten o'clock at night, could not travel beyond the five boroughs of the city without special permission, and could not socialize with anyone who had served time in prison.

That included many of the young people he knew who were still alive. His parole officer could issue a warrant for his rearrest any time she decided he was violating his parole, including if he did not report on time to her, and he could then be returned to prison, without due process of the law, after an administrative parole revocation hearing. He was also vulnerable to unscrupulous police and judiciary procedures when a crime needed to be solved, because he was easily available through the computer system. And this point is exacerbated by the perils he faced "on the street" from former convicts or middle-range dealers who with or without corrupt police complicity might finger him or maim him for a real or imagined grievance.

Eight months after his release, after receiving a Thanksgiving card from him, I invited him to my house for another interview. He came bearing a gift of his mother's homemade pasteles. Although the trip had been easier this time because I suggested he travel by bus—less claustrophobic—he appeared anxious and depressed. His options seemed even more restricted than before. Because of his continuing agoraphobia, he was unable to sit in a G.E.D. class. He had also been dropped from his drug program because he could not participate in its group sessions, though he continued to see a psychiatrist individually twice a week. I asked him how he spent the rest of his time.

"Well, most of the time I'm usually home," he said, his voice flat. "I go out once in a while and take a walk, just ride my bike, just anywhere. Sometimes I go up to the Village, or I go near the Twin Towers, right around there, or just take a ride down to my old neighborhood, down to the Lower East Side, East Fourth."

"How has the Lower East Side changed?"

"It has changed a lot as far as drugs in the streets. You don't see too many drug dealings going on as before. On Third Street, that's where most of the drug dealing used to be before, there is no drugs at all. But they're on Second Street now."

The old neighborhood looked a lot cleaner now, Miguel said, but at a cost. "The area looks good now, much better than before. They have restored the old abandoned buildings. It looks much cleaner, much, much better. When I came out it looked much cleaner, but . . . it didn't have the life it had before. The streets seemed so empty, so quiet. Most of the people I knew before, they no longer live there. So it's just new faces around."

He said it made him sad to go back there.

A lot of the people I knew that lived there are not there anymore. They either moved out, or went to jail, or are dead. . . . So, it makes me sad because I feel alone, they're no longer there. Some of the people when I lived or hanged around there are still there. But they are just people that used to live there that I never spoke with before. There were people who were using drugs when I went away, but they look much worse now, and some of them are just gone. They're dead. Young people, my age and older. Some of them died of overdoses, some died of AIDS. . . . In between the time that I was away I heard that they died.

He was looking somewhere within himself. Trying to bring him back, I asked him if he ever went back to his old house. His expression didn't change.

Yes, I have passed through Fifth Street. The building which I lived in before, it's now abandoned—it's empty and the windows are filled with cinder blocks. The whole building is covered with cinder blocks, the windows and the front door. There are two other buildings, one at each side, which are also abandoned. To see my old building, where I lived before, I just think of when I was a kid, when I lived there. I really don't feel anything—I just remember, when I was a kid, living there.

He sounded as if whatever clues the past held remained indecipherable. As if he was still marking time and had never left the box.

"I remember growing some there."

Epilogue:
Walking My Baby

Some of the people I knew on the Lower East Side over the past fifteen years or so, especially children, have emerged on conventional life paths. Yet the number of casualties in subtle or grosser forms is large. It is clear that the chain of causality begins with the political, social, and economic policies toward the poor designed at the highest levels of our society. Seemingly forgetting our more generous traditions, we have allowed our leaders to push our society to a historic low point of economic equality, construing the poor as a threat that can only be contained by increased reliance on armed "guard labor" (Bowles, Gordon and Weisskopf 1990). The effect of national policies that devalue the lives of poor citizens can be examined on several levels: The individual—how does a growing human organism react to endemic violence? The communal—what happens to a community that exists in a state of siege, subject to removal and potential internal refugee status? The systemic—what are the chances of achieving a healthy democratic society when increasingly larger sectors of its population are deprived of the means of making a sustainable living, and instead are severely punished for finding alternative ways to help their children survive?

First, on the individual level, my observations suggest a connection to a psychiatric area of research that has a small but increasingly sophisticated literature. The American Psychiatric Association officially published diagnostic criteria for Post Traumatic Stress Disorder (PTSD) only in 1980, and since then, research has mushroomed, including work with survivors of the Holocaust and of wartime bombings in England, victims of natural disasters in the United States, returning Vietnam War veterans, and victims of incest and family violence. A definition of PTSD and a wide sampling of the research can be found in *Trauma and Its Wake* (Figley 1985). My aim here is to draw attention to the fact that almost nothing has been said by anthropologists about the terrible suffering that poor children are forced to endure as a result of our undeclared domestic wars. A work edited by Cristina Szanton Blanc (1994) for UNICEF describes the lives of poor urban children in five countries, but not in the United States. The work that comes closest to engaging this subject is the research by James Garbarino and his coworkers. In *No Place to Be a Child: Growing Up in a War Zone* (1991), they document the life of children in war zones in Cambodia, Mozambique, Nicaragua, and Palestine—as well as in public housing in Chicago. The effects of endemic, warlike situations on the lives of children deserve immediate attention and joint action.[1]

Similarly and concurrently, on the community level, we need to address the effects on social life of chronic attrition and struggle, which unlike a declared war have no potential end in sight. Some consensus emerging from the research on natural disasters and victims of war suggests that a community that mobilizes itself against an "act of God" of brief duration has a much better chance of fast recovery than a community suffering from acts of man, but mobilization is the operative word, even against oppression by other human beings. Mustering against an enemy helps a community call upon the psychic and social reserves of its members and to regain its vitality (Quarantelli 1985). For the poor ghetto communities, who, what is the enemy? A community that cannot pinpoint and therefore mobilize against the sources of its oppression and depression is in deep trouble. It is urgent that clear analysis of economic and social inequality, written in plain English, once again finds its way back to working-class people. "Is this the death of the community?" Clara Valiente Barksdale asked us. It was only the beginning.

As I have indicated in the foregoing stories, the gentrification of the Lower East Side, followed by Operation Pressure Point, introduced paramilitary conditions for the poor people of the neighborhood, and swept the families away into the outer boroughs (DeGiovanni 1987), into "doubling up" on its edges in public housing, and in refugee-like shelters. Its young male population was moved on a massive scale into upstate penitentiaries. What chance was there to create stable community organizations that would help people weather the shocks of uprooting? Or give them a chance to organize and protest? To remain where they grew up, surely a human right?

The appearance of crack cocaine in the neighborhood at the time when these upheavals were taking place added a surreal dimension to them. Cheaper than cocaine, the drug of choice for the higher classes, and thought to be less addictive—or at least less degrading—than heroin, it became the drug of choice for young people who had previously smoked marijuana in friendly groups. In a climate of loosened community controls, when much of the community had already dispersed, young people flocked back to their neighborhood for socializing, for making money by selling drugs, and for taking drugs, which made this style of life easier to enter, accept, and endure.

A new dimension was added when young women, in much smaller numbers than the men, began to use crack as well, through their connections to the men who used it and dealt it. Young women are more responsible for the well-being of children than are men, and in stable communities, such as they were, they could count on the help of older women when they were too stretched or too young to cope. But the tearing away of young parents from their extended families into dispersed housing and shelters had overwhelming effects on the health of young children. The state's response to the situation its policies and neglect had helped create was to take punitive action against women, to take their children away and place them in expensive foster care (Susser 1992), and to institute moralizing policies attempting to control poor women's rights to bear and raise children.

At the same time, heroin—for years used in the neighborhood at a low, endemic level, supplying a small number of older local users and a growing number of consumers from affluent communities—now became attractive to younger users. It was cheaper once again, accessible and available. The devil himself could not have done a better job of planning the confluences that now came together, combining the spread of intravenous injections, dirty needles, men returning from prisons, cheaper drugs, loosened community controls over female sexuality, male homosexuality for money and favors, and the lurking presence of the HIV virus.

The first neighborhood casualty of the AIDS epidemic, which has since taken a large toll on the people from the Lower East Side whom we knew, was Cecilia, the former radical community organizer and later adviser to the Gatos group. Other women, men, and babies followed; at first, ironically, mainly from the ranks of the local-level "elite," people who had had earlier access to drug using and selling through their middle-class connections to middle-class whites. Delila, whose father had branched out from the bolita business into drug dealing, and whose family became wealthy by the neighborhood's standards, was infected with HIV from her drug-injecting boyfriend. Later, Señora Enriquez and her husband also became ill and lost all their fortune. Only Jojo seems to have escaped, living and working somewhere in New Jersey.

By the 1990s the AIDS epidemic had spread to the outer boroughs and to Puerto Rico as a result of the fluid migration between the island and the New York community. If one were to draw lines of the epidemic's spread, they would parallel the spread of drugs; from affluent middle-class enclaves to poor communities, to upstate prisons, and back to poor communities, subsequently radiating into the outer boroughs and suburbia.

By 1990 Lady Carpenter was taking care of scores of orphaned teenagers whose young adult parents had died of AIDS. She was doing this on a shoestring budget, in spite of looming legal problems (Jacobs 1996). She told me she was embattled against a local community board that received complaints about her teens. Some of the complaints originated with male pimps who had "stabled" teens, male and female, and made money by prostituting them. Ever the activist, she helped to prosecute several pimps and to send them to prison. Just feeding the children, who slept on cots in the large shop that had formerly been a site for training women in building trades, and making sure they attended school were overwhelming concerns. She got volunteer help from some of the adults attending the Alcoholics Anonymous and Narcotics Anonymous sessions now held twenty-four hours a day in the cavernous former trade school.

The active presence of the Grim Reaper on the Lower East Side was not confined to deaths from AIDS, "overdosing" on illicit drugs (usually the result of poisonous admixtures rather than overdoses per se [Haberman and Baden 1978]), alcohol abuse, or accidents. It was a combination of these factors and additional stresses that put the population at an increased risk. Real estate pressures on the housing for the poor that left them homeless and more vulnerable to infections in crowded or congregate housing, lawlessness by the police that ended in maiming and deaths, and the increasing push for "moving on," causing constant internal migrations, created conditions that were inimical to maintaining ordinary life. The space human beings need to perform the recurring rhythmic tasks that sustain life—a means to prepare their daily food, to provide nourishment for the upkeep of their bodies and a quiet space for the nightly refreshment of sleep—were also compromised. Life for the poor began to resemble some of the conditions of life in refugee camps. The emergency rooms of the local hospitals were overflowing with people whose physical and mental health had deteriorated, and the elementary schools coped with children who no longer had even a slum apartment for refuge.

Count Augusto lost his apartment in the late 1980s. His landlord bought him out for about $20,000, intending to co-op the building, which he did, probably making a million on the deal. Even though Gusto felt pretty flush, distributing the money hand over fist to his buddies, I was very sorry to hear the news because I knew the apartment was the only source of stability in his life. Its floors, walls, and ceiling painted in rainbow swaths of color, this railroad flat allowed Gusto to cook nutritious meals; provided a base for keeping himself neat and clean, a point on which he was fanatical; and above all, gave him a place to safely rant and rave and sleep off his bouts of drinking. On several occasions, when first Paul and then Nilda and her sister were homeless, Gusto had shared his technicolored inner sanctum generously with them for weeks on end. The apartment allowed him to conserve his energies, to recoup his mental and physical faculties, and to sail forth each day at 6 A.M. when he had work as a carpenter, happy to greet the morning with the birds.

Losing his apartment literally finished him. He moved from friend to friend for a year and ended up living in an abandoned house, his money all spent. Without proper rest and nutrition his alcoholism progressed swiftly. One Monday morning when his work partner, Lee, stopped in for Gusto on his way to work, as was his habit, he found only Gusto's distended corpse. Gusto was dead at the age of forty-two. The medical examiner determined that Gusto had fumbled in the darkness, hitting his head, and had bled to death over the weekend.

At the wake, held in a Brooklyn funeral parlor, Gusto's mother, a thin, dark woman with fierce Aztec eyebrows that formed a straight line over the bridge of her nose, looked lost. Gusto's twin sister, lighter-skinned than either her mother or brother, the one in whom the family had invested their upwardly mobile hopes, spoke to anyone who cared to listen about how often she had invited Gusto to mend his ways. Her husband, meanwhile, sat in their large car in the parking lot, working on tax forms. He was an accountant. This was February, when accountants are very busy; he had no time to waste. I said to Nilda, "If only Gusto could speak, he'd denounce the guy for a capitalist tool."

Gusto had not been well enough known nor his death spectacular enough to be rewarded with a public mural. But another man who died shortly after Gusto apparently did. Bimbo Rivas, a radical community organizer whom the cops singled out for repeated arrests during community protests against unreasonable police actions, died of a heart attack in front of the English class he was teaching, the stress of his unflagging activism probably contributing to his premature death. A huge mural on Avenue C, harking back in style to the democratic 1960s, celebrated his life's dedication to the poor and oppressed. Like Gusto, he was a poet. One poem he wrote, entitled "A Job," serves as a fitting epitaph to men of the Lower East Side. It ends

> *I only ask for a clearer path*
> *to put my hands and brain to work*
> *to prove my worth. (Algarin and Pinero 1975:93)*

Mr. Stern, our landlord, was another casualty. Although he had profited some from the misery of his tenants, he had been close enough and immersed enough in those miseries to succumb to the stresses of Lower East Side life. When I visited East Fourth Street in 1992, I was told by the tenant in our former office, a sculptor of wire horses, that Mr. Stern had died of a heart attack. His daughter was now the landlady. I moseyed over to Avenue B to express my condolences. The office was open, unlocked, with no one there. Apparently Mr. Stern's daughter was as comfortable with the locals as her dad had been.

I have already mentioned the deaths of the two mothers we knew as a consequence of losing their housing, but for the majority of people, the impact of their community's dissolution was more subtle and prolonged. Señora Moreno, for example, finally found housing in renovated apartments for the disabled below Houston Street. She now qualified on the basis of a severe asthmatic condition that had also undermined her heart. But her building had tough rules, enforced by nosy guards, about sharing living space with extra family; neither Paco, who was too disturbed to be quiet, nor Maribelle, with her young child, could stay with her for long. Paco began to flop wherever he could, and Maribelle, after leaving the warehouse hotel in Brooklyn, moved on to a rat-infested room on Fifth Street in an abandoned block, and finally to nights spent with her baby in welfare offices.

When she was at last allotted an apartment in the Bronx, the ratty room that had initially housed Lisa (who "passed it on" to Maribelle) was in turn passed on to Dolores, Maribelle's mother-in-law. Dolores lived there with Francisco, the boy traumatized by fires, who couldn't read or write too well at the age of twelve because he was too fearful to attend school regularly. Following the halcyon years in Puerto Rico and Queens, Dolores's partner, Cisco, and her oldest boy, Rafael, were sent to federal prisons after being convicted of big-time dealing. Rafael had become a Muslim in prison and changed his name to an Arabic one. The other boys were scattered between the outer boroughs and upstate prisons, and Dolores supported herself by working in a toy factory, earning $4 an hour, with frequent lay-offs during slow periods. Maribelle told me Dolores was hurting from performing the same movements over and over again, hunched over a conveyor belt.

Maribelle said that even though her new apartment was bigger, she didn't know anyone in the building and couldn't allow her children to go out because there was no way to monitor their safety from a seventh-floor window without good neighbors. The park—the usual "needle park" of poor neighborhoods—was out of the question for her and her children. She often took them by subway to visit her mother, whom she missed and worried about. She and Tico, who did various carpentry jobs and was, as she put it, "an all-around man," could not even afford a used car. He earned minimum wage, and the care of her three young children was a full-time occupation in this new, even more dangerous neighborhood. She and Tico had remained a loving and stable couple from the time of their young teens. For his little family, he built beds, cribs, and chests, all finely crafted and painted pink and blue. Those pigeon-coop building sessions had come in handy.

Besides Paco and her mother, Señora Moreno, the other living casualty in Maribelle's family was pain-in-the-neck brother Jimmy. His future had been predictable. Maribelle filled me in on how between Jimmy's stints in prison she had "tricked" him into attending family therapy sessions, and how he had said he would try to prepare for a different way of making a living. But in the end he even failed "shock camp," the latest New York State gimmick to prepare young men for a useful life without providing the jobs that are the major prerequisite for such a life. Jimmy signed up to do six months in the totalitarian training milieu in lieu of serving two years in an ordinary prison. It didn't take long before he told a guard to fuck off, and he was instantly sprung back to serve his full time in prison. He had assumed the role of a macho in his family too early in life to be able to change.

But some of the other boys were doing better. Maribelle told me that Myrna's son Adam (whose marine father, for all his veteran status, could not keep his family from falling into the dismal swamp of the Hotel Martinique) was married and worked two jobs. His primary job was as a paramedic, and he hoped to rise through the ranks to ambulance driver. Maribelle explained that "after he came out [of prison], he never went back in," and she gave credit to Adam's wife, a nice girl who was a chef and to whom he was married "by church." He owned a car and invited Tico, along with a few other young men who had stayed out of prison and landed marginal jobs, to go camping in the Adirondacks. They spent a weekend in tents, roughing it, and came back ecstatic about the experience. Paul's trips had attuned them to the call of the wild.

Like other young people I met who had been uprooted from their community of birth and childhood, Maribelle told me, "I feel so lost over here, I put in for a transfer to be closer to my mother." A few years later she got her wish and moved into renovated housing below Houston Street, close to her old neighborhood. She planned to get her G.E.D. and move on to work as soon as all three children were in school. She seemed much happier when I last saw her. She and her family came to a surprise birthday party for me. The best gift was the news that Paco had a room of his own and worked part-time in the craft shop of a venerable Lower East Side social agency.

Meanwhile, Isabel, Lucita's older sister with three young children of her own, was also homeward bound. Her husband had lost his manager's job when the supermarket closed down, and they could no longer pay for their New Jersey apartment. All five descended on Meri, who welcomed them in, but judging from the melees I heard in the background during phone calls, Meri was no longer as capable of taking care of the whole extended family as she had been when younger. Meri's long-absent husband, the father of her four younger children, was now out of prison, and he stepped into the breach. He used his connections to persuade housing officials to have Isabel moved up to the head of the line for an apartment uptown. I didn't ask how.

Fortuitously, using her intelligence, Isabel discovered before moving out from New Jersey that her Arab landlord had been overcharging on the rent during the entire ten years she had lived there. She took him to court and, appearing as her own counsel, won a judgment of $7,000 against him. (Whether she ever collects is another story.) But I was more than happy to write letters to court for her on my computer as her children and Lucita's first child gamboled in my house. These girls had turned into such beautiful, smart women. Those who had endured Nilda's boring Saturday classes in "proper" Spanish and English diction were fully conversant in standard English, rich Puerto Rican Spanish, and a smidgen of what might have passed for Castilian, to say nothing of Loisaida English.

Ginny, another of these diligent students, was also doing well. She now had three children. Her mother, Millie, had met another man after her divorce from Arturo, moved out to the man's apartment in Brooklyn, and left the project apartment as "inheritance" to Ginny, her husband, their children, and Ginny's two brothers, Marco and Chulito. The apartment was too small for so many people, and Ginny, although she loved to cook, got tired of taking care of them all. She put in for an apartment of her own, got it, and moved with her own nuclear family, leaving the apartment in turn to her brothers and their incipient families. At about the same time that Ginny gave birth to her third child, Millie had another baby. She was still very young for a grandmother, and her new husband had no children. I was not personally in touch with Millie because after her separation from Arturo she had set her eyes on Paul. She knew that Paul and I had had by then a steady partnership of over ten years, so I was not very understanding. But after all, even anthropologists are human.

Of all the young men we knew, one of the most spectacular successes was Lefty. During his visit to my house on his search for his child, he told me something about his life as a teacher and how he had arrived at that point. "Olie's death hit me like a ton of bricks. I almost got killed there [in the bodega] myself. Things didn't go better at first, it was a form of depression." But a piece of luck had connected him to a program that inspired him to finish high school and go on to college. He attributed a large part of his success to becoming a born-again Christian.

He still teaches math in an alternative high school, has a pleasant apartment in the Village, and listens to Mozart for inspiration.

Not that Mozart is necessarily a yardstick of upward mobility. Eti, *bochi-uchando* [gossiping] to me, said that Lefty "got religion in jail"—one item he omitted to tell me from the story of his life. For all her *bochinches* about Lefty, Eti and her children had had parallel experiences. José, the youngest and a macho, had served a small stint in jail and had given her trouble, but he was now settling down, with three children of his own. Her other children were doing really well. Our favorite, Emilio, was still with his woman and had three children. He had a full-time, poorly paid job, but he was also attending community college. His most spectacular achievement, however, was that he had become a preacher in the Pentecostal Church. He spoke fervently at street revival meetings, converting people to the faith, and managed to pull his entire family into it. Only the next to the eldest, Pablo, still drank alcohol occasionally; the rest were abstinent.

Nilsa's friendship was partly responsible for these positive changes. Beginning with the practical act of getting Pablo a union job through her husband (from whom she was now again divorced), and following up with a union job for Eti through her connections as a genetic counselor, she remained a steady friend to Eti through the most difficult times, helping with loans and empathy. She was there for Eti when her eldest son, a career officer in Puerto Rico, was shot to death, and again, a few years later, when Clara died in a car accident. Nilsa's religious convictions, the promises and energy that religious revival brings to people when nothing else is available to help them in a social vacuum, supported Emilio and his family's move into Pentecostalism. The radical left movements that had once been so helpful to earlier immigrants in organizing them to demand decent wages and living conditions had long ago been undermined, decimated, and compromised. Only the churches remained, pointing the way to individual upward mobility on earth and beyond.

I think that practicing his ministerial precepts has helped Emilio forgive me my treachery with Max the Wolf. After Olie's death, Ronna decided to cut short her stay in New York and return to her Indian reservation. Because we were all so overcome by the recent events, and because as a sweet person she wanted to make somebody's life easier, she invited Max to go and live with her. Emilio agreed, sadly, knowing he would miss Max, but then, hey, it would improve Max's chances in life, just like that movie *Papi*, you know, where the father puts his kids on a lifeboat so everybody thinks they're Cuban, and you know, they get adopted by a rich family? So Ronna left, her little Volkswagon crowded with books and Max. What I didn't dare tell Emilio until many years later was that during a pee stop in a Kansas cornfield, Max took off. And although Ronna spent several days searching for him, her last glimpse of Max was of his wolf tail heading east through the cornstalks. I like to think his ghost is still trotting toward the Lower East Side.

As hospitals began downsizing in the early 1990s, Eti lost her union job. But she found work in a senior citizens center, not precisely her first choice, because she was better at working with children, but a decent job nonetheless. When she gets home she is surrounded by her sons and daughter Maria, who with their children live in the same building and on adjoining blocks. (She had also tried to get Clara's two children to come live with her after Clara's death, but they elected to live with their paternal grandparents in Puerto Rico.) She has twenty grandchildren and says, "I have to give thanks to God, every day, every hour," for her good luck. She thinks that if she had remained on the Lower East Side she would have lost all her children, one by one. She has told them about what she had to do during the brief period when she was "without a man and without welfare" (at least the dealing, if not the bandit part) in order to feed them when they were little. She tells them it was bad and encourages them to come to her for help when they have problems. She can afford to help them now, in material and emotional ways.

The only one Eti wasn't able to help was Cheetah. She felt very bad about that. After another year of causing Eti increasing difficulties, this time in the Bronx, he disappeared without a trace. None of us wanted to think the worst, but there is an island between Manhattan, the Bronx, and Queens where prisoners from Riker's Island bury the city's anonymous dead. They use plain wooden boxes marked with numbers. When someone doesn't have a family who cares about him, this is where he ends up. To most poor people, this is a fate worse than death.

And Miguel. The last time I *almost* saw Miguel was just before Christmas 1994. In an ironic twist of fate, I was meeting Richie at the New York State Supreme Court at 100 Centre Street for Miguel's hearing on charges of (again) selling drugs. Since my last visit to this frightening building the nation had sunk even further into the conditions of a "garrison state," and everybody was required to pass through metal detectors.[2] Because the crowds tied into the criminal justice system had mushroomed, a huge line of people was stranded all the way into the street, waiting in the freezing cold to be processed. While waiting, I pondered about the changes that had come to pass in the United States during the past two decades.

I remembered a time during the Cambodian invasion when thousands of Americans from all walks of life had demonstrated downtown. It was on these very steps at 100 Centre Street that I and several other students had had our heads bashed by the cops. We had been caught up in a whirlwind when two cops in riot gear dragged a ten-year-old African American girl up the stairs, snatching her out of the line of demonstrators; those of us who ran after them to protest were beaten by about a dozen policemen. But twenty-five years later the middle class had withdrawn from responsibility: There were few foreign wars to protest, and the domestic wars raged on below the level of our consciousness. The policemen were our friends. We clamored for more and more of them, perhaps to protect us from the actions of the people we had abandoned to dire poverty.

Inside at last, I found the courtroom. Richie, a heavy man now, but his eyes still shining, gave me a big hug and introduced me to Tiny, Miguel's new girlfriend from the Smith Houses. Small and cute, she looked a little like Lucita. They told me that Miguel was already "in the bullpen" (a holding pen downstairs). The case was coming up very soon—Miguel's codefendant was already there with his lawyer—but Miguel's court-appointed lawyer had not shown up. Tiny was very nervous. The only way we'd get to see Miguel would be in the defendants' area, but only if his lawyer came. Miguel and the other guy had been arrested by undercover cops at Hester Street Park on suspicion of selling heroin. "They haven't got a case," said Richie. "They only found $30 on him, no product."

He was wrong, as usual.

Since our last interview, I had helped Miguel find a placement in a reputable halfway house recommended by people I knew who had gone through its substance-abuse program and who had been helped to obtain very spartan but clean rooms and modest jobs upon graduation.

But after a short period, Miguel signed himself out. His agoraphobia, coupled with the magnetic pull of his close family and Tiny, had been too powerful to keep him in the very cloistered atmosphere of the halfway house. Not to mention the pull of good old Hester Street, where a hundred years before, Jewish horse poisoners[3] dealt cheek by jowl with Irish, German, and Italian extortionists, pimps, and hired killers. Once again it was a marketplace where unemployed lumpen could find jobs.

Miguel had told me, in a phone conversation from Riker's, that he had been making a little money selling there, that he needed money for his mother and Tiny. He knew he was guilty and had said so to the district attorney. As a third-time offender he was facing eight years to life, but by agreeing to cop a plea he might only have to serve five. But the district attorney had joined his case to that of his codefendant, an expensively dressed stocky young man who did not want to plead guilty. This young man was represented by a cartel-funded private lawyer. They approached the bench and spoke to the judge, and shortly thereafter, the young man walked out on his own, apparently having posted bail, the lawyer sleazily hugging his arm. And that was it. Miguel would be transported back to Riker's Island from the pen that evening. "He's gonna miss chow," said Richie sadly. Tiny had tears in her eyes. The court clerk, a big Caribbean man, was coming in our direction. Richie whispered to me not to speak: "I told him you're our mother." The man took us outside the courtroom and very kindly told us he was going down to the pen to inform Miguel that we had all been there and were sending him our love. We hung around, waiting for him to return, me still trying, unsuccessfully, to reach Miguel's lawyer. Then I invited Tiny and Richie to have lunch.

There's a small Chinese restaurant on Canal Street where workingmen eat at round communal tables seating about twelve each. It's not that I have to turn every situation into a teaching opportunity, but what the hell—I wanted Richie and Tiny to see these poor, overworked guys who couldn't put even two English words together. My guests were a little spooked but did fine with eggs over rice. I asked Richie why he had told the clerk I was their mother. He said, "Well, you've been like a mother to us."

I told him that I felt very sad at not having had the power to help them more substantially. Richie disagreed politely, and to prove the point, he started telling the family history to Tiny. She listened, but what she really wanted to know was whether Miguel really loved her. As much as he had loved Carmen?

Then Richie said he had seen Lisa the other day. She had had another baby, fifteen years after her first. She looked good. Nice and full. Her boyfriend was "upstate" (in prison). She had given Richie her phone number. Should he call? He had never stopped loving Lisa, he said. I advised him to call her.

In a later phone conversation, Meri gave me more insight into the reasons for Miguel's return to Hester Street. He didn't earn very much there, but what he did was spent on buying new shoes, a new dress, and earrings for Tiny. The couple spent their days honeymooning in Meri's apartment; Miguel would go out in the evenings, make some money, take Tiny out to the movies or dinner, and back to bed they went. In the short time before his inevitable return to prison, Miguel wanted to "make a baby." Meri understood that, but why wasn't he concerned about his own mother's needs? Now that he was back in prison, Tiny asked her for money for presents and fare to visit him. "They want to touch each other, that's all they care about!" she complained. "And Tiny is too lazy to even get a job." Besides, added Meri darkly, "I think her mother told her to use [birth control] pills. If I see her on the street with some other guy, I'm going to mess her up. She says she loves my son, but she's just using him."

But back to prison it was for Miguel.

A lucid visitor from outer space would surely ask why, when illicit drug consumption had become de facto legal for middle-class people, the state refused to legalize it, to end the domestic killing fields of its distribution and the enormous profits at the top that didn't contribute to state coffers. This visitor would ask what magic was used to fill the prisons mainly with people with darker skin, and would surely pose the related question of why and how guns were made available to desperate and thoughtless young people. The answer, I think, unarticulated by politicians but feeding their nightmares, is that taking away the only available jobs from poor males would result in mass riots, in rebellions that would make the current crime-in-the-street child's play. To prevent that possibility, the white working-class electorate had to be persuaded that it is not the flight of jobs overseas but crime and the competition for jobs from immigrants and minorities at home that threatens their livelihood. Quite below the purely constitutional question of the right to bear arms, I think, is the white working- and middle-class conviction that race riots are just around the corner, better be prepared—while putting guns in the hands of dark young men is okay because they mainly kill each other, or their own.

We can come up with much better solutions to the problems of social and economic inequality. First, we should drop the rhetoric and symbolism of "war" and start talking about "peace." This is precisely the intent of a final recommendation of the distinguished National Criminal Justice Commission (Donziger 1996), who ask:

Who is the enemy in this war? Young men who hang out on street corners . . . teenagers who sell drugs? . . . The next door neighbor who sometimes smoked marijuana and wound-up serving a five-year mandatory prison sentence? The enemy in this war is our own people. . . . A war against the American people is a war that no-body can win. . . . The goal is not to declare a war and win it, but to declare a peace and bring with it the terms for lasting reconciliation. . . .

Peace can bring policies of renewal that have no place in warfare. One does not build parks or provide drug treatment for an enemy; one does not invest in job cre-ation for people one abhors. When we shift to a rhetoric of peace, we pave the way for the reform of the criminal justice system and what we hope will be a safer America. (Donziger 1996:218–219)

A restructuring of our society to provide decent jobs for all who want to and can work, undergirding a decent life for all our children, is a reachable goal that cannot be achieved by simply changing the rhetoric. But we can start by deciding as communities, as a commonweal, to do the right thing, finding words and sym-bols to express our intentions, and demanding action from our politicians. And if they drag their feet, throw the rascals out.

Lucita's first true love, and the father of the first child she bore at the age of twenty-six, is doing time upstate. This has not deterred Lucita from her real goal in life—neither her lover, nor her brothers; not even the constant state of her mother's anxiety. After finishing high school she continued to work to help her family, obtaining the low-paid jobs available to pretty young women, as a stock clerk, as a sales person. But her true ambition was to become a police officer. She applied to the police academy and survived five years of hiring freezes and re-peated exams to be eligible. A lot of people who applied to the academy when she did dropped out. "They couldn't take the wait and the roadblocks," she said, "but I have patience."

Meanwhile, on her days off from her tedious jobs, she went for long walks with her year-old son, Robert. One day they went to Pier 16, close to their home on the East River, and a bagpipe band was marching and playing. "The baby laughed and laughed. He clapped his hands and tried to make the sounds of the music with his mouth," said Lucita, ever alert to the sound of chirping.

Last May, Lucita invited me and Paul to the police academy graduation cere-mony in Madison Square Garden. We waited outside, nervous and excited, look-ing for Meri and Isabel among the finely dressed working-class people arriving in cars and on foot from all over the metropolitan area. There were heavyset women teetering on high heels, slender young beauties with huge manes of hair, older men with bellies and young ones with biceps, and children with slicked-down hair and baggy clothes—all obviously families and friends of the graduates. Meri finally arrived, in a car driven by a beefy young man, lugging Lucita's son, Robert, accompanied by Isabel with her youngest daughter. We all kissed and started our slow entrance into the mouth of this mammoth space, part of a huge, patient, wise-cracking throng. Meri said her sons couldn't make it. Julio had to be at work, they gave no time off; Richie was in court, and Miguel was upstate, where they give no time off either.

We watched the ceremony from very high up, not really able to distinguish Lucita from the smart rows of navy-blue clad cadets, marching in, standing up, marching around, saluting, all in tandem, all in precision, bringing roars of approval for their discipline from the spectators. Paul scurried around with the camera, his traditional function at all of the children's ceremonies, evading monitors who kept the public at bay (the children had taught him something in return) and actually getting a few shots of Lucita, as it turned out, in spite of the fact that her hair had been severely swept under her officer's hat. After the marching bands played and the officials, including the mayor, had spoken, the graduates threw their white gloves high up in the air, and for a second it looked like homing pigeons in flight. And then we were pushing our way down, Jagna the sap, wiping a tear on the sly, cutting into the nostalgia with a wry, ethnographic thought, "Well, well, threat labor and guard labor, all in one family."

But then we were out on the street, in the full sunlight, hugging, admiring and snapping pictures of Lucita, perhaps the fairest cop ever. I noticed then that Isabel, standing behind, was crying. I put my arm around her shoulder. She looked at me, her jet-black eyes of the Taino people, her icon Madonna eyes of Russian ballads, grave. She said, "I was just remembering how much our family had to suffer to get to this place."

Whenever I think of the Lower East Side, I think of Lucita. I can see her now, smiling at me, a fat baby face peeking out from between her arms, with shiny rascal eyes and a smile to match her own. She is alone and walking her baby into the future.

Appendix A: Methodology

A methodological goal of the research presented in this book was to improve the quality of the data by including culturally knowledgeable researchers and by practicing teamwork in all phases. In addition to the four primary researchers, a linguist and nutritionist were hired for specified tasks planned in the research design. The linguistic consultant, Dr. Bonnie Urciuoli, a graduate student then, joined the team in 1978 and eventually continued to work with the residents she met through our study in future research of her own. The results of her study are available in her book *Exposing Prejudice: Puerto Rican Experiences of Language, Race, and Class* (1996). The nutritionist, Ronna Berezin, MS, a practitioner on the Papago Indian Reservation in Arizona, spent only a few months in the spring and summer of 1979 consulting on the project before returning to her former work. She contributed a report on the children's nutritional status.

Although the team members came from different ethnic groups and seemingly disparate class positions, they had all experienced some hard times and worked well together. In addition to the clear advantages of minimizing the effects of the "observer variable" that haunts all science, support and intellectual vigor emerge through the discussion and contestation inherent in the process of working as a team. When ethnographers focus first on collecting etic information[1] about the society, as our team did following the cultural materialist paradigm of Marvin Harris, there is a greater likelihood of providing corrective perspectives to indigenous or visitor accounts that may be distorting the accounts of local life, glossing over taboo subjects, and exaggerating or sensationalizing others.

One of my conscious methodological project goals was to establish egalitarian principles for the way the team would work together. In the grant proposal, I requested approximately similar salaries for myself and all full-time team members. Similarly, each voice was given equal weight at prolonged staff meetings, where consensus could often be reached and each person's style accommodated. Self-initiated and self-conducted work produced energetic results because common goals were agreed upon and pursued. Deadlines and quantified studies had to be completed on time, so the project's time frame provided structure; but long-range and shorter-term tasks were always discussed and negotiated.

Two official reports resulted from our research. The first, *The Hispanic Study Project Report, Phase I* (Sharff 1976), details the results of the ethnographic work and the analysis of the socioeconomic census of the area. Dr. Bela Feldman Bianco, then a graduate student in anthropology at Columbia University, helped me design, collect, direct, and analyze the census data. The second phase of the research is described in a 100-page report, *Life on Doolittle Street: How Poor People Purchase Immortality*, completed in 1980 (Sharff). It ana-

231

lyzes and summarizes the quantitative and qualitative data collected in both phases of the research. Both reports were made available to the funding agencies, as well as to the academic and lay public through presentations, media appearances, and publications in the academic and popular press (see Sharff 1978, 1980, 1981, 1985c).

Chapters 1 through 13 of this book are based on the data collected by the researchers from 1974 to 1980. The frequent use of the word "we" is intended to convey the collective nature of the data-gathering, meta-analyzing, and concordance-reaching engaged in by the four primary team members (with the later addition of Bonnie Urciuoli). Chapter 7, "Blue Bayou," additionally contains the contributions of Bela Feldman Bianco and Ronna Berezin. Sequences dealing with events after 1980 in these thirteen chapters are the results of my subsequent follow-up research, with the occasional addition of a teammate's insights, as are the last three chapters and the epilogue. There the term "I" clearly refers to my own conclusions, as do the two short sections entitled "Reflections," composed later.

Appendix B:
Changes in the Patterns
of Incarceration in New York State

During the past twenty-five years the prison population in New York State has become overwhelmingly non-white. Today African Americans and Latinos are a majority in New York State jails and prisons. As Table A.1 shows, incarceration statistics for New York State reveal drastic changes in racial and ethnic composition beginning in the 1960s, when whites accounted for almost half of the prisoners. By 1990 African Americans accounted for a half, Latinos for a third, and whites for only a sixth of the men in the state's prisons.

Several other remarks are warranted about Table A.1. I included statistics for the years 1973 and 1983 because they coincide with recessions in New York State that make an earlier and deeper impact on the employment of the poor. For African Americans, 1973 represents a peak in relative rates of imprisonment, due no doubt to the demographic structure of their population, in tandem with the enactment of the Draconian "Rockefeller Laws" and the "Second Felony Offender Laws" as well as peaking of the activities of the "intelligence" agencies in response to the perceived "threat" of minority militancy. By 1990, the high rates of Black incarceration were rivaled by the Hispanic group, composed of the younger Puerto Rican population and newly migrating Latinos from the Caribbean and from Central and South America.

TABLE A.1   New York State Male Inmate Population Ethnic Distribution on December 31, 1960–1989 (selected years)

	Total Inmates		White		Black		Hispanic[a]	
	Number	Percent	Number	Percent	Number	Percent	Number	Percent
1960	18,017	100[b]	8,721	48.2	7,383	40.8	1,832	10.0
1970	12,210	100	4,024	33.0	6,521	53.4	1,609	13.2
1973	13,054	100	3,564	27.3	7,519	57.6	1,909	14.6
1980	20,938	100	5,764	27.5	10,902	52.1	4,062	19.4
1983	29,519	100	7,198	24.4	15,419	52.2	6,756	22.9
1989	48,769	100	8,537	17.5	24,172	49.6	15,693	32.2

[a]The category "Hispanic" was first used in the Department of Correctional Services reports in 1970 to indicate inmates born in Puerto Rico or of Puerto Rican parentage; it was expanded in 1983 to include "offenders born in Hispanic countries," in addition to persons of Puerto Rican birth or parentage.

[b]The category "Other" was omitted, so the percentage columns do not add up to 100. These figures exclude detainees in jails.

Source: New York State Department of Correctional Services 1990.

Notes

Introduction

1. The most influential work for students seeking to understand the causes of poverty in the 1970s were, and perhaps still are, Liebow's *Tally's Corner* (1967) and Stack's *All Our Kin* (1974). When Lewis's 1965 "culture of poverty" ideas were used by Moynihan (1965) to indict the structure of the Black family as a cause of poverty and to influence public policy away from the principles of economic equality, there was an outpouring of additional work in reaction to both publications, including Leacock (1971), Piven and Cloward (1971), and Valentine (1968), all of which tried to reposition the blame for poverty where it belonged—in racism and unequal distribution of national wealth. Some twenty years later these philosophical battles to restore the humanity of the poor are again being waged (see, for example, Gans 1995 and Wilson 1987).

2. Defining underemployment, Spring, Harrison, and Vietorisz write: "To gauge the degree of labor-market failure, it is necessary to know not only the magnitude of overt unemployment, but also the extent of worker discouragement . . . the number of people who can find only part-time work; and the number who hold jobs but at inadequate pay" (1977:67). They demonstrate that official unemployment statistics of 9.2 percent for ten ghetto areas in ten major cities "take a horrifying leap" to an average of 61.2 percent, when the other underemployment factors are measured (1977:68).

3. In her research with Puerto Rican women in Brooklyn, Lopez (1987) found that almost half had been sterilized and many were not fully informed about the terminal consequences of the procedure. Safa, working somewhat later with women in Puerto Rico, found similar rates of sterilization and notes that "none of our respondents mentioned pressure in their decision to be sterilized" (1995:94).

4. The most recent examples of research focused on young minority male dealers are Bourgois's *Buying Respect* (1995) in East Harlem and Williams's *Cocaine Kids* (1989) in Washington Heights, New York City. Both works locate the trade in its socioeconomic context of diminished job prospects in the licit sectors, but neither author expands his focus to the broader community. Williams's portrayal of his subjects is close to our own observations of young men—neither glorifying nor inflating the violence of the individuals or the trade, nor seeking clues for this choice of work in the men's character traits. Some of his young dealers have mainstream aspirations.

5. The "dual labor market" theorists describe the "primary sector" as stable, heavily capitalized monopoly industries that require and employ a disciplined, skilled labor force and allow unionization and promotional ladders. The "secondary sector" is composed of marginal unstable industries that are labor intensive and, in order to remain economically vi-

able, require a transient, unskilled, and nonunionized labor force (Bluestone 1977; Piore 1977, 1979). Harrison adds that the primary sector is surrounded by "peripheral segments" that include the training sector, the welfare sector, and the "irregular economy," or unreported and unreportable work (1977:103). He contends that underemployed workers frequently move from one segment of the periphery to another but are seldom able to penetrate into the primary work sector. Considering the recent trends of "downsizing" in the primary sector, however, the theoretical distinction between it and the secondary sector becomes blurred. The condition of underemployment helps to trap an available pool of potential workers who can be recruited to support low wages in marginal or faltering industries. Through the mechanism of discrimination the workers are relegated to work in the secondary labor market at substandard wages. Moving the analysis a step further, Bowles, Gordon, and Weisskopf (1990) suggest that the function of the underemployed in a capitalist society is tripartate: It supports marginal industries with its exploited labor and constitutes a reserve labor pool, and it fills the ranks of "guard labor" and "threat labor."

Chapter One

1. During her research with Puerto Rican women in Brooklyn, Lopez (1987) found that 47 percent of the households had one or more women who had been surgically sterilized. She attributes this high percentage to U.S. coercive population policies in Puerto Rico and on the mainland and disputes Scrimshaw's 1970 suggestion that some women may choose to be sterilized. While sharing Lopez's outrage at the way Puerto Rican women have been persuaded and/or coerced to participate in various schemes to limit their fertility, my data indicates that some younger women who have serious options and close role models for upward mobility may request sterilization after having had a child or two, and they will travel to Puerto Rico to obtain it if they cannot get the procedure performed here. But if the price for success is sterility at a young age, then their choices appear rather constricted.

2. The role of fertility for poor women in attracting and keeping a mate has been noted by a number of authors. I described it for the women of the Lower East Side in "Para el Futuro" (1986), and most recently, Nancy Scheper-Hughes noted it for the Brazilian women in her (1992) study.

Chapter Two

1. The practice of espiritismo has a highly prescribed ritual and rules of apprenticeship. Serious initiates are guided through a series of steps to achieve spiritual knowledge and ability to practice (Harwood 1987).

2. When I first made these observations in my field notes, Marvin Harris, my inspiring coprincipal investigator, took them to mean—and suggested in his book *America Now* (1981)—that the women of the Lower East Side would do anything, including prostitution, for the sake of their children. But I see their strategies in quite a different light. In a way similar to investing in the bolita, the women were gambling on the possibility of improving their life situation by marrying up. Hypergamy has a venerable history and indeed underlies the complex of male "honor," especially in Mediterranean patriarchal societies (Ortner 1993). There is no reason to suppose that poor Latina women would be exempt from or immune to its lure, especially when it offers a glimmer of hope in the midst of daily misery.

Chapter Nine

1. Sullivan (1989) provides a detailed comparison of the relative advantage enjoyed by white working-class youths who have access to apprenticeship positions in their neighborhoods, obtaining jobs subsequently as adults, as compared to Latino and African American youths.

Chapter Thirteen

1. From time to time clients are directed to meet with case workers of the Human Resources Administration in a "face-to-face" interview. Unfortunately, this human contact is usually invasive and humiliating because its covert aim is to decertify the client.

Epilogue

1. Although psychiatric researchers seem to be aware of the adverse psychic and possibly biological effects of prolonged trauma on poor children, like anthropologists their response seems purely "scientific" when, instead, immediate action is needed. A recent article reports that several psychiatrists plan to study inner-city children, among others, in order to discover whether people who suffer from PTSD experience cell death in the hippocampus region of the brain. It is thought that increased levels of cortisol secretion in response to traumatic events may cause a shrinking of the hippocampus. The report notes, "The researchers are now turning to prospective studies, where before-and-after images can be made of people who have not yet undergone trauma but are at high risk. . . . Dr. Charney . . . is planning to take M.R.I. scans of . . . young inner-city children, who are at a very high risk of being traumatized over the course of childhood and adolescence" (Goleman 1995:C3).

2. Bowles, Gordon, and Weisskopf (1990) caution that the United States is moving toward a "garrison state" in which "threat labor" (the unemployed, "discouraged workers," and prisoners) together with "guard labor" (people working in enforcement activities) now constitute 34 million people, in a fast-growing, nonproductive sector. They write, "An ever-increasing fraction of the nation's productive potential must be devoted simply to keeping the have-nots at bay" (p. 195).

3. In the early 1900s, Jewish immigrants, like other ethnic groups, carved out their own niches in the criminal sector. One of those described by Jenna Weissman Joselit in *Our Gang* (1983) was "protection" extortion from milk deliverers to avoid having their horses poisoned by the gangs.

Appendix A

1. *Etics*, according to Marvin Harris, are the "techniques and results of making generalizations about cultural events, behavior patterns, artifacts, thought and ideology that aim to be verifiable objectively and valid cross-culturally." *Emics*, in contrast, are "descriptions or judgments concerning behavior, custom, beliefs, values and so on, held by members of a societal group as culturally appropriate and valid" (1988:597). *Cultural materialism* is defined as: "The research strategy that attempts to explain the differences and similarities in

thought and behavior found among human groups by studying the material constraints to which humans are subjected. These material constraints include the need to produce food, shelter, tools, and machines, and to reproduce human populations within limits set by biology and the environment" (Harris 1995:280).

References

Adler, Patricia. 1993. *Wheeling and Dealing: An Ethnography of an Upper-Level Drug Dealing and Smuggling Community.* New York: Columbia University Press.

Algarin, Miguel, and Miguel Pinero. 1975. *Nuyorican Poetry: An Anthology of Puerto Rican Words and Feelings.* New York: William Morrow.

Auletta, Ken. 1982. *The Underclass.* New York: Random House.

Berezin, Ronna. 1979. "The Children Are at Risk: A Nutritionist's Assessment of the Status of the Children." Columbia University Department of Anthropology: Hispanic Study Project. Unpublished report.

Berreman, Gerald. 1972. "Bringing It All Back Home: Malaise in Anthropology." In *Reinventing Anthropology,* edited by Dell Hymes. New York: Random House, pp. 83–98.

Bianco, Bela Feldman. 1976. "Hispanic Study Project 1976 Census." In *The Hispanic Study Project Report, Phase I,* edited by Jagna Wojcicka Sharff. New York: National Drug Research, Inc., pp. 16–49.

Blanc, Cristina Szanton (ed.). 1994. *Urban Children in Distress: Global Predicaments and Innovative Strategies.* Langhorne, Penn.: Gordon and Breach.

Bluestone, Barry. 1977. "The Characteristics of Marginal Industries." In *Problems in Political Economy,* edited by David Gordon. Lexington, Mass.: D. C. Heath, pp. 97–101.

Bourgois, Phillipe. 1995. *In Search of Respect: Selling Crack in* El Barrio. New York: Cambridge University Press.

Bowles, Samuel, David Gordon, and Thomas Weisskopf. 1990. *After the Wasteland: A Democratic Economics for the Year 2000.* Armonk, N.Y.: M. E. Sharpe.

Bradsher, Keith. 1995a. "Low Ranking for Poor American Children: U.S. Youth Worst Off in Study of 18 Industrialized Nations." *New York Times,* 8/14/95:A9.

_____. 1995b. "Widest Gap In Incomes? Research Points to U.S." *New York Times,* 10/27/95:D1.

Butterfield, Fox. 1997. "Slower Growth in Number of Prisons: But Tougher Sentencing Tripled the Rate Over the Last 20 Years." *New York Times,* 1/20/97:A17.

Chagnon, Napoleon. 1968. *Yanomamo: The Fierce People.* New York: Holt, Rinehart and Winston.

Comitas, Lambros. 1973. "Occupational Multiplicity in Rural Jamaica." In *Work and Family Life: West Indian Perspectives,* edited by Lambros Comitas and David Lowenthal. New York: Anchor, pp. 157–173.

DeGiovanni, Frank. 1987. *Displacement Pressures in the Lower East Side.* New York: Community Service Society.

Dehavenon, Anna Lou. 1984. "The Tyranny of Indifference and the Re-Institutionalization of Hunger, Homelessness and Poor Health." New York: East Harlem Interfaith Welfare Committee.

Donziger, Steven. 1996. *The Real War on Crime: The Report of the Criminal Justice Commission.* New York: HarperCollins.

Federici, William, and Paul Meskil. 1979. "Hit Captain Who Failed to Cool Grocery Looting." *New York Post,* 5/1/79:17.

Figley, Charles (ed.). 1985. *Trauma and Its Wake: The Study and Treatment of the Post-traumatic Stress Disorder.* New York: Brunner/Mazel.

Fleisher, Mark S. 1989. *Warehousing Violence.* Newbury Park, Calif.: Sage.

Garbarino, James, Kathleen Kostelny, and Nancy Dubrow. 1991. *No Place to Be a Child: Growing Up in a War Zone.* Lexington, Mass.: D. C. Heath.

Garcia, Isidro. 1975. "Water Figure." In *Nuyorican Poetry: An Anthology of Puerto Rican Words and Feelings,* edited by Miguel Algarin and Miguel Pinero. New York: William Morrow, p. 171.

Garrison, Vivian. 1967. "The Puerto Rican Spiritualist: A Model for Psychotherapy Among Low Income Populations?" Paper presented at the 66th Annual Meetings of the American Anthropological Association, Washington, D.C.

Goleman, Daniel. 1995. "Severe Trauma May Damage the Brain as Well as the Psyche." *New York Times,* 8/1/95:C3.

Gordon, David. 1996. *Fat and Mean: The Corporate Squeeze of Working Americans and the Myth of Managerial Downsizing.* New York: Free Press.

Haberman, Paul, and Michael Baden. 1978. *Alcohol, Other Drugs and Violent Death.* New York: Oxford University Press.

Hamilton, Charles. 1976. "Public Policy and Some Political Consequences." In *Public Policy for the Black Community,* edited by M. Barnett and J. Heffner. New York: Alfred Publishing, pp. 237–255.

Harris, Marvin. 1968. *The Rise of Anthropological Theory: A History of Theories of Culture.* New York: Crowell.

_____. 1979. *Cultural Materialism: The Struggle for a Science of Culture.* New York: Random House.

_____. 1981. *America Now: The Anthropology of a Changing Culture.* New York: Simon and Schuster.

_____. 1988. *Culture, People, Nature.* 5th edition. New York: Harper.

_____. 1995. *Cultural Anthropology.* New York: HarperCollins.

Harrison, Bennett. 1977. "Institutions on the Periphery." In *Problems in Political Economy,* edited by David Gordon. Lexington, Mass.: D. C. Heath.

Harrison, Bennett, and Barry Bluestone. 1988. *The Great U-Turn: Corporate Restructuring and the Polarizing of America.* New York: Basic Books.

Harrison, Faye. 1995. "Writing Against the Grain: Cultural Politics of Difference in the Work of Alice Walker." In *Women Writing Culture,* edited by Ruth Behar and Deborah Gordon. Berkeley: University of California Press, pp. 233–245.

Herbert, Bob. 1996. "One in Four." *New York Times,* 12/16/96:A15.

Harwood, Alan. 1977. *Rx: Spiritist as Needed: A Study of Puerto Rican Mental Health Resources.* Ithaca: Cornell University Press.

Jacobs, Andrew. 1996. "Troubled Haven, Now Bankrupt, Still Fighting to Survive." *New York Times,* 2/4/96:7.

Joselit, Jenna Weissman. 1983. *Our Gang: Jewish Crime and the New York Jewish Community 1900–1940.* Bloomington, Ind.: Indiana University Press.

Kilborn, Peter. 1996. "Welfare All Over the Map." *New York Times,* 12/8/96:3.

Kwong, Peter. 1987. *The New Chinatown*. New York: Hill and Wang.

Leacock, Eleanor (ed.) 1971. *The Culture of Poverty: A Critique*. New York: Simon and Schuster.

Lewis, Oscar. 1965. *La Vida: A Puerto Rican Family in the Culture of Poverty—San Juan and New York*. New York: Random House.

Liebow, Elliot. 1967. *Tally's Corner: A Study of Negro Streetcorner Men*. Boston: Little, Brown and Company.

Lopez, Iris. 1987. "Sterilization Among Puerto Rican Women." In *Cities of the United States: Studies in Urban Anthropology*, edited by Leith Mullings. New York: Columbia University Press, pp. 269–289.

Melendez, Edwin, and Edgardo Melendez. 1993. *Colonial Dilemmas: Critical Perspectives on Contemporary Puerto Rico*. Boston: South End Press.

Mintz, Sidney. 1956. "Cañamelar, Rural Sugar Plantation Proletariat." In *The People of Puerto Rico*, edited by Julian Steward. Chicago: University of Illinois Press, pp. 314–417.

Moynihan, Daniel P. 1965. *The Negro Family: The Case for National Action*. Washington, D.C.: Office of Policy Planning and Research, United States Department of Labor.

Mullings, Leith. 1987. "Introduction." In *Cities of the United States: Studies in Urban Anthropology*, edited by Leith Mullings. New York: Columbia University Press.

New York State Department of Correctional Services. 1990. *Ethnic Distribution of Inmate Population on Dec. 31, 1960–1989*. Albany: NYSDOCS.

Norman, James, and Cynthia Fagen. 1979a. "The Death of a Deli." *New York Post*, 4/25/79:3.

———. 1979b. "Cops Hit Hands-Off Order During Deli Riot." *New York Post*, 4/26/79:4.

Ortner, Sherry B. 1993. "The Virgin and the State." In *Gender in Cross-Cultural Perspective*, edited by C. Brettell and C. Sargent. Englewood Cliffs, N.J.: Prentice Hall, pp. 257–268.

Oscar Alers, José. 1978. *Puerto Ricans and Health: Findings from New York City and Bronx Hispanic Research Center*. New York: Fordham University.

Piore, Michael. 1977. "The Dual Labor Market: Theory and Implications." In *Problems of Political Economy*, edited by David Gordon. Lexington, Mass.: D. C. Heath.

———. 1979. *Birds of Passage: Migrant Labor and Industrial Societies*. Cambridge: Cambridge University Press.

Piven, Francis Fox, and Richard A. Cloward. 1971. *Regulating the Poor: The Functions of Public Welfare*. New York: Vintage Press.

Quarantelli, E. L. 1985. "An Assessment of Conflicting Views on Mental Health: The Consequences of Traumatic Events." In *Trauma and Its Wake*, edited by Charles Figley. New York: Brunner/Mazel, pp. 173–294.

Riis, Jacob. 1951 (1890). *How the Other Half Lives: Studies Among the Tenements of New York*. New York: Hill and Wang.

Rivas, Bimbo. 1975. "A Job." In *Nuyorican Poetry: An Anthology of Puerto Rican Words and Feelings*, edited by Miguel Algarin and Miguel Pinero. New York: William Morrow and Company, pp. 93–94.

Safa, Helen. 1995. *The Myth of the Male Breadwinner*. Boulder, Colo.: Westview.

Sassen, Saskia. 1991. *The Global City: New York, London, Tokyo*. Princeton: Princeton University Press.

Scheper-Hughes, Nancy. 1992. *Death Without Weeping: The Violence of Everyday Life in Brazil*. Berkeley: University of California Press.

Scrimshaw, Susan. 1970. "The Demand for Female Sterilization in Spanish Harlem: Experiences of Puerto Ricans in New York City." Paper presented at the 69th Annual Meetings of the American Anthropological Association, San Diego, Calif.

Sharff, Jagna Wojcicka. 1976. *The Hispanic Study Project Report, Phase I.* New York: Narcotic and Drug Research, Inc.

———. 1978. "Families with Dead Sons." Paper presented at the 77th Annual Meetings of the American Anthropological Association, Los Angeles, Calif.

———. 1979. "Families with Dead Sons." *Amsterdams Sociologisch Tijdschrift* 12(3): 473–484.

———. 1980a. "Life on Doolittle Street: How Poor People Purchase Immortality." Final Report, Hispanic Study Project. Department of Anthropology, Columbia University, New York.

———. 1980b. "Exploring the Covert Economy of a Poor Neighborhood." Paper presented at the 79th Annual Meetings of the American Anthropological Association, Washington, D.C.

———. 1981. "Free Enterprise and the Ghetto Family." *Psychology Today* 15(3):41–48.

———. 1985a. "An Anthropologist's Chronicle of a Death Foretold." Paper presented at the Annual Meetings of the American Ethnological Society, Toronto, Canada.

———. 1985b. "The Role of 'Law and Order' in Gentrification." Paper presented at the 84th Annual Meetings of the American Anthropological Association, Washington, D.C.

———. 1985c. "Free Enterprise and the Ghetto Family." In *Annual Editions in Anthropology 1985/86,* edited by E. Angeloni. Guilford, Conn.: Dushkin Publishing Group.

———. 1986. "Para El Futuro." Paper presented at the Annual Meetings of the American Ethnological Society, Wrightsville Beach, N.C.

———. 1987. "The Underground Economy of a Poor Neighborhood." In *Cities of the United States: Studies in Urban Anthropology,* edited by Leith Mullings. New York: Columbia University Press, pp. 19–50.

———. 1995. "We Are All Chickens for the Colonel: A Cultural Materialist View of Prisons." In *Science, Materialism, and the Study of Culture,* edited by M. Murphy and M. Margolis. Gainesville, Fla.: University of Florida Press.

Sharff, Jagna Wojcicka, and Bela Feldman Bianco. 1976. "Getting High on the Lower East Side: Socio-economic Context of Drug Use and Commerce." Paper presented at the 75th Annual Meetings of the American Anthropological Association, Washington, D.C.

Sharff, Jagna Wojcicka, and Paul Van Linden Tol. 1976. "Burning a Historic Neighborhood for Profit." Unpublished paper.

Spring, Walter, Bennett Harrison, and Thomas Vietorisz. 1977. "The Crisis of the Underemployed." In *Problems of Political Economy,* edited by David Gordon. Lexington, Mass.: D. C. Heath, pp. 66–69.

Stack, Carol. 1974. *All Our Kin: Strategies for Survival in a Black Community.* New York: Harper.

Sullivan, Mercer. 1989. *Getting Paid: Youth Crime and Work in the Inner City.* Ithaca: Cornell University Press.

Susser, Ida. 1982. *Norman Street: Poverty and Politics in an Urban Neighborhood.* New York: Oxford University Press.

———. 1992. "The Separation of Mothers and Children." In *The Dual City,* edited by John Mollenkopf and Manuel Castells. New York: Russell Sage.

———. 1993. "Creating Family Forms: The Exclusion of Men and Teenage Boys From Families in the New York City Shelter System." *Critique of Anthropology* 13(3):267–285.

Susser, Ida, and John Kreniske. 1987. "The Welfare Trap: A Public Policy for Deprivation." In *Cities of the United States: Studies in Urban Anthropology,* edited by Leith Mullings. New York: Columbia University Press, pp. 51–70.

Taub, William. 1982. *The Long Default: New York City and the Urban Fiscal Crisis*. New York: Monthly Review Press.

Timmer, Doug. 1982. "The Productivity of Crime in the United States: Drugs and Capital Accumulation." *Journal of Drug Issues* 3:383–396.

Urciuoli, Bonnie. 1996. *Exposing Prejudice: Puerto Rican Experiences of Language, Race and Class*. Boulder, Colo.: Westview.

Valentine, Charles (ed.). 1968. *Culture and Poverty: Critique and Counter-Proposals*. Chicago: University of Chicago Press.

Williams, Terry. 1989. *Cocaine Kids: The Inside Story of a Teenage Drug Ring*. New York: Addison Wesley.

Wilson, William J. 1987. *The Truly Disadvantaged: The Inner City, the Underclass and Public Policy*. Chicago: University of Chicago Press.

Zimmer, Linda. 1985. "Operation Pressure Point." Department of Sociology, State University of New York, Genesco, unpublished paper.

About the Book and Author

In *King Kong on 4th Street,* Jagna Wojcicka Sharff chronicles an ethnographic team's involvement over a span of fifteen years with the people of a poor, largely Puerto Rican neighborhood in New York City. Anchoring her observations in field notes, she recounts the joys, fears, and disappointments of daily life as well as the drama of large events. Arson, the murder of a popular local teenager, the mobbing of a grocery store as an act of retribution for his death—all are projected onto a canvas of shifting local and national policies toward poor people and neighborhoods.

Sharff provides new insights into gender and family roles, how adaptations to available resources from the welfare state shapes the membership of households, and how children may be trained for specific adult roles that will advance the family's well-being. She also reveals how the underground economy, particularly the commerce in drugs whose profits are realized outside of the neighborhood, undermines neighborhood-wide solidarity and sends people scrambling against one another for jobs in the quasi-licit and illicit sector.

Following the lives of a number of families into the next generation, Sharff's ethnographic team documents how external political decisions that changed the war on poverty into a war on the poor affected them. Paramilitary sweeps of the neighborhood, in tandem with gentrification and declining social services, produced severe dislocations and relocation to homeless shelters, welfare hotels, and prisons. But the lives of the individuals and families are not all bleak.

The book's vivid style shows that the everyday reality in the neighborhood can also be joyous. People get real pleasure from raising children and taking part in the human drama around them. Kinfolk, real and fictive, keep each other afloat and reconnected to new neighborhoods and opportunities, including that of upward mobility through religious conversion. Adults and children achieve satisfaction and a measure of security through grit, wit, and acts of heroism and solidarity.

Jagna Wojcicka Sharff teaches anthropology at City College, City University of New York, and in its affiliated Center for Worker Education.

Index

Abortions, 145
Accidents, 67, 78, 113, 171, 182, 183
Adam, 75, 76, 128, 129, 223
Adler, Patricia, 196
  on drug addiction, 194–195
Adopt-a-Building, 16, 57, 109, 110, 111,
  139, 156
AFDC. *See* Aid to Families with Dependent
  Children
AFSC. *See* American Friends Service
  Committee
AIDS, spread of, 76, 109, 183, 219, 220
Aid to Families with Dependent Children
  (AFDC), 6, 180, 181
Albert Einstein Hospital, Paco at, 171
Alcoholics Anonymous, 109, 220
Alcoholism, 37, 62, 106, 107, 114, 192, 194,
  221
Alejandro, 44, 46, 47
  visits with, 53, 54
Algarin, Miguel, 109
All-Crafts, 109
All Our Kin (Stack), 5
American Friends Service Committee
  (AFSC), 121
  G.E.D. program by, 179, 187
American Psychiatric Association, PTSD
  and, 218
Andres Jr., 26, 27, 30
Angel, robberies by, 31
Animalito stories, 82–83
Arson, 139, 140, 165, 176
Arts and crafts program, 128, 129

Assimilation, 121, 158
Attica, Miguel at, 189, 204, 215
Augusto, Count, 16, 24, 36, 37, 47, 73, 76,
  77
  Adopt-a-Building and, 110
  apartment loss for, 221
  block party and, 134
  bodega raid and, 168
  death of, 221–222
  drinking by, 114–115
  machismo of, 75, 104–106
  poem by, 109
  prison life of, 175
  raps of, 74
  summer program and, 123, 125, 127
Auletta, Ken, 94–95, 173

Banneker, Benjamin, 60
Baptisms, celebrating, 69, 74–76, 78
Bare Hill, Miguel at, 204, 215
Barksdale, Clara Valiente, 138–139, 219
Bathing suits, story about, 100
Beatings, 83–84, 104, 143, 180, 182
  prison, 202, 203–204, 213
Beatriz, Miguel and, 187
Bellevue Hospital, 16, 67, 110, 154, 158,
  165, 184
Belmont, Harry, 93, 132
  bodega raid and, 168
  holdup and, 151
  Olie's death and, 161, 165
  prison life of, 175

Berezin, Ronna, 135, 158, 231, 232
  bodega raid and, 169
  Dolores and, 136
  gun incident and, 148, 149
  Max the Wolf and, 225
  on nutritional problems, 138, 145
  report by, 136–137
Beth Israel Psychiatric Center, Paco at, 179
Bianco, Bela Feldman, 231, 232
  on longing, 90–91
Biculturalism, 121
Biencriado, Señora: José and, 98
Birth control, 63
Blanc, Cristina Szanton: domestic wars and, 218
Block party, 58–59, 131, 134
Blondi I, 45, 47
  Juan's death and, 50
Blondi II (Mariel), 44, 45, 46, 50, 52
  pregnancy of, 54, 56
"Blue Bayou," 96–97, 99
Bob, drug trade and, 59
Bochinches, 166, 225
Bodega, 78, 79
  described, 21
  drug operations at, 172
  holdup at, 151–152
  raid on, 165–173
Bolita, 24, 69, 107
Breakfast program, 137
Bruno, 69
Buddy networks, 102
Bums, attitudes toward, 115
Buon, Nilsa Velazques, 7, 8, 23, 27, 28, 32, 48
  arts and crafts program and, 128, 129
  bodega raid and, 168
  car crash and, 41, 42
  drug operation and, 146
  Eti and, 29
  excursions and, 122
  Max the Wolf and, 22
  Olie's death and, 158, 163
  research by, 120, 121
  summer program and, 125, 126
  on superstition, 57

Caballero, Ramon, 83, 103
  addiction for, 91, 182
Capo, 51
Car crash, 41–42
Carlos, 129
  problems with, 128
Carmen, 194, 196, 228
Carpenter, Lady
  AIDS orphans and, 220
  All-Crafts and, 109
  on homicides/drugs, 55–56
Cartels, 184
  drug trafficking and, 176
  Operation Pressure Point and, 177–178
Cat man, 50
Census, completing, 136
Cestero, Marta, 91
Chagnon, Napoleon, 71
Chambers, Robert, 199
Charras, geodesic domes and, 83
Cheetah, 32, 126, 172
  caring for, 90, 142
  disappearance of, 141–142, 226
  Gatos and, 88, 156
  minibike for, 89
  Olie's shooting and, 160
Chet, 92
  bodega raid and, 168
  education for, 95–96
  ironing by, 94
  talent scout and, 108
Childraising, 97, 106–7
Children
  excursions with, 122–123
  safety for, 122
  violence and, 3–4, 83–84, 85, 97
Chinatown, 176, 197
Chinese, robbing, 189–192, 197
Chinese gangs, 144, 197, 200
Chino-the-socialist, 23–24, 36, 40, 94
Chino Two, gun incident and, 148, 150
Choochie, 75
Christian, Mr., 112
Christmas, visits at, 144–145
Chulito, 41, 59, 61, 64, 66, 91, 124, 224
  accident for, 67–68, 182
  bodega raid and, 169–170, 171

Head Start and, 65
Cintron, Mr.: bodega raid and, 168
Cisco, 142
    drug dealing by, 180, 181
    imprisonment of, 171, 222
Cocaine
    dealing, 58, 156, 176
    See also Crack cocaine
Cojo, birthday for, 105–106
Colon, Willie, 32
Comadre, 76, 77
Comitas, Lambros: on scuffling, 5–6
Community activities, 108–109, 120, 134
Compadrazco, 22
Cooperation, 82, 100, 102, 108–109
Co-parenthood, 102
Coreen, 74, 75, 92, 94, 127, 143
    bodega raid and, 168
    education for, 96, 97
Cortez, Ginny, 8, 59, 61, 62, 66, 69
    Chulito's accident and, 67
    loan for, 103
    molestation of, 104
    pregnancy of, 68
    sex education for, 63
    visits from, 70
Cortez, Millie, 62, 65, 81, 91, 98, 114, 118,
    124, 146
    bodega raid and, 168–171
    Christmas visits by, 144
    Chulito's accident and, 67
    dancing by, 134
    described, 61, 63–64
    marriage of, 66–67, 182, 224
    molestation and, 104
    reciprocity and, 103
    summer program and, 123, 131
    van incident and, 131
    "widow" story and, 89
    work for, 68, 95
Cortez, Nilda, 7, 8, 23, 25, 36, 46, 48, 58, 61,
    62, 71–74
    baptism party and, 77
    bathing suit for, 100
    bodega raid and, 168
    Christmas visits by, 144
    classes by, 224

Cojo's birthday and, 105
    dance class for, 126–127
    on dating, 33–34
    Juan's death and, 45
    minibike and, 90
    Olie's death and, 158, 159, 160, 164
    police and, 152, 166
    research by, 121
    rosario and, 57
    scholarships through, 121
    summer program and, 125, 126
    "trial" and, 150
Crabbing excursion, described, 100–101
Crack cocaine, 109, 219
    addiction to, 85, 189, 190, 191, 192, 194
Credit union, founding of, 107
Crime, 7, 64, 237(n3)
Criminals, raising, 106
Crocheting club, 101–102
Cuckie, 32, 142, 172
Cultural materialism, 120, 231
    defined, 237–238(n1)
Cultural relativism, challenging, 80

Daily News, on police problems, 167
Daniel, 9, 75, 87
    bodega raid and, 169, 171
    dancing by, 76
    Max the Wolf and, 80
    Olie's death and, 159, 161, 162
Dating, 33–34
David
    beating for, 143
    "trial" and, 149
Delila, 69, 70, 73, 75, 152
    baptism party and, 77
    beating for, 83
    disappearance of, 78
    HIV for, 220
Dental appointments, 137
Department of Social Services, 138
Depression, 140
Derelicts, attitudes toward, 115
Diet, problems with, 6, 87, 124–125,
    137–138
Disabled, aid for, 107

Dogs, 85
    attacks by, 80–81
    stealing, 82
    treatment of, 79–80
Domestic wars, victims of, 218–219
Dominoes, 70–71
Dropping out, toleration of, 29
Drug abuse/addiction, 15, 40, 71–72, 106,
        107, 140, 171
    problems with, 24, 31, 41, 59, 184,
        189–194, 196, 228
Drug dealers, 6, 24, 85, 141, 149, 176, 184
    addiction for, 177
    apartments for, 50
    counting, 120
    guns and, 147, 148
    imprisonment of, 171, 175, 177
Drugomatic, 145, 172
Drug trade, 4, 6, 14, 32, 50, 54, 58, 59, 108,
        161, 182, 215, 216,
        219
    development of, 143, 144, 145–146, 174,
        176, 184–185
    price of, 195, 196
Drug treatment, 179, 216, 229
Dry-cleaning business, 66, 68, 95
"Dual labor market" theorists, 235–236(n3)

East Village, 37
Education, 37, 65, 97, 106, 195
    adult, 14
    criticism of, 29
    subsidies for, 107
    See also G.E.D.
El Diario, on Olie's death, 167
Elena, 131
El Teatro Ambulante, 109
Emics, described, 237(n1)
Encampment for Citizenship, 34
Enriquez, Señor, 77, 78
    baptism and, 69
    beating by, 83
Enriquez, Señora: HIV for, 220
Environmental stress, impact of, 138–139,
        218–219
Errol, 93

Espiritismo, 24, 34, 179
    practice of, 236(n1)
Ethical Culture Society, 34
Etics, described, 237(n1)
Evelyn, 75, 83, 91, 103, 104
    education for, 97
    graduation and, 98
    marriage of, 182
    singing by, 96–97
Evictions, 176, 178, 179, 182, 183
Excursions, 122–123
    crabbing, 100–101
    Jones Beach, 65, 131–132
Exposing Prejudice: Puerto Rican
        Experiences of Language, Race, and
        Class (Urciuoli), 231

Families, 4–5, 108
Family Court, 142
Felipe, imprisonment of, 13
"Feliz Cumpleaños," 77
Fernandez, Señora, 19
Fernandez Funeral Parlor, 18, 47, 162, 163
Fertility
    limiting, 236(n1)
    premium on, 13–14, 236(n2)
Finelli, Vincent, 162
Fires, 139, 140, 165, 176
First Houses, 2
Flaherty, Father, 125, 126
Floating Hospital, 121
Florisol
    bathing suit for, 100
    dognapping and, 82, 107
Food Frequency Recall, 136
Food stamps, 6, 87, 107, 114, 133, 136
    problems with, 137
Foster care, 220
Fourth World Movement, 162
Francisco, 135
    bodega raid and, 169
Freddie, 24, 46, 50
    arrest of, 49
    Juan's death and, 44, 45, 51, 52
Fresh-Air Fund, 123
Friedlander, Miriam, 110, 112–113, 126

Friend's Seminary, 70
Fuentes, Arturo, 58, 61, 62, 81, 148
  conservatism of, 63–64
  drug trade and, 146, 149
  manhood lesson by, 65, 68, 83–84
  marriage of, 66–67, 182, 224
  "trial" and, 150
  work for, 68, 95
Funerals, 18–19, 47, 48, 53, 161, 163–165
  expenses for, 55

Games, 24, 67, 69, 70–71, 107, 148
Gangs, 3, 57, 156, 157, 178
  Chinese, 144, 197, 200
  formation of, 88–89
Garbage basketball, 148
Garbarino, James: domestic wars and, 218
Garcia, Commander: junior cadets and,
    128–129
Garcia, Reverend, 97, 98, 147
Garrison, Vivian: *espiritismo* and, 179
Gary, 51, 53
Gatos (gang), 37, 57, 88, 89, 111, 156, 220
  bodega raid and, 169, 170, 172
  Dominicans and, 165
  Olie and, 162, 163, 164
  See also Gangs
G.E.D., 28, 179, 187, 196, 200, 216
  obtaining, 14, 204, 223
  See also Education
Gender roles, 4, 100
Gentrification, 176–177, 219
Glue sniffing, 72
Goodwill, 95
Graduation, described, 97–99
Greenberg, Dolly, 24, 49, 50
Greenhaven Correctional Facility, 199, 203
  course at, 175
  Miguel at, 205, 215
Guard labor, 218, 236(n5), 237(n2)
Guiliani, Rudolph, 178

Halfway houses, 196, 227
Hanover Bank, closing of, 107
Harris, Marvin, 2, 47, 236(n2)

cultural materialism and, 231
  on emics/etics, 237(n1)
Harrison, Faye: on inclusiveness, 2
Harwood, Alan: *espiritismo* and, 179
Head Start program, 28, 65, 91, 94, 98, 124
Hector (Heckie), 38, 42, 72–73
  described, 37
Heroin, 31, 36, 58, 194, 219
  selling, 52, 53, 148, 190, 195
  using, 183, 189, 220
High School for Music and Art, Lisa and,
    145
High School of Performing Arts, Lisa and,
    53, 145
Hispanic Research Center, on homicides,
    172
Hispanic Study Project Report, Phase I, The
    (Sharff), 231
HIV. *See* AIDS
Homeless, 138, 178
  pressures on, 221
Homeless hotels/shelters, 85, 178, 180, 183,
    223
  regulations at, 181
Homicides, 3, 44, 47–48, 53, 54, 172
  drugs and, 55–56
  fraternal, 4
Homing pigeons, 38, 39–40, 43, 230
Hotel Martinique, 178, 180, 223
Housing, 107, 122
  allowances for, 176, 180
  problems with, 87–88, 120, 221
  public, 6, 110, 112–119, 177, 219
Housing Authority, 12, 68, 78, 119, 197
  interviews at, 110, 112, 117
Human Resources Administration, 17, 166,
    237(n1)
Hunt's Point Market, 92
Hypergamy, 107, 236(n2)

Immaculate Heart, 24, 65
Incarceration, 171
  changing patterns of, 233
Incestuous behavior, 32, 218
Ines, Señora, 69, 70, 71–72, 75
  baptism party and, 74, 76, 77

Housing Authority and, 78
Infant mortality, 69
Irregular economy, 236(n5)
Isabel, 8, 9, 11, 17, 19, 70, 75, 76
  apartment for, 224
  bodega raid and, 168
Ismael, 179
  income for, 24

Jack, 95, 96, 114, 115, 144
  employment for, 92–93
Jakub, 38, 39
Janie, program by, 55
"Job, A" (poem), 222
Jobs, 176, 218, 229
  competition for, 3
  construction, 111
  illicit, 6, 34, 106, 107, 108
  marginal, 6, 111, 235(n2)
John Jr., 96
John D., 60, 61
Johnny, 152
  "trial" and, 149
Johnson, Doug: bodega raid and, 169
Johnson, Lyndon, 146
Jojo, 69, 70–73, 76, 77, 127, 220
  accident for, 78
  beating for, 83
Jones Beach, excursion to, 65, 131–132
Jorge, bodega raid and, 168
Juan (Dodo), 42, 43
  death of, 44, 46–53, 70
  funeral for, 47, 48
  missing, 54, 86, 96
  work for, 45
Juan (Blondi II's son), 56
Julio, 11, 45, 46, 51, 52, 73
  accident for, 113, 118, 119
  death of, 17–18
  drug dealing by, 111, 183
  funeral for, 18–19
  health problems for, 110
  imprisonment of, 171, 183, 184, 195,
    199, 200, 202
  Olie's funeral and, 163
  thievery by, 112

Jumbo (security guard), 10, 17
Jump-the-shaft, Chulito and, 67
Junior cadets, 128–129

Kennedy, John F.: murder of, 56
Key Food store, 36, 88, 116, 133, 182
  working at, 10, 17
King, Martin Luther: murder of, 56
King Kong, 91, 99, 178
  painting, 96
Kinship, 2, 4, 50, 62, 82, 83, 84, 174, 177,
  188
  data on, 120
  links by, 102, 107, 108
Knife fights, prison, 206, 207–208
Koch, Edward, 167, 177
Koreans, dry-cleaning business and, 68, 95
Kurowitsky's, 61

Landlords, problems with, 138–139
La operación, 13–14
La promesa, 25
Latino males/females, image of, 33
Latinos Unidos, 201
La Vida (Lewis), 174
Lee, 114, 115, 221
Lefty (Eduardo), 87, 89, 113–114, 122, 126
  caring for, 142
  Chulito's accident and, 67
  minibike and, 90
  religion for, 224–225
Lewis, Oscar, 174
*Life on Doolittle Street: How Poor People
    Purchase Immortality*
    (Bianco), 231–232
Lily Pond, The (Monet), 91
Loans, asking for, 102–103, 107
Loisaida, 2, 197
Longing, 90–91
Long Island Railroad, 141
Loopy, 9, 73
  dog for, 80
Lucita ("Luz"), 9, 13, 15, 17–20, 59, 70, 73,
  98, 118
  bodega raid and, 168

described, 8
at police academy, 229–230
prison visits by, 198, 199–202
work for, 10–11
Lunch program, 124, 125, 127, 130–132, 137

Machismo, 14, 75, 80, 82, 102, 154
exercising, 15, 104–106
Madera, Señora Marta, 67, 72, 104, 143, 166
bodega raid and, 168, 169
Christmas visit to, 144
on dating, 34
death of, 178
loan for, 103
Malcolm X, murder of, 56
Malnutrition, 4
problems with, 6, 87, 124–125, 137–138, 158
Maloney, Captain: problems with, 166–167
Manhattan State Hospital, 11
Marco, 8, 59, 60, 61, 63, 66, 67, 224
accident for, 68, 171
beating of, 83–84
behavior problems for, 150
manhood lesson for, 64, 68
Maridel, 180, 181
Mariel. *See* Blondi II
Marijuana, 24, 114, 123, 194, 219
selling, 42, 45
Marriage, 4–5, 23, 33
Material constraints, 238(n1)
Max the Wolf, 23, 73, 105, 144, 168, 225
described, 22
masturbation session for, 80
Mayor's Task Force Office, 112–113
Mead, Margaret, 156
Medicaid, 15, 64, 68, 107
Medical care, 64–65
Medina, Clara, 26, 29, 30, 44, 46, 154, 158, 226
bathing suit for, 100
Christmas visit to, 144
death of, 225
Olie's death and, 162

Medina, Emilio, 8, 10, 29–31, 33, 34, 38, 42, 48
arrest of, 152
bathing suit for, 100, 103
bodega raid and, 166, 168, 169
Chinese gang and, 197
Christmas visit to, 144
dog for, 22
drug trade and, 146, 149
gun incident and, 148
job for, 23
Juan's death and, 47, 49
Max the Wolf and, 80, 225
minibike and, 90
Olie's shooting and, 160
preaching by, 225
Medina, José, 51, 59, 73, 75, 76, 77–78
education for, 97–98
gun incident and, 148
imprisonment of, 143
minibike for, 89
Olie's death and, 159, 160, 162, 172
as social broker, 103
Medina, Maria, 29, 32, 142, 153, 154, 166, 172
bathing suit for, 100
bodega raid and, 168, 169
Christmas visit to, 144
Olie's death and, 158–162
Medina, Señora Eti, 24, 28, 30–33, 90, 95
apartment for, 172
bodega raid and, 168
Cheetah and, 141, 226
dancing by, 32
described, 26–27
drug operation and, 146
gossiping by, 166, 225
gun incident and, 147, 148
job for, 34, 225–226
José and, 97–98, 143
Max the Wolf and, 22
Olie's death and, 165, 172
police and, 152
summer program and, 123, 125, 131
"trial" by, 149–150
welfare claim by, 142

Medinas, Olie's death and, 161, 162, 164, 165
Mental health, problems with, 140, 171
Mentorship, problems with, 128
Mercedes, Doña, 24–25, 55, 81
  Olie's funeral and, 164
  rosario and, 57
Meri, 11, 35, 98
  bodega raid and, 168, 171
  childraising by, 99
  Christmas visit to, 144
  drug dealing and, 183
  graduation and, 99
  hospitalization for, 183
  housing and, 110, 112–113, 119
  la operación for, 14
  marriage for, 19–20
  prison visits by, 198–204, 214
  problems for, 12–16, 18, 111, 182–187, 228
  Sito and, 111
  Smith Houses and, 115, 116–118
Met Food, 133
Methadone program, 183, 184
Mike, 45, 46
  arrest of, 49
  Juan's death and, 51, 52
Minibikes, 89, 90
Mobilization for Youth, 46, 52, 110, 113
Model minority, myth of, 197
Molestation, 103–104
Mollen Commission, 166
Mona, 42, 44, 45, 46
  Juan's wake and, 47
Montez, Cecilia
  AIDS for, 220
  housing and, 57
Morality, 30, 40
Moreno, Jimmy, 59, 60, 75, 86, 87, 88, 152
  bodega raid and, 168
  drug dealing by, 196
  eviction of, 179, 180, 181
  imprisonment of, 223
  Marco and, 150
  shooting of, 197
Moreno, Lisa, 8–10, 24, 48, 54, 59, 60, 70, 73–76, 82, 86–88

  acting career for, 179
  admissions test for, 53
  diet of, 145, 158
  drug dealers and, 171
  kidney infection for, 154
  mugging of, 181
  pregnancy of, 144–145
Moreno, Maribelle, 59, 67, 74–76, 87, 88
  bodega raid and, 168
  education for, 97
  job for, 223
  Paco and, 86, 180–181
  responsibilities for, 182
Moreno, Paco, 8, 9, 48, 53, 59–61, 70, 87
  beating of, 180, 182
  bodega raid and, 168
  collapse of, 171, 178–179, 181, 182
  creativity of, 88–89
  described, 86
  drug abuse by, 179
  job for, 224
  loan for, 103
  nightmares for, 86, 96
  painting by, 91
Moreno, Señora, 118, 196, 223
  apartment for, 222
  children of, 86–87, 89
  Christmas visit to, 144–145
  espiritismo and, 179
  eviction of, 87, 179–180
  hospitalization of, 181
  Paco beating and, 180
  rent allowance for, 88
Moynihan, Daniel, 84, 175
Muggings, 181, 183, 184
Murder. *See* Homicides
Muslims, confrontation with, 133
"My Glue Dreams" (poem), 72
Myrna, 23, 100, 128, 129, 223
  homeless hotel and, 178

Narcotics Anonymous, 109, 220
National Criminal Justice Commission, recommendation of, 228–229
New York Post, 200
  on bodega riot, 167

New York State Criminal Court, 186
New York Times, 55
Ninth Police Precinct, problems with, 80,
    141, 166, 167
Nixon, Richard, 64
*No Place to Be a Child: Growing Up in a
    War Zone* (Garbarino), 218
Novelas, 33, 62
    machismo and, 15
Numbers game, 24, 69, 107
Nutrition. *See* Malnutrition
Nuyorican Cafe, 109

Obligation, 4, 104, 154
O'Donnell, Officer, 141
Oliverio (Olie), 24, 32, 143, 156
    arrest of, 152, 153, 154
    bodega raid and, 169–170, 171
    death of, 158–165, 167, 170, 172, 224
    drug dealing and, 145, 161
    Gatos and, 162, 163, 164
    gun incident and, 148
    help for, 142
    rosario for, 165
    "trial" for, 149–50
Open chest (game), 70–71
Operation Pressure Point, 177–178, 219
Ortega, Dolores, 67, 126, 128, 135, 142,
    143, 145, 147
    bodega raid and, 169, 171
    drug operation and, 146
    job for, 222–223
    nutrition and, 124
    Olie's death and, 161
    Rafael's arrest and, 152
    Ronna and, 136
    Señora Moreno and, 145
    summer program and, 123, 131
    "trial" and, 149
Ortega, Rafael-the-Kid, 42, 48, 87, 101, 126,
    128
    conversion for, 222
    drug operation and, 145, 146
    imprisonment of, 152, 171, 222
    Lisa and, 145, 149
    minibike for, 89

Olie's death and, 160, 162
    "trial" for, 149–50
Overcrowding, pressures of, 84–85

Pablo, 21, 26, 29, 30, 32, 74, 100, 154
    alcoholism of, 225
    jobs for, 27, 172, 225
Padrone, 24, 49
Pam, 161
    described, 93
    holdup and, 151
    interview with, 132–133
Parole, 205, 215–216
Pasteles, 94
Pedro, 12, 19, 111, 113, 185
    craziness of, 11
Peripheral segments, 236(n5)
Peterson, Holly, 67, 114, 115, 118, 132, 133
    bodega raid and, 168
    Christmas visit to, 144
    described, 92–93
    drug dealers and, 143
    food and, 94, 125, 137
    Jack and, 92–93
    problems for, 93, 95, 108
    summer program and, 123, 131
    van incident and, 131
    work for, 95, 96
Pig, story about, 82–83
Pigeons. *See* Homing pigeons
"Pimpom" (song), 130
Platanos (plantains), 94
Plotek, Basia, 23, 36, 160
Police, 185, 229–230
    bodega raid and, 169
    problems with, 31, 140–141, 152, 153,
        166, 167, 173, 180, 182
Poor
    housing problems for, 221
    national policies on, 218
    war on, 146
Post Traumatic Stress Disorder (PTSD),
    237(n1)
    criteria for, 218–219
Poverty, 4, 56, 109, 124, 226
    blame for, 1, 174

culture of, 85, 174, 235(n1)
deepening of, 140
ending, 7
racism and, 235(n1)
structural conditions of, 84–85
underemployment and, 140
war on, 7, 140, 146
wealth distribution and, 235(n1)
Primary sector, 236(n5)
described, 235(n5)
Prisoner's Aid Society, Miguel and, 202, 204, 214
Prison life, 185
stories about, 175, 205–214
Prison populations, 7, 107
changes in, 233
ethnic distribution of, 234 (table)
Prostitution, 143, 174, 236(n2)
PS 63
attending, 65
graduation from, 97–98, 99
PTSD. *See* Post Traumatic Stress Disorder
Public Service Commission, Meri and, 110
Punishment, 83–84, 97
Puppet production, 129–130
Puppy (dog), 77, 80

Rag theories of culture, 102
Real estate, speculation in, 176–177, 221
Reciprocity, 4, 100, 103, 108
women and, 102, 108
Red Cross, 138, 140
Relationships, semi-durable, 28
Rene, 152
holdup and, 151
Olie's shooting and, 165
Rents, 108
allowances for, 87, 88
increase in, 176–77, 178
Rent strike, 58
Respect, 30–31
Ricardo (Richie), 11, 35, 37–38, 48, 51, 60, 70, 72–73, 75, 86, 87, 91
car crash and, 41, 42
dog for, 80, 82

drug abuse by, 183, 184, 187
drug dealing by, 145, 183, 195
graduation of, 98, 99
health problems for, 185, 188
hearing for, 186–187
homing pigeons and, 38, 43
imprisonment of, 171, 185–186, 187, 188, 198, 202
Juan's death and, 45, 46
muggings by, 183, 184
Olie's death and, 159, 162
"trial" and, 149
Riis, Jacob, 67, 118
Riker's Island, 183, 226
Miguel at, 193, 227
Richie at, 187, 188
Rip–off artists, 108
Rites of passage, 69, 97, 149
Rivas, Bimbo: death of, 222
Robberies, 89–90, 151–152, 189–192, 197
Rockefeller Laws, 233
Rocky, 24, 48, 77, 142, 156
Juan's death and, 47, 49
Rogerio
psycho attacks by, 115
street fights and, 111
Rojos, Olie's death and, 161, 164, 165, 172
Rosario, 57, 69, 165

Safety, 90, 122
St. Bridget's Church
baptism at, 69, 76
funeral at, 48
marriage at, 66
St. Mark's Church, 97
St. Vincent's Hospital, Jimmy at, 197
Salvation Army, 36, 95, 129
Sam, 24, 46, 50
arrest of, 49
homing pigeons and, 40
Juan's death and, 44, 45, 51, 52
Sanchez, Mr., 47, 48, 53
Sanchez, Señora, 53
Blondi I and, 46
Juan's death and, 47, 49
Scheper-Hughes, Nancy: on infants, 69

School breakfast/lunch programs, 137
Scuffling, 5–6
Sean, molestation by, 103–104
Secondary sector, described, 235–236(n5)
Second Felony Offender Laws, 233
Self–worth, gaining/preserving, 106
Sexual intrigues, 14, 63
Sharff, Jenny, 66, 77
Sharff, Maciu, 73, 77, 78
    dominoes and, 71
    teasing for, 70
SHU. *See* Special Housing Unit
Silver Palace, 197
Sito, 45, 46, 52, 110, 114–116, 119
    Adopt-a-Building and, 111
    role of, 15, 16–17
Slum clearance, 136, 177
Small Claims Court, 29
Smith Houses, 171, 184, 197, 226
    Meri and, 115, 116–118
Snowy (dog), 80
Social bonds, 102, 103
Social inequality, analysis of, 219
Social Problems (course), 175
Social security, 36, 95, 100, 108
Solitary confinement, 201–204, 210–213
    described, 193–194
Sosicho, "trial" and, 149
Special Housing Unit (SHU), 189, 203, 210,
    214
Speculation, 176–177, 221
Spiritual knowledge, 15, 24, 74, 236(n1)
SSI. *See* Supplemental Security Income
Stack, Carol, 5
    on kinship, 84
Sterilization, 13–14, 236(n1)
Stern, Mother, 35, 36, 37, 49, 141, 155
    apartments of, 39
    homing pigeons and, 38
Stern, Mr., 31, 36, 41, 49, 50, 54, 74, 94, 95
    apartments of, 39
    death of, 222
    described, 35
    dogs and, 81
    evictions by, 178, 179
    homing pigeons and, 40
    Max the Wolf and, 22

    problems with, 151, 155
Stolen goods, circulation of, 108
Stoney, Officer, 140
    gun incident and, 148
Street Ethnography (course), 120
Structural changes, 1, 174
Suffering, 26, 86
Sullivan, Miguel at, 198–199, 202, 204, 215
Summer program, 124, 125, 126, 132
    block party and, 131
    proposal for, 123
Superstition, 57
Supplemental Security Income (SSI), 6,
    179, 188
Suspensions, 97–98
Sweetie (dog), 85, 110, 168
    described, 79

Talent scouts, 108
Tallier Boricua, 122
Tessy, 92, 94
Third Street Music School, 121, 126
Threat labor, 236(n5), 237(n2)
Thrifty Food Plan (1975), 137
Tico, 180, 197
    drug dealing by, 181
    job for, 223
Tillie, 92, 94
Tiny, 228
    Miguel and, 226, 227
TNT, effects of, 178
Tol, Paul Van Linden, 7, 8, 11, 24, 46, 48,
    57, 58
    bathing suit for, 100
    block party and, 134
    bodega raid and, 168, 170
    Christmas visits by, 144
    drug operation and, 146
    excursions with, 122–123, 223
    gun incident and, 148, 149
    Juan's death and, 44, 47
    loans from, 103
    Max the Wolf and, 22
    Olie's death and, 159, 160, 161, 163
    prison visits by, 175, 201
    research by, 120, 121

summer program and, 125, 127
van incident and, 131–132
Tragic Magic, 190
Trauma, 218–219, 237
  biological effects of, 237(n1)
Trauma and Its Wake (Figley), on PTSD,
  218
Truancy, toleration of, 29
Twelfth Street swimming pool, 127
24 Hour Dietary Recall, 136

Underclass, 1–2, 174
Underclass, The (Auletta), criticism of, 94
Undercover agents, 31, 141
Underemployment, 3, 5, 235(n2), 236(n5)
  poverty and, 140
Unemployment, 3, 5, 140, 235(n2)
United States Department of Agriculture
  (USDA), shopping guidelines
  by, 136, 137
Urban pioneers, 85, 178
Urban renewal, 2
Urciuoli, Bonnie, 7, 61, 62, 64, 74, 77, 87,
  88, 92
  arts and crafts program and, 128, 129
  bargains for, 95
  bathing suit for, 100
  Olie's funeral and, 163, 164
  research by, 121, 231
  summer program and, 126

Valencia bakery, 77
Valiente, Isa, 59
Valiente, Miguel, 11, 18, 33, 42, 46, 60, 70,
  73, 75–78
  accident for, 183
  attempted suicide by, 198
  beating for, 143, 202, 203–204
  birth of, 13
  dancing by, 32
  disability claim by, 188, 195
  dog for, 79, 85
  drug abuse by, 194, 196, 215
  education for, 97
    graduation speech by, 98, 99
    imprisonment of, 191, 194, 198–201,
      203–215, 226–227
    narrative by, 189–201
    Olie's shooting and, 159
    parole for, 205, 215–216
    on Richie, 187
    suicide attempt by, 184
    "trial" and, 149
Valiente, Ricardo: Meri and, 12
Van, problems with, 131–132
Van Cortland Park, survival skill lessons in,
  129
Velasquez, Señor, 73
  dog attack on, 80–81
Velasquez, Señora: car crash and, 42
Victor, 45, 46
  arrest of, 49
  Juan's death and, 51, 52
Victoria, baptism party for, 69, 72, 74–78
Violence, 106, 107, 140, 193
  children and, 3–4
  endemic, 218
  family, 218
  societal, 1
Voodoo, 24

Wakes, attending, 19, 47, 48, 53, 55, 69, 161
Wald Houses, 118
Walkill, 199, 201
Ward, Benjamin, 177
War on crime, 7
War on drugs, 7, 39, 140, 141
War on Poverty, 7, 140, 146
Welfare, 6, 27, 32, 55, 86, 88, 107, 118, 142,
  150–151, 236(n5)
Welfare cheats, 64
West Side Story (Bernstein), 54
Wojcicka, Andrei, 135
Women, Infants, and Children (WIC)
  Supplemental Food Program, 136
Woodburne Prison, Julio at, 183, 199, 202

Young Lords, 157